Edna Croft

MARYPORT

ISBN 978-1-5272-6026-9

9 781527 260269 >

DEDICATION
To my capricious, wilful, wonderful mother, who drove
us to distraction and on to enriched lives.

INTRODUCTION

Here is a portrait of a small life in a small town and in the main I blame my son for it. He was lolling in front of the television watching nothing in particular when he suddenly turned to me and said,

"What on earth did you do in a little town like Maryport, and what on earth did you do before microwaves, mobile phones and television?"

I merely mumbled, "Dunno. We played a lot of cards and we did a lot of walking".

Even I felt dissatisfied with this feeble answer and thought and thought of a time that had gone.

We that were born just after the Second World War must be a generation that has experienced more changes than any before us. There are the obvious changes where we have had to learn to use different machines and modes of communication and we have had to modify or discard some skills that were thought would be essential. But we have also found that many of the attitudes and values that were instilled are now not acceptable. The History that we were taught was only moderately true and now we are told that we are politically incorrect. And yet we were nice people who were not deliberately unkind. I could see that we are in danger of portraying the past erroneously again. There *was* dissent and dissatisfaction and I am proud that my ancestors were some of the unsung heroes that fought and won better living and working conditions. I am amused when the media promotes the assumption that we were all true blue, rushing towards the gates of Buckingham Palace or cheerily enjoying street parties and adoring Winston Churchill. We are also in danger of romanticising some aspects that were simply uncomfortable such as public transport!

It was interesting to remember our naive attitude and our ignorance to those with special needs and the official approach to their care. It was horrific to know that a child could be certified and remain for all their lives incarcerated without having any specific difficulty. I thought of the education that was instilled and driven by the eleven plus and the opportunities that free further education was offering. Doors were edging open as never before and there was hope.

There were definite roles for male and female and this permeated everything including clothes, toys and pastimes. A strong woman was a harridan and an unmarried woman had somehow failed. There were many who were not ignorant but were simply not educated and had been unable to access the opportunity to choose.

In every walk of life there were fewer choices, not just for a career but in the goods to buy, and forms of entertainment. And yet with less choice there were fewer decisions to have to be made. Children had fewer decisions to consider and many areas were closed to them. And yet this meant that there was less worry for small minds, less to grasp and understand.

I am fully aware that there *was* physical and sexual abuse. There were drugs, paedophiles and pornography but I was shielded and ignorant of them. I lived in a small world, where, if I did not know the people around me then they were familiar strangers. It was stable and made all the more so by the events and traditions that marked the seasons. I lived in a wonderful part of the country that held its own beauty and rich history. And yes, we did a lot of talking, reading, listening to the radio, playing cards and walking. A small world in a small town.

CHAPTER 1
"I AM BORN"

There will come a time when time will be without me. And so, I think that I will write it down. And now that I've written that I am a little surprised to find that all the moments and the days of my life are not just stored somewhere in my mind, simply waiting there for the time when I wish to summon them. I did not suspect that many of the happenings and the petty events had gone; just gone. I suppose I thought that they were all lying there dormant and waiting to be revived. Now that I have at last sat down and thought quietly about that early time, I find much is hazy and unfocussed. What about all the clothes that I must have worn? What were the meals eaten? What was the weather and what was on the radio?

I put my head in my hands and squeeze my mind.

Come on Edna. Think.

This is my life. I know that it is there.

I happened.

I was. I am. And I want to write it down before I am not.

I decide to go right back to the beginning. Back to a time that has gone and taken so much with it. So many changes and so much that has evaporated since then. It is another time that is barely recognisable now. I lived the period of stability and optimism, wrapped in the warmth of those who shared my existence before the walls of elusion came tumbling down. I lived a way of life that is now viewed in museums.

There are some events where I am not sure whether they are my memories, or it is just something that I have been told.

Well, there's one event that I definitely don't remember.

I don't remember being born.

But I know this off by heart. I have been told the story over and over and over.

It goes something like this. "The War was over, bar the shouting".

Mam always added, "bar the shouting".

She said that everyone knew that it was over towards the end of 1944 even though Peace had not been officially declared, and far be it for me or anyone else, for that matter, to contradict her. If Mam said that the War was over, "bar the shouting" then it must have been.

My father had returned from Barrow where he had been serving in the Fire Service, which was his contribution to the war. Only the British army would have chosen a man with chronic asthma for such a task. Struggling through thick, choking smoke and fumes he was eventually blown into Barrow docks and was discharged and returned home, worse than he went away. His mother lent them a hundred pounds to buy the two up, two down in Grasslot Street and life was better with Rationing than it had been for them throughout the Depression. My two sisters were by then attending Cockermouth Grammar School and in many ways, life was seeming more settled. As Mam had always been interested in politics she was considering standing for the local Council.

From there the story takes a negative edge as her stories always did.

Dad was a quiet man who tried to avoid arguments, if such a thing were possible with my volatile mother. Not only was there little chance of winning a verbal exchange with her but it upset him so much that it apparently brought on his asthma. Mam maintained his solution to her new bid for independence and public interest was simply to make her pregnant. She was always convinced that this was his way of restoring his erring wife to the kitchen sink. Thus I was forever the cause of a lost and possibly great political career. Who knows, maybe my birth changed the course of British History!

She always told the tale as if she had had no part in the actual act of conceiving me but would slide over that and state,

"In the morning, I knew. I knew. As I got out of bed, I said to him,' I know what you've done you beggar'.

And he just smiled.

She never said how she knew but the statement was always accompanied by a knowing smile. Come to think of, I never asked either. You didn't. You didn't stop her.

You just thought,

"Oh, no. Here it comes again", and you listened, going glazed with boredom.

I tell you, my mother had senile dementia from an early age.

There is then a leap in the tale to the actual birth in December 1944 when it must have been cold and bleak. I know that, because it is always cold and bleak in Maryport in December.

Dad walked Mam to the Victoria Cottage hospital only to find that the doors were locked. With an untypical burst of spirit from the mild-mannered man he had hammered on the door. When the nurse opened it, he roundly told her that it was small wonder that babies had been born on the step, as one had been only the week before. This little snippet was important, as Mam liked to recall the few times that Dad acted with authority.

7

Of course, it was a long and difficult birth, what else?

I suppose Dad must have left her and gone back home to look after Mary and June but their welfare and whereabouts is never alluded to at this auspicious time. I once asked Mary about this and she said that Dad had seen them out to school the next morning. As she and June were in different classes, they had met at break time and asked the school secretary if she could find out for them if there was any news. The secretary must have been a considerate soul as she had rung Maryport hospital and then told them that they had a new baby sister. Mary said that she and June had hugged and hugged each other with delight.

So, there you go. Not one of them ever expressed anything but pleasure about my birth.

In later years I tentatively asked Mam if they had been sorry that I hadn't been a boy, when they already had two girls. She looked at me a little puzzled, as if not comprehending the question and then answered a little vaguely,

"I can't say we ever thought of it. Anyway, you had red hair."

As if that explained everything. But I knew what she meant.

Mary and June had inherited her jet-black hair whereas I was the only one who had a complete replica of my father's unusual, deep auburn hair. She once said that as I emerged into the world the nurse had said awkwardly,

"I think you should know, Mrs. Croft, that this baby has red hair."

Mam had laughed and said,

"She'd better have, her father has red hair."

Now what can that nurse have been thinking?

The tale continued.

"Of course, you were beautiful. In fact, you were so beautiful that Dr. Bird commented on it and your Dad paraded you round all the wards to show everyone his beautiful baby. Mind you when old Dr. Rattrie came into the hospital he came over to my bed and said

"I see you couldn't wait and managed to have it without me",

and I said,

"Aye, and just you come and have a look at a lovely baby".

He peered into the crib and straightening up he said in his rasping voice, "It's the ugliest baby I've ever seen".

And she would laugh and laugh at this memory, her faith in her perfect baby completely unshaken.

There didn't appear to be any disappointment in me at all. No jealousy from Mary and June that a new little person had come into their lives. Never any mention that they all had to move up and make room for another. But then psychologist's theories on sibling rivalry probably hadn't reached Maryport at that time. Dad had been delighted with his little red headed baby and having his wife returned to domesticity. Mam's political aspirations had been thwarted in a most satisfactory manner.

And so, I was taken home to the two up, two down in Grasslot Street.

CHAPTER 2.
"GRASSLOT STREET"

All did not go well.

Dad was unemployed and money was very tight.

Mary and June were at the Grammar School and this meant two uniforms, two hockey sticks, two tennis rackets and two of all the panoply of school needs. Mam didn't consider the expense as she knew that if you weren't born with a silver spoon gagging in your mouth then education went a long way to putting one there. Far better to live in poverty and be respectable. But this was at a time when no one in the house was earning a living wage and added to that a new baby. Mam did not recover, as she should have done from this late pregnancy.

And to cap it all, apparently ... I would not eat.

I could never discern what was wrong with me, but Mam maintains that I just got thinner and thinner after leaving the hospital with what she called a "wasting disease". The doctors were baffled and one night when bathing me June had looked with horror at my stark ribs and begun to cry.

"Do something. You must do something for her" she had pleaded with Mam and Dad.

The next day Dad had heard of a baby food called, "True

11

Food" which could only be bought in Barrow. He had got a lift in a friend's lorry and returned with the baby food. Whatever was in it, I began to thrive from then onwards. This little story was important to my mother. It was quite something that my sustenance had to be brought all the way from Barrow or I would have died and is another story that I know off by heart. There was a peculiar pride in needing something different from the common masses for her baby. She never tired of telling of my birth and subsequent decline, but the tale always ended with,

"And if it hadn't been for you, I'd have been on the Council".

It never occurred to her that she might not have got any votes!

When I had asked Mary if she remembered my birth and if she minded this baby coming into their lives she said,

"Of course, I remember you daft thing. How could I forget that? Oh, we didn't mind at all. It was exciting and we loved you so much."

But she stopped speaking and paused for a while. Then she continued with a passion that startled me.

"We loved you, but they should never have had you."

"They should have had more sense. Dad wasn't well with his asthma and Mam wasn't well after having you and that meant that June and I were left with you. Then Dad got a job at a factory in Aspatria, so he wasn't home much. Wherever we were going and whatever we were doing your bonnet was put on you and it was, 'take our Edna here or take our Edna there', and if it wasn't that then she was always round at her mother's house or her sister's and we were left feeding you or putting you to bed. It wasn't your fault and June and I knew that but just after you were born it was a bad time all round. Well, for me it was a bad time. I would have been happy to go to the Secondary School, but didn't our June go and pass for the Grammar. I didn't even mind that. I was pleased for her. Everyone knew that she was clever and oh, but she was a lovely sister for anyone to have. She was small and sunny. It was Mam getting into her head that we had to be the same. I can hear it now. I'd have a better chance in life. I'd meet the right people and have a career and not just a job. It wasn't June's fault.

For me the Grammar school was just a catalogue of disasters.

"I simply wasn't academic, I just graduated from bottom to bottom and then of course I resorted to getting into trouble. Mam should have just left me alone and she should have accepted that I just wasn't like our June. As for the "right people", that I was supposed to meet and hold as useful contacts for a later date in life, well they only grew up knowing me as the Grammar school Dunderhead. A Dunderhead that gravitated to the wrong friends who were also dimwits in trouble. I was a

13

constant failure and I knew it. My teachers knew it. I was a constant disappointment to myself and everyone else and I knew that too. And while June was flying through test after test I was staring at dismal results with a lump in my throat. When we were in bed, June would put her little arms around me and say, "Never mind Mary, never mind", but I did mind. I minded very much though I pretended I didn't "

"This was all happening around the time you were born and for all Mam's grand ideas, they simply couldn't afford two of us at the Grammar. We had the indignity of not having the right uniforms and of course you know Mam, she did some odd things. "For instance, she made us gymslips from one of our uncle's old navy suits. All very clever but they were a funny scratchy material and all the other girls could see that they weren't right. These things matter a lot at that age.

"Then when the time came for everyone to get on the school bus with their hockey sticks and those black rubber hockey boots, there we were with second-hand sticks that were split and a cousins hob-nailed-boots. I just hid or pretended that I was ill or something. Then I was in trouble for that. Always in trouble. June was so gentle and quiet, she must have been cringing at times to be my sister but she never said so.

"I brought home my terrible reports and Mam would shake her head and say, "Remember what Kingsley says", and Mary mimicked,

"Be good sweet child and let who will be clever".

"I hated that quote, it meant that I wasn't clever or anything. Oh, she did queer things. "While we were suffering agonies in school by being different, she went and made us appointments to be measured for matching suits at a proper tailor. It must have cost her a bomb. Maybe June being quieter suffered more than me. See I could lark about and make fun of myself, but June was just embarrassed about her clothes and that. "And it was so cold after the war. That made life more miserable and Dad had some terrible sieges with his asthma in Grasslot Street. You being born was about the only good thing that happened there even if they shouldn't have had another baby."

That was Mary's memories of Grasslot Street. Nothing at all really about the street or the people who lived on it. No one really reminisced about it. Just the odd tale like the one about Aunt Emily. She was Dad's sister and lived next door to us. Apparently, Mam and Aunt Emily had been sweeping their fronts at the same time; when Emily's daughter Gwen sailed past. Going into their house she gaily called in her polished voice,

"Hello Mummy",

Auntie Emily had leaned on her brush and looking at Mam had said laconically,

"It's been in the shit house and fergitten itsell".

The tale was told to show that Gwen had always had ideas way above her station and Auntie Emily was crude and common. There was no love lost between in-laws, simply because they were in-laws.

There are some rather faded black and white photographs of this period.

Mary and June posing holding hands. Always dressed the same as if they were twins. Then a rather surprising one of Mary, June and I in the Carnival. This was strange, as Mam was always contemptuous of the people who dressed up and took part in the Carnival Parade. Oh, she loved the Carnivals and always supported them but only the most "common" people actually made fools of themselves to entertain the better classes. She must have made a concession that year for there we are. Mary dressed as a man and wearing a black suit and a bowler hat and June dressed as his wife clinging self-consciously to Mary's arm. I am in a pushchair, a vision in a frothy white dress. The pushchair bore a card saying,

"Wot no Family Allowance for the first one?"

Trust Mam to give it a political flavour!

There are other photos of me with either Mary or June or both of them at the shore. It was never called the "beach" just the shore. And there are numerous photos of trips to

Auntie May's large grand house in Manchester. Now how could I forget something as momentous as a visit to such a large city? I am told that I skipped down the city streets singing, "Hey Bar Ba Ree Bop", which everyone thought very clever.

I don't remember any of it.

Maybe I was too busy having my wasting disease, indulging in True Food and learning and growing. I do have one vague and fuzzy memory, which isn't a photograph or a tale, told by someone. In my mind I am accompanying Dad to a large, grim building on Irish Street down on Maryport docks. We stood in an enormous queue. The queue wound along the road and then up some iron stairs that were on the outside of the building, like a giant fire escape.

That's all.

I don't remember what came before that or what came after, just standing in that interminable queue, while Dad chatted jovially with a lot of other men. I can see and feel the black iron of the stairs and peering through the holes in the ironwork down and down. Waiting, waiting and shuffling along now and then. Mam said that it must have been when he went to the Dole Office and added,

"Oh, the patience of the poor".

But I don't really count that, as it has a dream like quality.

17

Just a snippet that doesn't make much sense and doesn't fit anywhere. No, the first memory which I count as my first real recollection, all my own, is when we moved to Curzon Street.

At last Dad had got a job; and what a job.

Secretary to the local doctor's practice. How my mother must have loved saying that. Apart from the kudos of being Secretary to the doctors, it was agreed by everyone that this was a "good thing" and seemed to please everyone. He was not to begin work until late morning to open the surgeries. This was important as it could only help his health as he was "no good" in the mornings. Which was true. He got out of bed cough; cough, coughing and it took him a long time to get going. He coughed while he got washed and shaved. He coughed while he dressed. He then followed a little ritual. He coughed while he got out his special cup, with a lid to spit in, and a green tin of asthma powder. He coughed while he carefully lifted the lid of the tin and poured a little of the powder onto the lid. Then he set light to the powder and hunched over it to inhale the smoke and fumes curling upwards. While he was doing this Mam was downstairs lighting the fire. He was not allowed down until this was done, as the ashes and stew, "got on his chest." Neither was he allowed in the house while the carpets were being swept for the same reason. I can see him now standing in the yard lazily smoking a Woodbine while Mam created clouds of dust He was then clucked back into the house when she threw the smaller rugs over the washing line to batter them senseless with a very fancy, cane, carpet beater. So, a later start to his working day was a bonus. Another bonus was that it was a split shift meaning that he could come home in the afternoon and rest. This job also meant that he would always be in the warm in all weathers. However, with the job came the understanding that we had to live in the flat above the surgeries and my mother had to clean the surgeries along with another family who lived in a downstairs flat.

A recipe for disaster.

Still, it seemed such a "good thing" that Mam having to do this was rather skimmed over. Not only was the job welcome but there was kudos in going to live in the town of Maryport. Grasslot was a village in its own right, it just happened to be attached to Maryport by the New Road and the Railway Bridge. Village or not, Grasslot was the industrial area of the town and was therefore not a pretty village. It was a plethora of mining houses and factories. The Jam factory. The button factory. The Tickatee clothes factory and one where you could go and have your pennies polished. I haven't a clue what sort of factory that was; just the men would sometimes put your pennies in a machine, and they came out looking as new. Another part of Grasslot that killed any claims to prettiness was an area where there were the ruins of the old Iron Works. And frowning over it all were the Pit Banks and the Slag Banks. The Slag Banks were huge grey hills that looked like pumice stone and felt just as harsh to the touch. The railway line divided Grasslot from the Slag Banks and the Slag Banks sat on the shore.

Grasslot only seemed like a suburb of Maryport but it had its own identity. It had its own shops. Grasslot Coop, a Post Office that looked like the front room of a terraced house and a fish and chip shop. There was also Laird's, which was a rather fine grocer that had wonderful wooden shelves and still weighed out tea and sugar and folded them into deep, blue bags. Above the door was the proclamation, "Licensed to sell tea and sugar". Across the road from Laird's was the Miner's Welfare and beside it was Grasslot Mission, an outpost of Netherton Church of England. Further along from this and going towards Maryport was a small Weslyan chapel and beside this was Grasslot School. This was notable in the fact that the caretaker's house was round! It was a Pit village and though the Grasslot Pits had gone; the communal life generated by mining remained.

On the day of moving from Grasslot and over the bridge to Maryport we were all allocated our jobs. We were all expected to contribute, and I was no exception. My job was to carry my two dolls. These were both black dolls called Sam and Alma and I loved them dearly. Mary was pushing a pram laden with pots and pans and somehow managing to clutch a rolled carpet under the other arm.

We hadn't even left Grasslot when I tired of carrying Sam and Alma. The thrill of having a job to do had quickly palled and I tried to offload the dolls onto Mary.

20

She stopped and straightened,

"Look. That's all you have to do, so do it", and she marched on.

I was aghast.

I hitched the offending dolls under my arms and trudged after her in surprise. My beloved Mary who pandered to my every whim, was refusing me something.

And it is this amazement that stays with me and not the act of moving house!

CHAPTER 3
"CURZON STREET"

And so, we moved.

Over the railway bridge to Maryport.

Funny little town, clinging to the sea.

Every street a hill and if the street wasn't a steep climb it was a slope or a rise. And always the air moving. Either a gentle breeze or a body bending gale but always the air stirring off the sea. The wind-blown town rolled up and then tipped down to the docks and the shore. Solid buildings made from the local red sandstone. There were some fine buildings which told of the town's shifting fortunes and over a short period it had developed into definite areas. These organised the classes and made sure that where you lived in the town spoke silent volumes.

The main road from Carlisle to Barrow split the town. It was a wide road, which was in turn crossed by the town's main shopping street. This wide road was Curzon street. One half was made up of very large houses with bay windows and the other half was the same large houses along one side and the Coop on the other.

The Coop dominated this part of Curzon Street and was sectioned into different departments. It began around a comer going towards Mill Street. There; was the Coop

Cobblers and I can still smell its strange strong smell of glue and feel the slight disappointment that the shoes had been repaired but did not look as new. Wooden racks ran along the walls of the shop with each pair of shoes assigned their own cubbyhole and each pair having a fawn label dangling. The Cobbler always made quite a show of studying the label while you pointed and jabbed towards your own shoes. It was obviously very important that your label matched the one tied to the shoes. The fact that you knew that Cobbler and he knew you and all your family very well did not alter the slow process of checking the two labels. This large part of the Coop was also given over to the furniture department, household items, the Coop offices and a large room for, "Functions".

Around and onto Curzon Street came the Coop Butchers where it was a treat for a bored child to stand and watch the mincer slowly churning out lumps and strings of red meat flecked with cream fat. Fred, the master butcher wielded his lethal looking cleavers, chum, chum, down onto a joint of meat. Then he delicately shaped it with viscous knives and slapped it on a piece of paper for his art to be viewed. The grocery department was next to the butchers and was a large shop with two entrances. Next to this seemed to be a "walk around" store. Here was haberdashery, needles, wool, curtains, bedding, nylon stockings and school uniforms. Upstairs was the "Ladies" dress department. Next to this was the "Gents Outfitters" and upstairs the shoe department. Here ended the Coop. The street had a few other shops, Jean's Hairdressers with sun faded adverts for, 'Mason Pearson', hairbrushes and pictures of ladies looking sideways and advertising "Tweeny Twink," perms. The only thing that I remember about Jean was that she wore a big black boot giving her a distinctive awkward limp.

Next to Jean's hairdressers was a boring shop. It must have been boring, as I don't remember at all what was sold there. Next to the boring shop was the Bata shoe shop and this ... wait for it. This had a red neon light. Wow! Piccadilly comes to Maryport. Though this seemed very grand it was rather spoiled for me, as Mam would not allow us to choose shoes from Bata. She not only considered them to be cheap and nasty but an even bigger sin was that they were foreign. The fact that there was a Bata shoe factory in Grasslot did not alter her statement.

After crossing Senhouse Street, the first house on Curzon Street was the doctor's surgery and thus our new flat. This means that it rounded a corner and so the large living room windows gave a perfect view up and down both streets. This was of great advantage to Mary and June who rapidly realised that they could arrange, "dates" to meet them at Bata corner. They could then get ready and simply stand by the window to see if their current beau was there. This not only saved them from inclement weather but also saved them from the ignominy of being, "stood up." This was a faintly ridiculous fear which I don't ever remember happening. How could it? I thought them the most beautiful girls in the whole world. Not only had they youth on their side but they were bubbling and stylish.

24

June. Small, dark and incredibly pretty. In fact, everyone was agreed that she was the double of Jean Simmons.

Mary. An edge taller, an edge slimmer, an edge darker and full of fun and spirit. And everyone was agreed that she was the double of Elizabeth Taylor. Well, not quite, but close. It was very strange that the same people then said that they could not tell the two girls apart. To me they were nothing alike. They were clearly very different, not only in looks but also in their demeanour. June was gentle and nervy.

Sometimes Mam would shake her head and say,

"By that girl is a trial," or that June was going to be a trial. Which probably only meant that June had feebly countered a Mother command. June spent a lot of time in the bedroom listening to music, doing her homework, or she was out on a "hot" date, or over at Mother Tukes. Whatever, she generally absented her gentle presence when she could.

But Mary. Mary actually was volatile and spirited. Mary wasn't just an edge taller or slimmer, Mary was an edge everything including temper.

I could be playing quietly on the carpet when Mary would begin. Never slowly or tactfully.

Bang!

She stated her case. She got a sharp rebuff from Mam. She banged her fists on the table. The storm didn't gather, it just erupted and broke all over us. Mary demanded what was rightfully hers and on finding that she was no match for the scenes that Mam could create she would storm upstairs with much slamming of doors. I continued crayoning, listening and admiring Mary. At least she had the spirit to make a stand. It always amazed Mam that anyone dared to challenge her authority and house rules. However, amazement did not halt her ability to deliver blistering return volleys. It must have bewildered her greatly when her girls were feeling their pinfeathers and having the temerity to rebel in their different ways. Oh, Mary and June were not at all alike.

There seemed to be a myriad of boys waiting at Bata corner and there was much peeping around the curtains of the flat at Curzon Street. Getting ready to meet these boys was a "Big Deal." They flew up and downstairs, having great debates about what to wear, which included which shoes, handbag and gloves. Lipstick was applied where Mam could not see, invariably behind the front door just as they were leaving. Of course, they were the best-looking girls in the town, and I was not alone in that thinking. Mam may have demanded subservience but that was not to say that she did not care for us.

As the front door closed behind them Mam moved rapidly to the windows to give Dad and I a running commentary.

"There, I knew that dress would look right. Eeh, our June looks as if she has make-up on. No, it must be a trick of the light. Mind he doesn't look much. A bit skinny. Still he comes from a nice family so you can't have everything. Talk about, "a rag, a bone and a hank of hair." Oh, there they go. Must be going to the pictures."

And if this was happening while we had just moved to Curzon Street this means that both girls were still only in their early teens. There was no doubt that Mam with her penchant for the dramatic and the romantic encouraged them.

She always stayed awake for them coming in. Not because she was worried about them or to remonstrate on the lateness of the hour but so that she could hear of their exploits. As my bed was in the same big bedroom as Mam and Dad, I was often party to these whispered tales. Mam always kept the bedside lamp on all night, and I can see them now, creeping round the door and perching on the bed.

"What a night Mam, Edmundo Ross was brilliant, and I got his autograph."

"And that lad from Flimby said that he was the Tzar of Pica and we laughed and laughed..."

"And then Mam we..."

27

Dad, who, when he wasn't in hospital, always slept in his vest and long Johns, would stir and try to sleep through it all.

Mam wanted to hear that they had danced the night away, attracted all the young bloods, worn dresses that all the other girls envied and generally cut a swathe through Society. And all this in the Palace Ballroom in Maryport.

Eventually they crept off to their own bedrooms carrying their cripplingly high, high-heeled shoes and leaving Mam to turn back to her reading.

She was often reading.

She was often in bed.

She often combined the two.

Night-time and daytime.

June came home from school, dumped her heavy satchel of homework and read the note left on the table.

"Gone to bed. Go to the Coop for another pint of milk and make our Edna's tea." Some homecoming.

And Mary?

Mary remembered,

"You know, just as I was beginning to settle at the Grammar school, Mam decided that as I was fourteen, I should now leave and get a job. Dad had met someone in the street who had said that a factory at Aspatria was taking on summer workers for some fantastic wage and Mam thought with a toddler in the house we needed the money. So much for getting an education at the right school. Of course, she didn't go to school to tell them, I had the embarrassment of that. And it was really, really embarrassing. The school wouldn't wear it. I remember the Headmistress saying to me coolly,

"You cannot leave here until you are fifteen and even then, you should stay to sit your G.C.E. at sixteen. Why bother to come to a Grammar school otherwise?"

"She must have had an inkling of the state of things at home and she certainly knew that I had no chance of getting the G.C.E. I just sat it out until I was fifteen on the fifth of November and I left the very next day. So much for Mam's grandiose ideas and all that money spent sending me. Of course, the factory in Aspatria hadn't any jobs then so I got a job at a factory in Cockermouth. Mam demanded all of my wages. It was her way of keeping control. She took the whole wage packet and gave me a little bit of pocket money back. This meant that she continued to buy your clothes and that meant that she had a say in the styles

"He who pays the piper calls the tune;" she'd say when I objected to some ghastly creation. There would be an argument and you knew another was coming when you refused to ever wear the blooming thing. She had this notion of what the Upper Classes would wear for this or that and she tried to copy. Too many blooming Ginger Rogers and Fred Astaire films as well, if you ask me. Oh, it wasn't all bad. "She had quite good taste and knew how to put colours together, but you wanted your own choice at that age. Still, she took the wage and I raged inside working all week for a little pocket money. It wasn't so much that she didn't want you to grow up she just knew that the one holding the purse was the one in control and that kept us subservient somehow. I didn't stay long at the factory but soon got a job at Dearham School. I suppose now it would be called a Welfare Assistant. There I was really happy."

Mary may have been happy in her school job, but she was coming home to most of the work cleaning the surgeries and sidestepping the family arguments. She would come in from work, make a meal for us, if June hadn't already done so, and then begin work on the stairs and corridors. Mam said that she couldn't be expected to do this as she already had too much to do. The funny thing was that she always found time in the day to go over to her mother's house in Grasslot.

Every day.

It bordered on obsession

She was either there or reading a book or in bed or in bed

reading a book.

All of us were resentful.

Mam was the youngest of nine.

In fact, it was Mother Tuke's proud boast; *not* that she had, had nine children, but that she had, had nine children that had lived. Apparently quite an achievement.

Oh, but I was surrounded by family. My young life was overflowing with people. Though the new flat was a large one it was often filled with family. There were constant comings and goings of family that had come to town and found it a convenient place to call. The members of the family that lived further away, came to have their holidays with Mother Tuke and the overflow came to stay with us.

At the centre of it all was Mother Tuke. All her family returned to love her and some to lavish her with gifts. Everyone loved her and I loved her too.

There was Auntie May from Manchester. Mother Tuke had given birth to her, "out of wedlock," and it was said that May had married her cousin, Stanley, simply to acquire the same name as the rest of her family. She sometimes brought with her, her much pampered and only son, Robin. Robin seemed strange to me. He was a lumbering young man with only one eye. Sometimes he offered me his clenched fist and when he opened it, there was his glass eye staring at me. He obviously found my shock very funny and rolled about laughing. I didn't find it funny then and think of it with a shudder even now. Robin was garrulous and demanded attention from all. He was very interested in photography, an interest that his adoring Parents indulged, and he tried to use all of us as models for his arty black and white photographs. Uncle Stanley was a small Scotsman who sometimes came to visit in his car. Now that was really something! Auntie May always seemed very affluent and arrived armed with presents, making her visits all the more special. She was fat and round and laughing. It was always a pleasure to see Auntie May coming around the door. Not just because of the gifts but her jollity was infectious.

Not so Aunt Evelyn.

Taller and gaunter and much more severe, somehow her visits were a trial to all. There was no present from her. Well, there couldn't be because she was poor. She was poorer than anyone else and everyone was richer than she was. If anyone had more or better than Aunt Evelyn it was not because they had been more frugal or financially astute, she simply assumed that they were richer. In fact, it was hard to think that she was full sister to these smaller, rounder, jollier women. Aunt Evelyn and her family lived in Yorkshire, near Barnsley and their rich voices sounded strange and alien to my ears. Aunt Evelyn always seemed hard and bitter. This could possibly have something to do with the fact that she wore a wig.

Of course, this was never mentioned but we all knew.

Apparently, she had worked in the, "Munitions," at Gretna," throughout the First World War and it was said that the chemicals there had made her hair fall out. What a terrible thing to happen to a young girl and when I was deemed old enough, I was told that the wig had not to be commented on at all. So, I joined the others in pretending that we did not know or notice.

It was a man in Maryport who made her wigs and was possibly the only person that ever saw her without it on. This meant that she had to come to stay in Maryport while a new wig was being prepared and fitted. As the years went by, he cleverly added a little grey here and there. Mam grumbled that the people in Yorkshire must have thought that we were awful to Aunt Evelyn when she came to stay; so much so that she returned home greyer with each visit. As the wig could not be made quickly this mean that Aunt Evelyn had to stay longer and a longer holiday meant that her neighbours in Yorkshire would not notice the grey immediately. In consequence she often outstayed her welcome. Her caustic tongue and abrasive manner caused many family arguments.

Occasionally her husband Jack came to join her.

Now, I really liked Uncle Jack. A big burly man who smoked a wonderful smelling pipe. He had a deep, laughing voice and he would lift me high to touch the ceiling while Aunt Evelyn looked on sniffing and predicting all manner of accidents if he did not put me down. And while he talked to the others, he would take me on his knee and let me play with his pocket watch and chain to a murmured,

"She'll break that watch,"

"Gee oer. She'll not,"

He never took any notice of her.

But Uncle Jack always seemed to go back to Yorkshire earlier than intended. We would just get up to hear that he had suddenly returned home. When Aunt Evelyn was out of ear shot there were wonderful conversations with words like,

'British Legion."

"Spent all the money on drink,"

"Doesn't know where to stop."

"She's sent him home again."

"Not again."

"What drank it all?"

There was much sorrowful shaking of heads and sighing.

34

Oh, Uncle Jack provided much fuel for self-righteousness and everyone renewed their efforts to feed and keep Aunt Evelyn until the time was judged right for Yorkshire to have forgotten the original colour of the wig.

Of course, there were also her adult children visiting.

Her daughter Olive was the eldest and sometimes came with her two boys, Alan and David. David was a rather serious young lad, but Alan was about my own age and we had enormous fun. He was judged to be a "Very naughty boy," which was simply because he was either too noisy or too boisterous. Olive was also, "poor," and so she and her boys had to be fed and kept too but it was worth it as Olive had the great advantage of providing the family with many murmured conversations.

Olive had, "Had," to get married because she was having a baby. Apparently, this was an unforgotten and unforgiven sin. The fact that most of the women in the family, including my mother had, "Had," to get married was lost in the mists of time and gossip.

Then Olive added a huge bonus.

She was getting a Divorce.

A Divorce!

I had not a clue what a "Divorce', was but tea planters in

Ceylon must have blessed the day that Olive decided to make a bid for freedom from an erring husband. There had to be many family gatherings to discuss this unusual phenomenon over very strong cups of tea. Of course, this resulted in more notes for Mary or June to," get Edna her dinner".

There was also Aunt Evelyn's youngest son Malcolm.

It was said that when she found that she was pregnant, her two other children Cyril and Olive had asked if they could choose the name for the new baby. Aunt Evelyn had said that of course they could. She would write everyone's suggestions on scraps of paper and place them in Uncle Jacks Trilby hat. As they gave their choice of name. Aunt Evelyn carefully wrote the name, "Malcolm', on each piece of paper, thus ensuring that her choice was guaranteed.

We all liked Malcolm.

Tall with deep red hair, he was fun personified, and I can remember lying in bed at Curzon Street listening to him making everyone laugh and usually ending by singing something called, "Abdul de bul, bul de mere."

Yes, we all liked Malcolm, but it was judged that June and Malcolm liked each other a little more than was deemed healthy in full cousins.

There was also Auntie Lizzie. Another small round and

jolly woman. She lived in Coronation Street in Grasslot with her equally thin and taciturn husband. Uncle Bill Musgrave. Apparently, he was like he was because he had been blown up in the First World War and had a lump of shrapnel in his head. It was said that that he could take bits of it out of his ear. Now there's an achievement. Uncle Bill was a miner but also had a penchant for the sea. When we went over to Auntie Lizzie's house there were often buckets and enamel bowls in the yard full of seawater.

On closer inspection there was more than seawater in them. Sometimes I stirred the murky water and looked with fascination as crabs clawed the smooth sides of the enamel bowls. Another bucket was full of whelks, known in Maryport as, "Buckies," or there were small black shellfish that we called, "Cuvvins," never winkles. I loved the taste of them all. It was a treat to have a supper of cuvvins and I became quite adept at picking away the little hard bit with a needle and scooping out the fleshy part to eat with bread and butter. Auntie Lizzie's house was always calm and tidy.

In the middle of the living room was a large, mahogany, circular table and on the obligatory piano there was statue of Achilles studying his heel. This provided an early lesson in one of the Greek myths and I learned that I had to take special care of my heels.

Of course, she too had family and for some obscure reason they were always given their first name plus their surname. There was her son John Musgrave and his wife Amy Musgrave, a very thin couple who had no children. Then there was Kathleen Musgrave who was married to Terry Poland and they had one son, John Poland. Kath and Terry had rented our house in Grasslot Street.

There had been another daughter called Bunty, but we hadn't to mention Bunty as she was dead, and it would make Auntie Lizzie cry. Strangely for someone that was never mentioned I knew quite a lot about Bunty. She had been the biggest baby ever born which just goes to show that big wasn't "a good thing". On the day that Bunty was born, Uncle Bill Musgrave had paraded her up and down the street to show everyone her size. This tale was always followed by a slight silence and shaking of heads. Not only was it considered rather presumptuous, but the baby had shown more than a passing resemblance to another baby just down the street.

Bunty had then spent a lot of time lying on the couch in the living room and had finally succumbed to whatever was wrong with her when she was twelve. I never knew her, as it was all long before I had curtailed my mother's ambitions to serve on the council.

Aunty Lizzie's other son was Big Billy Musgrave. He had also had some bone disease and had spent much of his youth in the hospital at Carlisle. He wore a big boot and was married to Alice Musgrave and they had one son, Little Billy Musgrave. They lived in the flat below us in Curzon Street and as Little Billy was only a matter of months older than me, he was a built-in playmate.

There was always something amiss.

Either Alice Musgrave hadn't cleaned the surgeries and corridors when it was her week, or she had not cleaned them to Mam's satisfaction. Little Billy and I ploughed on with our friendship, regardless of the adult squabbles.

We were not only close to the earth in size but close to the earth in our play. We poked it with sticks, scraped it from between the cobbles, and created patterns in the muck. On hot days it was good to sit on the edge of the gutter and watch the tar melting and sliding down the slight camber of the road and mingle in the dusty muck. There was something satisfying to push the tar with a stick and watch it wrinkle and slide back.

One hot day I badgered Mam for a jam jar with holes stabbed in the lid. Billy and I stalked bumblebees in the fuchsia bushes. I watched them entranced by their colours and frantic efforts to escape their jam jar jail. Just as this form of entertainment was palling Billy suggested that we fill the jam jars with water to see if bees could swim. At least we had the good sense not to remove the lids but to stand at the tap in the yard filling them through the holes in the jar lids. The bees proved very disappointing and simply sank to the bottom of the jar without attempting to swim. Even a good shake of the jar did not result in any bee breaststroke.

As we were removing the lids to tip out the lazy bees, my mother appeared armed with a washing basket hitched under her arm. She paused to check our game and then bore Little Billy off to Alice Musgrave to report him for dangerous and cruel practices with bees. Alice was roundly told that the boy should have more discipline and had endangered her precious daughter with death by bees.

I felt uncomfortable as if I were to blame for this over reaction and so, later in the evening when Mam had gone to bed with her latest book, I sneaked down to see Little Billy.

He was sitting on the fender stool and looked as if he had been crying. He said that he had had a good hiding and he was going to leave home. How alarming.

As Alice made the supper Big Billy looked at the newspaper and Little Billy sat picking his nose. At one point, Big Billy called to Alice,

"It's alright Lass, he's not leaving home."

Alice came out of the kitchen drying her hands on a striped tea towel.

"How'd you make that out?"

"He's sitting here unpacking his trunk."

I couldn't see why this merited so much convulsed

laughter and I went back upstairs to our own domain.

Big Billy and Alice didn't stay living under us for very long.

My mother had had another sister called Madge, or Margaret Rose to give her, her correct name.
'

Madge had been very beautiful, well; she would be because she was dead. In later years when I looked with a more adult eye at a fading sepia photograph of Madge; posing with her head resting on her hands, she actually was very beautiful. It seemed more than a shame that her life had been cut short by poverty and childbirth. Mam occasionally found the photograph and wiping an imaginary tear quavered,

"Aye, there's many flower blooms unseen, beside a cottage door."

The story went that Madge too had lost her hair when working at the "Munitions," at Gretna but had then gone into, "service," at a farm in Wales. The kind farmer and his wife had allowed her time off each afternoon to walk the Welsh hills near the farm, with her head bare. The good fresh air had made her hair re-grow even redder and more luxurious than ever. So, there you go. There's a useful lesson. If you lose your hair working in the Munitions factory at Gretna and act like Aunt Evelyn, keeping it covered then you have to wear a wig and intermittently return to a little town called Maryport to have it replaced by a Master wigmaker. But if you walk the Welsh hills then your hair returns naturally and wonderfully.

Madge had returned from the kindly farm in Wales and married a Scallywag. Stories would have been nothing without the feckless who dared to enter the Tuke family. His sins mainly consisted of never having a job and keeping Madge in a perpetual state of pregnancy. Madge forever had to beg from her family for food or money to feed her growing family and pay the bills.

Mother Tuke wistfully wiped away a tear when she told of a day when Madge had arrived early in the morning with her boys. It had rained all day and Mother grew weary of feeding them all. Finally, she turned to Madge and said briskly,

"Now Lass it's ten o clock and those boys should be home and in bed. When you get home make sure you make yourself a good cup of tea, you've had a long day and it's like a Borrowdale shower out there."

Madge's boy John ran up and down the lobby saying, "Visht the vind," as the gale battering against the door frightened him. Harry scuffed his cracked boots against the wall. As Madge rocked the pram a tear slowly trickled down her cheek. Mother said sharply,

"You have some tea, haven't you?"

Madge shook her head. Mother Tuke sighed as it dawned on her that her daughter was braving the wind and the rain to enter a house entirely empty of food. Though she had little enough, she put some tea in a screw of paper, some sugar in another screw of paper, some bread and butter in a greaseproof bag and gave Madge these with a penny for the gas. If Madge had not spent the day there neither she nor her children would have eaten.

Madge died giving birth to her fourth boy, Basil.

Within the story of her dying hours it was recounted that Madge kept pointing towards a picture on the wall and no one could fathom the meaning of this. When the family was cleaning the house after her death, they found her set of false teeth in the cupboard under the picture. They then deduced that Madge had wanted her teeth in to go to meet her Maker. Not a very romantic solution to the mystery but there was a certain family pride in the fact that Madge had wanted to look her best for her final journey. The feckless husband had promptly, "taken off," never to be seen again. The local Salvation Army Major and his wife, who were childless had requested that they bring up the baby and the family relinquished him with some relief. The unfortunate little Basil had only lasted a few months before joining his mother, with or without teeth.

The other boys were simply farmed out around the family. There didn't seem to be any question that they would go anywhere else. The family simply moved up and made room for them. John Easterbrook picked the short straw and was borne off to Yorkshire to be brought up with rigour and discipline by Aunt Evelyn. Harry and little Jim went to live with Mother Tuke.

Harry proved too much of a rogue and was soon moved out to live with Aunty Lizzie. Jim was a similar age to my mother, and it was clear that she loved him dearly. But Harry!

Oh ... the tales of Harry were numerous and fearsome. In this supposed age of enlightenment. Harry would probably be analysed as having behavioural and emotional difficulties because of his early years of poor nutrition, an abusive father, the sudden loss of both parents on and on ad finitum. The fact that his other brothers were gentle boys who grew into fine young men always gave the family the lie to this. All were in agreement that Harry was a "bad un." The rotten apple in the barrel.

Mother Tuke and Auntie Lizzie tried. They tried hard to persuade Harry to become a model citizen. Both of them were kind and loving women who gave him a more stable life, but Harry moved from truanting from school and generally terrorising the neighbourhood to breaking the law. Auntie Lizzie had to go on more than one occasion to the local Police Station to plead for him. On one visit when she was again citing Harry's motherless state, the kindly Police Sergeant had put his arm around her and said,

"Mrs. Musgrave. I have known all your family and not one of them have been up these seven steps to the station except for help. Now you are just going to have to admit that Harry is just bad through and through. All I can see for that lad is either the army or jail."

It turned out to be the army where Harry acquitted himself quite well as a boxer. He even returned from the Second World War with a medal for bravery!

Harry told many stories of his war time adventures. He told of his capture at Dunkirk. The Germans had lined up all the British soldiers and proceeded to shoot dead every tenth man in the line. The rest were shot in the foot to ensure that they did not escape. What a thrill of horror listening to him and feeling the mounting fear as the Germans made their way along the line. Would he be a number ten or a hole in the foot? It transpired that he was a hole in the foot and so was spirited off to a Prisoner of War camp. The perforated foot must have healed as Harry and another soldier escaped. It was a thrilling story. And though this was also a time when it was agreed that the Germans were capable of inflicting all manner of cruelties against, "our lads," it was also agreed that Harry was a practised and accomplished liar!

However, his tales were later recounted in a book. One soldier who had accompanied Harry on the daring escape came forward and not only verified Harry's stories but added other tales of daring do. Apparently while Harry was a resident in the prisoner of war camp, he had

45

usefully occupied his time by learning to speak fluent German. On crossing a bridge, during their escape Harry had nearly given his companions collective heart attacks by stopping a German soldier guarding the bridge. Harry had calmly asked for a light for his cigarette. The guard willingly gave him one and then waved them across the bridge. His wild behaviour was admirably suited to the fortunes of war but certainly not peacetime. He returned home and for a while, lived off his stories and then got a job careering about in a lorry carrying dangerous chemicals. It was as we moved to Curzon Street that Harry got married. For some obscure reason Mary and June were chosen to be bridesmaids. I remember the wonderful long dresses and the coral beaded headgear but not the wedding. I do know it was a great relief to everyone that Harry and his new bride promptly moved to live in Bristol.

And of course, my mothers' brothers peppered my life.

John had been the eldest. Now John was actually a very large photograph that hung at the top of the staircase in Mother Tuke's house. There he stood in full uniform with a rifle plus bayonet, held smartly to one side. John had been very tall and very handsome, which he would be because he too was dead.

He had nobly volunteered to join up for the Great War before he was eighteen and had lied about his age. Two years later he was killed in the filth and mud of the trenches. Those that were left said that this was a great

46

pity as John had just been selected to return to Blighty to train as an officer at Sandhurst. John also had the unusual distinction of sending a letter to Auntie May after he had died. They all knew this as the telegram reporting his death had arrived before the letter. Not only this but in the letter, he had described himself as lying on a sun-soaked knoll listening to the birds singing. That was the proof, if proof were needed, that he was actually in Heaven. Why, everyone knew that there were no birds in Northern France at this time and certainly none near the living Hell that was the trenches. John never sent any more letters, so I assumed that maybe Heaven just granted you one last request and that had been his.

Apparently, Mother Tuke had been so devastated by the loss of her first-born son that she had, "taken to gin," for a while. When this little snippet was disclosed there was more sad sighing. Obviously, the loss of John was enough to exonerated Mother Tuke for falling about drunk and depleting the household money considerably. Father Tuke had been more than understanding and to help her overcome her passion for gin had bought her bottles of brandy instead. I didn't understand the logic, but they were all agreed that this had been a fine manly gesture to alleviate his wife's grief.

Uncle Ben came next and was a very shadowy figure to me as I only met him once. He and his wife lived, "down south," a term which covered a multitude of sins. They had no children. Many years later Mam slipped in upholding the perfection of her family by saying that Ben

47

couldn't have had any children as he had caught the "Pox." She quickly recovered this startling revelation by saying that, "it had been inflicted on him by wicked French women who preyed on our young lads in the trenches." Obviously, the young lads had no choice in committing the act that transmitted the "Pox." Certainly not the handsome and swarthy young Ben. Mam was a strange mix of feminism and fantasies of the dominant male brought low by a woman.

I do remember Uncle Sydney. A tall swarthy skinned man with a hoarse, rasping voice. The voice had been acquired when he was a Sergeant Major and screamed at the troops niceties like, "Come ere Quasimodo, you 'orrible little man". And the skin was an occasional family trait as Mother Tuke had been born in Cornwall and maintained that part of the Armada had been wrecked there. The soldiers and sailors had settled in the area thus producing children with a Spanish flavour. Hence the slightly darker skin tone in some of her children. She, herself spent much time trying to whiten her skin with lemon juice in Ponds cream. Sydney had been a great soldier and had served in China and India. When he came to visit, he regaled us with tales of the Khyber Pass and the Hindu Kush. We listened spell bound to flavoured descriptions of strange foods and scents and scenes. We wiped a tear when he told of seeing a crane in Hong Kong, which bore the sign "Cowan, and Sheldon. Made in Carlisle." Simply reading this had made him home sick for Cumberland as never before.

I never quite figured out Uncle Sydney's' private life. He had married another May and moved to Appleby to become a postman. Of course, he had married May against his family's' wishes. In fact, all the Tuke children had married against someone's' wishes. In consequence it was quite understandable that he had eventually left May to live with another. By the time I knew Uncle Sydney he lived with a handsome woman called, Marie and they lived in Surrey. He never did divorce May and continued to finance her, so there was some discomfort when Marie came with him and much pondering as to where she would sleep. However, before leaving Appleby to live "down south." May and Sydney had produced two sons, Kenneth and John. These two lads were a similar age to Mary and June and whatever the faults of May, Mam made them welcome to stay, along with all the others.

And that leaves Uncle George.

Unlike his brothers he was a small wiry, ginger haired man. Aunt Evelyn said that he had met his wife, Meg, in Glasgow and he was, "agin," the Government.

Any form of government.

Though he did hold a particular revulsion for the Tory party and the, "landed Gentry." It coloured his whole outlook and lifestyle. He was bitter, bullish and much given to heavy drinking, depression and the writings of Omar Khayam. Meg and George had four children, William, Rodney, Peggy and Ian and they must have sickened of the constant talk of principles, politics and poetry.

Mother and Father Tuke has begat those who begat more and somehow my infant mind kept a tally of them all.

All of them swirled and eddied in and out of my small life, forever tied by a thin invisible cord. Even at such a young age I had absorbed who belonged to who and the nuances of pleasure or tension when we were with them.

The living room in the flat in Curzon Street was large and opened into another area, which was the kitchen. In the living room was a large coal fire, which still had servant's bells, attached and at each side of the fire were bookcases. The three-piece-suite was made of green leather and had the added distinction of making rude noises if you jumped on it quickly. This was a practice that was much frowned upon, as one did not mention bodily functions in any manner. This was rather a shame as the rasps of air always proved excruciatingly funny, except to June, of course who merely found them excruciatingly embarrassing. In one of the window areas stood the radio, which was as large as a chest of drawers. This was invariably turned on and invariably turned on to the Light programme. This radio station followed a set format and now if ever I hear the opening music to the programme, "Music While You Work," I am transported back to that living room. Mam scorned, "Mrs. Dale's Diary," as "middle class claptrap," but it stayed on droning away in the window. Poor Mrs. Dale always seemed to be worrying about Jim! Though there were other radio stations they were not quite so segregated into specific music or talk stations. This meant that we were exposed to a variety that gave a broader base of knowledge. A silly song could be followed by Mozart, which in turn could be followed by Frank Sinatra bemoaning the stormy weather. I really liked a song exhorting someone to, "Put another nickel in, in the nickelodeon," I hadn't a clue what a nickel was or a nickelodeon, but I loved the catchy tune. Another favourite was "Poppa Picolino." But the radio wasn't the only music in our lives. In the same room was my fathers' piano.

How the removal men got it up there without causing hernias is a mystery.

Oh, what a piece of furniture.

It was called an "Upright Iron Grand Concert Piano." I know, because those words were written on it in gold leaf. It was built in carved rose wood, inlaid with Mother of pearl. There were scars where the brass candlesticks had been, and all the hinges and pedals were shining brass. The keys were made from ebony and ivory. Mam grumbled that it was a, "beast," to clean but it was always cleaned and polished with much reverence. The rose wood glowed with Lavender wax polish, the brass fitments shone with Brasso and the ivory keys were washed white with milk. No one was allowed to touch the inside of the piano but somewhere in the year Dad removed the front, "to allow the air in." Then it was fun to watch it being played and the hammers thudding the strings.

Everyone played the piano.

Mam and June played quite well, if somewhat self-consciously and now and then I plinked on it. Mary played the piano very well and also played the violin. But Dad was the pianist.

Oh, how he could play that piano.

He didn't simply play the notes of the music but added all the emotion or verve that was meant to be in each piece. He played anything and everything. Chopin, Beethoven, John Philip Sousa marches, the Internationale, Songs of the Revolution, tangos, modern Bing Crosby songs and of course, Poppa Picolino. Mam said that it was no wonder he could play as his mother had locked him in the parlour when he was a little boy. Even though it was cold and damp he was not allowed out until he had practised for the' allotted hour. Mam blamed this motherly viciousness as the cause of his asthma. But no one ever knew if these tales were true or not. Whatever his mother had done it had paid better divvy than the Coop. He was a talented musician and much in demand. He had his own dance band and was Vice President of Maryport Albion Band. His dance band had been quaintly called, "The Savoy Orpheans" but the name had been changed to, "Mossops' Melody Makers." This had come about when

Dad was on the dole. Apparently, Dad and his dance band were well known in the area and an over-zealous Means Test man had begun to keep a check on them and gauged how much they were paid. Dad's dole was reduced or non-existent according to information squealed. Fortunately, the violinist in the band, Stephen Mossop was in employment as a railway clerk and his earnings could not be reduced. Hence the name change; to combat such daft draconian measures.

Dad gave his services free to children's' parties and any events for the Chapel, but Mam was furious when Big Billy Musgrave came in with a proposition. He asked if Dad would play each Saturday evening at the British Legion and if he did, he would receive a pound for the session. This was a princely sum and Mam was already planning on how to spend it. Dad refused, saying that he could not play in that "den of iniquity." The British Legion not only offended his Socialist principles, but he was a Methodist and therefore teetotal. It didn't matter how much Mam ranted and raved at the loss of such a sum, he stayed resolute. However much she railed, he would not tickle the ivories for such ill-gotten gains.

He frequently played at home and I frequently stood by the piano watching his fingers rippling over the keys. I loved it if a piece of music called for him to cross his hands. He played Blaze Away or Night on the Bare Mountain with never a jarring note. I often went to bed and nodded off to the strains of the Indian Love Lyrics, Que. Sera, Sera, or the tango, "Jealousy," He made it seem so easy and his music permeated and enriched our lives.

Though it was comforting to hear my family making music while I was in bed, I was still very afraid of the dark. It amused them vastly if I woke and squeaked, "Puttee light on" and yet that became their chosen punishment! As it was an upstairs flat this meant that the landing had no windows and if I contravened the bounds of decency I was placed out on the murky landing. There I had to stand in the dim darkness until enough time had elapsed to allow me back into civilised society. I can't imagine what sins a three-year-old could commit to merit this, but Mam maintained that I once, "carried on," until I put myself out! It was this putting me out on the landing that brought a great revelation to me.

Suddenly Mam went into hospital.

Just like that!

For me, there was no build up to it. One day she was there sitting about reading and the next day she was gone. I knew nothing of words such as, "prolapsed" or "womb." Such words were not spoken aloud. In fact, whole conversations could be conducted with many words missing.

Auntie Lizzie would lower her voice and say,

"You know Ethel French? Well she's gone for an

operation on her..."

"No?"

"Hmm. She's got.............."

"Oh, I am sorry. Such a nice little body. That's terrible."

They seemed to know what they were talking about. I, in turn knew that it was nothing to do with me and got on pasting my latest scraps of angels and cherubs into a scrapbook. There were myriads of words that were totally excluded from polite conversation. Words like, hysterectomy, periods, pregnant, cancer, menstruation, or personal parts of the female anatomy. I was even admonished for saying, "belly." Obviously, men's bits must never cross any lips. God-forbid!

In consequence I was completely unaware that Mam was ill. She just seemed to go to bed a lot and for all the plethora of Tukes not one of them came to help. Why should they? There were two big lasses in the house. Now had they been sons it may have been different. Lads could not possibly be expected to look after their Dad or a little girl, let alone themselves. And so, Mary and June were left to organise and manage everything, but at least Mother Croft came round, and did the washing. Though this turn of events rather baffled me, there was a prize. I got to go to Dearham School with Mary. Three years old and going to school. Gee Whiz.

It was a strange time without Mam. And it was quite some time because when you went into hospital then, you stayed there. None of this staying for a day or three. There was the "pre op" period and after the event there was a period of "nursing" which could last some weeks. As I knew nothing of the reason for this sudden departure of my mother, I was not unduly worried. It was just rather odd.

The flat was constantly tidy and calm,

Not only was the dominant person away but the fractious Tukes absented themselves. Thus, there was less time expended providing teas and sitting talking.

Mary and June proved efficient housekeepers. Strangely, meals were on time and beds were made. Dad just continued to be Dad. It was never considered or suggested that I would be farmed out to another house. I would not have been happy with this arrangement. Though close family surrounded me they were not warm or demonstrative. However, something had to be done with me as Dad could not be expected to care for a little girl. Mary solved the problem by approaching the Headmistress of her school and explaining the situation. And so, each weekday, I was dressed and taken with Mary on the bus to school. Now I was a big girl.

All went well until one day when we returned to the flat Mary made tea for us and we sat in the cool, calmness eating it. It transpired that the pudding was Something and cold custard. Yuck! I hated cold custard. How anything so delicious when hot could turn into this slimy yellow stuff when cold I didn't know. I only knew that I didn't like it cold. I refused to eat it. Gentle June tried to cajole me, but I was adamant. June whispered a few bribes. Nothing would induce me to put that stuff in my mouth. June hugged me with one arm and lifted the spoon with the other.

Mary simply banged on the table and pointed an imperious finger to the door.

"Out."

I was aghast.

Out? Me?

Who was she to use the greatest of all punishments?

I would show her.

I appealed to my Daddy.

He just ploughed on with his Something and cold custard and quietly said,

"You do as our Mary says."

And I stood in the dark on the landing marvelling.

Why, he was nothing.

My father was nothing in the house.

It was the women that ruled. The women made the decisions.

He had upheld Mary's authority and when Mam returned, she would resume her rightful place as ruler.

He was nothing.

A nice man, a gentle man, a sick man and oh, how we loved him, but I knew on that day that he had no true authority.

He was just there being Dad and nothing more.

My great revelation in the dark.

That night Mary washed me and helped me into my best clothes. June brushed and brushed my hair and put it into little red stick plaits and we walked over to the hospital in Grasslot to visit Mam. I had to look perfection to show Mam that all was well at home and all that she had to do was lie there and get better. I was bursting to tell her of Mary serving me cold custard when everyone, but everyone knew that I couldn't eat it. Not only that but Mary had had the temerity to banish me onto the landing.

I didn't tell. Even at such a young age I knew to play the

game.

I didn't split on Mary and she didn't split on me.

It didn't matter.

Mam had long ago contracted the "I" disease and was detached from all other considerations. In consequence visiting her was difficult. It was difficult for me mainly because I was bored out of my skull. After the initial pleasure of seeing her and being turned this way and that, for her to approve of my well-being I just sat on a chair with my little legs dangling. I was given a "Peoples' Friend," or "Woman" magazine to flip through and look at the pictures and sometimes June walked me to the toilet. It was even more difficult for Mary and June. Assuring Mam that everything at home was fine only resulted in her peevishly whining that she wasn't needed and obviously we could manage without her. There then ensued much reassuring her that she was very much needed. If they tried another tack and spoke of meals that had not been as good as hers then they were berated for not learning more from her. If they used anodyne words and said that the place wasn't the same without her, she picked at the bed covers and said that they shouldn't be worrying her. How could they come and visit only to give her a catalogue of disasters when she was so ill? It didn't matter what they tried. Mam skewed off in another direction with much picking at the covers. Apparently, she had read that this was a sign of a person being very disturbed, so this little action was added to the deep drawn sighs. However ill, Mam had a great awareness of what other people would think of us. There were times when we were merely living representations of her and her goodness. We were walking examples of her proficiency as a perfect mother. And so much of the visits were taken with comments that became familiar. Mary shouldn't have come looking like that. Surely June could have combed her hair before entering the ward. Why put our Edna in that dress when it didn't look quite clean? I must have passed muster on some visits, as I had to be paraded around other beds or wards to be twirled and show everyone, "her baby."

A bell always rang to signal the end of visiting hour, whereupon we sprang into action, lavishly kissing her and checking all that had to be brought on the next visit. I was lifted up to kiss and be kissed and Mam stroking my hair would say,

"That's me lass a leather, when I kill me cow, I'll give you't blether."

We were mindful to leave slowly and regretfully, and then, with relief, scurried home in the dark. Well, I didn't do much scurrying as either Mary or June always gave me a piggy-back. As Mary or June took turns to visit every night, they had to side-step the exquisite torture of trying to say and do the right thing with regularity. I was only allowed to visit once per week. As no one under the age of fourteen was allowed in the pale green and cream walls of the hospital this was considered a great privilege for Mam. It was awarded, as Dad being the local doctor's receptionist was now considered part of the medical profession. This distinction alone may have contributed to Mam's recovery.

There were certain advantages to the practice of not talking in front of children or talking without certain words. I wasn't at all worried about Mam. Oh, I knew that all was not well, but I had no inkling that this was serious and anyway she often went to bed. For now, she was just in bed in a different place. The flat was relieved of the Tukes' political discourse and I was going to school. Apart from the weekly trail with Mary and June over to the hospital there were a few pleasures to be found in Mam's operation.

CHAPTER 4
"INFORMAL EDUCATION"

Here was my introduction to life outside the cocoon of family.

Mary and I walked to the Memorial Gardens each morning and caught the bus to the village of Dearham. As we alighted from the bus just as it entered the village, I saw nothing of Dearham. Then we walked down a very long lane called "The Went" and rounding a corner came to the school building. From the security of Curzon Street, comfortably sitting on Mary's knee on the bus and a companionable walk; the noise and hurly burly of the school Playground was a shock. I felt very small and everyone else seemed very tall Neither was there any pattern to their movements. I huddled against Mary as we weaved in and out of children. Some paused and looked with curiosity as they called "Mornin Miss Croft."

And then the biggest shock of all.

As we entered the building, Mary turned into another person.

Just like that! We crossed the threshold and she ceased being my big sister and became someone else.

It was very disconcerting.

As she knelt to unfasten my coat, she murmured that while we were in school, I had to call her "Miss Croft" and I hadn't to bother her too much. Oh.

I was allocated a peg for my coat that had a picture of a rabbit pasted beside it. The only way that I could reach it was to stand on the ledge covering wire cages for shoes. And I didn't work that one out until I saw another small person performing the acrobatic feat later in the day. The classroom was enormous with little desks arranged in the middle and toys large and small were standing along the walls. The floor was shining, dark floorboards and slatted wood was cladding the first part of the walls. The ceiling was very high, and the windows were like the ones that I had seen in the chapel. I'd have had to be the size of Goliath to even peep over the windowsills, as they were so high up the walls. To one side stood a black round stove, encased in a sturdy cage and near it the Teacher's desk. I don't remember any other part of the school and I don't remember any lessons. I do remember that after lunch. Miss Croft and the Teacher pulled out little green, canvas beds with folding legs. The desks were pushed back, the beds set up and we were exhorted to sleep. It seemed a very long quiet, time until Miss Croft allowed us to get off them and then we could choose which toys to play with. Within this room was a marvellous large, wooden, red engine. It was so special that there was a rota as to who could ride on the magnificent engine. Being a new and temporary member of the class, my name plummeted to the bottom of the rota. This did not at first trouble me. Our Mary would sort it out. Having a sister on the staff must mean that such things did not truly apply to me. Mary tried to explain the concept of fairness. She pointed out that it was a large class and some children still had not had their turn. So? So, why should they wait longer just because I had come into the class? I hung around the engine most days I tried to look pathetic. I hung around Mary, but Miss Croft remained unrelenting to my pleas. As my sojourn at the school was only until Mam came out of hospital I never did get to ride on that beautiful, big engine. It was tough lesson in knowing my place. May that Miss Croft never be forgiven.

Despite these puzzlements, I had a wonderful time at that village school.

I enjoyed having bigger toys to play with and the space to play with them. Except the big engine of course. I found that I enjoyed the company of other children and made friends quite quickly. I enjoyed the freedom of the Yard where I could make loud noises and shouts that were not allowed at home and out in the yard some bigger girls took me under their wing. They taught me things that I had never dreamed possible. They taught me how to tipple up against the school wall until my skirts fell down around my ears. Cool. The more accomplished could do this away from the wall and then go right over until their feet touched the ground and they skittered away upside down like a crab. This I had to learn, I practised and practised with the bigger girls catching me and holding me in position. It was no mean feat, gauging, exactly how much fling to give to my bum so that my feet not only arched over to reach the ground but also reached it carefully, without smashing every bone. At first a girl stood to each side of me and then just one stood holding the small of my back. Then came the wonderful day when I too skittered off across the yard. What an achievement. I proved to be very adept at Tippling Up.

I was also quite good at a game called, "Mum Jump." This was where one girl bent over and placed her head on the school wall and others bent behind her. Then with a long run and a flying leap I landed clump on their back. There was much shuffling up along the line of backs, making room so that another could take a flying leap and land somewhere behind you. This was considered a dangerous game and was banned, but we played it anyway.

Thankfully, as the school bell rang for the end of another day Miss Croft turned back into Our Mary and we "walked back down "The Went" to get the bus home. Even the walking time was not wasted. Mary showed me how to blow Dandelion clocks. One o'clock, phoo. Two o'clock, phoo, phoo. I learned how to pull upwards on the long grass, nipping and easing off the seeds. If there was a tail of seeds we shouted, "Cock" and if there was no tail, we shouted "Hen." A flat blade of grass placed between the fleshy part of my thumbs could be blown on to give a piercing wail or a cut lip. Buttercups held under my chin told the secret that I liked butter. All very useful lessons. But one that I never managed; probably because

I bit my fingernails was making a daisy chain. As we sat in the dyke waiting for the bus, Mary adorned me with daisy necklaces, bracelets and anklets. Her efforts were appreciated but did not make up for her strange behaviour inside the school.

Mam came out of hospital and promptly went to bed.

One day Auntie Lizzie came stomping up the stairs and found Mam leaning over the sink.

"Eh. Lass. Are you no better?"

"I'm not Lizzie. There's something very wrong down there".

"Well, you get back and tell them, you'll have to get that sorted."

"No. They've had one go at me and didn't get it right, who's to say it will be any different?"

"Listen, if you want anything done always go to the top. You tell them you want a Mr. Joyce seeing to you. For goodness sake get your Alf to talk to the doctors or something."

"I thought maybe if I could go into one of those Convalescent homes for a spell."

"Don't talk tripe our Edna. You know fine those are not

for the likes of us and where would the money come from? Always ideas above your station. Just get yourself fixed before you start thinking like that."

Mam must have been ill. Under normal circumstances she would have felled Auntie Lizzie with a look for such bald statements. But she must have taken in the part about going to the, "top man" as Dad was chased back down the stairs to "speak" to the doctors.

Whatever he'd said to them resulted in her going to Workington Infirmary to be operated on by Mr. Joyce. And I returned to Dearham school. It was not for long this time as Mam came home declaring that she was much improved. She still had to go to bed every day but the kudos of having been operated on by the "top man" had a wonderful restorative effect. Though the Headmistress had been very understanding and helped the family over the crisis she was not prepared to allow me stay longer. Mam was miffed but that was merely one of a life-time of being miffed about someone or something that had not complied with her wishes.

Life resumed its normal pattern. Dad at the surgery, June at the Grammar school, Mary at Dearham school and me at home. I missed all the little friends that I had made and the school routines, but this did not mean that my education ceased.

A major goal for Mam was always respectability. This was respectability with a capital R. and bordered on being a religion. The path to this sanctified state was more like an obstacle course and one which weaved along a crumbling cliff path. One slip and apparently, respectability was lost forever. The path was also either very icy or made of mirrored glass because whatever you did was reflected.

"Whatever will people think of me if you go out looking like that, our Mary?"

"Don't think you're showing me up, shouting in the street like a fish wife."

Of course, I had only put a teetering, tiny foot on this path and so had much to learn.

So much to learn in so many areas. And Mam knew them all.

She was especially knowledgeable about manners.

In fact, I think she knew all the table manners that were ever invented. It may have been the French who invented knives and forks but only the English could refine this into such a tortuous manner of getting food into the mouth. Trust the English to make anything as hair shirty as possible.

We had to at least try whatever was served on our plates and I manfully chewed a tomato or Brussel sprout rather than take the blast from Mam for not even tasting them.

We had not to voice our dislike for something but to leave it at the side of our plate - after we had tried it of course. Mam reasoned that someone else at the table might like it very much and it would be rude to comment adversely. However, manners were not Mam's sole prerogative. Mary and June entered into this with gusto and I guessed that I must have reflected on them too.

I hadn't to slump at the table, as it was bad for my digestion. Definitely no elbows on the table until after the food had gone from it.

"You can put your joints on the table when the other joint is off," June said.

"Don't hold your knife like a pencil. Hold it with your finger down and along it; so that you can press to slice and cut. A knife is not to tear food." Mary said.

"Remember a fork is to stab food and lift to your mouth, don't bend towards the plate and don't whatever you do put the knife near your mouth. No licking along the knife. You may cut your mouth and who wants to see your blood at the table?"

Not me, for one.

Not even peas could be scooped onto the fork. I ask you, who came up with that one?

"Don't eat like the Americans. You must use both knife

and fork."

Of course, fingers were totally out as a means lifting food.

I had to scoop soup away from me in case it spilled, and the soup spoon had to be turned over backwards to show that I had finished. I had to learn the correct cutlery for the correct course, and which sat on the left of my plate and which on the right.

There was no quarter given for my left-handedness. There was a myriad of turning away from the table to cough, sneeze, blow my nose or wipe my mouth.

"Don't hold your little finger out. It looks pretentious."

"Shut your mouth when you are eating. What makes yon think that anyone wants to see what's in there."

"Don't say, 'Can I have it?' We know that you can have it. You have to say, 'May I have it."

I hadn't ever to say, "I'm full." I had to say that I had had sufficient.

"Don't reach across the table. You must take the cake that is nearest you"

Mam solved that one by buying a revolving cake stand.

One would imagine that the knife and fork sitting neatly side by side on an empty plate, signalled the end.

No. I couldn't leave the table until I had said,

"Please may I leave the table?"

And of course, they had serious, mock discussions as to whether I could or not. Oh, very amusing.

Mam drew the line one day when Mary said that I was now old enough to say,

"Please may I leave the table? I'm satisfied and thank you."

"Oh, for goodness sake, leave her be. She isn't a pot dolly."

I learned.

I learned so much in a few short years and I don't actually remember learning them. Neither do I remember not knowing them. I mean, in this brief period I must have learned to walk and yet I have no recollection of not being able to walk. The quantity of times that I must have stumbled and fallen before taking an upright stance and a few faltering steps must have been numerous. Nothing stirs in my memory of what must have been a painful achievement. I had gained the dignity of learning to use the toilet correctly and promptly forgot what it was like to be incontinent. And I had learned to speak.

I cannot remember a time when I could not speak, and I can't remember actually learning to speak but I can definitely remember this being frequently refined and corrected. Through this I also learned that speaking could be very important in attaining respectability.

The way that you spoke denoted status. How you spoke gave a distinction as to your class or where you came from. It was still a time when accents or dialects were frowned upon and so we had not to speak in Cumbrian dialect. Even worse, was to speak with a Maryport accent. I did rather have a head start in the fact that the majority of people around me did not speak "broad" Cumbrian. What we did not realise was that though we did not use the local dialect, we still had a very Cumbrian flavour to our voices. The media seemed to have difficulty with this, or they were unaware that we had our own tones and so Cumbrian was given as a Yorkshire or Lancashire sound as if that came close. It was nothing like. It was nowhere near.

The Cumbrian dialect was almost a language of its own and this varied from area to area and village to village.

Attending Dearham School had introduced me to another language and one which felt very comfortable. Now, back at home, meant that all the good work that my little Dearham friends had accomplished had to be undone. Instead of saying, "divv'nt." I had to say "don't." I was not, "gaan yeam." I was, "going home." I had not to say, "gis yean uh them" but, "give me one of those." Which was all very well, but my family also appeared very proud of the Cumbrian dialect and also very amused by some who spoke it. The little lad who approached the School Inspector while I was a Dearham school and asked him to "lowse me brat," caused much hilarity. It had to be explained to the Inspector that the lad had wanted the strings of his apron loosened. Somewhere in my small mind I knew that to gain friends and be accepted, I had not to appear too different. In consequence I became bilingual. I learned the local dialect and then learned where not to speak it. Dad was very good at this and could slip from one to another like a second skin depending who he was talking to. However, it was something that caused Mam much pain. She was torn by the paradox of being fiercely proud West Cumberland and its uniqueness and denying her heritage to attain sedate refinement.

Every week the local paper published an amusing article called, "Jobby and Mary's Crack," which was written totally in Cumbrian dialect. Every week Mam read it and then read it aloud to us with much dabbing of her eyes as she laughed and laughed. Every week she cut it out to send to her sisters or brothers for their amusement and to ensure that they did not forget the language of the land of their birth. She bought what books that she could which were written in the local dialect and was proud that she could count in Cumbrian. But the only time that she spoke it was to harry home to us that someone was "common" or did not know any better. Mam had a nice voice, when it was calm. It was well modulated and very expressive with suitable shades and tones. She did not speak the Queen's English but certainly not broad Maryport And yet she was conscious of how one ought to speak and, in a different manner to Dad, changed her voice to suit the listener. Unlike Dad, she would not descend to speaking Cumbrian but often assumed what our June called, "Mam's Vicar voice." If we were out shopping and Mam met someone that she thought was a, "Personage" I heard her speaking in a clipped, alien, mincing tone.

"Mey, what a lovely day. Surely one would imagine that the washing would drey quickly in this weather."

It didn't bother me. That was just Mam. That's how she spoke to some people. It aggravated the life out of June. But it meant that, if I wasn't being told how to speak properly, I was subtly absorbing that we spoke to different people, differently. On the odd occasions that Mam used broad Maryport it was obvious that she was not comfortable and gave each word too much length and harshness of sound.

"I mean what can be done with someone who says, 'Aas nut juan that.' I ask you, how will they ever get employment?"

I didn't know either.

If Dad was well out of favour Mam mimicked his words in an exaggerated broad accent thus indicating her imagined gulf in their upbringing and her contempt. It was safer to make a rapid, mental check, if Mam sank into the vernacular, whether she was being amusing or verbally blistering. And though she corrected my speech, she had a great fear and faith that all local pronunciation would eventually disappear. Mam was convinced that the radio would educate all of England as to how to enunciate correctly. This medium was educating society as never before and soon the whole country would be verbal clones of Mrs Dale, worrying about Jim. The wireless would influence the whole nation. And to be sure the wireless was following a similar path to Mam. On the radio, only comedians spoke in local accents, therefore the impression was that speech in a local accent was amusing. Anyone but anyone who worked on the land had a very Southern tone with lots of "Oohs," and "Arrs." Anyone but anyone who worked in heavy industry and in particular the pits, spoke with a Northern flavour with lots of "Eee, by gums" and "thaas nobbut a wassick." Of course, all Cockneys were Spivs who went "dahn the Palais" or nobly kept the home fires burning while "our Arry " winked and said "Corr Blimey" even to the King. Naturally all villains had a foreign accent, the most damning being a German accent.

But "naice" people spoke "naicely." Therefore, if you wanted to gel on in life and be "naice", the message was quite clear. Crystal radio clear.

The cinema didn't count.

The clipped tones of Anna Neagle and Noel Coward were held in as much scorn as cowboys hollering, "Git them grits Maw." The cinema was something else and Mam merely sniffed that Hollywood speak was simply an adulteration of English speech. However, it slithered insidiously into our conversations, much to Mam's annoyance, though we were allowed to use quotes from the films.

Speech also appeared connected to intelligence and education. Therefore, to speak properly also gave a broad hint that one was educated, and it was imperative to be educated. Maybe the "naice" voice came with it.

The beginning of "real", education was definitely reading, writing and 'rithmatic.

It was while living in Curzon Street that I learned to count.

This had no connection to school or actual teaching from the three women in my life. It was a necessity resulting from Mam's lack of perseverance and conviction that she was much fatigued from the effects of forced labour.

Much struck by the fact that she could not afford to take up residence in a Convalescence home after her operations she came to the conclusion that something had to be done. She decided that she would have to contribute to the family coffers even though she was enjoying ill health. At this time, the local clothing factory offered, "outreach work", and so Mam felt that she could sit at home and comfortably earn what she called "pin money." The idea being that she "finished" the garments by sewing them together and adding buttons etc. As with most of Mam's ventures, it was one of these ideas that was good in theory. She could not be expected to actually go to the factory to carry the goods home nor could she be expected to return them. The happy solution was that Mary and June had to go. Of course, there were dates and deadlines for the return of the clothes. And of course, Mam did not meet anyone's deadlines other than her own. As the date and time drew near Mam began to panic. Initially this meant that she didn't trail over to her Mother's for a few days while her fingers flew, sewing the garments. As resentment set in, she was heard murmuring that she didn't think that the day would have come when she would have to do such menial work. If the factory wanted her class work, then it shouldn't set her deadlines. They likely didn't think that if a job was worth doing, then it was worth doing well. Mary and June had to add sewing to their already full lives. And me? Why my job was to find the buttons. The clothes came with a large box of assorted buttons, which Mam tippled all over the carpet.

"Now Pet, you find me five like that."

As she sewed, I sat on the carpet sifting through the mini mountain of buttons, glancing at the one on Mam's chair arm and back to the pile until, triumphant; I had a row of five, which were the same. So, there you go. Sorting, matching, one to one correspondence and counting, all in one fell swoop. I actually liked the little activity. There was a sense of achievement each time I found the correct button and of course I didn't know that it was Maths. Knowing that might have detracted from the pleasure. Before long, Mam announced that the pay was not enough to justify all the work and upset that was involved and Mary and June were relieved not to have to hurry over to the factory for the parcels. The box of buttons was not returned, and I continued to occasionally pore over it, sifting, sorting and counting. I was ill.

It was hardly surprising that I succumbed to contracting measles and mumps together. Mam did not believe in vaccinations. She stated that we should build our own immunity and anyway nobody knew what the Government was putting in us.

I only remember the illness in a haze. Everyone talked in hushed voices and the doctor frequently came puffing up the stairs. Somehow then, the doctors' very presence was reassuring. It was as if their visit alone would be sufficient to heal and worries lifted from the house simply by them stepping into it.

A problem with this was the tension and the work that had to be done before he rounded the door. Everything had to be exceptionally clean and tidy as Mam had once read that an untidy sick room made for a longer illness.

The sink or washbasins were given a birthday as he would want to wash his hands. Not a new bar of Knights Castille as we didn't want him to think that we didn't normally use luxury soaps. There had to be a pristine clean towel folded for his use and of course clean bedding and nightclothes. Not new nightclothes as we didn't want him to think that we didn't normally wear them. Being turfed out of bed, washed and changed also ensured that I had a raging temperature by the time he stomped up the stairs.

Mam always opened the door with a dramatic,

"Oh, doctor, I'm so glad you've come."

And we were.

He scrutinised my spots, which were even in my ears and in my hair. Then he tenderly felt my neck which was doing its level best to join my ears. Meanwhile Mam stood to one side keeping up a running commentary of my symptoms and all that she had done as a good mother. She looked suitably pained, wringing her hands to drive home her concern and occasionally blinking flirtatiously at the doctor. All that I remember of the actual illness is feeling very hot and miserable while the family trooped in and out commiserating with Mam.

But I do remember that as I recovered a little, Mam made me a bed in the big living room by putting the two armchairs together. I thought this very ingenious and it kept me part of all the family action. The afternoons were the best. Mary and June were out, Mam had gone over to her mothers' and all was quiet and peaceful. The only sounds were Dad's newspaper occasionally rustling and the clock ticking. I lay watching the fire flickering and glowing and it was almost worth having the measles and mumps to be so deliciously comfortable.

Though cleanliness was a great priority, teeth were not.

The dentist was simply there to address the occasional toothache. There weren't any six-monthly check-ups or scraping or polishing or anything that bordered on cosmetic attention. The dentist was like the doctor, you visited when something was wrong and that was that. June once bought me a little toothbrush with a Mickey Mouse on the end of it. Once or twice I nobly wet it and dipped it in the small round tin of Gibbs tooth powder. I scrubbed my little teeth and spat it into the wash basin, but this was just when the fancy took me. The Gibbs tooth powder smelled like Vim and was probably a similar abrasive. I don't remember toothpaste in tubes, just powder. No one exhorted me to clean my teeth, though I saw Mary and June cleaning theirs before a "heavy date."

I had hardly recovered from my measles and mumps when I woke with raging toothache.

The next morning Mam bore me off to Danny Watson's'. This was the town dentist and we hadn't far to go as the surgery was only across the road on the opposite side of Curzon Street. Again, there was no explanation given to me. No warning. I was washed, dressed and taken over the road, holding my little cheek.

Inside the Danny Watson's we sat on large dark, leather chairs until he looked around the door of another room and invited us in. Neither Mam nor the dentist thought to explain or forewarn me. He gently lifted me onto a very long black chair, while Mam impressed upon him the dreadful night that she had put in.

"Not a wink of sleep have I had. My poor baby has moaned and cried all night. I could hardly wait for you to open Mr. Watson. It hurts me so much to see her in this state," and she looked like Mary Pickford as she was strapped to a railway line.

"Now, now, Mrs. Croft. Not to worry. You know that I will sort this out and you can rest this afternoon. Of course, we understand your fears."

Mam just had a knack of wheedling around men. She could rapidly assume the demeanour of the weak piteous, woman desperately needing their manly skills and they fell for it every time.

A chair was found for her and she was patted and petted.

He looked in my mouth and announced that he could clearly see the problem. Phew that was a relief.

81

Suddenly this black thing with a strange pungent smell was bearing down on my face. I wasn't having any of that and I began climbing out of the chair. Strong arms pressed me back down and the black mask was pushed hard against my face. What on earth were they doing to me? The smell filled my senses and I could hear Mam crying. The sweet choking smell became stronger. Far away I could hear Danny Watson's voice kindly telling Mam to leave the room as it was much too upsetting for her.

She was upset!

What did they think I was?

The room spun and faded, and I was filled with the cloying odour.

A lady was offering me a drink. I was told that I must not swallow the liquid but spit it into a bowl that she was holding. The liquid came out of my mouth pink and bloody.

What had they done to me? Danny Watson lifted me from the chair, and I tried to stand but staggered about the room. I felt worse than I had done with the measles and mumps. Danny Watson led Mam by the arm out of the surgery assuring her that all was well. Mam was still crying copiously as she took my hand to cross the road. Out in the fresh air I could not keep my feet and my little legs buckled under me. I had to crawl on my hands and knees up the stairs to the flat. Then to add insult to injury Mam made me swill my mouth with boiled water and salt. Yuck!

I was sick, dizzy and disorientated.

Mam sat me by the fire and put a bowl on the floor beside me with the instructions that if I was going to be sick I hadn't to miss and hit the carpet. I just went on and on feeling dreadful. What on earth had they done to me? Finally, I lay on the floor with my head in the bowl. It was then that I found that part of me was missing. In my mouth was a large hole that felt like jelly. Oh, my poor little body had something missing. I cried and cried.

At last Mam stopped her own crying and laughed and laughed at my histrionics.

When Dad came in after the morning surgery, he took me on his knee and said that he would take me to town the next day and buy me an ice cream. Who knows what Mary and June would come up with? When they came in that evening, I tried to keep the momentum going. Oh, I was cuddled and kissed and told that I had been a good and brave girl. June promised me some new Plasticine from Woolworth's. Hey, this was O.K.

Of course, it wasn't long till Mam gave her version of events at the Dentists. Strangely my part had diminished considerably. She stressed how much she had suffered seeing her baby in such pain, how much I had dragged on her on the way home and how kind Danny Watson had been when he had seen her anguish. She worked herself up to another dose of tears. Then, to lend weight to her distress she announced that she could never repeat the exercise. It could not be expected of her. From now on Mary or June would have to take me to the dentist; in fact, it had to be Mary as she was the eldest. Mary and June cast their eyes to the heavens.

Later that night Mam redeemed herself greatly.

As she put me to bed, she drew from her pocket a blood-stained hanky. Carefully unfolding it she revealed an enormous tooth. She tore it away from the congealed blood on the hanky and instructed me to put it under my pillow. Apparently, while I was asleep a fairy would come and take it away and she would pay for the tooth by leaving a silver sixpence.

Fascinating.

She gently kissed my good cheek and stroked my hair and left me.

After she had gone, I took the tooth from under my pillow and turned it this way and that and round and round. How on earth had that lot got into my little mouth? It was smooth and creamy with a tiny black hole to one side. I carefully placed it back under my pillow. Once or twice I checked to see if it was still there. I watched the door for the fairy even though Mam had said that it would not come while I was awake. Then I watched the ceiling to see if it happened to be flying around up there waiting for me to nod off. I watched until my eyes were dry and scratchy and the sound of Dad playing Chopin in the living room was drifting and fading.

I faintly heard Uncle George stomping up the stairs calling,

"I see Paderewski's at it"

"Shut up George you'll waken Little Edna. She's had a bad day."

"Oh, not them measles again surely?"

"No, she's been to Danny Watson's"

"It'll be too many sweets, that's what. Them two lasses of yours spoil her rotten, well, spoil her teeth rotten."

"Sit down George and don't talk tripe, you know fine sweets are rationed. Anyway, what are you doing here?"

"Oh, just called in on my way to the Labour club for a drop of the amber nectar..."

And then it was morning.

I woke and promptly lifted my pillow. Sure enough, there was a silver sixpence and the tooth had gone.

It seemed a reasonable bargain.

Though teeth were not much of a priority, cleanliness certainly was. I wasn't sure what Godliness was, but cleanliness was next to it. Cleanliness joined other areas in achieving respectability. It was one area that transcended class. People could be incredibly poor and yet be admired for how clean they were. I sat through plenty of conversations that testified to this.

"It must be an uphill struggle in those old pit houses. The dirt just comes through the windows, but that poor Mrs. Sloan keeps it nip clean."

"Aye, and I bet she's glad that other slattern's moved up Ewanrigg, you know the one that lived next door to her? These Council houses have indoor bathrooms so that will make it easier."

"Oh, you can move that sort anywhere you like, they'll drag it down after a bit."

"Eeh, our Alf was laughing the other day. He'd gone round the doctors door with some cards, just as the doctor was saying, 'Now Mrs. Peet, you really are going to have to clean yourself and she said,' You know I aven't a bath doctor, and I'm way down the council list and the Dr said, 'Of course you can be clean without a bathroom. You simply have to wash yourself up as far as possible and then down as far as possible' and she went into gales of laughter and said,' Aye doctor but oo'se gonna wash Possible.' I think he was stunned into silence. Mind you, you know me, I'm no snob but I am about dirt and a bar of soap is cheap enough."

I think Mam proclaiming herself not a snob stunned them too into silence.

It also seemed that some could go too far in the other direction. Aunt Evelyn was always being mocked for being too house-proud. It was said that she even polished the coal that sat on the top of the coalscuttle. Likely there was a happy medium somewhere between obsessive cleanliness and slovenly dirty habits, where one attained respectability.

"Tide."

That was the only washing powder that Mam used. I can even picture the orange, swirling pattern on the box. She was very particular that it had to be "Tide" and there was much grumbling if Mary or June came back with Omo or Oxydol. Even the adverts had no influence on her faith in, "Tide." Mam was always singularly unmoved by adverts, maintaining that all advertising was based on fear. She also said that, adverts were anti women and she did have a point. There was the advert for Persil where two boys were passing each other; one with a snow-white shirt and one with a dingy grey one. The words,

"Somebody's mother doesn't use Persil," damned that poor boys' mother forever. Note, not his father. It did nothing to make Mam change her choice of washing powder.

But we didn't just use washing powder for washing clothes. It was also used for washing the dishes and though we lived in a soft water area it was also copiously sprinkled into the bath. This made a Hollywood style bubble bath.

If the bubbles began to disappear June taught me how to bring my knees up, put my arms underneath them and then roll my hands furiously over and over each other. The white foam returned rising up and up and around both of us.

I cannot remember bathing alone.

Either Mary and June were kneeling by the bath, washing me or idly playing in the water, or even better, I was in there with one of them. This was not an exercise in saving soap and water, it was quite simply if I knew that one of them was having a bath — Woohoo, I was in there. More often than not, they announced that they were going to have a bath and did I want to come.

Did I want to come? Try stopping me.

It was wonderful.

I had one of them all to myself in a most intimate atmosphere. We were comfortable and easy with each other. Oh, I wasn't too keen on the hair washing part and so June pretended that we were in a proper Hairdressers.

"Now Madam and what would you like today? Of course, before we do any styling Madam, this hair must be washed."

Oh, shucks.

Still, it got the crummy part over with and then came the luxurious time when we were simply playing in the warm water. After our arms had pummelled the water into foaming bubbles we lay in the mountains of white. It was really quiet. Then without warning whichever one of them was in the bath with me swooshed down under the water and I was tangled in their legs. Mary taught me how to put my thumb and forefinger together and make a tunnel with my other fingers and blow. With enough soap lathered on, we could blow the most enormous bubbles. This was quite a delicate operation and required much gauging of breath and blow. And it was a good time to teach me rhymes and songs. My prune like toes and fingers were little piggies going to market. They gently drew their fingers around the palms of my hand slowly, but slowly,

"Round and round the garden" and then shot up my arm to tickle.

Oh, the delicious anticipation.

They always got out first. There was such a sense of disappointment when it was over.

Often, I refused to join them and sat in the bath getting colder and colder.

"Aw, come on our Edna,"

"No. You come back in."

"I'll shout of Mam."

"You willent."

"MAM, our Edna won't get out."

Clattypyat.

Mam came bustling in, aghast by the towels strewn about and warnings of the dire consequences of water flooding the floorboards.

"Out me lady."

Mam didn't even try to persuade me to leave my watery cocoon. She simply continued to admonish Mary or June whilst expertly folding up her sleeves. Then whoosh, I was yanked out and plumped dripping and shivering onto the bathroom floor. I can still feel the big towels wrapped around me and being shooed into the living room, for Dad to dry me by the fire.

I seemed to be washed a lot. Often, I instigated this as I could not stand sticky hands, or the feel left from Plasticine or wax crayons. Mam was very particular that we washed our hands after using the toilet.

Toilets were something else. They were extremely private places. You never, but never went in when someone else was in there and you most certainly did not talk about what went on in there. This was still the days of the large tank of water up near the ceiling and I jump, jump, jumped to reach the chain rather than ask someone to come in and help me flush the toilet. Words connected with using the toilet were a minefield of what was allowed and what wasn't, in respectable company. I learned.

Sometimes this was by copying those around me or it was just a frown from one of the adults. A variety of euphemisms could be used but never, never the correct terminology. You could say, "Poo," or "Jobby," or even "a number two" but June told me that there was really no need to say anything. The thing to do was to just quietly leave the room. If you absolutely had to say anything then it had to be, "I'm going to the X.Y.Z." or "I'm going to wash my hands," This last one puzzled me, as there was no wash basin in the unmentionable place.

Mam said that common people called it the "lav" and

posh people called it the "lavatory." I guessed that we must have come somewhere between common and posh as we called it the toilet, when we called it anything. They were just places to get out of. There was no attempt at making them attractive. They were just kept clean. The toilet paper was either "Izal" or "Bronco". It came in rolls or single sheets, which were ingeniously folded into a box with an opening, like a letterbox. It was fine, slithery and scratchy. Not everyone bought toilet paper. In fact, Mother Tuke sat cutting up newspapers into rectangular pieces and these were hung on a nail by the toilet. Sometimes I was commandeered to help her and found it really difficult. Not just because the large scissors were awkward and heavy in my left hand, but the pieces had to be just the right size. Not too big and not too small. Thankfully, a lost form of recycling.

After Big Billy and Alice Musgrave left the flat downstairs another family moved in. Their daughter proved too old to become a playmate for me but one warm day we happened to be on the fronts together. Maybe she was bored and decided that I would do for that moment and she offered to teach me a rhyme. I had to clasp her hands around the nearest lamppost and dance around it. She instructed me to repeat after her,

"Red, white and blue, you dirty kangaroo,
You went behind a lamp post and did a number two."

I was scandalised.

I felt dirty and tainted. Why; everyone knew that you didn't say words like that. Strangely I memorised the shocking rhyme immediately and never forgot it, but it was rude, and I knew it was not to be repeated in company. I didn't play with her again, simply because she was the girl that said toilet word out loud.

When I asked June what she remembered of Curzon Street, she said that even though it was a flat, it had seemed very spacious after the little two up, two down in Grasslot Street.

"As soon as we moved in, Mam allocated us our jobs. If it was our "duty" week for doing the surgeries either Mary or I had to do this. We had to clean down all the stairs, the hall and the doctors' rooms. We had to thoroughly polish their desks and chairs. In that period, doctors gave out medications as well as the chemist and so we had to dust and clean all those bottles including the famous A.D.T. bottles. The doctor said that that stood for "Any Damned Thing" and usually worked wonders.

"Funnily enough none of us were very ill when we lived there. Oh except for you having measles or something. Dad certainly didn't have any crisis in that time. And of course, having a bathroom was a pure luxury.

"Mam used to call me "Cinderella" because I always liked to see the fireplace tidy. Mam wasn't dirty, far from it, but she didn't seem to mind if things were a mess. Somehow the fireplace a mess, made everything look worse and so I really didn't mind sweeping the ashes and washing the tiles. Floor clothes had a certain long life of fireside smells. Mam was just scornful of me doing this as she thought it was a criticism. You couldn't win no matter what you did to please.

"It was an impressionable time. School was the big build up to the school Certificate and my satchel always weighed a ton. In fact, school should figure largely at this time, but it doesn't. This was partly because I wasn't scientific or sporty and those were the qualities that were valued at the Grammar school. For me, it was just a case of following the timetable, liking some teachers and heartily disliking some others. I guess I just went there and got on with it. I must have had some sort of illness as Mam had a thing about convalescing afterwards and she sent me to Auntie May's at Appleby. This was a bit odd as Auntie May was so embittered about Uncle Sydney. But, one visit that stands out in my mind was to Aunt Evelyn's at Hoyland. She was different in her own house and nice to me in a brusque way. I travelled in a grey suit with an emerald green blouse and a matching jelly bag hat. I thought I was the bee's knees for Malcolm to meet me at the station."

"All Malcolm's' friends wanted to meet his cousin from the country, and I felt very popular. Of course, there was always that frisson between Malcolm and I that held the promise that 'Something' might develop. We reckoned without Mam and Aunt Evelyn deciding that it was sinful for cousins to form an alliance. Mam was forever trying

94

to get us away somewhere. Well, either that, or being at home working. There were always undercurrents with various family members. One polite word to one of them could easily mean that you were being disloyal to Mam. We were often told to go up to our bedrooms while shocking family events were being turned over. Everything hinged on the Tuke side of the family and the only calm Tukes were the ones that lived at Flimby.

"It was always Mam's family that surrounded us; not Dad's, but I remember seeing Aunty Emily and Unck Eph on a concert in the Baptist church and wishing that we saw more of the Croft side. They always seemed such fun. Auntie Emily was blacked up; singing 'Lazy Bones,' and Uncle Eph sang 'the Floral Dance' with great gusto. "Then he recited an hilarious monologue about a lad called, 'Albert,' and a lion. "Cousin Gwen was in the Maryport Operatics and Dad was often playing the piano for some charity concert. Put together they must have raised more money than enough for good causes. I can't imagine the Tukes ever losing their dignity to raise money or provide entertainment for others. The Crofts' were much more "hail fellow, well met," types. Well, apart from Mother Croft. There was no getting rid of her, no matter how hard Mam tried. As well as helping Mam, we had to help Mother Croft clean various churches. I remember helping to stoke the big church boilers and dusting interminable pews with her. And Dad? Well, Dad was like most fathers, he was just around. He was busy doing his surgery shifts, doing some house repairs and there was his music. Like most men living with a harridan, he found ways of being busy elsewhere.

"He was very well liked in the town and he knew everyone. I suppose with his job and his music he would know everyone. He was well liked in his position at work and this was probably an area where Mam couldn't interfere. Funny he was always loyal to her.

"Nowadays, Mary and I would be called, 'lad mad,' but we enjoyed getting ready for dances and we danced well with each other. I think of them as a time of music and colour and sometimes Dad was up on the bandstand playing the piano. I was so proud of him I could have burst. At the Palace ballroom in Maryport, there was such a crush in the cloakrooms. Only two toilets and two mirrors for all the combing and putting on make-up. Phew, there was no need for Gyms then with so many nights spent dancing. Our 'dates,' at that time seemed to be confined to lads from the next town, Aspatria. After the dance we walked them to the bus stop and that was the excitement over until the next dance.

"My big romance at this time was with a nice but inarticulate lad called David. When I visited his house, I was much struck by how calm and light the atmosphere was, compared to the tension in our house. I was very puzzled when his mother sent me a letter on my fifteenth birthday saying that I was too clever for her David and I should be concentrating on my homework instead. I was totally devastated for a few days and then I recovered and met another lad called Jacky. He took me to a very posh 'do' at the Freemasons' Hall and then bought me some 'Innoxa' smellies. I felt very grown up. That's how it was. You knew you were too young to get serious and Mam encouraged us to play the field. I think she was afraid we would make the same mistake as she did and get married at eighteen. At this point, even going to church was another way of meeting a lad. And the dances and the cinema were a way of forgetting the drabness. After the war, life was dismal, dull and colourless. As if the war hadn't been bad enough, the winters were very harsh, long and cold. So very cold. To add to the drabness, the bombed houses in Maryport hadn't been cleared away. There were shortages of everything, we were so sick of 'make do and mend.' "We couldn't help but be aware of politics and World events, but I think the Tukes talked politics so much that Mary and I went the other way. There were times when you wondered who'd won the blooming war. We seemed just as badly off as before. "There were no luxuries. It was a time before fridges, tissues and proper hair curlers. "It wasn't just the viscous cold, I was always hungry. School dinners were very small portions. Honestly you came home from school just about ready to eat a scabby horse and there was nothing but a note for you telling you to go to the Coop or something. I was particularly sorry for Mary at this time. Being the eldest she caught it more than me, and Mam was forever rearing at her about some domestic job that she hadn't done. Mary must have been just as hungry as me but Mam's rearing and shouting about anything and everything just went on and on. She was forever getting at us about our manners and appearance. We had to be

97

just so. She once nearly had hysterics because she found out that I had been 'Downstreet' where the docks are. Crikey I'd only gone there with a friend to leave a message for my friends' Auntie. Mam was more worried that someone had seen me down near the docks. It was nothing but a relief to escape. Somehow, I had acquired a wireless for our bedroom, and I enjoyed going there and listening to American Forces Network. That was the station that played all the popular tunes. I liked, 'Twelfth Street Rag' and 'So Tired' and of course Frank Sinatra and Frankie Laine.

"Thankfully I got a little job at English's' cafe and had some really good, filling meals there. Then I worked on a Saturday in Woollies. I was on a variety of counters, but I liked the electrical counter the best. At that time, you had to test every light bulb before they were sold. When I got my money at the end of the day, I sneaked something out of it to buy some food for myself before Mam got her hands on it. Oh, and I usually got you something from the toy counter. Oh, but we just loved having you around. You were sweet and funny, and I can't remember you having any tantrums. It was nothing but exciting when you were born, and you just got more and more interesting as you grew. Mary and I were as bad as Mam for wanting you to look and act your best. We didn't really mind taking you places, well, not much.

"I can only once remember having a day out with Mam by myself at this time. Her nephew Jim had got married and moved to Carlisle and we went to see him. She'd more or less been brought up with Jim and she loved him dearly. For some reason she was much calmer with him, and I saw a different side to her. Riding on the train back to Maryport she taught me the words to the song, 'Stay as Sweet as you are.' "We had a lovely day together.

"A major event in the year was the Maryport Amateur Operatics. Whatever the show, we learned all the words and sang them on the school bus. "The Merry Widow," "The Bohemian Girl," "The Arcadians." That was real live entertainment and so colourful."

"Luxury for me, was a night at the pictures with a Kit Kat from Annovazzis' ice cream parlour. Hollywood was so very glamorous. There were two cinemas in Maryport at this time. The Carlton and the Empire. As the Carlton was known as the "flea pit," then the cinema to go to, was the Empire and if we could afford it, we sat upstairs. "Pictures took years to reach Maryport. I remember going to see, "The Outlaw" with our Malcolm in 1948 and it had been released in 1943. The most memorable ones were the musicals like "On the Town" and the ones set in exotic locations like Hawaii. "I loved the pictures; I even thought the name, "Curzon Street" sounded like an Anna Neagle film. Yes, it was escapism, but it was also warm in there with comfortable seats. I somehow always found the money to go to the pictures. Even better when a boyfriend paid. Really we were paying for a bit of dark to canoodle in comfort"

June's account was similar to Mary's but from a different perspective. Trust self-effacing June not to mention that this was a time when she was actually a high-flyer at the Grammar school and gaining very high grades. As Mam ate into her homework time and June worked at weekends then she must have been clever indeed to achieve anything academic.

June and the cinema.

It was a lifelong romance for her.

Correction.

June took Hollywood orders. She was a devotee.

A communicant film fan.

Hollywood's' glorification of a supposed way of life soaked into June and never left. The cinemas' high moral tone and the smug portrayals of what they thought life should be, permeated her thinking and stayed. She became dyed in the Doris Day image of the sparky, virginal girl who married the bumbling but brilliant male. They should have lived happily ever after. June was to strive forever to recreate all that was portrayed on the silver screen. They had sold her that that was life and she innocently bought into it. There should have been the capable, generous husband. A large, old house tumbling with freckled, beautiful children. A raggedy dog and

Mary Wickes stomping about being a gruff treasure in the kitchen.

And, the Christmases. A tree up to the ceiling with mountains of presents underneath it and mountains of snow outside. And in the background of their lives would be a kindly mother who supported but did not interfere and only put in an appearance at Thanksgiving.

It never existed. June was forever to be let down by real life.

Likely, Mam did not share June's impression that Curzon Street sounded like a film title and once again we moved house.

CHAPTER 5
LAWSON STREET

"I'm telling you. Lizzie. I didn't miss him and hit the wall."

"So, what did you say?"

"Well, when Alf came upstairs, I said that we were moving. I'd seen this house for sale in Lawson Street and I'd had enough of being nothing but a skivvy for those doctors, not ust that, but I can't get away with those new people that have moved in."

"What did Alf say?"

"Oh, you know Alf. First of all, he was mad, he said 'Frizzling Hexham woman, you doing the cleaning is part of the job, we can't move.' I said,' Don't you swear at me.' "Because as you know Lizzie, there's dirty swears and clean swears and I know what he means by 'Frizzling Hexam' Then he said I was changing the subject and he wasn't going to move no matter how much I carried on. I said, 'If you don't go and see those doctors, I will. You are only happy when I'm miserable and I'm miserable being a domestic drudge. That's all I am. And what's more I can't do it anymore. If it isn't cleaning the stairs it's up and down them to answer every bell and every telephone' and it is Lizzie, I'm sick of it."

I sat on Mother Tuke's sofa and tried to look engrossed in stroking the cat.

Auntie Lizzie and Mother nodded sympathetically.

"Mind, Edna, he has a point. You don't want him to lose his fine job and you've hardly been there any length of time."

"I've been there long enough to know that all I am is a servant and it's unputupable. I told him, I said that he had to tell them doctors."

"And did he?"

"Of course he didn't. As long as everyone thinks well of Alf, that's all that matters. "When he came back upstairs after his shift, I knew he hadn't, so I took off my apron and I went downstairs to old Dr. Rattrie."

"You never?"

"Oh, but I did. I just stood there and told him. He asked me to sit down but I wasn't having any of that. I said, 'Do you know how many stairs there are? I have just had these big operations and I can't do this anymore.""

"What on earth did he say?"

"The beggar said, 'It appears to me that your two girls do most of the cleaning and you do realise, Mrs. Croft, that you did agree to do this as payment for the flat and as part of your husband's position.' I didn't even lower myself to point out that Mary and June were well capable of doing the work, but I said I'd get a letter from Mr. Joyce to say I shouldn't be doing such menial, physical work."

"Ooo. That was a good one."

"Oh, he wasn't one bit mismade. He just smiled and said.' Mrs. Croft, I am the senior partner here and Mr. Joyce has little influence. I see no good reason why you should want to move to Lawson Street. Might it be out of your league a little?' Well, that was like a red rag to a bull."

"It would be. What a cheek."

"Then he said,' I must remind you that if you go ahead with this, your husband may be out of work."

"I just straightened up and said, 'Well, doctor, we never died at winter yet." And I walked out."

"That was another good one. I bet Alf was worried though."

"He might have been, but I wasn't. They'll have to go a long way to find a better than Alf and they know it. I just put on my coat and went to the Coop to see how much was in the Savings account and then I went up to old Mr. Crerars, the solicitors and told him that I wanted to set

104

the wheels in motion to buy Lawson Street. I'm telling you Mother, my girls are going to have a good address however happy Alf is to stagnate and keep us in squalor."

Alf wasn't allowed to stagnate.

I was not party to any of the details and arrangements to buy Lawson Street but this time I was aware of the upheaval of moving house. I remember tea chests being packed. The crockery was wrapped in newspapers and the best china carefully rolled in the tea towels. As Lawson Street ran parallel to Curzon Street everyone was commandeered into carrying as much as possible there. The flat took on a hollow, bereft air and looked bigger than ever. I was allowed to ride in the front of the enormous removal van. Dad lifted me up into the front cab and I sat with him and the driver all the way around the corner. Wizard.

And now, my memory doesn't play tricks with me. It was, and still is, a large, imposing house. A long terrace of sandstone houses with bay windows and a tiled forecourt, leading to each front door. Each house had a low wall with scars where the railings had been before they had been removed for 'the war effort.' A quiet, sedate, street and the residents mainly made up of widows and spinsters.

This was, "Something."

This was a, "good address."

Inside the front door was a vestibule. Not a porch. A vestibule.

Mam insisted that we call it that, and so we did.

The vestibule door was half dark wood and the top half stained glass. This meant that you could peer through and see a blue or red visitor at the open front door. There followed a long hallway, which Mam said that we had to call a 'hall' and not a 'lobby' and so we did.

To the right was the first room. This was the sitting room. Mam said that we had not to call it the 'front room,' as that implied that we only had two rooms, a front and a back room. The sitting room was all the grandness that the name implied.

A most beautiful room. It had a large, black, marble fireplace. The ceiling was ornate with carved patterns and a large carved light rose. The doors were something else. They were panelled and in each panel were pastel coloured carvings of flowers and peacocks; their tails sweeping down the doors. The piano was manoeuvred into this room and stood against the wall. It finally looked as if the magnificent piece of furniture had found its spiritual home.

Next to the sitting room was the living room. Again, this was a large room. It had a door at each side and a large, sash window looking down a long back yard. From this window we not only had full warning of anyone strolling up the yard to visit but also full view of the backs of the houses of Curzon Street. In the living room was a black leaded grate, which Mam declared she was going to keep. Apparently bread and teacakes were not quite the same taste when cooked in a gas oven. In one of the alcoves by the fire was a cupboard and then shelves reaching up to the high ceiling. Mam announced that this was the shoe cupboard and that's what it became. The best china was unwrapped and placed on the shelves above it. For all the years that we lived there, there were shoes in that cupboard and the best china displayed on the shelves. The opposite alcove had large drawers and a cupboard above them. I was given the bottom drawer for my smaller toys. I solemnly unpacked them and placed them in the drawer while the others whirled and carried and emptied and unpacked.

From the living room there was an under-stairs pantry and two steps down to a small kitchen. This had a pale green gas cooker, a large cream sink and a door leading to the yard. It wasn't really fair to call it a 'yard,' but it wasn't a garden either. Outside there was a washhouse attached to the kitchen and a stick shed attached to the washhouse. Then the yard opened out to a square of grass and the yard was divided by high green trellis. This had an arch covered with 'Seven Sisters,' roses. At the very end of the yard was a coal house and a toilet and then the back door into a narrow, cobbled lane. Near the living room window in the yard was a trapdoor leading to two large cellars. I can only ever remember being down them once. They were just as dusty and creepy as the word "cellar" implies. Dad kept all manner of things in them that he may need for repairs to the houses that he had bought, like the odd toilet lying on its side.

Moving into Lawson Street I was given my own bedroom which was above the living room and next to Mam and Dad's bedroom. Mary and June were to share the big bedroom on the next floor, next to the bathroom. Here was a potential minefield for dissent, which never transpired, as they were so agreeable with each other. When the bedroom suite was move into the room, Mary pounced on the mirrored dressing table and said triumphantly,

"Bags I this."

Mam held her breath until June pounced on the chest of drawers and said,

"All right then, bags I this."

Mam looked balefully at the one wardrobe. Ouch!

But Mary went outside the room and placed her hand on the floor to ceiling cupboard on the landing and said,

"June, you can have the real wardrobe and I'll have this out here."

Mam breathed a sigh of relief.

So, it remained until they married and left home.

The bathroom was a veritable monument to Edwardian grandeur.

The enormous iron bath, with large brass taps stood on claw like feet. The washbasin looked like a large white shell with smaller brass taps and small shell shapes indented on each side of the taps for the soap. As this had once been a bedroom it was very large. Mam soon had a dividing wall built in it to make a box-room, but this still left us with a very big bathroom. All the door handles, the round light switches and stair rods in the house were brass as was the bell and knob on the front door. We had not been there long when Mam had a plaque made of brass exactly like the ones outside the doctors' and dentists'. This was screwed onto the front door and boldly stated, "CROFT." We had not been there long before Mary, June and I vowed we that would never have brass to clean, when we owned our own houses!

Oh, but I loved that house and I was much loved within it.

Though every room, except the bathroom had a fireplace, these were only ever lit if it was Christmas or someone was very ill. In consequence here we were in this huge house and the only mode of heating was the living room fire. I remember spending ages perusing Jack Frost patterns on the windows, their delicate patterns and intricate tracery. Long icicles hung where the sash windows divided and slowly dripped onto the windowsills. And that was inside.

It was a cold house and I really felt the cold. Mam said that it was because I had red hair and as everyone knew, red headed people felt the cold more. Oh.

She never blamed the fact of feeling cold on the house or the lack of heating. If we huddled by the fire, she'd stare and say,

"You lot must be made of bad stuff."

Or worse was her exceptional gift of piling on the guilt.

"What's wrong with you lot? Haven't I fed you well enough? All that good food that I pour into you should keep you warm. Is it my fault?"

She was a past master at drawing anything to herself until we lost sight of the original discomfort. We'd be there protesting that her meals were fine while our teeth chattered almost as loudly.

Even the living room fire wasn't always a haven of warmth. Winter washing days found it commandeered to dry the clothes. We were shooed away from the fire while the clotheshorse took pride of place and clothes were draped over it, while we shivered at the back of the room. There were no such things as fitted carpets. We had patterned linoleum, with mats placed at strategic places. The trick was to hop, skip, jump, over the ice, cold lino to reach the nearest mat. Of course, there was always the off chance of misjudging and shooting off the edge of the carpet across the polished lino and smashing into the wall or a piece of furniture.

Going to bed we left the warmth of the living room.

Mam always filled me a hot water bottle in consideration to my red-haired coldness. We were modern enough to have rubber hot water bottles and Mam wrapped mine into one of my dolly blankets to ensure that it wouldn't burn me. I lay cuddling the bottle while my feet lost all sensation somewhere in the bed. I didn't dare stretch out as the rest of the bed was freezing but occasionally, I gave my nether regions a treat and wriggled the bottle down there. The trick then, was to pull the covers over your head and warm the air under the blankets with your breath. I went to sleep semi warm and woke up thinking I had turned into Scott of the Antarctic. I had my own method of keeping warm until it was time to get up.

Simple.

I just sneaked past Mam and Dad's room, up the next flight of stairs and crept in with Mary and June. They never complained. They just drowsily pulled me closer and wrapped me in their love.

There was so much love.

As one little girl, I had so much love poured all over and around me.

Of course, no one ever said the word, 'love.'

No one ever said,

"I love you."

"We love you,"

"You are much loved."

But I was.

And I knew it.

I was utterly safe and secure in the knowledge that I was much loved. It didn't need to be spoken out loud.

Their actions and their care were more than enough without words.

And anyway, this was not only Cumberland but also Maryport.

Soppy words were for soft people living 'down South,' or in the films. They were a different species and could voice such emotions, but we did not.

There were a variety of loving terms like, 'Pet' or 'Pettle' or 'Pet Lamb,' and on rare occasions we advanced to 'Dear,' but even that was mainly kept for letter writing. Often the intonation was enough and so the terms,

'Lad', or 'Lass' could hold a wealth of warmth.

No, no one ever spoke of love for me. That would not only have been incongruous but very embarrassing.

Still, I knew.

I was petted and pampered and loved in their easy manner and their actions.

And my small world was rich in touch.

I can feel my Dad's scratchy tweed jacket as he cuddled me close to his wheezing chest. Mam's hands helping me dress. Pulling the dress over my head, pausing for a few seconds while I was in the gloom of the cloth and then, 'Boo' as my head popped out. As she fastened my coat, she'd gently push me and pull me and laughingly say, "Oops, you're drunk You're drunk! Stand still."

And I helplessly tottered backwards and forwards.

Lifting me onto a table; then, with her back to me, expertly grasping my bare leg under her arm and cutting my toenails. I liked Mam to fasten my shoelaces as she always did them tighter than anyone else, firmly holding the sides of the shoes as she did so. And she had her own funny way of putting on socks, which I never mastered. She folded the foot of the sock inside out and then placed it on my foot and rolled it upwards, always rubbing the calves of my legs warm with both her hands when the sock was in place.

Sometimes she'd look at my small feet and say sadly,

"I wonder how many miles these feet will eventually walk?"

Mary and June would cast their eyes to the heavens.

They did a lot of that.

I can feel their hands holding mine when we walked anywhere and everywhere. And if I tired, it was a carry in their arms or better still, a piggyback.

At that height I was master of all I surveyed. My legs clasped in their arms and my smaller arms around their neck. Dad would crouch down, and I knew that this was an invitation. I could quickly run behind him and scramble on his back while he stood up, hitching me higher.

Sometimes the touching was rougher.

Mary or June, or both together, tickled me until I could stand it no longer and I had to shout for Mam. She'd come to the bottom of the stairs,

"Are you two tantalising our Edna?"

We all knew by her tone that she wasn't cross. And as I squealed that they were, they shouted that they were not and carried on. All of them blew loud raspberries on any bare part of me. Sometimes Mary grabbed my ankles and turned me upside down, holding me high in the air and saying mockingly,

"Your eyes are going to drop out, your eyes are going to drop out."

They never did.

But, oh the delicious fear that some-day they might.

They threw me on beds. They threw me on the couch. They sat on me, and in mock surprise announced to the world in general what a funny cushion they had found, while I wriggled and gasped for breath under or squashed behind them.

"Mam, Mam, there's something weird about this chair."

"Give over you two and leave that lass alone."

They nipped my bottom as I wandered past, tweaked my plaits, nibbled my ear lobes or grabbed my waist and rolled me over and over on the floor, while Mam shouted, "You two stop that. I didn't have her just to be a punch bag for you two."

It wasn't even any good appealing to Dad as he just lowered his newspaper and laughed at us. They counted my fingers and toes. They gently nipped my nose and then presented me with their thumbs, as if my nose had come right off.

"Mam I'm famished. Oh, it's OK this will do,"

and they pretended to gnaw and chew on my arms or legs. And all this was additional to the touching when I was washed or dressed. Physical pain was only something that happened by accident or when I was ill. But there was one, which always took me by surprise.

Every morning I had to sit on a stool while Mam brushed my long red hair and firmly plaited it. One wriggle or protest from me and the brush was smartly overturned to thwack me on the head.

That's all.

That's all I can remember of being admonished in a physical manner. My small world was relatively untroubled, safe and secure. There was no deliberate physical pain but there was tension. There was the constant not knowing when the next eruption would occur or why. And then there was the not knowing what to do about it when it did occur. There were bewildering charged atmospheres, which either heralded a gathering storm or were the aftermath of an unresolved argument. Sometimes there was just an atmosphere and no-one but Mam knew its origins. Even in my infancy I knew that I was a minor player in the dramas that unfolded. I was more an onlooker, but I was there. I was there in Lawson Street.

Dad didn't appear to nurture any devious plans to ensure that we lived in filth and degradation but if he had married a different woman, he probably would have been happy to ramble through his life in calmness and tranquillity. However, once Mam's desires had been achieved, he was more than accepting of the new situation. Not only was he inordinately proud that he had had two girls at the Grammar school but was rapidly very pleased with his new address. I know that because he somehow managed to weave it into his conversations with anyone and everyone when we were out walking. Probably moving house had left Mam too exhausted to ponder her achievements, when she went to bed for the first time in Lawson Street. But she had certainly come a long way from her own early life and must surely have felt a great sense of pleasure when simply looking around the spacious rooms. What she would not have pondered or ever conceded was, that every move forward was achieved by employing her volcanic upheavals, heavily laced with toxic emotions. Mam was the catalyst for all the changes, but others had to provide the practical means of achieving and sustaining them. Even with his laconic demeanour. Dad rose to the occasion and contributed his earnings, his energy and his health. It also seemed that there was no further to go. This was as respectable as one could get in Maryport without moving to the very large mansions just outside the town and as these were owned and occupied by the same generations of local wealthy families, there was no point in even considering this. No, Mam had, 'arrived' and dragged us with her. All that there was to do now was to slowly but surely replace the shabby furniture and bring joy to the hearts of all the decorators, joiners and plumbers in the town by trying to turn an old house into a new one.

Mam loved that house and was settled as never before. If she noticed its defects, she never alluded to them and admonished us if we complained. Mam would rather have sat in her boots and coat rather than admit that it was cold in there.

And it was.

Even in the height of summer, that house never felt warm. Well, only right at the top, in Mary and June's bedroom. The heat rose and collected there until it became stifling and stuffy even with the window open and the net curtains drifting lazily.

That room was never tidy.

Mary and June whirled in and out of it, leaving a trail of evidence that they had been. With her hands on her hips Mam looked around it and said,

"Those drawers look as if they are being sick!"

It was a good description.

Either the drawers were not closed and the contents bulging out or they had been hurriedly, rammed shut, with sleeves of something trailing out. Odette could have left coded messages in the clouds of face powder that had settled on the furniture. Even the mantelpiece of the bedroom fireplace was merely another ledge to hold discarded earrings, the odd glove, and letters and lists were nudged behind ornaments. Their bed often remained unmade, while June announced that it was a pointless exercise. Very daring considering the dramatic reaction any opinion other than Mam's would receive. Now and then Mam blitzed the offending room and they were roundly told to, "keep it like that." She might as well have talked to the wall. They were always rushing, rushing, and bedrooms were bedrooms. You slept, dressed or undressed in there. None of this having your own type of bedsit. They remained cool, supposedly tidy places that were empty for most of the day and evening. For me their bedroom was an Aladdin's cave. I hitched myself onto the chair at the dressing table and primped and preened. I awkwardly scraped my lips with lipstick, gouged Max factor Pan stick across my cheeks and hung

Mary's dangling earrings that were like baskets of fruit on my ears.

"Mam! Our Edna's ruined my good lipstick."

"Well, you shouldn't have left it there."

"Mam! Our Edna's had my diamante necklace and bracelet."

"If you put things away properly, she couldn't have done."

I was never to blame, and they were very forgiving, so I was never banned from their untidy emporium.

My own bedroom remained tidy and neat, but then there was only one of me. And Mam and Dad's bedroom was so big that there was always part of it that was untouched by human hand. That was, until Mam decided to clean.

Was it worth it?

I was never very sure.

It was an orgy of activity and she could destroy the order of the whole house by doing just one room. And of course, she could not be expected to do this alone. We were all commandeered into doing something while she directed operations.

Oh, how my heart sank when I heard the words,

"And you, flower of my flock, can be my hanmagitma."

Which was a term for "hand me this, get me that."

She said it with a beaming smile as if bestowing some great honour. Now for some children, it may have been a pleasure to be involved in cleaning, but I was not "some children" and Mam was not quite your ordinary mother.

She just began.

Not the most organised of people, well, not organised at all; she stomped off to the unfortunate chosen room and then bawl,

"Mary, come and help me move this furniture."

Much thumping and grating noises.

"June bring the soft brush and dusters."

June putting her homework away and trotting upstairs, never to return unless it was for more cleaning materials.

"Mary go to the Coop for some Vim and Edna bring the Lavender polish."

Trot, trot, trot.

The house was particularly freezing at these times as windows and doors had to be flung open, "to let out the stew." At least the trotting kept us warm for a while.

Mam justified our inclusion in these activities by saying that she was teaching us in readiness for when we had our own homes. She always added that she hoped that we would be able to afford servants to do the "rough," housework.

Mary and June cast their eyes to the heavens.

But we learned.

And some of it we learned not to repeat. All three of us vowed not to ever own a house with more than one flight of stairs. All of us vowed not to own brass that had to be polished with regularity and all of us vowed not to include our own children. Some of these learned skills became obsolete or unnecessary as cleaning materials and a way of life changed and some of it was a lesson in how not to do it. Like the vows to exclude areas of Mam's practical lessons it became an upside-down type of learning. All three of us learned to have all we needed before beginning. We learned to plan for meals that would be needed and to stick with the job until it was finished.

Mam just began cleaning and you were lucky at some point when hunger was gnawing at you, that she remembered food.

"Mary. Nip over to English's cafe and get us a ham sandwich and a Fancy each."

Or

"June, away to the Coop and get a tin of Corned beef and make something with it."

Mam could not be expected to clean and cook as well. Heaven for-fend!

And just when she had allocated us our cleaning roles, she downed tools and flung her coat on to go over to her mothers'. We continued the cleaning with much resentment and grumbling to each other, but we would not have dared leave the job undone. Anyway, it was sometimes easier and more relaxed without her.

Though the cleaning may have appeared haphazard; it gradually dawned on me that it happened at very prescribed times in the year.

There was spring-cleaning and "back end" cleaning which ensured that the house was "bottomed" twice in the year. As if that wasn't enough there came the Christmas cleaning as Mam quite reasonably pointed out,

"To greet the Christ Child."

Rather like Santa, he never did put in an actual personal appearance, but the house had to be ready just in case it was the chosen venue to celebrate His birthday.

I once pointed out to Mam that Jesus never came.

"Don't be so ridiculous. He's here all the time."

Pardon?

Life could be very confusing.

Then there had to be a mini repeat performance in the days after Christmas, as the house had to be clean,

"To greet the New Year."

In this constant commotion the house was never just right, but the timing gave another sense of security and order in life.

And yes, I did learn. With all that timed cleaning I'd have had to be one thickhead not to have absorbed something.

Not only was there a time for cleaning but also there was a sequence to it. It had to be done from the top of the house to the bottom and from the top of a room to the bottom. As much as possible was cleared from the room. Various items were taken down to the kitchen to be washed including the light shades and bulbs. Material items were consigned to the washing baskets or just flung down the stairs to be scooped up later. Mattresses and base cushions were tipped off and upended and furniture was pushed and shoved into the middle of the room. After the dust was battered and bashed from the mattresses, someone teetered on the top of the stepladders to wipe the ceilings and walls. All the paintwork was washed, and a skewer used to ease the dirt from edges and comers.

"Mam. It doesn't really need all of this."

"Do it me Lass and then we know it's done," which held a sort of Mam logic.

The furniture was washed inside and out with warm water and vinegar to kill the grease from the previous polishing. When it was dry, it was polished inside and out with the Lavender polish and its soporific smell. Even now I can picture the round, lilac tin with a funny little key at the side which had to be turned to prize off the lid. The polish was rubbed on, a little at a time in a circular motion; left to "dry in," and then polished off with a soft cloth and rubbed and buffed. It was a pleasure to see the sheen, but it didn't happen without much elbow grease and standing back to check that there were no streaks of polish showing.

All the round brass switches and brass ornaments were polished with Brasso, leaving the cloths black, black, black and feeling sordid and dirty to the touch. The linoleum had to be washed from the furthest point of the room to the door and when it was dry, that too was polished to dangerous, ice rink perfection. It was all physically exhausting and there were few labour-saving devices. I suppose Mary, June and I were Mam's labour-saving devices.

There were compensations.

When the mattresses were tipped against the wall, they made excellent tents, caves or hiding places. Inevitably Mary or June would lock me in an empty wardrobe and airily wonder to the others where Edna had gone. Empty drawers became brilliant boats and Sam, Alma and I sailed off down the Amazon. Mam threw a blanket over an upturned table and I sat within it with a torch, pretending that I was in a gloomy forest. Even better, I just sat silent until Mary or June came around the door and I could burst forth. Yaargh! Either there was much clasping of bosoms in mock shock or genuine fright and I was threatened with a dire future.

Alongside this timed deep cleaning were all the daily and weekly jobs, which contributed to respectability. One that I liked was swilling the fronts. This had to be done very early in the morning, as one had not to be seen cleaning the front of the house; it had to just appear clean. The only exception to the invisible outside, cleaning was occasionally emerging with a soft brush to tut away the odd leaf. Otherwise, Mam tottered up and down the hall armed with buckets of soapy water and the hard yard brush. The water was flung with some vigour and then swooshed into the gutters with the brush. Then came buckets of clear water to repeat the exercise and the postman or milkman sidestepping with alacrity.

"Give over Missus. I've had yan wesh tuhday."

While the tiled fronts dried, the entire paintwork and front door were washed. Then the step reddened with Cardinal polish and the brasses cleaned and buffed. The back yard received similar treatment but that was on washing days and the timing didn't matter, as the general public could not view the activity. One job that sickened me was when the gratings were lifted from the drains. They had gungy, slime and hairs dripping from them, which had to be scraped, and persuaded away, then washing soda and bleach poured down and around the drains.

Mam may have been disorganised, but she was certainly thorough. For the time we were considered clean and my mother would have been horrified and deeply wounded if it had been suggested otherwise. Most houses had a particular "Washing Day." Not ours. According to Mam, women, who had to have a day for this and a day for that, were obviously wanting in some area. In consequence washing day was not every Monday as in other houses; it just sort-of happened when Mam decided that there was enough to wash. I suppose it was called "washing day," because it took all day to complete. Mam got up very early in the morning and lit the little fireplace under the set pot in the washhouse. The set pot was filled with water and a round wooden lid placed over it and then while the water was heating, everything was sorted into whites and coloureds. There was much flinging of "Tide," into the set pot while some white items were left steeping in a bucket of cold water and "Dolly Blue." There was always something standing about in a bucket of cold water, as Mam said that this lifted the dirt and stains before the actual washing. She wore a funny little uniform on washing days. Ankle length wellies, a big wrap around apron and on cold days a heavy overcoat and a headscarf were added. There seemed to be much lifting of clothes and bedding from one place to another, one of them being a large Dolly Tub with ribbed sides. Into this was balanced a scrubbing board and the clothes rubbed up and down along the grooves. I quite liked doing this but best of all was the poss. This was a wondrous thing, with a sort of upside-down colander stuck to the bottom of a long pole. When it was pressed into the clothes the water squelched and belched up and out. I was not allowed near the set pot while the water was bubbling and boiling but as the water cooled, I was invited into the washhouse to help but I had not to go too near the mangle. This was a big hand mangle that stood over the dolly tub and I was allowed to stand at the other side of it and catch the clothes coming through. Using the mangle was some skill, as the clothes had to be fed through in a straight manner with one hand while the handle was turned by the other hand. Quite a feat with wet, heavy bedding or curtains and Mam muttering,

"Blooming men, call themselves the stronger sex."

The clothes were always hung on the washing line running down the middle of the long yard, unless it was really pouring with Cumbrian rain. Apparently, the sunlight bleached just as well as any chemical.

Mam said so.

How much a bleak, watery Maryport sun bleached, I was not very sure.

When it was hung in the yard it became quite a feat negotiating a path through it. In winter the clothes hung, stiff as boards until they were brought inside and then they melted into a sopping mess only to take up residence around the fire and dangling down the banisters.

When they were eventually dry it was time to fold them as Mam maintained that an item folded properly didn't need ironing. I liked it when it was time to fold the bedding, as Mary and June held the sheets or blankets at each end and I was invited to roll inside and be swung back and forwards and then unceremoniously tipped out. Although I can remember Mother Tuke having flat irons, Mam had a new-fangled electric iron in black and silver. She didn't have an ironing board but ironed on a table. When the clothes were ironed, they were placed carefully on the pulley. Even this had a format; for instance, knickers had to be placed with the gusset facing to the back and therefore not in view to offend.

Important items of clothing were taken to, "Johnsons' Dry Cleaners," up in Senhouse Street and there was always the Co-op Laundry. This was not the height of laziness; people just did send some items of washing to the laundry. These were parcelled up and placed on the front doorstep and then disappeared! They returned in a much better parcel and the shirts folded as if they were new and placed in cellophane. Gosh. The Laundry van with the picture of the cheery little man waving his cap was as common as the coal lorries.

I do remember some children missing school to help with the washing, but this was much frowned upon by schools. It was a very physical activity and some women must have had muscles on their muscles. I never knew any men who took part in it. Dad came into his own when the washing was dried and gathered in from the washing line. Then he was called on to lift buckets of the water from the set pot and fling them down the long yard, while Mam, or Mary or June hurriedly grabbed the hard yard brush and swept vigorously. The water rushed and gushed into the diamond grooves of the navy tiles and down the slight slope towards the drain grating, carrying whatever stew had dared to settle since the last washing day. That's all I remember Dad doing on washing day. The means of being clean belonged to the world of women. There was this paradoxical message given out of the strong, all knowing male who could not be expected to know about washing powders. Men were intelligent and dependable but incapable of understanding the intricacies of what polish to use for what and some women actively fed this to keep their domain a mystery and their own preserve. And while men earned the women the money, by the sweat of their brows and muscular bodies, only women apparently needed the new deodorants and bubble baths. The new adverts told us so. And yet what counted for clean then was not quite the same as now. Sunday was the major night for having a bath and washing hair and clean clothes were laid out ready to be worn on Monday morning.

Not in our house!

I had to suffer this indignity more frequently especially on Thursday night. You see, Mam felt that by Friday, teachers would only be seeing and working with children in grimy clothes and possibly rather smelly children at that. We were giving our teachers a treat by turning up at the end of the week sweet smelling and dressed in something fresh. A nice touch, but I don't think my detached and lofty teachers ever noticed this extra effort on their behalf.

We wore clothes longer and thinking of the method of washing clothes, it seems reasonable to cut the amount down to the minimum. I didn't change every day; in fact, you wore things until they were dirty. There had to be evidence of dirt before the clothes passed muster to enter the washing cycle.

"June! You can take this back upstairs. There isn't a mark on it, get away with you. "Too much washing takes the stuffing out of clothes you know. And anyway, a new item stays clean longer than an old one."

Mary and June cast their eyes to the heavens but took the clothes back upstairs. Many clothes were worn and then carefully hung on a coat hanger and put back in the wardrobe. The only items where sweating was admitted was the bedding and the beds were completely changed every fortnight. However, as the bottom sheet was supposed to be the one that caught all this sweat, it was changed every week and the top sheet put onto the bottom of the bed. This meant that there was perpetual bedding hanging over the banisters, waiting to become an exhilarating swing.

Personal daily washing was either a "lick" or a "good wash."

A lick was just the hands and face, but a good wash was everything and seemed cleaner than sitting in the bath. I watched with great admiration, Mary or June suddenly fling their leg up and into the wash basin to wash their feet and legs. This was obviously a very grown up thing to do and when I was in the bathroom alone, I forgot that my legs were too short and tried to copy. After a few flings, resulting in my ankle thumping the edge of the shell wash basin and practically wrenching my ball and socket joint asunder I wandered around, limping like one of the new Polio victims.

Men, other than my Dad washed differently.

I knew this because when we visited other houses men were occasionally in the back kitchen with their chests bare, braces dangling by their sides. This type of washing was very vigorous and noisy. They always snorted and snuffled into the soapsuds and loudly blew their noses.

Mam was horrified when Uncle Jack came to stay and though we had a perfectly good bathroom, he insisted on continuing to wash in the kitchen. Telling Aunt Evelyn that Alf was not allowed to do such a thing made no difference. Jack may have had many failings as a husband but his wishes or his washes, were not to be crossed. He continued to snort and energetically wash his naked torso while Mam squirmed indignantly waiting to have her kitchen back. He was declared terribly common but what could you expect from a Crellin from Downstreet?

Oh, but the shades and grades of life were myriad, and many were dependent on cleanliness. Often a compliment for a woman was,

"By but she's a good worker and clean" or,

"You know you could eat your meat from her floors."

I was never very sure who would want to visit and eat meat from the floor but the woman that received that accolade was clean indeed. This transcended all class barriers and a clean woman could even be a lady and live Downstreet.

As our bathroom was way up on the top floor and incredibly cold, I had the enormous treat of sometimes having a bath in front of the living room fire. There was always a tin bath hanging on a large nail in the washhouse. This was lifted down, placed by the fender stool and filled with many kettles of hot water. Towels were strategically placed around it and Mam knelt down to test the water temperature with her bare elbow. I hopped about naked and ready for the signal to slide into the warm water. I sat there in the warmth and the light of the fire with my boats. Wonderful. Of course, Mam always spoiled things somewhat by insisting on washing me. She knelt down by the side and scrubbed me. Well, it felt like that.

Washing for Mam was a very energetic affair and I simply became another commodity to be washed. The flannel was roughly rubbed around my face and the corner of the flannel poked in and around my ears and even in and around my tummy button. The nail brush was caked in soap and scrubbed across my fingers and toes. My legs were yanked out one at a time a vigorously rubbed up and down and my arms stretched upwards to receive similar treatment. The final indignity was the hair.

How I hated having my hair washed.

Soap in my eyes, naked and now blind and vulnerable. By the time Mam had finished soaping my scalp it was tingling. Then she disappeared to the kitchen to return with jugs of warm water with drops of vinegar in it. This, she said, not only killed the soap but gave a good sheen and preserved the red colour. I believed her. Then Dad lifted me out and wrapped me in a big towel, telling me that I smelted like a parcel of fish and chips. Thanks Dad.

I stood by the fire dripping while he and Mam lifted the tin bath out into the yard and swooshed the soapy water away.

Then the best of times.

Dad rubbing me dry between his tweedy trouser legs, while Mam cleared the wet towels and restored the room. A clean nighty and onto Dad's knee to have my hair dried. This always culminated in a cuddle and listening to the radio.

"Rays' a Laugh."

"Educating Archie."

It didn't matter if it was a play that I didn't understand. It was the warmth. The clean feeling. The intimacy.

This was Dad and I sharing.

Sharing and loving.

My head laid on his wheezing chest.

His arm around me.

There was no-one but us two.

I never remember Mary or June there. Maybe they were out on a "Hot Date," but these moments were all his and mine while Mam busied in the kitchen making the supper.

We never had the twee suppers that were mentioned on the radio. I was never an "Ovaltiney." Supper in Cumberland was not milk and biscuits. It was supper with a capital "S."

Mam said that in Cumberland we had four meals a day and, in our house, it was a fact. So, while Dad and I cuddled, Mam was in the kitchen peeling potatoes and cooking a full-blown meal. Maybe with Dad working split shifts at the doctor's surgery, he was probably hungry for a proper meal. Whatever the reason, I always got a smaller plate of what they were eating and when the radio programme ended Dad carried me to bed. This was either clutched to his chest with my arms around his neck or a piggyback where he dropped me onto the bed from what seemed a great height.

Mam eventually came up afterwards with my hot water bottle and often released the bedding that Dad had firmly tucked in and was by then cutting off all circulation.

The drive to attain respectability via cleanliness was not easy. Many roads were not made up with tarmac so that they were often either sludgy and pitted with mud puddles, or dusty dry. The old pit houses seemed to crumble dust from the walls and a windy day brought fine sand and coal dust through the ill-fitting windows and doors. Women all over West Cumberland waged their own war against a difficult and uncaring environment that constantly mocked their energetic efforts. Nothing was easy. The adverts and the films from Hollywood held the promise of, "labour saving," devices but they either had not arrived in our area or the ones that were in the Coop were much too expensive. Though we had won the War and were told that the country was going forwards, there still wasn't much evidence of this. Well, road signs were being put back up, after being removed to confuse any stray German roaming around the area. Otherwise everything seemed much the same, including the methods of cleaning and heating. Coal was King and was essential in every house; especially to heat the water to clean away the dust and dirt that it had caused in the first place. It was a glorious paradox. Coal made work to earn money to survive. It provided the means to earn nearly enough to buy it, after digging it from deep underground. Then, while it was being used, it created its own market all over again in dirt, dust and disease.

Coal carts were everywhere. It was a common sight to see a coal lorry paused in a street and the black faced, coal men standing with their backs to the lorry edge. Another coal man stood on the flat back end of the lorry and dragged and scraped the heavy bags until they were level with the man's back. As the sack was leaned against him, he gently bent forward, grasped the top corner of the sack and walked away from the lorry. They had their own uniform of flat caps worn backwards and a leather piece down their backs, tied around their shoulders and waist. I can hear now the black diamonds rattling down into the coalhouse and then Mam scurrying out armed with the money to pay and the yard brush.

"Here you are lad and a copper or two for yourself. Oh, and tell Mr Towers, there was a bit too much dust and dross in last weeks', to say nothing of a few stones. And you can tell him, if it's the same this week that Mrs. Croft of Lawson Street will be calling to remonstrate."

He touched his backwards cap with a black finger, his teeth showing white against the black dust on his face when he smiled.

"Now, yuh, know that Towers and Southwell don't cheat and yuh know we're the best there is, else yuh wouldn't av us."

"Yuh daft beggar, you're the only one, after Coop. And don't you touch your cap to anybody lad, you're working for your living and that makes you as good as anybody."

"True, true. See yuh next week, Mrs Croft of Lawson Street."

Mam took a swipe at him with the brush as she began to sweep around the coalhouse and then slammed the door shut to keep the coal dry. And would you believe, at some time every summer the coalhouse was allowed to become empty and Dad lime washed it, white!

Of course, the coal men dropped coal and there was always Mother Croft to pick it up.

Mother Croft was an obsessive recycler. The Green Party or something similar should be honouring and raising sacrifices to her memory. She constantly carried a capacious basket, which she gradually filled with whatever she saw in the street. It was a constant source of pain and shame to Mam that Mother Croft subsidised her income and heating in this manner. But everyone was adept at knowing what could be salvaged and saved to keep the home fires burning. Fruit and vegetable peelings that were not being saved for the Allotments were left to dry to burn on the fire. If we were going out or going to bed, the peelings were put on the fire while they were still wet to dampen down the fire and make a slower burn. In fact, there was very little left to go in the ashbin, except ashes.

The fire was one of the most important items in the house. Not just for heating and cooking but it gave a focus to the room. If the grate looked neat and tidy then so did the whole room, but how dismal the room looked with a burned-out fire or an untidy grate. The fire was beautiful, romantic and dreamy and I would never return to the blooming things unless some ghastly world event forced me to.

Getting up in the morning, the whole house was cold and what a pantomime to achieve a spark of warmth. I feel a nostalgia for something that has gone from many homes, but I remember too well all that it took to achieve lighting one and keeping it clean. The numerous failures. The frozen hands trying to strike matches. The whole body frozen while scuttering down the yard for more coals and putting the ashes in the bin. Architects invariably placed the outside toilet and the coalhouse furthest from the house making going for a shovel of coals a real trial in inclement weather. Of course, buckets of coal were filled and placed just inside the house, by the back door, on a piece of clean newspaper but even these had to be refilled now and then. Also, there were the mock brass coalscuttles standing in the grate itself, but these were more ornamental than useful, especially the ones where the top coals had been polished for effect. Neither did it just sit there giving out a gentle clean heat. Now and then it gave a belch of smoke and the soot motes drifted around the room. The ashes crumbled and sank and spilled out into the grate and just to keep you on your toes a piece of coal suddenly flared and sent out blue, green flames. Often it was giving out the best heat just when it was time to go to bed.

Most fireplaces boasted a "Companion" set. Hanging on this was the fire irons. A small shovel, brush, tongs and a poker. Often hanging on the fireplace was a pair of bellows and a toasting fork. In Aunt Evelyn's' case these were vigorously polished with regularity but never used. Mam said her sister wasn't a housewife, she was house-proud. Sniff.

Fireplaces were very large affairs and dominated the room. They were always black. To the left was the oven and to the right was a warming cupboard and leading to the fire itself were ledges for kettles and pans. Above all of this was the mantle-piece and slightly before this was a long pole which often held smaller clothes drying or airing. Nearly every mantelpiece had a Holy Trinity of ornaments. Usually two large spotted dogs at each end glaring balefully out into the room and a clock in the middle. Among these were a pot of spills, long coloured sticks used instead of matches. In Mother Tukes house there were still gas lamps on each side of the mantle-piece, and I looked with fascination at the delicate white, mesh gas mantles nestled in a box of six.

There was usually a large, part blackened kettle, bubbling quietly and when it was lifted, drops spit and hissed into the fire. I don't remember anything being cooked on the coal fire even at Mother Tukes; our cooking was done in the pale green gas cooker.

June saying that she remembered being hungry puzzled me, as I don't remember being hungry at this time. Maybe Mary and June made sure that I wasn't. But Mam was a good cook; when she remembered or bothered. Well, she was a good cook as far as cooking went then. Not only was there little money to be adventurous but there was still Rationing and so few could experiment even if they had wanted to. Mam was a lifelong devotee of the frying pan. And as we have all been reasonably healthy it gives a strange pallor to the Puritanical view against fried food. There was always some dish or cracked cup standing about with fat congealing from something that had been rendered down and this eventually joined the fat in the frying pan.

I didn't know that fried eggs were meant to be white and yellow until I was visiting a friend's house and was offered one for my tea. Almost everything went into the frying pan. The egg being fried alongside black pudding gave it a distinctive taste and a black speckled appearance. Even Mam's chips were fried in the shallow frying pan; she simply added some more fat. In consequence homemade chips were always bronzed on one side a pallid white on the other. Oh, and the odd bit of blackened onion from the last meal thrown in for good measure. She boasted to others that Edna didn't really care for chips and in truth I did avoid the homemade ones. The grill section of the cooker was never used for anything but toast. But she could make good plain English meals. Mince and potatoes, Cumberland Tatie Pot, Steak and Kidney with dumplings, Sunday roasts and a variety of fresh fish dishes. Mam could make a Sunday joint stretch until Thursday. There was the traditional Sunday lunch and then there were sandwiches from the cold meat for Sunday tea. On Monday the remaining vegetables were fried and served with cold meat. Then came a plethora of meals where there was some evidence of the roast meat lurking somewhere. Meanwhile the bones were boiling ready to make soup with dumplings. Mam often made what she called "Lob Soup," meaning that she lobbed anything in that came to hand. One meal that I loved was a Cumbrian meal called "Tatie Hash," which was a white stew made with lamb, turnip and onions. I thought that this was the meal that came after Pancake Tuesday for Hash Wednesday. There was also "Fatherless Stew," and this was just onions and potatoes stewed in a frying pan of water, called "Fatherless," because there was no meat. They were all plain but very tasty and filling and it wasn't until much later when I was married that I realised that there was an art to cooking even the plainest of meals. Mam was an artist.

She could also bake.

She baked what she called "plate cakes." Any fruit that was in season went into the lightest of light pastry. Then there were savoury pies, mince, steak and kidney, cheese and onion or egg and bacon. She had a light touch and they were always good, hot from the oven. I was encouraged to, "help", and when she tired of my ham-fisted attempts, I was given a lump of pastry and told to go away and play with it. I fashioned this into all sorts until it took on a grey look; then I ate it. Mam would look to see what I had modelled and then squeal,

"You silly lass, you'll be ill."

I never was.

If she was baking sponge cakes, I was hauled in to unconsciously practice pre maths lessons in weighing and counting. I wasn't too keen on the stirring, but it was worth it to be given the dish to lick out. I always liked the taste of things just as they came out of the oven and in later years Mam laughed and said shaking her head,

"Remember when you used to run after me with the big kitchen knife saying,' Cut it Mammy, cut it."

I didn't remember but gritted my teeth and smiled through them.

She had one recipe that she called a "Cup Cake" as it was made from a cup of this and a cup of that. This gave her the basic sponge cake mixture. All she did was to make a large amount of this and then divide it into other bowls. Into one went coffee, and in another cochineal and another ginger and another Rowntrees cocoa powder. And lo, we had lots of different cakes from the one batch of mixture. After all that ingenuity I just liked her plain sponge cakes.

There was always a cheesecloth bag dangling and dripping over the sink. I hated this, as it was milk going sour. This was left to either partially solidify to make cottage cheese or it was used when she was making scones. Whatever was in that sour milk, it made wonderful scones. She made a variety of jams but mainly rhubarb and apple and of course she made rum butter. This was especially welcome when I coughed and coughed all night. I was hauled downstairs and commanded to eat a spoonful of it. Often a little vinegar was added, which I thought was to ensure that the homemade cough remedy wasn't too pleasurable. Mam stood shivering and scooping the spoon into my mouth saying that the sugar was to scratch the itch in my throat, the butter to grease it, the vinegar to break the phlegm and the rum to send me to sleep. I believed her and it usually worked.

Apart from the disgusting bag of sour milk, I only ever remember one type of cheese. Mam called it "Red, " cheese, and all she did was chop it into chunks and place it on a nice dish on the table. I don't remember much fruit. I do remember Auntie Lizzie bustling in to excitedly say that Grasslot Coop had bananas. Whether Mam couldn't be bothered to hurry over to Grasslot, or it took her so long to make herself what she called, "presentable," I don't know but I can't remember getting one. Occasionally I was given an orange as if it were a huge treat. I thought that they were horrid. They were cold, sour things and made my hands sticky. That's all that an orange meant to me.

The only biscuits that I remember were Kit Kats or plain biscuits. It was a family joke that if Dad went to Woolworth's for them, he asked for a bag of plain, mixed, cream, assorted. The counter girl always smiled rather wearily. What I do remember is standing in the Coop wishing and wishing that there would be enough coupons in the Ration book for sweets.

Mam always just bought for the day. The pantry was never full. She bought what she needed as she needed it. June and I had a standing joke that the only thing that we remember in the pantry was a lonely little nutmeg rolling about. Maybe it was with living through the Depression and then the War. Maybe it was not having fridges or freezers that made her do this, but other people did a big weekly shopping trip and had shelves laden with food.

Not Mam.

It was, "common," to be seen with bags laden with groceries, or so she said.

Mam said a lot of things.

She was so full of contrasts and so exquisitely complicated.

For instance, if it were Sunday tea or visitors coming to tea, or Christmas, or a special occasion, she could really set a table. I mean really set a table. She was very proud of what she called her "table linen" and these were kept in a specific drawer. There were hand-embroidered tablecloths or pure Irish linen or Damask tablecloths always with matching serviettes. There was "good", crockery, jam dishes, cheese dishes, bread plates and cake plates. The best bone china tea service or the dinner service with matching tureens and gravy boat. There was all the correct silver cutlery, all in the correct positions and her best sugar and jam spoons polished to perfection. It was a pleasure to sit down to such a table laden with the homemade jams and cakes and chunks of "red" cheese.

I once asked her where she has learned to set a table and Mam, being a past master at not answering a question said,

"Oh, I suppose from my own mother."

"Yes, but where did she learn it?"

"I don't know. Somewhere."

I wondered if some of the women in the family had learned it while being "in service" to the local Gentry. Whatever the reason Mam could set a table absolutely correctly.

But that was when it was an "occasion."

Otherwise on an ordinary day she shouted,

"Dinner's ready."

And we tumbled to the table only to find nothing on it but steaming plates. The dinner got cooler as we jumped up and down, running in and out of the kitchen for salt and pepper and cutlery. Sometimes Dad shouted,

"Where's the eating irons woman,"

but we would not have dared and scurried finding them for him.

And then the ritual began.

"Does this taste right to you?"

"It's just right Mam"

"Hmm, I think it could be hotter."

"No, no Mam, it tastes fine."

"These Brussels could have done with a bit longer."

"Mine are O.K."

"Well, I've tried to get this meat tender."

"And you have Mam."

"There's not much you can do with cheap meat mind. Not too salty?"

"No, no. Its' lovely."

On and on and on. I grind my teeth just thinking of it. I don't know why she did it, but it was a litany that accompanied every meal. Sometimes we tried to halt the flow by immediately taking a taste and passing a compliment. That didn't work as we hoped. "Well, all I can say is, you're easily pleased. It doesn't seem right to me."

And woe betide any of us if we did actually advance to making an adverse comment.

"A hungry man doesn't quarrel with the cook. You can't be that hungry or you'd eat anything."

I used to think that that was such a daft thing to say. I mean how if the cook had made something with a dash of Tide thrown in? If we tentatively said,

"You're right Mam, mine could be a bit warmer."

"Aye well, it's a poor stomach that won't warm it."

She was so quixotic and contrary that I still don't know what she was looking for by doing this. I only know that it ruined many a good meal. Whether she set the table, or we did, the milk bottle had not to be seen on it, or the sugar bag and definitely no reading material while we were eating. Only people from the Council estate and Downstreet did that sort of thing. Mam said.

Mam was not only adept at baking and cooking, but she was actually very clever with her hands in other areas. She could sew. My goodness, she could sew. She had a Singer treadle sewing machine, which magically turned in on itself and made a table. Occasionally it turned back became a sewing machine and Mam could suddenly produce suits or dresses. There were neat lapels, collars and many features that others would have found extremely difficult. Always resting somewhere were matting frames. Long and short pieces of super smooth wood with fat wooden pegs to fit into the holes of the longer pieces of wood. Mam, or all of us sat clipping strips from old clothes or nylon stockings and they were separated into colours and placed into individual bags. Then Mam sat behind the matting frames with the bags around her feet and lo, a mat emerged. She often drew her own patterns on the base material and sometimes personalised them with our names. They were beautiful and a ton weight to shake clean.

Mam had, "taste." She instinctively knew which colours to put together and many times she was ahead of fashion. The decor of the day was chocolate and margarine.

Brown doors and virulent yellow skirting boards. Soon after we moved into Lawson Street Mam changed all the paintwork to stark white, including the front door. Very avant-garde for the time.

Oh, yes, in practical areas Mam was very talented. If we needed an article of clothing she set to and made it with dexterity and ease, often adding a little item of flair and originality. Meanwhile we were wading through threads and mat clippings and Mary and June were making all the meals and doing the shopping.

She could cook but scorned doing it. She did not recognise any of these as skills to be proud of. She looked for compliments but did not truly value such attributes. In her mind these skills were learned and done simply from necessity or poverty. It was not a talent to be proud of but simply something to be done. It irked her that she had to do these things. The "Rich" did not need to do it. The "Rich" would have serving maids to do such menial work. In consequence the very act of making something was placing Mam into a certain position in life that grated on her. For all her life she did not appreciate that she could have developed these accomplishments. They were just another statement of poverty and were not to be encouraged in her daughters. We learned housework and cooking from necessity while she read avidly but not because she actually wanted to teach us such skills.

We ate her meals and learned our manners and sometimes she said,

"Alf are we going to say Grace?"

We bowed our heads over the plates and Dad solemnly said,

"For Gods' sake start."

"Alf!"

"Oh, alright. Cumbrian Grace. "Lord mek us yabble to eat o that's ont tyabble"

"ALF!"

CHAPTER 6
"Nearer My God to Thee"

Religion permeated everything and Maryport seemed to have almost as many religious places as it had pubs. They were all Christian. Some more than others. There was only one Salvation Army Temple, one Presbyterian Church, one Baptist Church and one Roman Catholic Church. But there were a plethora of Methodist Chapels and three large Church of England churches. Oh, brave people to be of the Roman Catholic faith in Maryport. Maybe Dr. Rattrie and his family being of that faith eased their lot. As there was also a segregated Roman Catholic school, I knew little of them and even that was only what I overheard. I heard that they were supposed to have large families, which they certainly appeared to have. In consequence many Roman Catholics were very poor. It was also rumoured that their school curriculum was so punctuated by learning their religion and holidays for Saints, that they did not learn very much. Added to that. Aunt Evelyn muttered darkly that screams could be heard coming over the walls of the convent when the priests were running after the nuns. Nuns were strange creatures who were rarely seen. When they were spied wandering out of the convent, they wore long black habits and their faces had starched white wimples coming so well forward that they had to turn their whole faces sideways when looking to cross the roads. Their rare appearances and mode of dress left them open to much speculation and much fear. A slight oddity was that the Roman

Catholic Church was smack bang opposite the Presbyterian Church at the top of a rather narrow street. The two buildings of solid sandstone stood glowering across the road at each other. I don't know who chose this arrangement, to site two churches opposite each other with such opposing religious views, but there was a time in Maryport when they had to have staggered entrance and exit times.

Mother Tuke had been brought up as a Quaker but had, "fallen from grace." On one gin-soaked journey through Grasslot she had literally fallen in to Grasslot Chapel. As the speaker of the day, was thundering on about the evils of drink and the virtue of temperance, her sudden appearance must have seemed a Godsend to him.

He had hurtled down the Chapel and led her to the altar rail to give her testimony. She confessed all to the Lord and to the congregation. She described her difficult life, the deaths of Madge and John, and on being forgiven her sins, she went forth as Wesleyan. She always maintained that the Lord had led her feet into that chapel and saved her from the demon drink. From the time of her conversion, her children were encouraged to follow her lead but at some time in her teens my mother decided to be confirmed in the Church of England. She just had to be different.

Dad was a strong Methodist, but Mam and Dad were not averse to patronising other religious establishments; well, all except the Roman Catholic Church. They did not switch their religious allegiance, but visits to other churches were more for the entertainment value. There were flower shows at the Baptist church and we wandered along rows of Pom Pom Dahlias and giant onions. At the end of the long rows of trestle tables were shining tea urns managed by the ladies of the church. They always wore hats and highly flowered, wrap around aprons. Or there were evenings of music and song and in the intermission, we climbed over benches to sit at the trestle tables now covered in snow-white tablecloths. The same ladies bustled between us holding aloft steaming plates of pies and peas and still wearing their hats. Nearly every church or chapel had Jumble Sales where the clothes had a foisty, musty, mothball smell but there was the promise of finding a prized item. There were even plays.

One dark evening we all walked over the New Road to Grasslot Mission to watch a visiting troupe giving a rendition of, "Maria Martin and the Red Barn." I thrilled to see a perfect villain, twirling his black moustache. I wasn't very sure what dastardly deed he had done to poor little Maria, but I was very sorry for her plight and cat called with the rest of the audience. At the Presbyterian Church we went to see, "An Inspector Calls" and on another evening the play, "Dear Octopus". These were very social occasions and the beginning and end of these visits to alien churches were a ceremony of meeting old friends and being introduced to new people. Dad was comfortable in any company, laughing and gently slapping backs while Mam cordially shook hands and kept herself rather aloof. She had taught us that we had to wait to be invited to use a person's first name before having the temerity to do so. She rarely extended this invitation to include herself and always insisted on being called Mrs. Croft. In consequence we were often standing to one side simply waiting for Dad to finish his conversation or joke. If Mam was drawn into conversation, she was pleasant and polite but not encouraging.

"Did you enjoy the play Mrs. Croft?"

"Indeed, but such a shame that we are so starved of live entertainment in this part of England."

"Oh, I thought it was very good," some bewildered soul answered, and not a bit mis-made, Mam replied,

"Yes, all very well for a small-town amateur group, but not quite the standard of Manchester or London."

She must have left many abashed after they had acted their socks off that evening. All church Halls whatever their denomination, were used for a variety of purposes. There were Brass band concerts, Flimby Male Voice Choir concerts, dances, Variety concerts, beetle and whist drives and educational classes.

In this period of my life I can't remember attending a Church of England service. The church at the end of Netherhall corner marked the end of the town. It stood in it's own large grounds which were full of seemingly drunken and mould covered grave stones. It was said that this church was High Church. The Vicar insisted on being called Father and incense was used. Obviously too close to the Roman Catholic faith for comfort. Mother Croft was also strong Methodist but swallowed her principles to earn hard cash. She was a church cleaner and though Mam squirmed at this indignity she consoled herself that cleaning a church was far nobler than being a charlady. In fact, not the same at all.

I often accompanied Mother Croft and while she dusted the pews and rubbed Brasso on the candlesticks I tottered up into pulpits and gave forth. I turned open the massive Bibles and put many a desultory Vicar to shame, flinging my arms about and giving whatever tripe I chose to shout full welly. Mother Croft always totally ignored these dramatics. Christ Church was built right on the harbour and designed as a ship. I thumped the lectern in there too, enjoying the freedom to sound my voice without the embarrassment of anyone listening. Mother Croft drew the line at cleaning the Roman Catholic Church but now and then I sneaked in with friends, just to have a look. It smelled funny and the flickering candles cast ominous shadows across the statues. We diddled about in a dish of water in the wall near the door and then hurried out, running off down Crosby Street as fast as we could, alarmed by our boldness. Mam said that the statues and woodcarvings that I had seen were, "graven images," and reminded me of the Ten Commandments. It puzzled me that they could worship the same God but not adhere to his Commandments. Having such a segregated church and school meant that we were of the same town but very much apart and it created and promoted misunderstanding and superstition.

It was a time when there was still an interest in predicting the future or trying to contact those who had "passed over to the other side." And so, there were two Spiritualist churches. Although this did not sit easily with our family faith it somehow passed as another form of entertainment. There was also the small added thrill that mainstream religions would not have approved and the bigger added thrill that it may be true. Aunt Evelyn was supposed to have "the Gift," and was proficient at reading tea leaves. Sometimes on her long visits she could be persuaded to sit at Mother Tukes table peering into the teacups. The fire was stoked, and everyone pulled up their chairs and squashed around her. She must have had a turn for the dramatic as she began by announcing that the "Gift," had left her but after being exhorted to try harder she put her wigged head in her hands and breathe deeply. Aunty Lizzie bustled about, pouring everyone very strong cups of tea; well it had to be very strong to leave plenty of leaves in the bottom of the cups. A dish waited in the middle of the table for the slops to be gently drained in and then the cup was carefully and slowly turned three times on its saucer. As the "gift," miraculously returned in time. Aunt Evelyn solemnly peered into the cup. She increased the tension by slowly turning the cup this way and that.

"Hmm. There's definitely a man in here."

Increased interest from the single ladies at the table. She turned the cup towards them to show a splatter of black leaves up its' side.

"Can you see him? Just there."

"Ooo. It does look like a man, well fancy that. Look Elsie, it is a man."

"Hmm. Now this man looks dressed for an important occasion. There can you see him wearing a bowler hat?" and she gently placed her index finger at the top of the splatter.

"Eee. Evelyn, you are clever. I would never have seen that myself but now you point it out, there it is. It's definitely a bowler hat on him."

"Now I'll just turn the cup."

Silence hung in the warm air.

"Come on Evelyn, what can you see"?

"Well, I really don't like to say."

"Oh, go on. If it's bad news, I'd rather know."

"It looks like a baby to me."

"What's wrong with that? That's nice news."

"It's just... no, I'd better not say."

"Whadya mean?"

""There's a baby but no wedding here."

Scandalised silence.

It was never good news from Aunt Evelyn.

As she had the "gift," this meant that she had to visit the Spiritualist churches. She did not care to go alone, and Mam was dragooned into accompanying her. Mam got ready, telling us all that she didn't believe in such things but was only doing it to keep her sister sweet And of course the Spiritualist churches also had sales to raise funds.

One winter evening we all accompanied Aunt Evelyn to a Sale of Work at the Spiritualist church. It was warm and packed with people and the wares were far superior to those of any other Rummage sales. Whilst wandering along the stalls I spied, standing proud at the back a very strange soft toy. It had a very fat tummy, elephantine arms and legs and a large pixie head with floppy ears. I fell in love with it. The lady must have seen me looking and looking and she handed it down to me. It was made from soft midnight blue velvet, had large black button eyes and felt so soft and squashy.

"How much is it?"

"I'm sorry but it is rather special so it's three pounds."

Three pounds! I could hardly comprehend such a vast amount of money.

Deep inside I wanted and wanted that strange, soft toy but I knew that this was far too much. Even though I was well adept at wheedling most of my material desires out of Mary and June I knew that this was going too far. There wasn't even any point in bringing them to look at it. After a while, Mam said that it was getting late and Mary had to take me home and put me to bed. I regretfully left the wondrous toy, still standing looking down at us all. June has bought me some Pontefract cakes and I ate them as I walked down Church Street beside Mary but wishing and praying that I could have had that toy instead. Still I said nothing.

On Christmas morning it was there beside my other presents.

There it was. Amazing. I hadn't told anyone that I had wanted it. Talk about "Ask and you will be given."

For a while I thought that Santa must be a Spiritualist.

Though we were not a deeply religious family or fanatical and bigoted; Christianity was all around me.

The days, the weeks and the year were woven around it. It permeated our lives. It peppered our speech with quotations from the Bible, the Hymns or the Prayer books. Anything could happen and you could guarantee that someone would sigh and say,

"Ye know not what the day will bring," or "The Lord works in mysterious ways, his wonders to perform." If Mary swirled out to a dance in a cloud of, "Evening in Paris" perfume. Dad lowered his paper and said to Mam,

"By this time, she stinketh."

Or he stood at the back door about to go to work and call,

"In a little while I shall see thee and in a little while I shall not."

I was given "Adams' Ale," to drink and found it to be just water. If June patiently tried to explain something to me, she'd look helplessly at Dad and say,

"I'm casting pearls before swine."

There was a healthy irreverence that made our religion all the more comfortable and pertinent.

Of course, living in such a Socialist family, I could not help but be aware that some did not share this belief. I overheard many discussions and ploughed on with my little life.

"Now look, I don't deny that He lived. A good man, a nice man who had a lot of good things to say but as for being the Son of God. Rubbish!"

Mother Tuke listened and then leaning her knuckles on the dining room table she'd shake her head and say, "George lad, your tongue will get you hung."

Obviously, it wasn't too wise to ponder the truth of Christianity and certainly not out loud.

"Opium for the masses, isn't that right Father?"

Taking the pipe out of his mouth Father Tuke said,

"All very well kept in its place, it's when men get hold of it that it all goes wrong. You know George that your mother likes the chapel, but they don't take it to extremes. The state things were in, in Russia, well; something had to be done. People starving and freezing from the cold while their church had silver and gold and asked for more. It had to go. But don't mistake that for every religion. Sometimes people have to have something."

"Get away Father. It should be got rid of everywhere. Causing nothing but dissension and wars."

"Oh, give over George."

Mam said,

"Jesus was a pacifist. Didn't he stop Peter slicing that Roman soldiers' ear off? It was later when men saw it as a means of getting some to go to war that they conveniently forgot His teaching."

"You think what you like, our Edna, I think it's just something to stir us up or to keep us humble. Whenever did the meek inherit anything? Stay meek and you get nowhere. Jesus promoted grovelling and accepting your lot. Me? I can't do that. "There's the Pope wandering around in finery we'll never even see. Russia is quite right, it should all be shared out."

"Well, in that case Jesus was the first Communist."

George nearly had an apoplectic fit.

"Jesus a Communist. Where did you get that piffle, Edna!"

Mam delivered a direct hit.

"Didn't he say that if you had two cloaks, then you had to give one to the poor?"

Father winked at Mother Tuke as Auntie Lizzie and Auntie May came around the door.

"Is there a cup of tea on, we've been round Workington Market till my feet are killing me. By our George you're smart today. You look like the Duke of Buccluegh."

George preened himself.

"I had this tailor made at the Coop Gents Outfitters. Real Harris Tweed it is and cost a small fortune, I can tell you."

"I hope your Meg hasn't gone without, for you that suit, you little Dandy,"

"May, I might dress like the Duke of Buccluegh, but I wish I had his Bank balance or even a bit of his land."

Mam looked at Auntie May wearily,

"Don't you start him off again. How's your Stanley? Is his stomach any better?" Auntie May eased herself beside me on the couch and gratefully took a cup of tea from Mother Tuke.

"Better! I'm telling you this new National Health is grand. Can you remember Mother, bringing the doctor out and him standing in the doorway saying he wouldn't see anybody until there was two and sixpence on the table for him and us with hardly two pennies to rub together? I

165

knew Stanley wasn't eating right for a while and then the other day I just shouted from the kitchen,' Stanley do you feel like a bit of sausage', and he said, 'Dear God May, how do I know what a bit of sausage feels like?' No. no, you can stop laughing, I knew then; he was off his food. I just went to the kiosk and rang for the doctor and not only did he come right away but it was free. He gave Stanley a grand chalk bottle that seems to have sorted him."

Father Tuke flashed a look at her.

"Free? Free! You daft woman it isn't free. Don't ever get that into your head. It's a wonderful scheme to pool money for those who can't pay, but all of us in work are paying something."

George was on safe territory here.

"Aye, a sort of insurance but not just a private one for yourself. And the good thing about it is, it will get cheaper."

Aunty Lizzie looked puzzled,

"How do you make that out?"

"Well, as the nation gets healthier, there won't be as much need for the doctor will there?"

"Good point George."

"You see, it's good Communism. We give what we can to the State, and it all goes into one pot to help the weak in society not just to buy old Lord Lonsdale yellow cars."

"Or the Duke of Buccluegh, new Harris Tweed suits?" I ventured.

Father Tuke looked at me ominously.

"Children should be seen and not heard and little pigs have big ears."

"What, so that they can listen to big pigs talking?"

"Take that child home, Edna. Now."

Mam flushed while the others smiled.

"She has a right to give an opinion." But she went for my coat. As she held it for me, she said,

"So, George you think it's good to give to the State?"

" Are you deaf or daft? I've just said that. Good Communist principles from Marx and Lenin."

Mam shrugged her own coat on.

"Hmm. Funny, I think it was before them that Jesus said, "Render unto Caesar, that which is Caesars."

167

We walked down the lobby leaving all but George, laughing.

Back and forward it went and I was obviously considered too young to be included, I was just around absorbing it all, like a process of osmosis. Still, it was nice to know that Jesus would have approved of the National Health Service. I could never quite work out how the "feckless," suddenly turned into "the weak in Society" or the ones who had been cheated and put upon by the Upper Classes. But Mam managed to marry her Socialism with Christianity quite comfortably and had a warm view of a gentle Jesus. She'd say,

"That poor Jesus, he gets the blame for everything." or,

"That poor man. All he left us to do was to love one another and we just can't do it. We have to wrap it up in services and fancy clothes and then go and fight to keep it like that. He just said to love each other, and it was so simple it was too difficult."

Mam taught me how to say my prayers. I had to kneel down by the bed and put my hands together with my thumbs crossed. My hands had to be down by my chest so that they did not cover my mouth and stop Jesus hearing what I was saying. I had to shut my eyes so that anything else would not distract me. Then I had to bow my head and repeat after her.

"Gentle Jesus, meek and mild,
"Look upon a little child,
"Pity my simplicity,
"Teach me Lord to come to Thee."

Mam and I went over and over this little prayer until I had memorised it and then I had to kneel by the bed to say it, every night. When the prayer was finished, I had to add,

"God bless Mammy.
"God bless Daddy
"God bless Mary and June."

After that I was at liberty to ask Jesus to bless anyone I cared to add. But by that time, I was so frozen that I leapt into bed hoping that Jesus and the rest of my large family did not mind. It was a nice prayer and a nice one for her to teach me. Later when she thought me old enough for more, she taught me the second verse only to make kneeling by the bed even longer.

"Fain I would to Thee be brought,
"Gracious God, forbid it not.
"In the Kingdom of Thy grace,
"Give this little child a place."

I wasn't too sure about adding this verse as there was portents of my mortality in there but there was a pleasure in knowing it off by heart. Of course, there came one winter evening when I gave up on the kneeling part in favour of bodily warmth and suffered the guilt of lying in the bed murmuring the prayer and all the God blesses. It became like a Mantra and spelled that now it was time for sleep.

Mam liked Jesus and promoted the impression of a gentle man who looked down on our misdemeanours with understanding and sadness. She told me stories of Jesus from rather battered books, which had beautiful pictures. One book practically told the whole story in pictures. The first picture was of a man walking all unsuspecting, through a barren ravine. Well, he might have known a place like that was non-too safe. The next picture was of viscous looking men, belting seven bells out of him, while he cowered with pleading eyes looking upwards. Then came a picture of a haughty man hurriedly crossing over the road to avoid the bleeding body and another picture of a man looking into the far horizon so that he needn't see the bleeding body. Then a picture of a man heaving the body onto his donkey, ending with him by a Pub, exhorting the Landlord to care for the wounded man. I totally missed the point of the Samaritans being a race vilified but certainly picked up the point that we should help in times of need. Or, if we were ever traversing a barren ravine and came upon an injured person, we should heave them on our donkey and get help.

All good stuff and not only that but Jesus was magic. All that he had to do was to touch someone and they got better. In fact, sometimes he didn't have to even do that.

They could just touch the hem of his skirt and there was no need even for the National Health Service.

Sunday School was something else!

Every Sunday morning. Dad and I walked up the long hill to Brow Street Methodist Chapel. This was called a, "lantern Chapel," as it had once had a light to guide the sailors towards Maryport. Mam said that the sailors had sighed with relief whenever they had spied it, as it meant that they were nearing home. This was said with much suppressed emotion. Likely sailors and their harsh life were worthy of much sympathy and a tear dramatically wiped away.

When we got to the Chapel Dad handed me in to the little Sunday school, at the side, while he went into the "grown ups'" service. It was another cold place. By the teacher's desk there was a tall, round paraffin stove that emitted a cloying smell but not much heat. We shuffled onto long rows of wooden benches and kept our coats on. If we were required to colour in a picture, we simply had to twist sideways and lean our paper on the bench. The Sunday school teachers were Annie and Winnie Robinson. Annie was so devout and devoted that she kept a long thin stick by her desk, to beat the religion into us. It was never used on me but the sight of it; or the sight of it being used on a lad who had squirmed and sniggered too much, was enough to frighten me into submission. A gaunt lady with fading ginger hair fashioned into a Victory roll. She had a harsh, strident voice and shouted and exhorted us to love the Lord. Rote learning was very popular, and we had to learn the Ten Commandments and then stand to recite them to Annie. I was shaking in my shoes as she pointed her stick and said,

"Number six? Yes, you. Number six?"

and the chosen one had to stand and recite it, word perfect. I can still feel the rigidity of fear that the stick may be pointed in my direction and I would be found wanting. We learned prayers in the same manner though I cannot remember learning the Lords' Prayer. It was almost as if I was born knowing that one. Eventually Winnie played the wheezing organ and then we had to learn a hymn. There was no quarter given to our age and we simply learned the hymns that we would need to know when we joined the grown-ups in the Chapel. We coloured pictures of Bible stories and were given stamps to stick in our books and of course sat to listen to Bible stories. I heard of Adam and Eve, but the implications of the story were not conveyed. I just concluded that women were to blame for all the evils in the world and maybe we shouldn't share apples. I really liked the story of Samuel though I did think it a bit thick of his mother to give him away after so desperately wanting a baby. And there was poor old Eli waiting and waiting for his sons to make good and inherit his job when Samuel was there being good and ending up as the Chosen One. That night I lay in bed listening and listening, but no deep booming voice called, "Edna. Edna. Where for art thou, Edna." I was not to be a Chosen One, which seemed a bit of a shame. Now

172

David was really good. All that trouble with the Philistines and he sorted it with his little sling. The lad had only been taking sandwiches to his brothers at the Front when he suddenly he had to deal with Goliath. You see; you never know what world events you may affect when you are running an errand. Well, as long as you don't forget your sling. I can visualise the picture now. Plucky little David by a large boulder with a fearless stance and across the plain, a huge man in full, long ago, armour holding his bloodied eye.

Ooo, gruesome.

I promptly went off Abraham when he decided to sacrifice his son. I mean all that time waiting and hoping and poor Sarah having a baby when she was well past it. What does he go and do when he finally gets his son and heir? Walks him up a mountain and builds a fire to burn him to death. I didn't just go off Abraham, but I was none too sure of God. What sort of request was that to make of anyone as proof of their love? This did not sit easily with the nice gentle stories Mam had told me. Sometimes there was a change to the weekly programme, and we were told stories of little brown babies in far-away lands. Apparently, they did not have much water but even worse; some of them did not even have a Chapel. Occasionally we had to buy a little black and white picture of a, "brown baby" and the money was to fund missionary work. I was mildly interested but it all seemed too far away and sad.

The prize for itching about, cold and uncomfortable, on the bench was right at the end when the door opened, and Dad was waiting for me. He was usually talking and laughing with another parent. I was well used to this. Any walk out with Dad was frequently punctuated with some jovial chat with someone. Before long he took my hand and we left Brow Street Methodists and walked down Wood Street and into Bob Harris' shop.

Correction, no one walked into Bob Harris's shop.

He had a strange system of ordering goods for his shop and then simply piling the delivered boxes anywhere and everywhere. In consequence it was a matter of going around the door with its' jangling bell and then squeezing and shuffling among the boxes. These rose higher and higher until some sweetie skyscraper was wobbling precariously above you. Bob Harris was a portly man who wore a long fawn shop coat and, on his head a black beret perched jauntily to one side. Often, he was leaning near the doorway and as we came in, he manoeuvred his bulk around the boxes to station himself behind the counter; as if this was the most normal arrangement in a shop. I can only think of that shop with the counter above my line of vision and Dad and Bob Harris way above me, passing the time of day. Sometimes from boredom I managed around the boxes and went back outside to look at the shop window. There were sun-faded packets of Acdo beside bottles of Silverkin shampoo, Bero flour and Fullers Earth Powder and no evidence of any deliberate window arrangement.

174

Eventually the transactions began, and I had to be back in the shop for this. Dad bought something for all us. Pear Drops for June, and Merry Maid caramels for Mary. I had to make a wise choice, as these were the only sweets bought for the whole week. Hmm? Black Jacks? Horlicks Tablets? Aniseed Balls? Mint Balls, Bumper bars? Treacle Toffees? The choice was rather reduced, as it was safer to choose something from jars on the shelves just behind Bob. Otherwise it meant him having to ease himself, with much huffing and puffing, around the shop to peruse the sides of the wobbling boxes. For some reason I was allowed two quarters of sweets but never Bubbly Gum. Mam said that if I swallowed it, it would clog up my insides. Dad always asked for himself a quarter of "Long Lasters" and for Mam a bar of Rum and Raison chocolate He was much too loyal to buy her Bitter Lemons or Acid Drops. When we returned home Dad ceremoniously gave Mary, June and Mam their weekly sweets but mine was, always placed in the china tureens, high on the shelf above the shoe cupboard. In the following week I was allowed some sweets each day. I must have been quite an accepting soul as it never entered my head to climb up and help myself.

Sweets became synonymous with Sunday and sweetened the pill of Sunday school.

And that was official religion over for another week with the occasional exception throughout the year.

175

An annual event was the chapel Anniversary.

Hmm.

This was delivered as another form of entertainment. That is, if you weren't actually one of the entertainers.

The Anniversary consisted of certain factions of the chapel doing little "turns." Someone singing a solo or giving a "recitation." Two stout ladies performing a duet. And what appeared to give the most pleasure and amusement was the inclusion of the children from the Sunday school.

I wanted to be chosen.

I wanted it to be acknowledged that I was capable of being part of the annual concert.

And then, when I was chosen, I was terrified.

And I was always, but always, chosen to perform on the Anniversary.

Oh, the agony. Oh, the terror.

Many hours were spent learning my, "piece," off by heart.

I had to stand on a stool, by the living room window and have a, "practice go," as Dad called it.

June dutifully listened and then softly interrupted.

"Lift your head a bit more. You are talking into your chest. You must project your voice. Right, start again

"QUINQUIREME   OF   NINEVEH   FROM DISTANT............"

"For crying out loud. I didn't say shout. I said project. That means that the people at the back have to hear you, but you haven't to shout. Lift your head so that the sounds travel in the air."

Later I had to climb up on the stool for Mary to listen.

"Wait. What are you doing with your head?"

"Our June said I had to look up."

"She didn't mean up at the ceiling, you clown. Look dead ahead"

Dad listened to me.

"Could you not put a bit more expression into it?"

I might have done if I'd known what an "Isthmus," or, "moidores," were. To say nothing of a "Quinquereme."

But the most fearsome of all was Mam.

Oh, she didn't scold or abuse too much, but she pulled up a chair and watched while I recited. What she was actually doing was weighing up what hairstyle would be most admired and which dress could she manufacture to add to my torture.

On the appointed morning out came the curling tongs; invented by Torquemada himself. Long steel tongs, which lay across the gas ring until they glowed orange and red. Mam gingerly held them with the handle wrapped in a tea towel and grasping a lock of my long red hair, she clamped it into the tongs and curled up and up.

"Whaaagh! That's my ear."

"Shut up. It's no-where near your ear."

"I'm burning."

"No, you're not. Oh yes you are."

There I was, with the most ghastly curling ringlets hiding my singed ears.

If it wasn't the curling tongs it was another curious agony called, "Bobs." The night before the Anniversary I was directed to sit on the stool and while Main twisted my wet hair into long strips of torn sheeting and tied the loose ends into a knot. Then I was expected to sleep with

178

these lumps of cloth wrenching my hair from my scalp. The next morning, I was back on the stool for Mam to unwind them.

"You're pulling my hair."

"Of course, I'm not, you silly girl."

"Aaagh. It hurts."

"It'll hurt even more in a minute if you don't stop squirming."

June tried to intercede on my behalf.

"Leave her alone Mam."

"You mind your wisht."

"But Mam, you're hurting her."

"All pride is painful."

"It's not her pride that's hurting her though."

"Don't speak to me like that my lady. Alf, Speak to her."

And Dad lowered his paper and said,

"Hello June."

"I didn't mean that and well you know it."

Dad and June smiled at each other but didn't stop the descendent of Attila the Hun twisting and twirling my hair.

Oh … the ignominy of seeing myself with the ridiculous dangling curls. Which was nothing compared to the ignominy when the dress appeared. While other children trooped to the chapel in a neat kilt and Fair Isle twin set, there was I looking more like a latter-day Shirley Temple. Mam embraced shotte silk and satin sashes wholeheartedly and to my utter amazement had her simpering reward when all the old ladies swooned with admiration. When Mam was eventually satisfied with my appearance. Dad walked me up the long hill to the Sunday school and handed me over to my fate and Annie Robinson.

She was having an orgy of organising.

We were shoved and pushed into the chapel and then shoved and pushed into our appointed places on the tiers of forms. I don't know who built them for the annual event or where all the towering seats resided for the rest of the year but they were set at such a dizzying incline that we should all have been smitten with vertigo for the rest of our lives.

"Frank, you sit next to David. Stop doing that, you dirty boy. Edna, remember you speak after Mrs. Eliot.

"Marie, get your shoelaces tied, you slovenly girl."

On and on she bullied little children for her fifteen minutes of small-town glory.

When we were finally in some semblance of order, Annie took her place, hiding down by the organ and I didn't have butterflies in my tummy but a flock of Solway seagulls. How if I forgot my place? How if I just looked silly? And worse than that, how if I forget my lines? Some children did and the silence while they Annie Robinson hissed at them was, for me, an endless agony of sympathy for them and more worry about my own performance.

On one occasion a little girl faltered, repeated the last line and then sank into silence. The tension in the chapel rose and as she began to cry Annie's arm snaked out and dragged her off. Down by the organ she gave her a good shaking and sat her down beside her with a thump. I watched and watched Mrs. Eliot, waiting for my cue and by the time she reached the last line of her song my legs were physically shaking. I was also fully aware of Dad, Mam, Mary and June sitting there with adoration, waiting for me to bring the house down.

It's amazing that my legs ever held me long enough to recite my piece, but they always did and I got through it without mishap. And that was that for another year. There was never a word of praise or a pat on the back from

Annie Robinson. She was too busy accepting her own accolades and we were simply discarded to join our families. The next week we were presented with a book, with a piece pasted in the front acknowledging our performance but better than that Dad took me to Bob Harris' for a more tangible reward.

Of all the religious places that we visited; my favourite was Grasslot chapel. Dad was also an Elder at this chapel and the congregation were less aloof than Brow Street. It was a very small building and in consequence always seemed full. Another bonus was that it was always warm. There was a large, round; black pipe running along the bottom of the wall which was really hot. If I got beside this, I could put my feet on it until the heat burned through and then I placed them on the wooden floor, feeling the warmth soak through. Another trick was to place, hats, mitts and scarf on the pipe so that they were deliciously warm to put on at the end of the service. We always went as a family and always ensured that Dad had the seat at the end of the pew. It was another venue for him to be talking and laughing at the beginning and the end of the service and anyway it was agreed that you got a better sing at Grasslot chapel.

The chapels provided seasonal entertainment and the Harvest Festivals were big. And I mean Big! The gifts made a veritable hillside of goods at the front of the chapel and the pride of place always went to a sheaf of corn made of bread. Naturally local industries were represented and among the groceries there was always a bag of coal and plates of fish.

Oh, how we sang. I loved those hymns. We fairly belted out our gratefulness to the Lord.

"We plough the fields and scaaaarrrter, the good seed on the land."

Or,

"Fair waved the golden corn. O'er Canaans' pleasant land."

I had not a clue where Canaan was, but I knew that golden corn waved over it.

Both Mary and June had very good singing voices and I chortled away with them. Dad joined in for a while and then quietly slipped from the pew to go and stand outside, "to get his breath back." It was not unusual. All the chapel people knew that he had a bad chest and they just nodded and smiled sympathetically as he wheezed his way out.

The next night the goods, freely donated, were sold. Dad and Mr. Parkin, a man with a large thumb and thinning hair, auctioned the goods, banging on the table with a small wooden gavel.

"Sold to the lady in the lovely dress."

They always knew who it was, but their impromptu comments made for a more comic and entertaining evening.

"Just look at the size of these carrots. Remember they help you see in the dark. Have you ever seen a rabbit in glasses?"

"Now, what am I bid for this fine basket of eggs?"

The fact that most people had their own allotment with a hen pen mattered little and the bidding went on and on.

And last of all came the sheaf of corn.

"Come along now dig deep for our final item. Made and donated by Robert Studhoime, Master Baker."

Which was doubly charitable, as the Studholmes were Baptists. It never ceased to amaze me how much that sheaf of corn realised, and I never quite knew what the successful bidder did with it as it did not seem a likely candidate for slicing. Neither could I equate the story of Jesus turning people out of the Temple for selling goods with the Harvest festival auctions. I just assumed that maybe he had a special dispensation for Methodists.

CHAPTER 7
"SERIOUS EDUCATION"

I began attending, "real", school in the September after my fourth birthday. The only preparation for this was a few trips to the Coop for new clothes and shoes. There was no preliminary visit to the school and no forewarning of what was to come. Mam walked me there; up Senhouse Street and then up High Street to a large house called the Settlement, on the top of Moat Hill. The River Ellen ran around the bottom of the hill making a natural moat and the Romans had immediately and sensibly seen the advantage of this position and built a Roman settlement up there. Much later, the local aristocratic family had built a large dower house. A stray German bomb had obliterated the towns' Primary school and now this house was being used as a school until a new one was built.

We stood about outside while Mam talked to Alice Musgrave and I renewed my friendship with Little Billy. Then the doors opened, and Mam ushered me in and went away. We went into a classroom on the left of the entrance hall and I was given a seat at a desk, which had a lid that lifted. At some point in the morning someone came around and placed a small bottle of milk on my desk. Cool.

I began to pick off the foil cap.

"You. Edna Croft. What do you think you are doing?"

I nearly jumped out of my skin

.

"N, n, nothing."

"Of course you are. How dare you. You naughty little girl. Who told you to take the top off your milk?"

"N, n, no-one."

"Exactly. Nobody told you. See that? See that on the wall."

She pointed to the wall and hanging on the wall was a leather thing with strings of leather hanging from it. She reached for it and told me to stand.

"This my girl, is a Cat o Nine Tails and waits on the wall just for naughty little girls like you," and she slapped it hard across my leg.

I was stunned.

I had never felt deliberate physical pain before. Added to this, I was aware of the others looking at me and I felt embarrassed and silly.

"Sit down you bad girl and in future you wait until you are told to open your milk."

186

The Cat o Nine Tails was returned to the nail on the wall while my leg reddened and burned. At lunchtime, I walked back down the hill home and indignantly told Mam and Dad of my public indignity.

I did not return to school alone.

Mam marched into the school and was met in the hallway by the Headmistress. Mam twirled me round to display the welt on my leg.

"Can we have some explanation please," she said icily.

"Ah, I'm sure you know that we are in a difficult position here in this building, Mrs. Croft and the children must learn to comply, for us to keep any semblance of order."

Her tone was very much that of a person with some, "position," but no one was a match for Mam when she was in full flight and a Headmistress was no exception.

"Is this any way to treat a small child on her first day? What an introduction to school. "What on earth are you women thinking of? Is there no warmth? Is there no understanding that this is a momentous day in a child's life? Our Edna has never, but never, been physically punished..."

"Then it strikes me that she should have been as she has not learned to be an obedient child."

187

"She can hardly be obedient if she wasn't told first what to do."

Then, I was shocked to hear an adult telling lies as a defence.

"Of course she was told, she is simply telling you lies to save her own skin."

I wasn't. I knew that I wasn't.

"My child does not tell lies, so somebody else is and I suggest that you investigate. If she comes home just once more like this, I will take this further, much further. And don't imagine that that is an empty threat."

It ended when the Headmistress condescendingly said,

"Mrs. Croft I have had many children through my hands..."

Mam quietly intervened saying,

"But you have never had one of your own. Not one,"

And she turned and left.

It was probably a bit below the belt to a childless woman, but I just knew that Mam had scored a brilliant hit. I was never bothered again with the Cat-o'- Nine-tails but the Class teacher occasionally taunted me.

"Oh, and we mustn't touch, 'Our Edna,' must we? Or we bring our Mammy to school." I cringed but was not sorry. I knew that I was safe in the knowledge that my family would rise up for me against strong forces. Even more amazing was the fact that Mam had stirred herself to intervene without leaning on someone else to do this. Serious indeed.

There was no empathy from the teachers for small children. They were simply there to impart knowledge to conforming little minds. Much of the conforming depended on us being clairvoyant. How we could do this without prior knowledge of their rules, Kafka only knows. But it worked. As a lesson it worked. The foil top never left my milk bottle again, until I was told to remove it. I just happened to be too dim to generalise this concept of guessing the rules and then giving total obedience.

In a courtyard, outside the make-shift school, a wooden structure was being demolished to make way for a long, brick building. At break time we were all sent out to play in the courtyard where there was very little space, and even this was diminishing by the day as the old building came down and the new one went up. We were exhorted not to bother the workmen, we were exhorted not to go near the wall looking down, down, to the docks and we were told not to ever leave the premises. Nobody mentioned the growing piles of rotting wood and new bricks.

I had quickly found that boys were better to play with than girls. They thought up much more exciting games, so when Little Billy Musgrave and his friends decided to climb the stacks of discarded wood and attack the Hun; I was there with them. As George Clark refused the third light for his imagined cigarette, known to be an unlucky delay in war, I wrenched the pin from my invisible grenade with my teeth. Just as I was about to lob it and end a decisive skirmish with Jerry, the mountain of wood began to slide from under me. A large rusty nail sank deep into the soft flesh at the side of my knee and pain exploded in my head. My friends quickly gathered round to investigate, and Little Billy Musgrave wrenched me away from the nail. They twittered and clucked me into school while the blood ran down copiously.

It was made very obvious to us that we had disturbed the teachers having their cup of tea. I was roundly told that I should not have been on the wood in the first place and given a wet piece of paper to hold on my knee.

"And you lot, go back outside. It doesn't take eight of you. Stop that wailing and sit there Edna Croft until it is time for class. That's what happens to little girls when they cannot behave." and she wearily disappeared back into the makeshift staff room.

No one actually looked at the wound, never mind administer medication. I sat through the rest of the morning with my sock soaked in blood and then I squelched my way home. There I got a similar response.

190

Auntie May and Auntie Lizzie were drinking tea in the living room while Mam was grudgingly throwing something on the table for Dad and I. She wiped the around the wound and slapped on a plaster. She tut-tutted at the state of the sock and after much wringing it in cold water, threw it into a bucket of Reckitts blue.

After lunch I limped back to school. The reaction of the adults was scant and casual, though it was a deep wound and took many plasters and forever to heal, leaving a pale, white scar. There was no thought of hospitals or doctors, never mind a Tetanus injection. Well, my jaw didn't seize up and my leg didn't drop off so maybe I was reasonably healthy. Anyway, Mam said that a little dirt didn't hurt anybody before they died.

That's all that I remember of Infant school. Incidents, just incidents, and none of them connected to education. I can't remember learning how to read but then, neither can I remember a time when I could not read. I just did. In later years if I saw an old "Janet and John," primer something stirred in my memory and I presumed that I had learned reading from this at school. Mam roundly squashed that idea.

"It may have been the school reading scheme and you might have been given one to keep you quiet, but you could read when you went to school. Those daft teachers couldn't cope with a child that already knew something and probably ploughed on teaching you how to read. For goodness sake, we were all always reading. You were surrounded by books, and good books at that. Of course, with our Mary and June being at the Grammar school you already knew that learning came from reading. "None of us were behind the barn door when brains were given out and you just sort of soaked it up."

So, I didn't learn to read at school, it had been another process of osmosis.

There was nothing made of my left handedness with the exception that I was allowed to turn my exercise book to the side, so that I was writing away from my body.

One happening that stands out, was when we were all hustled into a long crocodile and walked to see the new school. This was built on the far reaches of the town, keeping children well away from civilised society. It was at the top of a hill and looked down on Netherhall road. There were few houses near, and the school had a long driveway leading to the centre of the building. It was a cream building, long and low with flat roofed classrooms. A larger, taller section divided the Infant and junior schools. As it was built close to the site where there had been a Roman camp and at the end of Camp Road, the Local Education Authority truly taxed their imagination and named it, "Camp Road School." It was a very hot day when we were frog marched up the hill to view the new school. I sat thirsty and uncomfortable on the hard parquet, floor of the new Hall listening to the Headmaster giving a speech to "open," the school. We were urged to squirm around and look at the windows in the Hall doors. These were round and he likened them to portholes. Apparently, we were on a vessel of discovery searching for knowledge and they were a fitting tribute to the history of the town. We sang some hymns and then walked back to the Settlement. In the following September I began attending Camp Road school.

It was not only light and airy but also very spacious compared to the Settlement and of course there was a large Hall. It was here that I experienced my first bewilderment at being educated in a proper school building. At some point in the first week, we all had to go to the Hall where we were told to take off our clothes. I had never done such a thing in public. Everyone began dutifully divesting themselves of their raiment's and I did so very reluctantly. What a strange thing to have to do and in front of other people. I was very uncomfortable. Thankfully we were told to stop at our vest and knickers and there we stood shivering. Then we were told to skip round the Hall. How odd.

All of us went around the edge skip, skip, skipping. It appeared that quite a few of the boys could not skip and were hauled into the middle of the room and were exhorted to try harder. The order to skip was changed to hopping and on we went hop, hop, hopping. The hop failures were also consigned to the middle and told to watch those who could hop and try to copy. This was not funny. I began to worry that something was coming that I could not do and would end up in the middle too.

Thankfully it always seemed to be the boys that came later in their hopping and skipping development. After some time of vigorous exercise, we were told to sit on the cold, brown, wooden floor and curl up like hedgehogs. I had never seen a hedgehog, but I curled up on the hard floor, glad that the energetic round and round the Hall had ceased.

Some were exhorted to,

"Get those elbows in," and I rapidly tucked mine in too. Maybe hedgehogs didn't have elbows.

There was a great sense of relief when we were told to get up and put our clothes back on. Scorn was poured on those who could not fasten their shoelaces and they were told to get their mothers to teach them. Apparently, this was not a teacher's job. No one had explained what was going to happen to us. No one had said that we would be required to strip or why this was necessary. No one explained the benefits of physical education. It was as if, one minute we were sitting at our desks reading and the next minute we were walking to the Hall to prance about semi-nude. I was quite an accepting little soul and I just assimilated that somewhere in the week we had to walk to this Hall, take off most of our clothes and fling ourselves about.

I also remember being allowed to paint. I had watched others and waited for my turn to come with great anticipation. At last my name was called. I had to go to the back of the classroom and stand by a painting easel, which was squashed between the rows of desks. As I donned the red plastic apron, I savoured the pots of paint resting on a ledge on the easel. It was not what I expected. The paint ran down the paper until the colours merged. Whatever I had decided to paint was lost in a haze of red seeping into white and green. I watched the person in front of me carefully scraping her brush against the side of the pot and I copied. It was a better result but still very unsatisfactory. We were not taught any painting techniques and I don't know what happened to my mock Kandinsky as we did not take work home. This was the era of the "Bulge," or "Baby Boom" and there were forty-five in my class. Small wonder painting was only an occasional event and the easels squashed between all the desks.

It was as if the move to a new school also signalled the sorting out of friendships. No longer did I just play willy nilly with anyone but began to select and be selected. Little Billy Musgrave and I were playing less and less with each other as we made new friends. A favourite of mine, was a lad called Donald who lived near me and was good for the long walk home. I often went to play at his house and at some point, in the evening his father called us through to the living room and we solemnly listened to Dan Dare on the radio. Another favourite friend was called George Clark. I had such a warmth and fondness for George. He lived up past Cuetos' Chip shop and so whenever I think of playing at George's house, I also have a memory smell of fish and chips. His Mam was a nice woman who made me welcome and always set me so far home in the evening.

In Camp Road school I began to spread my favours to include girls in my circle of friends. My "best," friend was Pam and she *was* the best. The chemistry was just right and sparkled and crackled between us. In fact, it was this that first alerted me to the fact that school was not fun. Fun was something that happened somewhere else. Fun had to be put away for break time and lunchtime and after school hours. Fun had not to be conducted in the actual building and most definitely not in the classroom. Any signs of this phenomenon were quickly squashed. And Pam and I frequently committed the gross sin of laughing in class. We had the temerity to display evidence of enjoying ourselves and were roundly castigated for doing so. We were forever being, "split up," Oh not to another class, but sent to various parts of the same room. "Edna Croft. To the back until you can stop being silly."

Not "silly." Heaven forfend!

Of course, the great unwashed and snotty nosed always sat at the back so this really was a punishment. It was a great relief to go out to play at breaktime, not only to meet up with Pam and legitimately enjoy ourselves, but also to breathe unpolluted air.

On one occasion there was no more room at the back for "silly," people and Pam was told to sit just across the aisle, whereupon we advanced to "A" level silliness and made faces at each other.

"Pam Ferguson, one of these days the wind will change, and you will stay like that."

The thought of someone going through life cock eyed and their tongue lolling was too much.

"That's it. That's it. If you two girls don't stop, you will be sent to stand outside Mr. Crellins' door."

Couldn't she see? Couldn't she see how funny it was? Likely not and we were despatched to stand making faces at each other outside the Headmasters' door. Nothing else happened, so at breaktime we shrugged our shoulders and went out to play. It was a better punishment than sitting, watching green snot sliding down someone's' upper lip.

Pam was definitely the best for fun and added to that she had naturally curly hair of a rather non-descript colour. I was so envious. Mine was long, straight and always in plaits. And of course, it was this odd colour. It wasn't violent red, or sandy but a deep, red, mahogany hue. I disliked being different, a feeling made worse by the lads, cat calling, "Ginger," or "Ginger Nut." Mam said that they were only jealous as my hair was my crowning glory and I didn't believe her at all.

No, Pam was definitely the lucky one not having such a public burden to bear. Not only that but she lived the closest possible to anyone to the school. In fact, her garden ran right down to the edge of the school playground. This meant that often after a substantial school lunch we could walk round to play at her house and then run pell, mell back to school when we heard the bell. The position of Pam's house had quite another significance for Mam. This was the area of the town where Maryport's aristocracy lived in large, heavy detached houses. Oh, not aristocracy in the sense of landed gentry but certainly the families that owned the local cinemas, theatres, garages and shops. I was most definitely encouraged to further my friendships in this area. It was no trouble to comply as we all shared the same class for seven years and a certain group of us just gravitated to each other.

Mary and June were probably quite relieved that I was beginning to make contacts of my own and they were more able to pursue their own interests instead of being commanded to "mind," me. My circle of friends had grown, and the companionship begun in school was to be extended to invitations to visit their homes. I gradually realised that Mam was older than other mothers were, and other homes were not as charged with atmosphere and angst. I really enjoyed playing in these calmer houses and though I also enjoyed the act of inviting friends back to my own house, I was never comfortable with this. I was increasingly aware that Mam was noting my friends' speech or manners and then discouraging those who were not suitable. Away from Mam's influence I swirled around various groups and always including or returning to a small circle of special friends. One was called Miriam and was known for being a "delicate," child. It was said that she had been born prematurely and though I didn't know what this meant it obviously left you delicate which seemed deliciously fine. She was slender and pale and was often absent from school and had the added interest of being "an only one." This was a great advantage when I went to play at her house, as we were not required to include siblings who were a decided nuisance in our games. By now my own life had taken on the flavour of being and only child and at home I mainly entertained myself.

For a while I had an imaginary friend until one day when waiting to cross Curzon Street, I had invited my friend to hold my hand for safety. The man standing next to Mam and I looked down at me as if I was crackers and Mam decided that the time had come to call a halt to outward evidence of daftness.

"Stoppit and stoppit now," and I was yanked over the road. No counselling in our family; just "Stoppit." And stop it I did. It brought home to me that others could hear our conversations and apparently others did not do this. Occasionally Mam and Dad played cards or Ludo with me but otherwise I kept myself occupied. Once Mam agreed to join me in making an imaginary tea. I made a cup of tea from cold water, milk and sugar, in my tiny china tea service. It tasted ghastly.

Mam daintily held the tiny cup and pretended to drink from it. It was an uncomfortable affair and we never repeated it. It didn't matter. Mam and Dad were these asexual beings who provided for me and loved me, and I loved them back. That was the deal. They were not your friends. Teachers were not your friends either. They were not even friendly. Teachers were aloof beings that taught us and that was all. They were not remotely interested in your personal life and you knew not to reveal home events to them. School was school and therefore something different. You were not required to like it or love it. Oh, when we met other adults in the street they invariably said, "And does she like school?"

And Mam assured them that I did, that I loved going to school, in fact couldn't get enough of it. I learned that this was the sort of answer that I was supposed to give if the question was ever addressed to me, and I lied beautifully. But no one truly wanted to know; it was just a question to ask small children.

There were some pupils who didn't attend on a regular basis and if they weren't like Miriam and known to be delicate then the School Board Man paid them a home visit. Now here I was at a distinct advantage as my Uncle Eph was the School Board Man. He was a very big man who looked like Victor McClaglan and could intimidate by simply filling the door of the truants' house. He was frequently seen at school chatting to the headmaster and disappearing into the office to check the registers. If I happened across him, he continued talking to the teachers

200

but magically managed to slip a silver sixpence in my pocket before marching off down the drive to search out malingerers. Uncle Eph carried with him a small black book that had a pencil fitted down its' spine. He had a wonderful way of taking the pencil out with a flourish, licking the end of it, leaving his tongue a beautiful purple hue, and writing importantly in the book. Later in the day he could be seen like a doom-laden Pied Piper, marching back up the drive followed by a string of small, scruffy children. He only once called to see me in his official capacity and having established that I was not fading away from some infectious disease, he whirled me onto his knee and covered me in slobbery kisses. He then drank quantities of strong tea and gladdened Mam's heart by describing some of the houses that he had to visit in the course of his duty. According to Uncle Eph there were some houses where the smell was so bad, he had to light a cigarette as he entered to deaden the effect.

"Dear God Eph, soap and water is cheap enough. There's no need for it in this day and age. Now you know me Eph, I may have some faults, but dirt is not one of them."

Which was true.

"And anyway, I don't know why their Mam's want them at home round their feet or scadging around the streets. It's always the very ones who need to be in school."

Which did appear to be also true.

There was always a little knot of children who were bottom of the class and exuded a nose-wrinkling odour. They came to school in cheap plimsolls even when it was snowing. Their shirts were an off white and their jumpers milled until they were tough as bulls' lugs. They also had a peculiar achievement that I found fascinating to watch. A trickle of green snot was always sliding from their nose and with split second timing, just as it reached their lip, they sniffed it back up their nose, whereupon the process began again. Snake belts were very popular with them. A strip of striped elastic with a curved silver clasp. I really would have liked one of these but there were definite girls' clothes and boys' clothes. Snake belts were definitely for boys, as were balaclavas and pullovers. Otherwise, there were few concessions for the weather, boys came to school shivering in short pants and girls came to school shivering in skirts. Trousers were for adult men, unless you were Katherine Hepburn in the films. A few women in Maryport who were very daring, wore trousers but these weren't called trousers, these were, "slacks." Children's clothes were for covering

and not for fun. In consequence there were children at school who either had clothes trailing to the ground for them, "to grow into," or skirts up to their backsides showing lines where the hems had been let down.

And so, there were always children around the school looking either very cold or very overheated. Their poor footwear was a clear indication of their station in life, to say nothing of the pungent odour seeping from them and of course the green stripe under their noses.

Soon after we moved into Lawson Street, Mary went to College. She had proved to have quite a flair for her job at Dearham School and so had applied and been accepted at a College in Bolton in Lancashire.

Oh, how I missed her.

Not only was she vivacious and passionate but it broke the family unit. There was no question that I loved June just as much, but it was odd not to have Mary around. She wrote frequently, telling us of her exploits. Mary didn't live, she had exploits. Mam always read them out loud to us as we sat around the dining table and then said that she must write back and tell Mary that her handwriting was terrible. In one of her letters Mary had enclosed a photograph of herself, holding a baby at a Bolton Nursery. I made the gross mistake of thinking that my Infant teacher would be interested in my personal news and took the photograph to show her. A few days later when Mam and I were on our way to the Coop we met my Headmistress who mincingly enquired after Mary. Surprised and pleased at this sudden and untypical.

Interest, Mam told her that Mary was doing fine at College.

"Really? At College? I had heard that she was not at College at all but had moved away to have a baby. In fact, Edna brought a photograph to show us. Or wasn't she meant to do that?"

Mam was aghast.

"I can assure you that my daughter is in College and not some unmarried mothers' home. Though I really should not grace such filth with any reply."

And grabbing my arm she moved away saying just loud enough for others to hear,

"Some people have such dirty minds."

I don't know why that Headmistress kept trying to wrong foot her. If she had only asked us, we could have told her that there was no victory in a verbal exchange with Mam, or any other exchange for that matter. I learned. I learned that school was not a place to reveal even family pleasures and successes. The only other memorable incident in the Infants school always brings a sense of discomfort.

The number of the pupils in the class fluctuated and one day we were introduced to a new girl. I had to squash along my desk to make room for her. As she had newness value and was sitting right beside me, I courted her for a few days, along with all the others. She was very girlie and sweet with little interest in the Great Maryport Apache Uprising to be enacted each playtime and soon I slid back to my original friends. Then, one day we were told that we all had to stay in at play time unless the person who had stolen her beautiful new necklace owned up. There was a long silence. I looked around for the thief to identify himself or herself. Nothing. Everyone just sat there. It was all very uncomfortable. We just sat and resentfully missed our beak time.

At lunchtime it was cold and as I made my way down the long hill home, I stuffed my hands in my gabardine coat pockets. To my horror there was the necklace. I felt it but did not take it out. I knew exactly what it was and fingered it, not knowing what to do. If I went back, not only would I miss my lunch, but also would anyone believe me? I was stunned by this strange problem and plodded on feeling miserable. As I walked round our back door, I was enveloped in sheets drying on the long line. Disentangling myself I suddenly thought of a solution and I hid the necklace under the rest of the washing in the basket. There was a great sense of relief. If it wasn't in my possession anymore, then everything was all right. I cheerfully ate my fried bread and black specked fried egg and wandered back up the hill to school. It was very disconcerting to find that the search was still going on. Now I was suffering. I had never had such a dilemma. I was sorry for the girl, but I could hardly confess that it was in our washing basket. I had already witnessed teachers' swift judgements and surely this would sound as if I were guilty of the original theft. There was also the uncomfortable feeling that someone else in that class knew that I knew where the necklace might be. I stayed silent even though I knew that she was upset and that my silly actions had deprived her of her necklace. When I got home after school, the necklace was lying on the table and there were deep discussions as to how it had come to be in the washing basket. The favourite theory became the accepted one. According to Mam, some birds were known to like shiny things and so a bird must have dropped it. At no time did any of them ask me if I had the solution to the mystery and I certainly did not volunteer the answer. I was awarded the little necklace to play with. I never did. It was as big a worry to me as it would have been for an adult to get into gross debt. I was quite relieved when the girl eventually left the school and moved to another town, minus her necklace.

And that's about all that I recollect in the Infants school.

Just incidents and none of them related to reading,writing and arithmetic.

My little world was stunned. Some were dismal, others enraged, and many were bewildered. I sat on Mothers' fender stool busy folding my hankie into a rabbit as the debate swirled around me.

"I don't believe it. I just don't believe it."

"You'd better believe it Lizzie. And look out for all we've gained going down the Swannee."

"I don't believe it."

"Oh, stop saying that. It's a fact. It's happened. After all we've worked for, they go and vote Winston Churchill in again."

"I don't believe it."

Uncle George blasted round the lobby curtain.

"I see you've all heard."

They nodded miserably.

"That drunken old reprobate back in power. You know what he said about the miners? You know what he said? He said that they were worms that should stay in the ground. I'd worm him if I could. I don't know where it all comes from this adulation for the man. By God he never did a thing right until the blooming war started and even then, all he wanted to do was go through Norway and drop leaflets in Europe. "He knew fine that we weren't ready."

Mother put a cup of tea near him.

"Now it's no good George getting yourself all het up and anyway here comes Father from the allotment and he's bad enough so don't set him off again."

Father came in, washed his hands and sat down heavily in his chair by the fire. "Well, lad, what do you think? A bad day for the working man eh?"

Mam decided to enter the fray.

"Well, I hope he passes nothing thicker than thread for a month."

"Edna!"

Mother was scandalised, but Father smiled.

"No, you know what I'd like to see? I'd like to see him getting vaccinated with a pint of Lenin's blood. The war that would go on in his insides would drive him crackers."

Everyone laughed but quickly resumed their dismal air. Uncle George's eldest son William came swinging in and stood rocking on his heels by the fire. He was a stocky, bullish young man and he leaned down and ruffled my hair.

"Hyah blood nut. How's your fettle? Any chance of a cuppa Mother? What's the crack then?"

"Need you ask?"

"Aw, get away. The old fella won the war for us."

The air was suddenly charged, and everyone stole a glance at Father. Even I felt a flutter of concern.

"You daft, unthinking young man. Wars are made by old men like him for young men to fight. Won the war indeed. The only thing that he did in any war was to get captured and then run away. Then, when he found he couldn't get elected he changed parties. Nobody likes a turncoat. Oh, very noble. And he'll probably be written for History as a great thing like Dunkirk. That was nothing but a retreat. Only the British could turn it into something to celebrate I'm telling you it's a black day for us and we can only hope that he's got too old to have any effect. I don't know where the country's brains are."

Auntie Lizzie tried to soothe.

"Well, Labour got in in Maryport."

"A blooming donkey wearing a red rosette could get in in Maryport."

Father was looking thunderous, but William was too full of himself to notice.

"Me? I reckon, if you can't beat them, join them. I'm going places and I'm going to have things. What has all your socialism got you?"

"It hasn't got us anything individually, but it has got the whole country a Health Service and Nationalising industry for us to benefit."

"Oh, yes Aunt Edna very true but me, I'm going to have things for me, and I see you've got yourself a fine house to bring Little Edna up in. Where was your Socialism when you were buying that?"

"Honestly William, you don't half talk some rubbish. Socialism doesn't mean that we all have to live in a Council House. Don't you know the story of Marx visiting Paris? "The French Communist Party waited and waited to greet him on the station platform and were aghast to see him stepping out of a First-Class carriage. One of them rushed over to him and asked if that was a tactful thing to do and Marx said, 'You've got things wrong. With Communism, I want everyone to be First Class and get rid of any lower classes. I want everyone to pull together to have the best'. So, thank you very much William I'll stick with my house and keep looking for the best but still working for better conditions for everyone."

William just shrugged, unconvinced.

"All right maybe things are a bit better, but Attlee wasn't against keeping all those German prisoners of war here as cheap labour. Like, I know they did some terrible things in the war but it's about time they went home."

Father clicked his tongue.

"William, it's amazing what terrible things you will do out of fear."

Uncle Bill Musgrave wiggled a bit of shrapnel from his ear and said softly.

"I couldn't vote Conservative because of the name."

Mam looked bewildered and everyone was surprised that he had even opened his mouth to speak.

"All they want to do is bloody conserve. Conserve the bloody establishment. Bloody status quo. Them up there and us down here serving while they bloody con."

There was a stunned silence.

"You've made a very good point Bill, but you should mind youre language in front of the women."

"He can't help it Father. It's the way he was left."

There was an air of such disappointment, but I had worries of my own and they had little to do with a Government far away in London. I was moving up to the Junior school and to my horror had discovered that I was to be in Annie Robinson's class. As Mam and I walked back to Lawson Street I pondered my dismal future.

Not only was I unsure of the teacher but the educational system ensured that just as I had risen to the top class of the Infant school now, I was to be flung back to the bottom of the heap in the Junior school. Once again, we would be the smallest and the most ignorant in the building. A guaranteed mode of repetitively diminishing any assumptions of achievement. And anyway, being a little star in Annie's Sunday school was no guarantee that I would be favoured when in her class. I was right. If that woman ever had favourites, then she took that knowledge to her grave with her. In fact, when I was chosen to be on her concerts or to speak in Assembly, I assumed that she had divined that I found this publicity a peculiar form of torture. I was never given the impression that she thought me capable; I did not feel flattered or favoured. But, if ever I learned anything I learned while I was in Annie's class. It was a diligence generated from fear.

Though it was a new building, we still sat in rows facing the teachers' desk. We had new rectangular tables, which had a little inlet at the top that slid aside to reveal an inkpot. We were given new rulers, pencils, rubbers and exercise books and many exhortations that the school could not afford more. The only item that I can remember as a wall display was a very large, shiny map of the world. Annie frequently pointed out to us that the map was nearly all coloured pink. Pink meant that that country was ours. I was so proud to be British. Australia was pink, Africa was pink, Canada was pink, a spattering of smaller countries were pink and India was pink. Obviously Ghandi had never happened for Annie Robinson. She continued to encourage us to view the whole world as ours. On Empire Day she brought in a very large Union Jack and we had to stand and sing all of the National Anthem to it. We cheerfully sang about our strength and might and dismissed the very idea of a united Britain by promising to also hammer the Scots into submission, whenever the chance arose. She lauded and praised the Royal Family, which made me develop a dual personality.

At home Mam was teaching me to sing,

"God save our gracious cat,
"Feed him on bacon fat,
"God save the cat,"

And at school I was being exhorted to revere the very people and practices that my family despised. Annie described to us the wonderful little Princesses. They were jolly Girl Guides and baked for the war effort. They had all been so brave throughout the war and we had to admire King George and Queen Elizabeth because their house had been bombed. They had even given up their time to visit bombed areas in London. And weren't we lucky to have Winnie back in power? Why when the war was on, if anyone felt a bit down, they only had to pull their chair up to the wireless and listen to Winnie and they immediately felt better."

At home I tried to speak up in their defence, but Mam promptly flattened my new Royalist fervour.

"Bombed their house? Bombed! Waken up our Edna their house is big enough to take ten bombs and they wouldn't feel it. Anyway, they probably weren't there at the time. As for mincing around bombsites after the event, well, anybody could do that. "The Queen there in all her finery and that daft hat tipped to the side, dressed like we; or the Eastend never could. Great example of make do and mend. And don't you talk to me about Winston Churchill, the old warmonger. He probably had shares in Krupps."

If it wasn't Mam it was other members of the Tuke family, preaching seditious libel into my little ears. I never repeated it at school. I cheerfully chortled the National Anthem and wrote in my exercise book of my great sadness when the old Queen Mary died.

But Mam was genuinely sad when the King died. She said that he was never meant to be the King and being the King had killed him. She said that he was a quiet man with a terrible stammer, and it was all Wallis Simpson's fault that he had been thrust into the limelight. I didn't understand what she was talking about, but I did understand that there were some things that I had not to repeat in school.

There was already enough repeating in school as most lessons were based on rote learning. A quantity of trite little poems were memorised, moving to a more mature, "Daffodils" by William Wordsworth. And not a mention that he was a son of Cumberland. Maths followed the same method as learning the Ten Commandments.

"Thirty days hath September,"

Da, dee, da, dee, da, dee, da.

Eight pints to the gallon, sixteen ounces in a pound. Rods, poles, perches, chains and furlongs. I didn't tax myself too much over these as Mam said that I hadn't to marry a farmer and so would not need them. Apparently, Mam thought that a farmers' wife was simply cheap labour for the farm and I would have to get up very early in the morning. I resolved not to fall in love with a farmer and then I could stay in bed if I wished. We chanted tables over and over. I didn't know why we did it but trusted that the adults knew what they were doing and there must be some future purpose to all this memorising. Twelve inches made a foot and three of these made a yard, not only that but a yard was from the tip of the nose to the tip of thumb when your arm was outstretched. We were exhorted to peruse the patterns on the coins, a wren for the farthing, as this was the smallest coin and our smallest bird. Good old Britannia sitting sturdily on the back of a penny and on them the letters in Latin for, "Defender of the Faith," which was comforting to know. Money was not difficult to learn as it was an everyday item and I had already absorbed its importance. It was large and heavy which made it seem all the more worthy of having. The white five-pound notes were beautiful, large and felt like crisp tissue paper. Another everyday necessity was time, but this proved a little more difficult.

On my Birthday Mary bought me a watch with a slim grey strap. Watches were very expensive, and I was proud to own one and show it to all and sundry.

Aunt Evelyn looked at it and then at Mam,

"Well, you say your Mary hasn't as many brains as June and you just might be right. What was the point in squandering her hard-earned money on that thing until Edna can tell the time?"

"Well if that's the criteria, I won't let her go in the water until she can swim eh?"

Go on Mam you tell her.

Even with my own watch I found this difficult. I eventually devised a mental picture of time as a circle, with January at the bottom, climbing to June at the top and then sliding down to December. This was just something to be got through as a necessity. "Real," maths were pages and pages of sums. I loved adds, take-aways, times and share-bys and when we eventually came to long division, I was sure that I could have given Pythagoras a run for his money. But my greatest pleasure was the lessons in History and Geography. Here there was no confusion and much to be proud of.

We learned the sequence of the Kings and Queens of the United Kingdom and it gave a sense of time and continuity.

We did not have a time for listening to fictional stories, but Annie regaled us with tales of noble people full of

216

daring do. Florence Nightingale was the "Lady with the Lamp;" risking dread disease and bringing succour to the soldiers in the Crimean War. Grace Darling risked her life and rode the waves in her little lifeboat to save sailors. Shackleton risked everything to not get to the Pole. That one really did confuse me as something to admire. They were all British; they did not have feet of clay, they had gone the extra mile and it was good to learn of people who had a certain superhuman something.

Annie also embarked on teaching us the history of Maryport. She taught this with enthusiasm and her pride in the little town was infectious. We learned the names of the docks and made awkward little diagrams of them. We learned that the Romans had had an important camp to defend Maryport from the marauding Scots. We learned that the town had once been called Alauna, until one Lord of Manor had decided to rename the port after his wife Mary. Gee whiz, how romantic. Annie even claimed Fletcher Christian for Maryport, and her reason was that we had Fletcher Street, Christian Street and Bounty Avenue. It sounded logical to me. At no time did it appear to occur to her to take us to actually see these places, all learning was classroom bound. She may have been a tartar, but she certainly tried and, in my case, succeeded in giving us a pride in the little town.

Geography was equally simplistic, certain and in many cases patriotic.

Eskimos lived in cold countries. They built their houses from blocks of ice and called them igloos. They cut holes in the thick ice and sat for ages beside them, fishing for seals and walrus. They had kayaks and harpoons and on a good day they caught whales. They made their clothes from the skins and fat from the whale's blubber. Simple and fascinating.

In Africa there were black people. Some were small and called Pygmies and some were very tall and called Zulu's. They lived in round straw huts and didn't wear very much at all. Simple.

Things got a bit muddled for me when we moved further afield to the Far East and in my mind both the Japanese and the Chinese had small feet and wore Kimonos. The men had pigtails and wore cone shaped straw hats. All of them ate nothing but rice and lived in boats called sampans. Simple. I can still visualise the books that we used which had little ink drawings at the top of the page of igloos or African huts.

There were even some countries that had been empty until we had found them. Australia and New Zealand only began when Captain Cook had happened across them. The same could not be claimed with any comfort of India but Annie cheerfully ignored whatever had been going on before the East India Company set up shop there. India seemed to be our complete opposite, our other half. Unreserved, flamboyant, colourful and so exotic. I thrilled to words like Samarkand, Jaipur,

Kashmir and Shalimar. I rolled them around my mind like delicious sweetmeats and murmured them with reverence.

Once in a moment of boredom I perused the shiny pink map on the classroom wall and was suddenly struck by how very tiny Great Britain looked.

At home I commented on this to Mam.

"Aye that's right Lass. Everywhere is bigger than us, but we're such cheeky beggars, we've given them all a hiding."

I swelled with pride.

Mam may have despised the class system, but she was very patriotic.

CHAPTER 8
"ALL THE WORLD'S A STAGE"

June was sitting sniffling into her hanky.

"Oh, but Mam it was so good, I'll never, never forget it."

"You silly lass. How could it be good if it made you cry like that?"

"But it was Mam. She just fell in love with him and they couldn't do anything about it because they were both married. It's the best film I've ever seen."

"Aye till the next one."

"No, no. This one is the best ever and the music was so, well so lush. I'm going to go to Eliot's' and get the sheet music. I think it said Rachmaninov's Piano Concerto. I even sat long enough to see what the music was. And don't worry I didn't stand for the National Anthem"

Dad looked up,

"That's me lass, but which Rachmaninov Concerto?"

"Whad'yuh mean? Oh, did he write more than one? Trust you to know that. Anyway, I'm going to get it and if I can't play it, then you or our Mary can, and I'll cry all over again."

Mam put her hand on her arm,

"You'll have to stop this June there's enough sadness in the world without going to see it in the films. Just remember, 'laugh and the world laughs with you, cry and you cry alone. For this sad old earth has little of mirth and sorrow enough of its own."

Mary jumped up,

"Oh, give over Mam. It was a good film and even I had a little weep at the end. I just kept wondering why she kept calling him Eric when his name was Alec."

June looked at Mam despairingly,

"Mary, she talked posh. She was saying "Alec," but in a posh voice, so it sounded like Eric. Anyway, I'm going to see it again on Friday night with Tom Ackerley."

"What a waste of money and I'm not too sure of that lad, his eyes are too close together. Edna stop playing with your food. And if you are going again, remember to take a clean hanky to cry into when the music starts" and she slyly nudged June, "If music be the food of love" eh?"

Sometimes Mam's pearls of wisdom were more like chokers.

It was small wonder that June was addicted to the cinema. There were the obvious reasons that she was escaping into a fantasy world and away from the fraught atmosphere at home and of course occasionally buying a bit of dark where she could snuggle in warmth and comfort with her latest beau. But Mam had already set the scene for such a deep interest, as she too loved the cinema. The whole medium fascinated and entranced her and she introduced us to it as soon as she could.

Some evenings she washed her hands and face, flung her coat on and just hurried up Senhouse Street and watched whatever happened to be on that night. She did not seem to have any particular genre as a favourite and occasionally returned home having been terrified by Voodoo zombies or ants radiated to giant proportions. She then kindly shared the terror by slowly wandering after me with her arms outstretched and mumbling creepy noises. She reminisced about someone called Valentino and told of her amazement when she saw her first Talkie. And after reading her large red book of Shakespeare over and over, it had been a revelation to see it acted at the Lonsdale in Carlisle. She laughed until she had to dab her eyes telling us about someone called Charlie Chaplin. These stories left me mystified, as I could not see anything funny in someone being so hungry that he imagined his companion as a chicken or cooked his bootlaces for spaghetti.

Mam said with contempt,

"I don't know why they keep calling them "Silent Films." O.K, there wasn't any spoken dialogue from the screen but there was plenty going on in the cinema. For a start, not everybody could read, so they had to take someone with them who could. In consequence there was a constant noise as the words came up and somebody read them out loud to their neighbour. It could get very annoying to those of us who could read, and it sometimes even drowned out the pianist. Silent my foot."

But there were so many films being churned out at this time, that it was very rare that an older film was repeated and so, many of Mam's favourites remained memories for her and simply stories for me. After reading, it was her favourite form of entertainment and if Mam liked something then everyone had to. My first film was "Bambi," and, though very young I was much struck by the beauty of the scenes and cried and cried all over her when his mother died. Of course, Mam was just as contrary about films as she was about anything else. She did eventually succumb to going to see, "Brief Encounter," but disgusted June by declaring it, "middle class clap trap."

There were two cinemas in Maryport, the Carlton and the Empire. We rarely went to a film at the Carlton even though it was cheaper. It was a beautiful, grandiose building, standing opposite the Town Hall, and had once been the Cumberland and Union Bank. Now it was very shabby as if the owners had lost interest. The Empire, on the other hand had plush red velvet seats which were even more plush upstairs. There were two showings each night and the films changed three times per week, the best being saved for the weekend. Through the week you just went to the pictures, but Friday and Saturday night was more of an event where you dressed up for a "proper," night out.

Soon after moving to Lawson Street, Mam made a stand.

Added to the atmospheres and tensions that Mam could create she occasionally threw in, "a stand."

These were big.

"A stand," was bigger than simply whining for anything and everything to be done for her. "A stand," was bigger than the feigned illnesses. It was bigger than all the slammed doors and drawers for no apparent reason. But at least a stand had the advantage of being a clear demand or command.

I sat miserably on the fender stool trying not to hear and failing.

"I've just about had enough of this. Everybody has a life but me. There's our Mary and June putting on the La la and flying out to dances and you with your Chapel dos and the Town band. Even our Edna goes out to play. But me. What have I got? Eh, what have I got? Nothing. That's what I've got. Nothing but work, work and more work. Well I want a night out. A proper night out. And I want it every week. I've decided we are going to go to the Empire every Friday, you, me and little Edna. At least it will be something to look forward to. You can just get those doctors told that you are finishing early on Fridays. Just you tell them that you have a wife to consider. I get nothing. Other women get nights out and holidays. Me, what do I get? Nothing. I tell you, you ask for nothing in life and that's precisely what you get. Now get those doctors told that the surgery closes early on Fridays."

"I can't do that you daft woman. I don't set the times. And anyway, when am I supposed to eat?"

"Aye that's it, worry about your stomach. Don't worry about me."

"You can go out yourself and you went the other night with your Lizzy. Why make life difficult for me."

"Because I want a proper night out with my husband. Dressing up nicely and going in the best seats. You never take me anywhere. Of course, if you are ashamed of me just say so. Maybe you don't want to be seen in public with your wife. Do I cramp your style? You, blooming well wouldn't have any if it wasn't for me. Think on that. "Just say. Just say if I'm not fit to be taken anywhere.""

Would he dare?

"Oh, for crying out loud, woman, you're the best hand at twisting things."

"Well, things are going to change or I'll..."

"You'll what?"

There was an ominous silence coming from the kitchen, then Dad struck terror into my heart.

"I know what you were going to say, I've heard it plenty times. You'll leave that's what you were going to say. Well, if you don't like it the way things are, you can leave."

Longer silence.

"Well, Alf, you might have heard it plenty times and I've done it plenty times before."
"Aye and you can do it again."

Silence.

"No. I don't think so. You're right. I've done it plenty times. It's your turn. This time you can leave."

I held my breath.

Amazingly they both began laughing. They laughed and laughed, and then Dad went down the yard shaking his head and laughing and laughing.

I was bewildered. I was unaware of their turbulent young married lives. Mam frequently returning to her mothers', with Mary and June until Dad capitulated to whatever she had demanded. I was fortunate to have arrived on the family scene when they were mellowing somewhat.

Whatever Dad had said to the doctors, it transpired that he did begin to return home earlier on Friday evening. Mam's part of the bargain was to have his meal ready on the table as he came in and she stuck to it. Thus, we began going to the Empire cinema every Friday. I was washed and changed and all three of us trooped up to the last house of the pictures. Every Friday. It didn't matter what was showing. It didn't impinge on their thinking that the film may not be suitable for a little girl. That was the arrangement. That was Mam's big night out. They both dressed in their best and Mam entered the cinema armed with a bar of rum and raisin chocolate from Annovazzi's Ice Cream Parlour to set the seal on this special night out. It was fortunate, for Mam, that Dad was so friendly and so respected in the town, as children were not normally allowed into the last house. I was just shuffled past the ticket office while Dad winked at the usherettes.

Now it was my turn to ripple with fear while luscious ladies in diaphanous gowns, had the lifeblood sucked out of them; or Triads, high on opium, ran amok, chopping up everyone in sight.

But Mam had made a stand and won. That was what mattered.

I learned.

The cinema added to my knowledge and enhanced my understanding. It supplemented adult conversations and stories. It contributed to assimilating my own time in history and my own place in geography and fleshed out my school lessons. Now, I could see, instead of imagine, modes of dress, differing architecture and climates. Forever more, Florence Nightingale looked like Flora Robson and the light bulb was invented by Spencer Tracy. Henry VIII *was* Charles Laughton, wrenching the meat from a large leg of pork and throwing it to the dogs around his table. A young Elizabeth 1st looked like Jean Simmons but sadly and rather shockingly ended up looking like Bette Davies. Robert Taylor as Ivanhoe and Errol Flynn as Robin Hood, exhorting his Merrie men to join him in the greensward, enabled me to visualise the period. Cecil B. De Mills films; Nero would forever be Peter Ustinov, weak lipped and fearsome in his power and insanity. And of course, Charton Heston was ... well, anyone biblical or even just anyone being stoical and strong. But I knew just how a Roman soldier would have looked. I knew just how Rome would have been as a thriving city with a packed Coliseum and the lions snarling and racing forward to feed on Victor Mature. I totally confused any films of India with Arabian countries. Howard Keel meeting his Kismet could have been in India. The colours, the architecture, the mode of dress and the manner of speaking were exotic enough to be anywhere in an eastern direction. I fought in India with Kenneth More and repulsed the Chinese with Ava Gardener. Deborah Kerr and I marched through the heat and the dust with Stewart Granger, to find King Solomon's' Mines. And I galloped through France, laughing and slapping my thighs with The Three Musketeers.

It didn't really matter whether Hollywood had tampered with the facts they gave colour and detail to the facts being taught in school.

The programme at the cinema had a definite pattern. It began with a "short." This was usually an information film or a documentary. A cartoon and then the Movietone news followed this.

The Movietone News. Ta ra. "Here come our gallant boys, back from Kwalalumpa. All of Britain gives them a joyous welcome." Ta ra. " Jamaica greets Churchill for a well-earned holiday and a plentiful supply of well-deserved cigars." The air in the cinema froze and someone murmured that they knew where they'd put his free cigars.

"This summers' new look for our ladies is Dior. Tangerine and orange will be the order of the day."

"Hurrah! Stanley Matthews saves the day. And just look at Mike Hawthorne go at Silverstone; even Fangio can't catch him." Ta ra. It was all very jolly; delivered in clipped, precise tones and I couldn't wait for it to finish.

229

As the adverts came up the usherettes moved to the front of the cinema with their ice cream trays strapped around their shoulders. I was volunteered to stand the queue; a tub for Mam and choc-ices for Dad and I. Even the adverts were on the cusp of change. There were scrolls with beautiful cursive writing advertising local shops followed by more sophisticated mini films telling us that Brylcream put life into dry hair or exhorting us to try the new "Drink on a stick." As the lights dimmed the usherettes strolled very slowly up the aisles still selling their drinks on sticks. Then everyone settled down for the big picture.

I was gone. I was clean gone. The Empire faded around me and I entered another world. A strange world where telephones and doorbells were answered immediately. And if they weren't then that was a sure sign that "something" was very wrong in there. Matches shone as much light as a hundred and fifty-watt light bulb. People thrust money into taxi windows, slapped it onto shop counters or bars and never received any change. The slightest cough was a sure sign that something very serious was amiss, usually a terminal illness. The hero could stand any pain until the heroine dabbed him with iodine, whereupon he winced; but nobly. A lady appearing a little faint was a sure sign that before long there was going to be a baby. Of course, the men were delighted and rushed home with flowers then pampered and petted her and placed cushions behind her head. " Bring plenty of hot water," heralded the baby's arrival but

I never quite knew what they did with all that boiling water. No-one ever needed the toilet, which was probably a good job for Deborah Kerr and Stewart Granger in all that heat and dust and not a bush in sight to hide behind. No one ever had a snotty nose, handkerchiefs were for dabbing a genteel tear or to slyly drop and be retrieved by a dashing nobleman. There was no foul language, but the sense was conveyed somehow. I saw what I wanted to see and as much as I understood. I was unable to interpret the sexual innuendoes or implications. A train rushing through tunnel was simply a train rushing through a tunnel and I didn't know why it merited Mam giving Dad a sly nudge.

The weather was very definite. None of this smattering of snow on the pavements. When it snowed on the films, it snowed. Wallop! Huge snowflakes the size of saucers and all neatly piled into three-foot heaps by the side of the road or in the driveways. The Americans were so lucky as they always had the right clothes for just such an eventuality. Lurking somewhere in their houses were beautiful fitted red coats trimmed with white fur on the collar, cuffs and hems; often accompanied by matching muffs. Lakes froze over safely and completely and Lo, the same people had ice skates just waiting. They could all skate very professionally but only until they needed to fall with perfect timing into the arms of the hero.

When it rained, it rained and Mam called it, "Hollywood rain." In America the wind could turn with sudden ferocity into a tornado and Maw could be heard shouting,

"Git them kids in the root cellar, Paw." Most American houses had cellars, and someone was always disappearing to stoke the boiler down there. Most American houses had attics and Americans never threw anything away but kept it in the attic; especially Grandmas wedding dress. This was found in some trunk and viewed with awe and reverence then used for the next wedding whether it was in fashion or not. And of course, the sun always shone for the special day. If the sun shone, no one was sunburned, and they lounged by their own private swimming pool. To be sure America was a perfect place.

Well, except for the, "baddyies" and there were plenty of them in Hollywood. I never quite knew why the F.B.I, needed finger printing or identity parades, I could have told them immediately whodunit. It was fairly obvious to anyone that any man wearing a black shirt and a white tie was up to no good. A woman who was dressed skimpily, sucked on a long cigarette holder and looked through a curtain of peroxide hair was definitely a gangsters' moll and could have fingered the bad guys any day. And if it wasn't their outward appearance it was the actors themselves who gave the game away. Any self-respecting Irish cop should have known that Sydney Greenstreet and Peter Lorre were plotting some nefarious deed. Anyone with a foreign accent, fat men or oriental gentlemen were invariably leading wicked lives. And you just knew that the black man who wasn't a shoeshine boy or the trusted house servant must be, at the very least, assisting the villains. Me? I knew who they were in the first reel.

I somehow knew that there wasn't really a Frankenstein with his monster and so didn't suffer any long-lasting terror, I thought it a shame that creatures from another planet were always portrayed as evil. It would have been nice if just for once they had made that long journey to be friendly and share their knowledge, but some films did leave me having nightmares. One that really affected me was about a "Black Hand Gang". The gang always left a picture of a black hand beside their murdered victim and for some time I woke sweating and worrying that there would be one on my bed. But the worst, the very worst villains of all, were the Germans and Japanese. The recent war was the greatest gift ever given to the film industry and they made full use of it. There was no playing hopscotch with political correctness. They were bad and we were good. Simple. Occasionally and very grudgingly Mam conceded that, "we were on our knees," when the Americans entered the war. But it was more usual to believe that we had paved the way, done all the spadework and all that they had to do was the final mopping up. If anyone was late for anything someone was always heard to say, "Oh, here comes America." It was then quite annoying to watch John Wayne winning the war again and again... and again. Some of them were magnanimous and a British star was thrown in to help, but in the main it was Uncle Sam who had liberated the whole world. Pinewood and Elsetree countered with Jack Hawkins and John Mills sporting their stiff upper lips but they did not have the panache of the American versions. And rather like the puzzlement over the F.B.I, not realising who was the baddy, I was not very sure why we had worried so much about losing the war when we had Richard Todd and Kenneth More to sort things out. These films taught me that Europe was dark and bombed. People did a lot of trudging about with handcarts piled high with their possessions. There were Disney like castles teetering impossibly on high mountains and German soldiers spoke broken English until they needed to shout. "Shnell, shnell," I learned that France caved in immediately and I wasn't very sure where the Italians stood. It was quite clear that Switzerland was a good place and a great relief to get there. Many films ended with the actors beaming at the sight of chalets and Alps. I don't know what happened to them after that, but it was obviously a great relief to step on to Swiss soil.

In some respects, it was all very comfortable and reassuring. We were the good guys and once again we had vanquished the baddies. Oh, there were a few near misses but this only added to the thrill of winning in the final reel.

The cinema left us with no doubts. A man with very blonde hair had to be a German. Red hair was either Scottish or Viking. Any female with a tan could be a Polynesian maiden and in the next film an Indian servant of the God Kali or an Arabian dancing girl. The majority of the actors were type cast and you could rely on Jimmy Stewart to deliver the goods. Oh, Cary Grant gave the occasional murmur of something a little more sinister but came good in the end. And Alec Guinness was, well, just

Alec Guinness in everything he did. There was a slight feeling of disappointment if the big picture was a British film. They lacked the gloss and verve of their American counterparts and we did not particularly want to see life as we knew it. There were occasional forays into educating the cinema going public with Shakespeare and Dickens, but I preferred Victor Mature murdering early Christian history. The British comedies often relied on slapstick, which I found rather embarrassing, or they were heavily laced with innuendoes that I did not understand. No, I definitely enjoyed the more colourful and vibrant films such as "Anchors Aweigh," or "On the Town," even though Mam said that Gene Kelly wasn't a patch on Fred Astaire, he just thought he was.

Occasionally we went as a whole family. This was when the film had opened in London to heavy publicity, then toured the cities and finally reached our little town in the far, far north. By the time it came to Maryport we often already knew the plot or had memorised the songs that had been aired on the radio. There was a ripple of excitement when a long-awaited film was advertised in the local paper and we greedily studied the stills outside the Empire. For these we willingly queued on the windy incline that was Senhouse Street and crossed our fingers that we could get five seats all together. So it was with "The Quiet Man," We queued; way, way past Woollies and somehow managed to sit together even though Dad had to sit behind one of the columns supporting the upstairs, Mam loved Ireland, often wishing that she could one day visit, and she drank in all of the film. As Mary and June had recently had a day trip to Dublin, they assured her that Ireland was just like that. It was a memorable evening. All of us together as a family and ending with fish and chips from Cuetos, setting the seal that this was a special event.

Though there were definite boy's toys and girl's toys, I had a little tin train set and a few Corgi cars but best of all were my guns. One Christmas I received a full cowboy costume with a leather holster and belt. This was far better than drippy dolls and teddies and I often donned the costume and whined for someone to fasten the belt for me. Then it was off to shoot anything and everything. I lurked around the wash house, then with my back flattened against the wall and after some surreptitious peeps around the corner, I leapt out shooting. Of course, I took the occasional hit, but this had to be in the shoulder so that I could live to fight another day. There had to be much staggering about clutching the wounded area and sinking down the wall. Dad, passing down the yard on his way to work shook his head with silent mirth. Most of my toys resided in the big bottom drawer but my best guns lived on the windowsill. There was a very good reason for this. They had to be kept in readiness for Dad saying, "Right get your six shooters, we're going to see a shooty bang shoot film." Resplendent in holster with revolvers slapping at my sides. Dad and I went to the Empire. Mam declined this treat. She generally scorned Westerns saying that it was the only history that America had and even that was just killing people. It didn't diminish our enjoyment; we just went without her. We spent many evenings with Richard Widmark, Gabby Hayes and the daddy of them all, John Wayne. There was nothing better than the wagon train rumbling through the Grand Canyon and an unending line of Red Indians silently appearing along the hills. High Noon, oh, I was there absent-mindedly munching my sweets and sympathising with Gary Cooper's dilemma. Sometimes I got so caught up in the film that my guns just lay on the floor until we left the pictures. Then I whooped my way down the street blasting the odd Apache in Craig's Fancy Goods shop doorway.

Often, I went to the first house with friends. A particular choice was the Tarzan films. It didn't matter whether it was Lex Barker or Johnny Weismuller, it was Tarzan. Cheetah was the comic relief and Jane a minor irritation, but it was worth it when he finally gave his elephant call. I could think of nothing better than being able to summon a thundering herd of elephants to your aid. I left the Empire. I WAS Tarzan and warbled and yodelled my way down the street. For some weeks afterwards, the Comanche and the Arapaho had a rest from defending their buffaloes down our back lane, while I swung on vines, wrestled lions and saved white explorers from the cannibals.

It was understood that there could not be any pictures on a Sunday, that would be too sacrilegious. It was also understood that there were no films at all for one full week, to make way for the Maryport Amatuer Operatic Society.

Mary's face had turned all shades of red.

"Mam."

"What?"

"Mam, come here a minute."

Mam came from the kitchen.

"What now? Surely you can iron them yourself. Oh, my God!"

Mam looked with horror at the butterfly costume with its flesh coloured body stocking that Mary was holding up for her to view.

"You can't wear that revealing thing in public."

"But I can't let them down after all the rehearsals. Mrs Williamson will go mad."

"Never mind Mrs. Williamson, your Dad will go even madder. Try it with the wings on and see if they cover anything."

Mary pulled on the costume, attached the wings to her shoulders and looped the wafting chiffon to her middle finger.

"What do you think?"

"Not much better, but you can't see, well, anything definite. Jump about a bit."

Mary obliged around the ironing table.

"Mam, Dad'll not let me go on like this, you know he won't."

Mam thought for a minute.

"Look lass, what the eye doesn't see. Just iron the thing and say nothing."

"Oh, very funny, he'll blooming well see it when he comes to the Empire."

"Aye well, the deed will be done by then. He can hardly drag you off the stage, can he?"

The deed was done. Dad viewed his eldest daughter prancing about the stage for all Maryport to see and later took her aside.

"Mind that was a bonny carry on wasn't it? All I can say is, it was a good job your Mam didn't know beforehand or there would have been no Operatics for you this year. I'll do what I can to square it for you. O.K?"

Mary looked suitably grateful.

Year after year the Empire ceased being a cinema and became a theatre. The "upstairs," became the "Upper Circle" and the screen disappeared to reveal a stage. Marlon Brando and Montgomery Clift were given the heave ho and a live light operatic show appeared. Somehow the little town produced an orchestra, chorus, dancers, comedians and leads singers. Maryport Amateur Operatics was high date in the social calendar. Broadway eat your heart out.

"The New Moon," "The Vagabond King," "The Desert Song," "The Merry Widow," each year a new delight. Costumes, lights, music and action but this time for real. There was the added interest of knowing the actors and singers and trying to recognise them in their costumes and heavy stage make up. There was also the added interest of the occasional whiff of scandal if the current hero and heroine showed more than a theatrical passion for each other.

Mrs. Williamson stopped serving in her husband's newspaper shop and became a choreographer. Wilf Brinicombe hurried from his Gents. Outfitters to conduct the orchestra and the local undertaker turned into the comedian. They all gave of their time willingly and voluntarily and introduced many to live theatre, drama, comedy and music.

Mam said that it wasn't worth going on Monday evening as this was only a glorified dress rehearsal.

But each, "first," night she flung her coat on, hurried to sneak in and watch her two daughters strutting their stuff as dancers and then, after a quick costume change, swelling the chorus line. Mam said it wasn't worth going on Saturday night as that was the last night and at the end of the show, you had to sit through various speeches, and everyone being presented with their bouquets. But each Saturday night Mam flung her coat on, hurried to sneak in and watch her two daughters receiving the bouquets that she had ordered earlier in the week. No, the night to go, according to Mam was Friday night. By then the orchestra had stopped scratching and squawking and played more as a team. All of the amateurs were sure of their lines, positions and dance routines. And so, Dad was instructed to get three tickets for the best seats in the Upper Circle for Friday evening. This time she didn't just fling a coat on but had her hair done at a proper Hairdresser and wore her best costume while I agonised in the Shirley Temple dress and singed ears.

The foyer was a whirl of Maryport "Society," buying programmes and making small talk It was quite a feat to get Dad to his seat in time for curtain up. However long the show was on, it didn't begin for me until I had spotted Mary and June. I was so proud of them and followed their every move. I wanted to tell the whole theatre that they were my sisters. And of course, there was Cousin Gwen.

Gwen was quite a leading light in the Operatics, not only having a good singing voice but proved a very good

241

comedienne. Mam grudgingly swallowed the rather unpalatable truth that one of her in laws was also one of the leads each year. The intermission was more time to mingle.

Aunty Emily and Uncle Eph came across.

"I reckon this year's is about the best yet, don't you think?"

"Oh, undoubtedly." Mam minced.

"Aye, our Gwenie is just about bringing the house down and your Mary's a grand dancer, very lish."

With spurious charm Mam said,

"I believe Angus has now emigrated to America."

I dedicated myself to my choc-ice and wondered why Mam felt that she had to mention their bombast of a son. Angus had not only left behind a wife and five children but also a variety of scandals. Quite unabashed Aunty Emily laughed and said,

"Aye, he's got himself away and nut doin see bad as far as we know. Me and Eph are keeping an eye on May and the little ones. Mind you when he told me he was goin, I said to him 'Angus if you think yer gitting away from the heat, yer nut, cos you're teckin yer trouble in yer trousers."

Mam nearly swallowed her ice cream whole as they returned to their seats for the next part of the grand performance.

We were thrilled if there was an encore. At the very end we clapped and clapped our hands until they tingled, and the lights went up to reveal that we were still only in the Empire. However tired, I stayed up that night until Mary and June came home. They banged around the door with entrancing apprehension.

"Mam. Mam. What did you think? Good eh?"

On this special evening of the year Mam always laid out what she called, "a cold collation" and as she carefully lifted the cloth that was covering it, she shrugged.

"Aw, come on Mam."

I sat up at the table fascinated by their faces. Not only were they aglow with the exhilaration of the show but were still wearing their heavy, heavy make-up. Deep tan foundation, cheeks violently rouged red, deep purple coloured their eyelids and a large black spot at each end of their eyes. It was Mary and June in glorious technicolour.

"Aye well, it wasn't so bad. June use your serviette, you know how you drip."

243

"Not so bad? You know it was good. I thought they were never going to let us off the stage. And did you hear the applause for the Riff song?" And together they chewed their cold collation and hummed, "Daaah. Da, dee da, dee da, dee da dee da."

"Give over now at the table. That Sheikh's desert might be waiting but so is your bed, there's been enough excitement for one night. June watch that teapot; your cup might runneth over tonight but not on my tablecloth. And don't forget to cream that muck off your faces before it gets on my pillowcases."

She couldn't, she just couldn't praise them.

Mary eased off her spiked high heels,

"What a show, but I'm glad to get those off. My feet are killing me."

"Mary I've told you and told you. Ill-fitting shoes show on your face."

How anything could show on those make up caked faces I wasn't very sure.

Dad, chewing on his cold Cumberland sausage and rough carved ham said,

"Your Uncle Eph said you were very good."

"Hmm. But your Auntie Emily rather spoiled it by being crude about Angus," and she told the tale. June looked embarrassed but Mary said laughing,

"If I'd been his wife, I'd have taken the carving knife to bed with me."

"Mary! You're as bad as Emily. And I've told you before; people mustn't laugh at their own jokes."

"Why not, it's the first time I've heard it?" At that, we were all laughing.

When Monday dawned, the films came back on the Empire and though we were devotees, the cinema just wasn't the same as the theatre. The town talked of the show for some time afterwards, then interest sank and Mary and June eagerly awaited rehearsals to begin for the next year's performance. I marvelled at their enthusiasm and pleasure in participating. They were my sisters, but I could not summon the same relish for public acclaim.

There was no escape. My loving family trustingly delivered me into the hands of State education and then was delighted with the reward of seeing their little gem starring in each school production. Annie the Hun continued to torment by devious means. She not only produced seasonal school concerts but also repeated them in the evenings with a small charge for charity. If I'd ever met Charity and her growing bank balance at my emotional expense, I'd have blasted her with my silver six shooters or summoned my herd of African elephants.

"Right. Jonty and Frank. You are to be the chief gnomes."

I stifled a snigger.

"Tanis, Ann, Pam, Brenda, Miriam and Eileen, you will be the fairies."

My face was going purple with the effort of keeping it straight and my feet shuffled ready to go out to play.

"Oh, and Edna Croft, you will be a fairy. Ask your mother to look out your tutu."

Purple rapidly drained to ashen.

Valuable lunchtimes were lost rehearsing in the cold school hall so that Cochis and his tribe were able to roam Camp Road without restraint. Desperados blasted their way out of the Last Chance Saloon and held up the Coop Divvy queue, while cannibals heated a big black pot and feasted on missionaries down on Maryport Prom. The Cavalry was too busy treading the boards in tutus and Tarzan was preparing for another school smash hit. It was all very worrying.

Even moving through the school and on to other class teachers did not save me from the doom of Annie's concerts. Now and then names were read out.

"The children whose names are called have to go to Annie Robinson's room at lunch time."

I was a gypsy, a pirate, a Snow Queen and a hand maiden to Pharaoh, but mainly a fairy prancing through paper fluttering leaves in the ignominious blooming tutu. And my doting family appeared to have some silent conspiracy to hasten my death by public ignominy.

From somewhere Mam produced large yellow melons. She scooped out the seeds and gushed water over them in the colander. When the jelly stuff around them had slithered down the plughole she placed them on a tray in the oven to dry. Later that evening while she sewed strips of raffia to an elaborate waistband, Mary and June were given the unenviable task of stringing the tiny seeds on thick thread to make anklets, bracelets, and necklaces. Crepe paper was fashioned into garlands of flowers and lo, I was the best-dressed Hawaiian hula dancer in Cumberland. Granted the most surly, but efforts were made to camouflage this with liquid coffee.

Oh, the excruciating embarrassment of prancing about on that stage and the jangling worry of being in the wrong place at the wrong time. Even worse, my whole family always, but always, came. They clapped and cheered as if Vivian Leigh had walked on the stage. Oh great. As if I hadn't enough to think about, there they were being wonderful for me.

One year I was accorded the honour of being chosen as Mary in the Nativity play. After sitting dressed in blue in the school performances Annie decided that this particular performance was suitable to cheer the sick and dying in the Victoria Cottage Hospital. Nice idea, but pretty nerve wracking for the mother of Jesus.

Disorganised as usual, Mam decided that I had to wear my new grey serge coat with matching soup bowl hat to walk to the hospital. June chaffed at the time being lost in primping and preening.

"Mam it doesn't matter. She's going to change as soon as we get there."

"I'm not having my baby looking like a trollop when she arrives. She has the lead role and she's going to look like it. And anyway, it helps your nerves when you look your best. "Screw your courage to the sticking place and we will not fail," remember that pettle."

We were late and Annie was smouldering with fury. Mam blanked the tyrant.

All of the others were changed and waiting in line in the corridor to enter the ward. Annie grabbed my grey serge shoulder and rammed me at the front of the line hissing,

"I refuse to waste any more time. Get on as you are, you silly little girl."

I solemnly leaned on Joseph's arm and slowly walked onto the make-shift stage. I stared miserably at the doll in the crib as Annie apologised for the delay to the bedridden and walking wounded. She traitorously pointed and named me as the cause and I wished that the shining floor would open up and swallow me, plus grey hat and coat. Being centre stage and one of the major players was bad enough but the elastic from the hat was slicing into my neck while it nid,-nodded on my head. A case of Hail Mary full of greys.

Afterwards June hugged me and said that I had been a little trooper. Annie almost felled me with a look and Mam had disappeared to bestow succour to the sick.

Just as I was recovering from learning lines for this or that it seemed that Annie came up with something else. I was mortified to be told that she had entered me for the Workington Speech and Drama Festival. More break times were sacrificed while I stood at the back of Annie's class and spouted memorised lines. She had chosen a piece from Pilgrims' Progress. I hardly understood what I was required to learn and had some difficulty getting my mouth around the words. Mam made me a purple velvet dress and crochet a white collar and cuffs for it. My hair was brushed and plaited and I really should have been wearing brown knickers. I sat alone on the bus with

Annie and at least understood the Slough of Despond and the Forest of Despair.

I'm not sure where the Festival was held in Workington, but it seemed like a cinema with the lights up and very little audience. I had to stand in the wings while others stood on the stage and recited their pieces with efficiency and flair. When it came to my turn it was useful that Annie pushed me onto a white cross drawn on the boards, but I felt very alone and vulnerable. My beloved family was not there. It was an Annie Robinson thing. Somehow, I said my piece. I don't remember coming off the stage, but Annie said that I had, "acquitted myself reasonably."

Praise indeed.

Mam cut my picture out of the local paper and put it in the big family Bible.

"There you are. Pet. "All the Worlds' a stage and we are merely players on't."

She had a wonderful penchant for the dramatic. She pushed and shoved the three of us towards it but would never have gone on't stage herself.

CHAPTER 9
"I HAVE THEE NOT AND YET I STILL SEE THEE"

Mam grabbed my arm and yanked me after her.

"Just going up to our Lizzie's. Mother" she called back down the lobby.

My little legs plaited as she dragged me along the street, and we burst round Aunty Lizzie's door.

"You'd better come and look at Father." Mam held a stricken hand to her forehead.

"Oh, dear God Edna. What now?"

"Come back with me Lizzie. There's something wrong with him."

""I can't. I've old Mrs. Armstrong coming for her dinner, surely you can manage. Honestly, you and your dramatics."

Mam looked suitably miffed.

"I'll give you dramatics. You could take the time to come and have a look, it's only down the street."

"Alright, what happened?"

"Well, I was pegging out the washing in the back lane when he came down from the hen-pens. Just as he got to the back door, he leaned against it and he looked funny. I put out my arm to him but you know what he's like, he just brushed me away saying, "get away with you woman," then he stumbled into the house and went to lie down in the front room."

"So? Edna he's eighty-four, maybe he was tired."

"No, wait. I went after him to see if he was O.K. and he asked me to go down to the corner shop and bring him a pint of porter".

Aunty Lizzie looked up sharply.

"Give over, he wouldn't ask a woman to do that".

"For crying out. Lizzie, I'm telling you he did. Well, I went down and got it and mightily embarrassed I was; like I said it was for Father and he wasn't well, so that didn't make it as bad. But when I came back, he'd gone to sleep so I just put it on the table by the sofa."

"Where's Mother?"

"Mother? Oh, she's in the kitchen making his dinner. He didn't look right to me Lizzie."

Aunty Lizzie stubbed out her cigarette.

"Bill, away up to Mrs. Armstrong's and tell her not to come today, something's up."

Uncle Bill Musgrave shrugged his shoulders and said nothing as usual, but he put his flat cap on and went out of the front door as we hurried out of the back.

The three of us trooped into Mother's front room and Aunty Lizzie leaned over Father. He lay looking towards the wall with his arm flung carelessly down his side. She straightened up.

"My God, Edna, he's dead. Didn't you know he was dead?"

Mam looked miserable.

"Well, I knew he looked funny."

"Does Mother know?"

"She's still in the kitchen."

There was silence while Aunty Lizzie thought.

"Look, I'll make him look more comfortable. One of us will have to tell her, then you go over and get your Alf to send the doctor over to do a certificate. And leave that little lass somewhere, she shouldn't be among all this."

"You sort him Lizzie, you've had plenty practice laying folk out. I'll go and tell Mother and your right I'll away to get Alf after that."

She was still holding my arm and drew me with her towards the little kitchen.

"Mother. Mother. I think Fathers' dead."

Mother looked up from the plate.

"He can't be Lass, he hasn't had his dinner."

Mam let go of me and gently pulled the old lady towards the front room.

Mother just stood in the doorway looking at the big man and said softly,

"Johnny. Johnny. Oh, my Johnny."

No-one had ever heard her call him such a pet name and in that unguarded moment she revealed her great love for him.

She had met him when she was thirteen, had their first child when she was fifteen and eventually run away to Scotland to marry him. Somehow, they had stayed together. She could not go to the funeral. She did not parade her grief; she did not express her devastation in any manner. She simply lived on.

The Tuke funerals had their own peculiar pattern. There was the chapel service, the long drive to the wind-blown cemetery outside the town. There was a tongue and ham tea and then they all fell out. Eventually the men repaired to the Station Inn while the women vowed never to speak to each other again. Mam came home and wailed that our Sydney had said this or that to her. And Aunt Evelyn had come for the look of it, but she had hated the man and if she'd found him in a gutter begging for water, she'd have kicked him and walked on.

"And as for our Lizzie. Said I was a drama queen. I'll give her drama queen. I was right, wasn't I?"

It seemed quite satisfying that her father had died to prove her right.

Dad listened, knowing that it would all calm down and before long they would all be trooping up the long yard at Lawson Street looking for freshly brewed tea.

"Walter Carter was down here before."

"Walter Carter? What did he want?"

"Well, being the local scribe he though a bit should be in the paper about Father."

"Oh, very nice."

255

"On Monday the Rev. K. Crane officiated at the funeral, at which there was a large attendance, of Mr. John Tuke aged 84 of Collins Terrace, Grasslot. Mr. Tuke was, in many ways a remarkable man.

"In times of war he put the integrity and safety of his country first; in times of peace, he was an advanced Left Wing Socialist and few living in Cumberland today have given such long service to the Labour Party and Trade Union Movement.

"His military record was excellent. Six feet tall, strong and active, he served in the Black Watch and in the Boer War. He was then living in Distington, though his family originally came from County Wicklow in Ireland. He went right through the Boer War, was besieged at Ladysmith and always maintained that the hardships and privations of that campaign were the worst that he had ever experienced.

"In 1914 -18, when he learned that two of his older sons John (killed in 1917) and Ben, had joined the Army, he reported immediately to the Black Watch depot and was in France with a section of that regiment three days later. Another son, George, was the fourth member of the family to serve in that war. Sidney joined the Army, subsequently serving in India, Singapore and China.

"By occupation, he began as a miner part time at the age of nine and full time when he was eleven. Then he turned to soldiering and was later a metal worker and a sailor and finally a miner again. He retired 21 years ago. In sport, walking was his strong point. One of his biggest successes was to leave Ellenborough Colliery after a hard shift in a wet seam, walk six miles to Workington, then win a three-mile walking contest and walk back home to Grasslot.

"It was however in politics that he is best known in Cumberland. He spoke from the same platform of Keir Hardy in his younger days. He was one of those instrumental in introducing Robert Blatchford, Bruce Glacier and other Labour speakers to Cumbrian audiences. He was one of the right-hand men of Robert Smillie when he fought the old Cockermouth Division for Labour.

"Mr Tuke carried the marks for years when they were stoned out of Maryport in the

Smillie campaign, for then Labour was a most unpopular party.

"He was the first man to be approached to stand for Workington Division for Labour. He declined and the mantle fell to the late Mr. Tom Cape who won the 1918 election with Mr Tuke as one of his most active supporters.

"Mr. Tuke was largely self-taught but he was exceptionally well read, a good conversationalist and a man who many people liked, even though they may have disagreed with his politics. He was an upright man of strong principles. He had the fullest respect for the strong religious views of his wife and others. He abhorred foul language and vulgarity. He held the view often expressed in the mine or Inn that it was a sign of ignorance for anyone to swear when they had language as strong as the English language.

"In addition to Mrs. Tuke who is also 84 and in good health for her age, he is survived by a family of seven. The sons mentioned earlier and four daughters, Mrs Tuke of Manchester, Mrs. Crellin of Barnsley, Mrs. Musgrave and Mrs. Croft of Maryport."

They sat in our living room while Uncle Sydney read it out.

"Aye. A fine obituary." Mam sighed.

"Fine indeed," said Aunty Lizzie.

"Well, you may all be struggling with your loyalty, but I am not. He gave us all a life of Hell and you know it. "Man of principle." Never marry a man of principle, that's what I say after living with him. They say every man has a mistress of some sort and politics was his. Where were we while he was promoting the Labour Party? And what did it get us? There's poor Mother; never known what it is to have a hot water tap in a house and still ending her days in a pit cottage."

"Oh, Evelyn give it a rest. The man's hardly cold in his grave. What's the point in reaping things up now? He did do some good things for Cumberland even if he was a hard man."

"Hard? He was a blooming woman hater if you ask me. I can't remember him doing one nice thing with me. He never took me to the shore, never gave me a gift, never even gave me his time. He did give me a few good hidings and when he was around, I knew what it was to be cold and hungry. He took himself off to war and left us with nothing. Then Mother started selling her baking and before long we'd that little shop in Distington. What happened when he came back? Got drunk and hammered the Vicar. There we were, sneaking out of the village that night to start all over again with nothing. But there was always money for drink. I'll not forget, I'm telling you."

259

"Dear God, Evelyn. You know well enough he'd deserted to run away to marry Mother and the only way to clear his name was to join up again. Mother was having our Sydney and begged him not to go but the man was sick of being on the run. And you know that the Army had been sending money to the Vicar to give to Mother and the old beggar hadn't handed over one penny."

"I know, I know, but there was other ways he could have handled it. The only time we were all right was when he was away. How Mother stayed with him is a miracle. Go on. Go on. You tell me one nice tender tale about him."

I waited in the silence with the others.

A fine man. A fine upstanding man. They respected his capacity for hard work. They admired his political views and supported his drive to attain socialism but love? No. That emotion was never voiced or even intimated. He was simply their father, a stern man whose home was for his comfort and not theirs.

Mam stroked the back of her hand.

"You know, I thought our June the prettiest baby ever and when I took her over to Collins Terrace, I put her on his knee and said, "Just look what a pretty face she has Father." He didn't even lower his paper he just said," If you don't move her, she'll fall off and her face won't be so pretty then will it?"

"See. Those are about the only sort of stories we can tell of him."

"What's the story about Ireland? Can't say I know that?"

"Course you do Malcolm. Surely our Evelyn's told you that?"

"Maybe I have done at some time and he's forgotten, it doesn't matter, it never did any of us any good. In fact, I always think it harmed us thinking we were from aristocracy."

"How come?"

"We all thought we were something better. We weren't happy to be servile."

"Just tell the tale."

"It isn't a tale it's true. His father was one of three brothers. Their father built ships and they had a mansion in the Vale of Avoca. He was sent to Trinity College Dublin, and while he was there his father died. The other two brothers argued over the inheritance and one killed the other. The mother rapidly got him away on one of their ships to America and he changed his name to Dempsey. Meaning that we are also related to the boxer Jack Dempsey"

"Get away!"

"Shut up Malcolm and let your mother finish."

"Our Grandfather had little interest in the estate and he too fled to England. While living in Yorkshire he became a miner and met and married a widow called Mary Brown who had one son called Willie. Together they produced three more sons and two daughters. Father once said that they had scraped the money together to return to Ireland to see his mother. He was proud that he was now doing well and wanted his mother to see his family. When they arrived at the big house his mother had been so horrified that he had married an Englishwoman that she would not allow them even over the steps. She had said that she could not forgive him for leaving her and his two sisters to manage the estate and she would neither look nor speak to his children. That night they had slept in a barn in the grounds of the house. The next morning, they resolved to try again, hoping for reconciliation. It was a very hot day and Father said that they had washed in what he called a little burn. The door of the house remained closed to them and they all had to trail sadly away. Father said that he could remember how overgrown the drive was and as he looked back, he could see the two sisters sitting in the long grass with parasols. It seemed that, unused to physical or menial work, the three women tried to live as they had always lived, while the house deteriorated around them and the unmown grass grew taller, than themselves. Father called it 'the crumbling pineapple.' I don't think it was called that, he

262

just meant it had been something as exotic as a pineapple but wasn't anymore. And that's our past in Ireland. "

"And Father never went back?"

"Oh, him. He was too busy squandering money on drink. Then he would come home and bang three times on the door and shout, "I've just returned from Paris." We knew then what state he was in and we all scattered. It was either that or a good hammering for the first one that he could get hold of. I've slept on more neighbours' floors than I can remember. And don't tell me that just because he's dead that you've forgotten either."

"You can't speak ill of the dead Evelyn."

"Can't I? I've just done it."

"Mother said he never touched a drop until after the Boer War."

"Aye, well. He made up for it after that, well and truly," laughed Uncle Sydney.

"You've no room to talk. All his shenanigans didn't put you off it like the women of the family."

"Now Lizzie, you know there's a very good reason for that. Being down the pit sweats all the salt out of you and water won't put it back but beer does. All of us lads started down the pit, so we had to drink beer."

Uncle Jack lazily pulled on his pipe and suggested that the men repair to the British Legion and replace salt in memory of the old man.

I sat on the fender stool and remembered Father. I wasn't sad. No one around me was sad. A very tall imposing man, serious and scary. He had allowed me to help stir crowdy that he made in a big tub for his hens. The hot yellow liquid was carried in buckets up to the allotments by the pit bank. While he poured it into shallow troughs, I went into the hen pens to search for eggs. I gingerly lifted them warm in my hands and carried them to put in a basket to take home. I sensed the smell of the crowdy and the hen-pens and remembered Father. I guessed that he had just got old and died. I guessed that now he would become a sepia photograph.

"Well, Evelyn, there's just you and me and little Edna here. Do you fancy going to the pictures?"

"We can't do that the night of our father's funeral, Edna, what will people think? No, I tell you what, there's a service on at the little Spiritualist Hall we'll go to that and have a laugh."

"Now Evelyn, you know I don't hold with that sort of thing, but I do feel like doing something so, 'give me my robe, put on my crown, I have immortal longings in me', as the Bard says."

"You and that Bard. Are you going in that coat? Never mind it will be dark soon and no one will see you."

We walked up Church Street and into the Hall. It was very full, but we found three seats near the front.

A man holding on to a tall lectern was well into his stride passing messages from, "the other side," and we listened with interest.

"I have a Maggie here with a message."

Aunt Evelyn leaned and murmured in Mam's ear.

"The other side must be full of Maggie's. He's bound to be on a winner with a name like that."

"Shh."

A woman at the back put up her hand and claimed Maggie for her sister.

"Maggie is worried about you and says that you have to look after your health."

The woman at the back looked grateful and began to quietly cry.

"Anybody could have said that. He's not very good."

"Shut up Evelyn. It was you who wanted to come."

The man at the front suddenly put his head into his hands and began to breathe deeply. I watched fascinated.

He looked up rather wildly,

"There's a John coming through. Does anyone know a John?"

Aunt Evelyn rolled her eyes,

"There must be a John in every family."

She was right, as most of the congregation put up their hands.

The man did not respond but breathed deeply again and then said,

"Does anyone know a John from Paris."

Now we looked around with interest. Fancy knowing someone from Paris.

No one claimed him. The man was struggling.

Then he said,

"Does this help?" and he banged loudly, three times on his lectern.

Mam went white and Aunt Evelyn tentatively raised her hand.

"He says you have to look after Mary and tell her that he is well and happy."

Aunt Evelyn nodded dumbly and gathered up her coat. We fled home.

Back in the house they looked at each other.

"I told you; you hadn't to speak ill of the dead Evelyn. Now look what's happened."

"How the hangment was I to know. I got such a shock I nearly joined the old goat on the other side. I'm not telling Mother. You can."

"I think we'd better ...he did send the message for her after all. Eeh, wasn't that queer? I tell you 'There's more in heaven and earth than is dreamed of in your philosophy Horatio.'"

"Oh, I never heard him mentioned Nelson."

CHAPTER 10
"POOR TOM'S A COLD"

Mother Tuke lived on.

Sometimes she stood on her front step watching the children playing on the Green and sometimes she sat by the window of the front room with the net curtain drawn back, watching the world go by. She lived on, surrounded by her family, her furniture and her memories.

Mam had tentatively given her the message from, "the other side," and Mother had smiled a slow smile. Then she wandered into the front room and opened the door of her china cabinet. She took out Fathers' numerous medals for bravery and gallantry and tenderly stroked them with her old fingers. Her large, expressive, brown eyes had a wistful, far-away look and everyone worried about her living alone in her decaying house.

"That's it, Alf I've decided. Mother is coming to live with us. It's not right her being there by herself at her age and with Mary at College our Edna can get in with June. Mother can have Edna's room."

My room? What a cheek.

"You know how independent the old lady is. She'll not leave that house now. Why bother her. And anyway, our

Mary comes home for the holidays, what then? And she's not going to be at College forever."

"We'll manage somehow, and I've thought about it. As our Mary comes home June will be going to College so there will still be room. No, my mind is made up."

I vaguely wondered if June knew that her future was already planned.

Mam and I marched over to Grasslot to give Mother the joyous news.

Mother protested while Mam packed Robin's old National Service suitcase for her.

She stayed three days and on the fourth day Mam had to concede defeat and take the unhappy old woman home. Mam was enraged. She was incensed by this ingratitude. She was seething that she could not dictate to her mother. She was baffled that all her ministrations had not resulted in her mother living with us permanently instead of any other members of her family. That would have been glory indeed. We listened to all that she had done to make Mother happy, all the sacrifices she had made and was prepared to make. Sacrifices? It seemed to me that it was Mary, June and I that were the ones that would have made the sacrifices. I may have loved Mother Tuke to the point of adoration, but the house had a temporary, artificial air while she stayed and now, I was pleased to have my own room back. Mam did not try again and as

269

Mother never again left her own house, the walking over to Grasslot resumed.

Mothers' was a coarse house that refused to look good however much it was cleaned and decorated. Maybe the end houses being bombed contributed to its weakened state. Doors and windows did not fit properly; they rattled in their frames and allowed the dust in from the Green. Though she was in her eighties. Mother kept it neat and tidy and her children made sure that it was clean. But in the morning, silver fish darted, and the occasional cockroach trundled across the lino. Her old cat, Darkie, wearily watched as mice skittered across his paws and Mother laughed and laughed at his uselessness. The walls were almost covered in pictures. Deer majestically striding Scottish mountains and cows wading at the edge of lochs were a favourite. There was a framed picture of laburnums and under the flowers were the words, "To greater things some men aspire but this would be my hearts-desire." Another wooden plaque had the words burned into it; "Keep your temper. Nobody wants it." Obviously, Mam has missed reading that one.

Mother was very proud of the contents of her china cabinet. There were small, pale Goss ornaments with the coats of arms of towns that she had never visited. A little Welsh lady whose apron turned pink when it was going to rain. A small wooden chalet with a man and woman at each side. Mother told me that this was Robin and Janet. Sadly, they never met as Robin only came out when it rained, and Janet only came out when the sun was shining. There were Willow pattern plates and Mother recited the story of the lovers that turned into birds and flew away. She pinged her bone china tea service, to prove that it was bone china that she had paid for weekly but never used. Against another wall was her harmonium. This had to be pumped by foot before it wheezed a note, and everybody had pedalled it into life at some point whether they could play or not. Mother laughed and laughed at their attempts and polished it with reverence but never played it. After Father died, the horse-hair sofa was sold, and Mother's bed was brought downstairs and placed in the front room with all her treasures.

It was the living room that was the hub of the house. It had a coarse wooden dining room suite and a three-piece suite somehow squashed into it.

Aunty Lizzie eased herself down onto one of the upright dining room chairs.

"I wonder how long it will be before one of us can sit on Fathers' comfortable chair?"

"It's a wonder our Evelyn didn't chop it up."

"Shush, don't let Mother hear you. Eeh, but Evelyn can be a trial. I went up street with her this morning and stopped to talk to a neighbour. As we walked away, I commented what a nice little body she was, and do you know what Evelyn said? She said, ' She might be nice, but her face is a wrinkled as tripe.' Then when I said that the poor woman couldn't help her face, she said that she could have stopped at home and given us all a break."

Mam could hardly breathe for laughing.

"Oh, Lizzie I know she's got a tongue on her but it's the way she says things. The other day we met old Mr. Shimmings as he was going up the allotments and Evelyn stood stock-still and said that his face looked as if someone had stood on it to wind the clock up. I wouldn't care she's no oil painting herself for all the creams that she slaps on her face. Mind I do envy her slim figure. In fact, when I was in the Coop, the other day, buying Mother her ten Capstan, I was tempted myself cos there was an advert saying that Kensitas helped you slim."

"Oh, give over Edna, everyone knows that when you are over forty you go stout. "Well, every normal woman does. Trust Evelyn to be the exception. It's the Change that does it. I tell you, you suffer the Curse and when that's gone you get these funny turns and go stout. There's no justice."

Mother came through from her afternoon sleep.

"Anybody for a game of Whist?"

"Aye. I'll make us a cup of tea and have a quick hand with you before I go to make Bill's tea."

"And bring a bit of that nice rhubarb pie back with you."

"Mother you are no help. I'm just telling Lizzie how fat I feel."

Mother expertly flicked out the cards.

"Edna, do you feel well?"

"Much better since those operations."

"Well, then, go out and buy some bigger clothes."

Aunty Lizzie came back through with the tea and pie. Mam made my cards into a fan and I struggled to hold them.

"Talking about fat. As old Mrs. Wilkinson squeezed her bulk around the Doctors surgery door yesterday he said,' Mrs. Wilkinson you are not fat, you are obese. You are digging your grave with your teeth,' and she wheezed and laughed and said, ' Dr if you follows me up to Annovazzis Ice Cream Parlour, after this; you'll see me take the biggest shovelful out of me grave".

Mother dabbed her laughing eyes as the front door burst open and Uncle George came up the lobby calling,

"In came the King laughing and dancing."

"He's in a good mood today. Sometimes it's easier when he's sober and miserable."

"Stoppit you two" said Mother as her precious son came around the curtain that made the entrance to the living room.

"I see Phil the Greek might be coming up here."

"George, careless talk costs lives."

"I live in a country of free speech and I am merely exercising my right. And anyway, he is Greek. If Mountbatten had his way it wouldn't be the House of Windsor, but it would be the House of Mountbatten. I bet that's what he was hoping for when they married the young lass off."

"Don't talk piffle George. They can't change back to a German name, they've only just got the English one."

"Aye and that was only because they were terrified of the Russian Revolution being repeated over here and spoiling their way of life. I tell you, they don't make any changes willingly and they do nothing for the likes of us. Apart from taking our money. That young Elizabeth has already given us two other mouths to feed, let's hope she stops at that."

Aunt Lizzie got up and put her coat on.

"You can finish my hand of cards, I've to go and make Bills' tea. I don't mind her, just she seems a bit serious and stodgy."

"You're all a load of sheep. Baa. Baa. You say whatever the newspapers tell you. "Next you'll be saying they do a good job. What job? I'd like to go to Ascot and Africa. I'd do that job."

Mam shrugged,

"They are saying, now that things are getting better, that it will bring people here for their holidays; you know Americans to see the changing of the guard. They like that sort of thing."

"What a load of balderdash. Are you telling me that if you had the chance to go to America or France you wouldn't because they hadn't a Royal family? People just go on holiday."

I was bored. I placed my cards on the table and told them that I was going out to play.

"Don't go near those end houses or the factories."

Me? Go to the bombed houses, never.

Little liar.

There were so many attractive places to explore in Grasslot. Most of them were actually banned but you couldn't ignore them, as they were so interesting. The Germans had come over to bomb the Naval Armament depot and had miscalculated disgracefully and dropped their deadly loads quite some miles short of their target. The end houses stood drunkenly with some of the walls wrenched clean away. They reminded me of my dolls house when the front was open, showing both upstairs and downstairs. Wallpaper that had once been lovingly pasted on the walls now hung flapping in the wind. The small upstairs fireplaces teetered away from the hearth walls, threatening to crash downwards. Floorboards splintered inwards and occasionally the wind moved beams until they shattered down among the bricks, filling the living areas. Adults just could not see that it was a veritable treasure trove to play in. There were so many children in the area that there was always someone mooching about willing to play, though I preferred my best, Grasslot friend, Betty.

We scrambled into the bombed houses and settled down to make shops. Among the rubble was shattered glass and crockery and we made numerous cakes and pies. Patting the muck into old saucers we decorated them with sharp, shards of coloured glass and pottery. These were laid out and friends were invited to buy. The buying part was boring; it was the hunting for the right colours and the designing that was intriguing.

Of course, there was the added frisson that a roof slate may just slither downwards and slice someone's head off.

If we heard an adult calling,

"Are you lot in there?" there was much scrambling over the bricks and rubble to escape before detection.

When the pie making palled, a good expedition was to cross the Green and make our way up a hard, narrow, black trodden path, past the allotments. This brought us out where the old Gussler pit had been. All that was left was the pit bank and large concrete squares, walling off the pit shafts. The banks were by now covered with coarse grass and were good for rolling down.

"Come on. Bet you can't."

"Corse I can."

"Go on Betty, you first." And we climbed the concrete walls surrounding the pit wells. I only ever managed to sit with my legs dangling as I threw pebbles and loose concrete into the depths. It was a very long time before they splashed into the sump. Some brave lads stood upright and ran around the narrow edge and occasionally a passer - by shouted frantically,

"Get down you silly buggers."

We obliged with alacrity, then waited until they wound out of sight towards the Cottage hospital before climbing back up again and peering down into the darkness.

"Me? Up at the pit bank Mam. Oh, I just walked up past the allotments."

Phew, a half lie.

And who could resist the factories?

Occasionally the word got around that the large factory gates had swung open and this was the signal to run there and then just hang around. Eventually the lorries arrived bringing the fruit for the Jam factory and as they careered round and into the factory grounds, we scrambled to gather anything that dropped. Braver souls leapt up and snatched apples or strawberries and some hung onto the back of them and threw what they could grab, back to us. I'm not sure what sort of jam was made, but a favourite lorry was the one piled high with pea pods. As I didn't care for fruit, these were the prize lorries for me. The man guarding the gate and the lorry drivers bawled and shouted at us while we filled our pockets and stuffed more down our coats and jumpers.

"I know who you are, and I'll tell your Mams."

I didn't query how they all appeared to know our Parents and ancestry but scattered with my purloined peas.

"Me? Down by the factories. Never. Peas? What peas? Oh, these peas in my pocket, Martha Weaver gave me them."

Hell and Damnation stared me in the face, but both were preferable to Mam's wrath.

The front of the factory wasn't much good for anything else. In fact, when the shifts changed it wasn't a safe place for a band of wandering children. Men and women poured out.

Some wheeled out on bicycles. Most of the women moved in packs. Some linking arms. Some walking turned slightly backwards, trying to light a cigarette in their cupped hands, which was no mean feat in the constant sea winds. There seemed to be a factory uniform. The men mainly wore an old dark, suit with open necked shirts. The women wore pastel coloured overalls hanging under their jackets and quite often they were also wearing a headscarf wound around hair curlers and tied at the top of their heads. Even when the factories were in full operation there was always someone wandering about the grounds that would spot the stealthiest child.

"Ere! Go on. You want nothing in here."

How very short-sighted. Of course, we wanted something in there, if only because it was banned.

"If I see your Mam's I'll tell them. Now go on."

It was a very nice entrance to the factories. These were no, "dark satanic mills." Each factory was set back from its own little road and footpath and in between were lawned areas with flowerbeds. If a factory area could be attractive, then an effort had been made on this site. There was spaciousness and ordered neatness, which also spelled death to any proposed expedition there.

No, the preferred mode of making an assault on the factories was over the back wall. Thankfully the sandstone wall had weathered to leave perfect footholds and we climbed them with agility. Climbing the wall was discouraged but not banned, so we often sat like birds on a fence, chatting until the coast was clear and we could drop down the other side. This had to be done with care as the factory beck ran alongside the wall leaving us only a few inches of hardened dirt to land on. One slip and we ended in the fast-flowing water. Teetering on the other side of the wall, we removed our shoes and socks; stuffed the socks in the shoes and either put them in our pockets or tied the laces and hung them around our necks. Then into the mighty Umpopo River to wade across, murmuring to each other that crocodiles were coasting the far shores. With my dress tucked into my knicker elastic, I felt the base of the beck with my feet, to avoid bricks and sharp metal. Small black eels darted and slithered and refused to be caught and orange, yellow canker that floated on the surface stained our legs. Much further down was a large, round, black, pipe which would have made a brilliant crossing point, but some killjoy had wound barbed wire around it. There was nothing for it but to paddle in the forbidden beck, flowing with all the filth and chemicals from the old mines.

Though the front of the factory site was carefully tended, the back was not and so grass and weeds grew taller than we were. Old forklift trucks lay drunkenly on their sides. Columns of wooden pallets were piled high and all around was the debris from all the factories.

"When you've got your shoes on Edna, we'll fan out a bit. Keep in touch with bird calls."

"Which bird?"

"I don't know. Any bird."

"An owl?"

"Don't be daft, they only come out at night and anyway there isn't any in the jungle."

"Oh. Is this a safari?"

"It's safari so goody."

I rolled in the long grass stifling my laughter at Betty's amazing wit.

We were always rumbled and chased back towards the beck. It was part of the thrill.

Sitting on the high, factory wall, looking down into Mother's back lane, we fumbled our shoes and socks back on and tried to wipe away the orange canker stains with lumps of grass.

"Don't look, but here comes Old Bobby."

I studiously gave my whole attention to my laces.

Old Bobby had a habit of flashing at anyone who looked his way. If you didn't look, he didn't do it. Everyone said that it wasn't his fault as he had been shell-shocked, so that was all right.

When he had gone past, I made to jump down from the wall and found my descent was halted for a few seconds and then was accompanied by a ripping, tearing sound. My dress had caught on a piece of sharp glass, cemented to the top of the wall, and was torn from waist to hem. We all tried to think of an explanation to deflect Mam's reaction. Betty offered the nail on her back door but as this was about level with my ankle it did not serve as a useful nail. Steeling myself, I marched bravely back to Mothers' to face my nemesis. Entering the back door, I encountered a strange phenomenon.

Mother was alone.

She was rarely alone. The house was never easy. The rent man, the insurance man, the man who surreptitiously took her bets, neighbours and family were in and out.

I sidled round the door.

"Where's Mam."

"Gone to Lairds for me some butter, why? Oh, dear, what's the matter lass?"

I swivelled round to show her the stripe of fresh air where my dress should have been.

"Dear God. Our Edna will go mad. You always have to be that perfect. What on earth have you been doing?"

Between sobs I confessed all.

As I cried, she pulled me to her. She wiped my tears with her hanky, warmed from the fire and pulled the dress over my head.

"Go and get my tin of sewing stuff and we'll see what we can do before she gets back. Mind you'll have to thread the needle for me."

At that moment, I'd have threaded a million grape pips for her if she had asked.

I sat in my vest and knickers while she sewed swiftly and neatly.

"There. Get it on quick. Mind she'll see it the next time it's washed. Just say you tore it at Mothers and Mother mended it. That way it won't be a big fib."

Just as she was tying and arranging the sash to cover the sewn area, Mam breezed in.

"Sorry I've been so long Mother. I've just had a grand crack with George Menhams and Yoight Shimmings. It's very good of George to take over Father's allotment and he says he'll still bring you eggs and the odd chicken and that."

She talked as she went into the little scullery and Mother winked at me.

"Do you not think it's time you were getting home now Edna? That man of your will be coming in soon surely?"

Mam made a mild stab at defence, but this was Mother Tuke speaking and carried more weight than any others.

"Oh, June could see to him. Still maybe I should. Edna get your fair isle cardigan and we'll go."

As we left Mothers' I turned to blow her a kiss and she in turn, put her fingers to her mouth to remind me to keep quiet. On the way home I emulated Prince Philip and walked a few paces behind.

It had been a hot day and everyone's windows were still open.

"There goes Ella," said Mam.

As we neared and passed Ella's house, we could hear her strange whoops and laughter. She either did this or stood on the front step endlessly twirling a piece of string. We all knew the story.

One day her Parents had been walking towards the docks, down Shipping Brow and paused to speak to some friends. They had inadvertently let go of the little girl's pushchair and it had careered down to the docks and smashed into a large capstan. The beautiful little Ella had lived, but the brain damage that she had suffered had left them with a half-life of strange noises and an infantile adult. There were far bigger and wearying tragedies being eked out on that street than a torn dress.

Then, as we neared a gap in the terrace of houses, Mam, unconsciously drew me close to her and we hurried past. There was always a man stood there. That's all he seemed to do, just stand there. But if you were passing when it was dark, his lurking figure could be amazingly frightening. Dad usually called, "Evening Lad," and the figure shrank closer to the wall and stayed silent. That's all. Mam said that he was just simple, but there was threatening air about the murky figure and so we simply hurried past. There were oddities in the town, like two women who dressed as men, but we knew them and as they were nice it didn't matter how they dressed. There was one woman who had never grown to adult maturity and her family always dressed her as a little girl. Mam said it was to stop strange men doing strange things to her and though I didn't know what she meant; I thought it was a kindness. But her old wrinkled face peeping out from luxurious ringlets and bonnets was startling. I really couldn't imagine anyone wanting to hurt her, she was ours, just one of our "funny folk" and we accepted that every town must have some.

Not all of them lived in their own homes. The majority lived in a large mansion set in its own grounds in a village between Cockermouth and Maryport. We nicknamed it, "The Colony," because it was virtually self-sufficient. I was a little afraid of the people, but Mam said that they could not help it and only the safe ones were, "let out." Being, "let out," happened one Saturday in every month, when they came to spend the day shopping, having a meal in Annovazzis and generally trailing about. If it was raining, they generally trailed about Woolworth's for most of the long day. Mam said that if they spoke to me that I just had to speak back nicely and walk on. It was not difficult to walk on as their unpredictable movements and sudden noises startled me and their appearance troubled me. It seemed that being, "funny," also made them physically misshapen. I once wondered if this meant that people who were very beautiful were also very clever. Well, our June was both, so it seemed a logical conclusion. I knew it was nice of Mam to accept these people but not knowing them or why they were like that made me uncomfortable.

Maybe Mam was more tolerant because we had a vague relation that lived in, "The Colony." As well as the Saturday for being, "let out," there was another Saturday when family and friends could visit them. The Tuke family took it in turns to visit Marjory or have her to their houses for her tea. She wasn't at all frightening, just a very small, old, lady and if she hadn't opened her mouth, others would have wondered why she lived there. Marjory talked in a strange, stilted manner and frequently added, "Darling." Which she pronounced as, "Tahlin." When she came to our house for her tea it was very difficult to drive a conversation with her. She knew little of our everyday lives and we knew less others. After a few pleasantries about the weather and health, we all ground to a halt. Mam had her own solution and she disappeared to the kitchen to take a very long time to prepare the tea, leaving us to "entertain," Marjory. I was exhorted to play my latest piano piece and June was told to show her the wonderful essay she had written at school. While I was being a veritable Sparky on the piano, June was pretending that she'd left her books at school and delighting Marjory, by producing the latest magazines instead. On one visit Aunt Evelyn surprised us by announcing that she wasn't daft at all. And then unfolded the horrific tale of how she had come to live there.

287

"Oh, her father was always into politics. Not our sort of politics. He was a Tory through and through. Her mother died when she was only about ten and he started on her instead. Well, when she was about thirteen, he was voted Mayor of the town where they lived, and she said she would tell what he'd been doing to her. The nasty, old goat promptly had her certified and that's how she came up here to live in that place. It saved his reputation and his political career, and he never visited. No wonder the poor soul is like she is. Institutionalised by now. That's all that wrong with her. "Each time she'd tried to tell people what had been going on they were scandalised with her instead. Said she was making it up because she was crackers. It's all so long ago now. Marjory thinks of it as her home and she's be upset to live anywhere else."

For once everyone hurriedly agreed with Aunt Evelyn and murmured that they just hadn't the room for another. Coming for tea once a month was enough for them to do Marjory always seemed very proud that she had family in the area and a definite somewhere to come while the others were sheltering in Woolworth's.

Once she patted my arm and whispered,

"They all think I'm daft. But I've no gas and electric bills to worry me, so which one is daft?"

There was the uncomfortable feeling that she had something with that thought. It was a relief when the time came to set Marjory to the bus for, "The Colony." We made a great show of kissing and hugging, as we knew that she wanted all the others to see that she had people somewhere who cared. Then we stood waving and blowing kisses as the bus drew out.

"Talk about more sinned against than sinning. "Tis a great stage of fools."

I walked alongside Mam.

Looked more like a bus of them, to me.

CHAPTER 11
"SET IN A SILVER SEA"

I painstakingly scrawled in my school exercise book, "Our new Queen has two children. King George was her father. Queen Mary has died. Princess Margaret will never be Queen. There are four Dukes. The Queen has a dolls' house big enough to get in. She is the second Elizabeth. The Queen is going to Westminster Abbey to have oil put on her head." Which rather reduced the great occasion. While the school and some of the town entered into an orgy of flags and tea parties, my family was deliberately doing as little as possible. Mam said that only common people had street parties and so on the day of the Coronation we might go for a walk on the shore if it was fine. Which it was not and so we stayed in the house.

At school I was given the choice of a free, commemorative Coronation mug or a spoon. Mam said that I had to choose a spoon as June had fallen and broken her mug when the old King had been coronated. I obeyed and chose a spoon. It came in a very smart box and languished in a drawer for some years before being thrown out. At Sunday school Annie presented us with a small book of the "New Testament," to celebrate our new Queens' accession to the throne. A nice gesture but I would rather have been given, "The Famous Five." Some while after the event, we all walked in crocodile, down the long hill of Camp Road to watch it at the cinema. I thought it very poor fare and not a patch on the films I watched with Mam and Dad. It was simply a change from being in school and I quite liked the music. But it did appear to herald a new optimism. We were told that this was the new Elizabethan age, and everything was getting better. We had spent so long having it hammered home to us that to be the winners and victors of the war, then there had to be sacrifices. Rationing had gone on much longer than expected and Mam was deeply wounded to hear that butter was freely available in Germany. Now, it really did seem to be getting better.

"Here you are my Lass you can have these to play with."

And Mam flung the Ration books into my toy drawer. Everyone was greatly relieved by this and new and strange items began to appear in the shops like tangerines, which did not impress me in the slightest. I began to dodge more cars as I crossed Curzon Street. These were becoming more outlandish their squat designs being replaced by elongated styles with wings at the back. The flashy Zephyr Zodiacs flashed by, desperately trying to emulate the American Cadillac's and failing. Wings were popular everywhere, even ladies' glasses now had wings and the really posh ones had diamantes in the wings. Spikes were popular. Clocks had spikes around them. The new "Contemporary," furniture gave a spiked impression and curtains were designed with jagged lines and zigzags. Dresses and skirts became longer and fuller as more cloth was available and there were gadgets. The Movietone News showed us machines that would do the washing and then dry the clothes. The Coop displayed machines that would hoover the carpets and television aerials were appearing on chimney pots all over the town. Optimism was everywhere. All around us there were concrete expressions of what could be done with full employment and Peace. And there was the impression that this could only go on and on.

At school we were taught that we were the best. The local pits were still churning out much needed coal to fuel progress and the Iron and Steel works at Workington were manufacturing the finest rails to be exported all over the world. Carrs of Carlisle made the most delicious biscuits and the Hornflowa factory provided all the buttons that were ever needed. In General Knowledge lessons this was extended to learning that Sheffield made the most coveted cutlery, Kendal and Northampton the sturdiest shoes and the strongest nails came from Wednesbury. Evidence was all around that our country was the greatest. Even Edmund Hilary conquered Everest with a little help from Sherpa Tensing. And just down the coast something was being built that would bring employment, not just to hundreds, but thousands.

We had been chosen. At last, poor little Cumberland had scooped the jackpot. The new and wonderful nuclear power was to be manufactured here. Not only would it bring more employment but cheaper electricity than anywhere in the whole country. It was so important that even our new Queen was coming to open it. Of course, it had nothing to do with those nasty bombs, that was another sort of nuclear power. We were assured that this was benign and only for useful purposes. We smugly munched our sweets in the cinema and watched atomic bombs mushrooming in the American desert or some tropical island, safe in the knowledge that we had found a safe use for splitting the atom. As part of the nuclear plant was called Sellafield, I thought that they manufactured Selotape and so there couldn't possibly be any worries. It was simply "a very good thing" for us and in all innocence, we sold our souls for employment.

It was onwards and upwards and our little family was no different from the rest of the country. The old black leaded grate was ripped out and a new tiled grate replaced it. Mam said it looked like potted meat, but I was so proud of it that I brought all my friends to view the new fire. The Coop Divvy bought Mary and June a new portable gramophone. This greatly intrigued me. Certain parts could be unscrewed and slotted into the main case, enabling the lid to close. Of course, by the time this was done it would have taken Charles Atlas to lift it, as well as the fragile seventy-eight R.P.M.s. In consequence it wasn't ported anywhere but lived in the sitting room. The selection of records gradually grew. "Rhapsody in Blue," "Slaughter on Tenth Avenue," "Caramia Mine," Frankie Laine singing "Jealousy," and Frank Sinatra singing everything. Mam insisted on having some Kathleen Ferrier songs simply because she had lived in Silloth. I enjoyed winding the handle to hear

Mario Lanza singing falsetto moving to baritone and bass and his voice slowly, grinding to a halt as the handle wound down."

"Mam. Our Edna's ruining my records."

"Well, you should have made sure it was locked."

"Mam. Our Edna's using up all the needles."

This was a real cheek, as we must have had needles coming out of our ears. June now had a grand passion for the man that served in Eliot's' record shop and when she couldn't afford a record, she sidled in to charmingly purchase more needles. Mam told her to stop it, as he looked constipated.

Mam sent for a joiner who made a carved corner cupboard to hide the ugly electricity meters in the sitting room. Dad said,

"If I'd known that was what that cupboard was for, I'd never have agreed to it"

"Aye well, you did agree and there's going to be a telephone on it by next week."

"And it'll come out just as fast."

Mam made the pots rattle as she banged her fist on the table.

"Do that Alf and I'll be up to Annovazzis' to buy my first packet of cigarettes."

"Give over, woman. If it comes in here, I'll not pay one bill for it."

"Who asked you to?"

The telephone was installed. A white one. And as none of my friends would believe me, I had to troop them down to see the wonderful phenomenon in our sitting room. The women in my life then decided that I had to learn telephone manners to add to all the other manners. I made awkward little calls to my friends and was thrilled when they called back. Mary and June gave our number out with alacrity and Dad was forever wearily coming around the living room door saying,

"It's for you."

Somehow the freezing conditions in the sitting room didn't bother them then.

Mam stopped decorating the house and instead, "commissioned," a proper painter and decorator. This was after much wailing that she had had nothing but a life of being a charlady and should not be expected to climb ladders after her big operations. Mr. Thorburn left cumbersome wallpaper books and we all perused them, made our choice and then came in to find him and a callow youth, expertly decorating with Mam's choice. The reasons to justify Mr Thorburn also served to justify Mam employing Mrs. Routledge.

Mam called her, "my woman that does" or "my little woman," which may have been patronising, but Mrs. Routledge certainly was very small in stature. She came once each week and the night before was an orgy of tidying so that she did not think us too slovenly. And as all of us were still doing the majority of the housework I wasn't very sure why this woman was needed at all. It was rather worth it as she was much given to malapropisms, that kept us all amused.

"Mrs. Croft. I've done the front brasses. Do you want to come and expect them?"

"Do you know I said till my sister last night, if you think my mother is going in a porpoise's grave, she's nut."

At least Mam had the grace to keep a straight face until she went home.

Mam was also able to lie down and read her "Complete Works of Shakespeare," for the umpteenth time. A slight problem to this being that she quoted this to her little woman whenever the opportunity arose.

"Mrs. Croft. I can't swill the fronts today in all this rain,"

"Mrs. Routledge,' the sun for sorrow will not show his head."

A bemused Mrs. Routledge hovered in the doorway.

"Err, so, do you want them swilled then? Shall I go and do it?"

"Stand not upon the order of thy going but go."

"Oh."

We were used to Mam's barmy answers, but Mrs. Routledge must have been frequently baffled by them.

It seemed a safe time where adults made the decisions and you were not required to influence them. The evidence all around was that they were not making too bad a job of it. We lurched forwards with the rest of the country dragged along by Mam's determination. But even that was in a haphazard sort of way. We never did fathom Mam's finances. However, disorganised in other areas, she could have taught the Chancellor of the Exchequer many valuable lessons. Dad's little brown pay packet had to be placed on the table each Friday and she allowed him his pocket money with great munificence. And though he was not earning a large wage, he had by now acquired seven houses in Maryport. Mary and June were awarded the job of collecting the rents in all weathers. I was usually with them as they stood at the doors, writing in the rent books or wearily listening to why the money wasn't there this week. Mam took the money and carefully perused the small books, checking on the non-payers and putting a little of the money away, "for repairs."

It was a feast and a famine.

"June! It takes as much effort to switch a light off as it does to switch it on."

"Get off that phone for a full week, the bill was terrible."

"Money doesn't grow on trees you know."

"New shoes? New shoes. Get your others to the Coop cobblers."

"Do you think your Father is made of money?"

"Don't ask. We can't afford it."

And June murmured again to Mary,

"I'm telling you, darkness and hypothermia solves all her bills."

Mam would not have anything that could not be paid for then and there.

"I'm telling you this Hire Purchase and "Buy now Pay Later" is just to keep you servile. It's just a little bit here and a little bit there and before you know it you have to work whether you want to or not, just to pay it all off. You'll not get no Tallyman at my door. And as for insurance, you won't see that man at my door either. All based on fear. Oo, you might have a flood. Oo you might have a fire. And the best one, Oo you might have an earthquake. Earthquakes in Maryport. What rot. Anything to get money out of you. Next time we have a day in Carlisle, just you look above your heads at all the buildings. The finest of them all are the finance buildings, and all built with money dragged out of the poor for what might happen."

They didn't come to our door, but others did. A French onion seller, a man to sharpen knives and scissors and the rag and bone man. Mam sometimes took out her own insurance, buying pegs from the gypsies that called, because she thought that it was bad luck not to.

There were weeks where Mam could not afford the money for me to stay for school dinners and then the Coop furniture van drew up and delivered the latest fashion in three-piece-suites for the sitting room. There were weeks where we ate every permutation of egg recipes, because the eggs were free from the allotments and then we were all going to Reays at Workington to have a proper afternoon tea with silver service. A feast and a famine.

We were at our appointed places at the dining table.

"Well, I think you should know. I've booked us a holiday at Silloth."

June choked and my jaw dropped. Dad just paused and said,

"Then you go on your own. I've never been further than Barrow and much good that did me."

"Please yourself. It's booked."

June's eyes shone as she asked numerous questions, but I was bewildered. Holidays. We only took holidays with Mam's family in Barnsley or Manchester. And anyway, it seemed that only men travelled. With the war and National Service, they visited places that women could only dream of. Malcolm was doing his National Service in Malta and had sent me a doll in the National dress. The ticket around her waist stated that her name was "Natalie," and I knew from his letters that Malta was very hot, and cigarettes were very cheap.

"Are we not going to Aunt Evelyn's'?"

"No. I've had enough of that. Some holidays. Working in the house all morning so that we don't feel guilty for eating free. Then trailing round more family in the afternoons and sitting playing cards at night. No, this is going to be our holiday in a chalet near Silloth. The holiday camp is called Blitterless and Mary can come as she'll be home then."

"You daft woman. You'll be cooking and cleaning in a chalet, but you'll be paying for the pleasure. Either get it cancelled or go on your own."

This time Dad had no allies. June and I were so excited about the proposed week and Mary wrote from College.

"After working in Woollies in Bolton on Saturday, I rushed back to my digs and Maureen and I got ready for a Tea Dance. Oh, Mam, it was exhilarating. It would have been better if I'd had those new red shoes, I told you about that I saw in Kendal Milnes in Manchester. They would have matched my dress far better, but I just don't have enough saved. Still, I haven't enough, and your news means I'll have to save some for our HOLIDAY. I can't believe we are going on a proper holiday. I don't care if it rains; good weather will be a bonus. Give my love to June and Edna and of course Dad. P.S. If he doesn't want to come it will mean more room in the chalet. Ha. Ha."

Mam shook her head.

"What a dizzy beggar. Not a mention of College work. She'll fail and nothing to show for two years there. You try to give them a career and what does she do? Blooming tea dances. I'll give her tea dances and Jazz Clubs. Wasting her time. And our Edna's nothing but a plodder. Thank goodness June has brains. I'll give her red shoes when I write back."

I munched my eggy bread.

"I think that's what she was hinting."

Mam glared.

Oh, the preparations for that holiday, almost everything that could be carried on a bus was packed and standing in the hall. Each week Mam had bought a little extra from the Coop so one case was full of things like tins of Corned Beef, packets of tea, sugar and of course, Tide. I had dreadful decisions to make. When the day came to walk round to the bus station. Dad shrugged on his jacket and announced that he would come and see the chalet. Strangely, Mam had already packed for him.

We had a glorious week.

Dad rapidly got to know other men on holiday on the site and they sat in the sun, smoking and putting the World to rights. Mam announced that she would do as little housework as possible as it was a holiday and she sat in the sun reading. Mary and June quickly found the dance hall and most evenings disappeared in clouds of perfume and swirling dresses to sample the delights of Silloth nightlife. It was a dream. I played on the long shifting sand dunes with my bucket and spade. We all walked along the long straight promenade to see a whale that had been washed up. And we stood shading our eyes watching schools of porpoises leaping in the Solway

Firth. I happily squandered my holiday spending money in the Amusement Arcade. I particularly liked one machine in there where, for sixpence, an elephant trundled from a plastic jungle and tipped a gift down a little chute. I thought that I was so clever winning every time, not realising that it always delivered a gift. Every day we had home-made ice creams from Longcakes. Every day!

Silloth was crowded with people and trains chugged in from Carlisle disgorging more with their suitcases and carrier bags stuffed with holiday packing and buckets and spades tied to them with string. It was as if the whole country was at last allowing itself to relax a little and being an island then the seaside was the place to do it. This was Britain at play and for one week in the year politics and austerity was set aside. On the caravan site there was no class system, well apart from the Swells that had managed to afford a week in a railway carriage. These fascinated me. I wasn't very sure how they had got there but, on every site, there were a couple of railway carriages parked. They had been converted into living quarters and were more spacious, and grand than the little chalets and roly-poly caravans. I commented to Mam that when I was grown up, I hoped that I could afford a week in a railway carriage at Silloth.

"Don't be silly. I hope when you are grown up you can afford to see other countries and other cultures, Things are just going to get better and better and this will seem

303

very small beer indeed by then but for now this is just grand."

Mam didn't half say some daft things at times. Other countries? That was so far-fetched that I couldn't even comprehend it. Silloth was the most wonderful holiday place to be and for that first holiday, Silloth obliged. The sun shone and danced on the silvered Solway. Across the water Scotland looked hazy in the heat while Mary and June lay on blankets by the chalet recovering from last nights' dancing but assuring us that they were actually getting a Hollywood tan. By the Wednesday, Dad announced that he hadn't felt so well in years and all around us every one was in fine humour, well, except for the odd children wailing for a plastic windmill on a stick or a giant lollypop with the words iced on them, "Welcome to Silloth."

On the Thursday June had to get the bus back to school to get her exam results. Mam paced the chalet and Dad kept telling her that it didn't matter. Now and then Mam walked to meet buses in from Maryport and came back alone and wringing her hands. As Mam was too worried to make the meals Mary made the corned beef sandwiches and we all mooched around the chalet somehow putting in the day. Eventually June burst around the chalet door to set the seal on the wonderful holiday. "Mam. Mam I passed. I passed all of them."

Mam shrugged and said, "No more than I expected," and she went to put the kettle on.

CHAPTER 12
"0, TIME THOU MUST UNTANGLE THIS"

I swivelled on Dad's office swivel chair while he finished the filing for the day. He talked to Dr. Rattrie as he pulled and pushed the drawers of the filing cabinet.

"I'm telling you Sandy, I haven't felt so well in ages. And sleep, I think we all slept better than ever"

"I'm not surprised at that, Alfred. There's a very good reason why there are Convalescent Homes in, or near Silloth. Apparently seven airs meet there so for your complaint you should either go there or to Switzerland. I don't know why I haven't recommended it to you before but at least you had the foresight to arrange it for yourself."

My lips were sealed.

"That's another day in and a long one it seemed. Pumping Red Biddy out of that dreadful fellow just about sickened me. I'm glad Dr. Robert is doing the house calls, people don't appreciate how many stairs we have to climb with each visit. I'm ready to put my feet up right now. See you tomorrow."

He waved cheerily and left. Dad hung his short white jacket on the door and pulled on his own tweed jacket as the phone rang.

"Hurry. Come fast. The Wife's just had a bad bout."

Dad looked blankly at the humming mouthpiece.

"Drat. Now I haven't a clue what to do. Somebody somewhere in the town is in trouble and I don't know where. I keep telling folk to give their names first."

He worried as we walked home and then told Mam.

"You know it sounded a bit like Billy Charters. I wonder if I should have a walk up there."

"Now, that's enough of that Alf. You've done your days' work. If you trail about after other folk, you're going to ruin all the good work Silloth did for you."

"I tell you what, I'll eat this and then me and Edna will have a stroll as it's a nice evening."

"Aye, and you wouldn't happen to be strolling past Billy Charters' house, would you?

"Don't answer that, I know you will, you soft beggar."

Dad and I did a lot of strolling, and he was right to stroll to Ewanrigg that night, as it was the house desperate for the doctor. Dad rang the doctors' home number, for them to somehow find Dr. Robert and send him to the address. The Charters were grateful and told me that my Dad was a good man, but I already knew that.

Sometimes when we were walking, I looked up, and around his mouth there was a bluish hue. Even the slightest rise in the land meant that he had to stop and gather his breath. We didn't talk much. We were just comfortable; my hand in his strong clasp while he slapped his walking stick against his leg in time to the music in his mind.

There was little encouragement to write freely at school but on one startling occasion we were asked to write about our homes. I wrote,

"My Mammy pegs out the washing. I went for a walk with my sister June. My Daddy has no wind."

And he certainly had very little. He had given up running the dance band and now only played very occasionally for the Chapel. Dad going into hospital every winter just became a fact of life. Sometimes I came home from school and he had already gone. Sometimes I woke in the dead of night to hear the ambulance men lifting him down the stairs. Occasionally I crept out of bed and watched through the banisters. Dad on a stretcher wrapped in a white cellular blanket and looking like a large baby Jesus in swaddling clothes. Mam awkwardly following and trying to hold his lolling head and whispering,

"See our Edna's alright and I'll be back when I can."

Dad always went into Workington Infirmary and there was definitely no visiting from children under fourteen there. I just had to wait until he returned home to see him. His return was similar in reverse order. He was lifted back upstairs and then the ambulance men went back out and hoisted in a trolley with a large black cylinder of oxygen. This was bumped up the stairs and parked by the bed with the mask dangling daintily over the headboard. It was not a surprise. Just as other people had bedside cabinets my Daddy had an oxygen cylinder. It happened every winter.

And in a crisis Mam was perfection.

She ministered to Dad better than any qualified nurse. She carefully made him small invalid meals and sat on the bed persuading him to eat a little. She timed each spoonful just right to allow him to turn his head aside to gasp the air. She spooned quantities of honey into him saying that it was a natural antibiotic. She added a squirt of lemon telling him that it would cut the phlegm. We all suffered the arctic cold as she flung the windows open, saying that the sea air was good for him. Mrs Routledge came more frequently, and the house was unusually tidy. It had to be ready for the doctor puffing up the stairs each day and possibly noticing the cleanliness. Much to

Mam's chagrin, Mother Croft also puffed up the stairs to visit her only son. Dramatically clasping him to her bosom she cried,

"Oh, my Lad. What? What can I get thuh to mek thuh better?. Just say the word Lad.

"Anything. You say the word and it's yours."

"Mother," gasp, "Oh, Mother I had such a good holiday in Silloth," gasp, "If I had my own caravan there..."

She leapt off the bed.

"A caravan? Do you think I'm made of money?"

and she stormed down the stairs and slammed the front door after her.

Mam sat down on the edge of the bed.

"Well, she did ask. Never mind Lad. You'll have a caravan. It will be like a hobby till you finish working, with a small garden around it and you me and little Edna can go along whenever we like eh? In fact, maybe we could get a little car just to do that. "Mary and June will be finished College and in really good jobs, maybe married to some chaps with a bit of money and prospects. Oh, it's going to be so good. Just you lie there and get better for now."

I lay listening, beside Dad. I liked what I heard and thought about it.

It seemed very important to get a job. Then when the job was secured, it had to be kept secure. You weren't expected to like it or even enjoy, you just had to get a job and stay there. You had to work at being at work. Fun was something else. Fun could only happen after work. Which was a bit of a paradox, as the work was never done.

Well, frequently in Mam's case, it was never done.

She carried the working-class guilt that reading should not be done until all the work was completed. Yet she downed tools and simply sat reading. Then she created dramatic scenes to cover her guilt. Or there were her illnesses. These often occurred just as she was tiring of being our Dad's Edith Cavell.

"The tea isn't ready as I had to lie down. I felt a bit funny."

"Oh, what's the matter Mam."

"Oh, you know."

"No. Should we call the doctor?"

"Don't be so ridiculous. Why on earth would I want a doctor?"

"Because you said that you were ill."

"Well, it's a bad job if I can't have a lie down without a load of fuss and histrionics. I'll come around when I finish this chapter."

"Is it a headache. Should I get you a Cephos powder?"

"Oh, for goodness sake I'll have headache listening to you. Just get away with you and leave me alone".

"But you said that you were ill."

"That's it! That's it! I'll get up and you'll all be happy."

"No. No, you stay in bed. I'll bring you a cup of tea."

"Oh, no me lady. Never let it be said that you had to do anything for me. Never let it be said that I had a cup of tea in bed for no reason at all. I've spent the last few days running up and downstairs after your Dad and now when it's my turn there's a big fuss. I've worked all morning for you lot. Bad job if I can't have a lie down now and then without suffering the Spanish Inquisition about it."

Then she would fling the covers back and push me out of the door, slamming it behind me. I didn't know what to do. I didn't like to think of my Mammy being ill but offering the only sort of help that I knew, was, more often than not, rejected.

311

As June came around the front door she said,

"What's the matter with you? Oh God, is she in bed again?"

"No, it's worse, I think she's getting up."

We stood listening to the drawers slamming and heavy footsteps crossing the bedroom floor.

"She's mad because I asked if she wanted the doctor," I whispered.

"Silly lass. There's nothing wrong with her Edna. Those blooming operations will last her for years. She's just as fit as you or me but she's bone-idle. Just let her stew. "Come on I'll see if there's anything in for our tea."

It was all very well for June to suggest that we let her stew, but I knew that, that didn't work either. If we didn't go to enquire as to why she was in bed or if she needed anything, that was not acceptable either.

"Doesn't anyone care? You get on with your lives. Don't worry about me ill in bed. "Not even a cup of tea or an aspirin. Well, I'll have to get up if only to please you. "One of these days you'll find me lying at the back of the door and then everyone will be happy."

It puzzled me greatly. I fluttered around her trying to hug or kiss her to see if that helped but she pushed me away, tossing her head and banging into the kitchen to vigorously wash the dishes.

If Dad came in and sensed the atmosphere, he handed me my coat saying,

"Edna and I are going for a walk."

"Aye. Go on. You think if you go out that will answer it. You don't take any responsibility. You go and trail about as if that will make things better."

But we didn't know what was wrong to make it better. I worried and chewed my nails. How if she was "behind the door when we came back?" This was only marginally better than the other threat that we would find her floating in the dock. I never knew why these eruptions happened. And no one else seemed to know either. It just happened now and then, and we could not take the chance and totally ignore her. Maybe she was ill. Maybe she would be found in the dock. Whatever it was, we spent the next few days or weeks trying to pamper and appease her and slowly it ceased. It affected June. Mam said that June had, "nerves."

"Either there's something wrong with your nerves or mine. If you don't stop dathering your foot, I'll have to walk out. You're like a jelly bag. And cut that out or you'll be down to the knuckles." Mam delivered a sharp

313

slap to June's hand, which was rising to her mouth to nibble her nails. And yet it was June that made her own stand.

"You're WHAT?"

"It's no good shouting Mam. I can't stand the sixth form and I just can't get away with "A" levels. Have you any idea what it's like? Studying Shakespeare in depth is killing it for me."

Nice touch June.

"I saw a job going a Workington Library, so I've been down to ask about it and they've offered me the job. I start on Monday."

"You silly lass. I wanted you a career."

"It is. I'll train to be a Librarian."

"Oh."

And so, Mam's prize intellectual left the Grammar School and was travel sick on the bus to Workington instead. Mam repeated to everyone that studying subjects in depth killed them and her daughter was now studying to be a Librarian. It gradually became of some concern to her that there didn't seem to be much actual studying going on at all.

314

"All you seem to be is a dogsbody carting heavy books about. Spending your days stamping tickets and mooning over the lads that come in. That's no career."

June dathered her foot even more.

June wasn't, "mooning over lads;" she was dreaming of one in particular and was glad when Mary came home to confide in her.

"He's everything I ever dreamed of. He's six-foot tall, dark hair and so gentle."

"How did you meet him then?"

"He's in the R.A.F. doing his National Service but he belongs in Workington so when he comes home, he comes to the Library. The last time he came in he asked me to go to the pictures with him. My heart was fluttering but I went. I can't even remember the film. He'd booked those back seats in the Ritz, you know the ones that hold two. I was a bit embarrassed, but they were very comfortable, and he'd brought me a box of Black Magic. Then he set me to the bus and said he'd see me again when he was home."

"Wow. So, what do you know about him?"

"He's got two older sisters that are married. He likes cricket and I can't think of anymore. I don't need to know anymore, I'm in love, truly I am."

Mary shrugged,

"Better get your story ready for Mam then. I mean does he live in a posh house? Is he Roman Catholic? What are his prospects?"

"I don't care."

"You'll care when Mam starts."

"Maybe I could invite him for his tea and then she'd see how wonderful he is."

Mary did not appear to think that viewing June's new Adonis would answer.

"You'd better come up with more than that. She has to have her own way and you'd have to be a better man than I Gunga Din to cross her. You've already managed a job that she didn't choose but how long will that last?"

"You know Mary, I've sometimes thought it would be easier if she had a whip behind the door to belt us. At least that would be over with but this never knowing whether we are doing right or wrong is driving me up the wall."

"Don't take so much notice June. She only wants the best for us and have all that she didn't have. I know it's hard when she's in that humour but there's other times that are good."

"Like what?' I never know what I'm coming in to. I just want to get married and live far away from her."

"You might be jumping out of the fat into the fire doing that. I've a mind not to come home when College is over. I love going to Aunty Mays' in Manchester and I might try for a job there. I haven't screwed up the courage to tell her. I thought I'd wait until I've passed the exams. If I ever do, you know me; I'd rather go off to the Free Trade Hall to see Ella Fitzgerald than study. And then there's Dad and little Edna to think about. I mean maybe I should be home to be a buffer for them."

I lay very still between them listening to them whispering, in bed. It was all very alarming. I couldn't think of life without Mary and June. I didn't mind them going to College because this had a temporary air and I didn't mind the thought of them getting married. That would be good and exciting, and everyone got married and just lived nearby, but for them to live far away was unthinkable. And Mam was just Mam. I hadn't thought that you could criticise your Parents. I was aware that June was very affected and troubled, but Mary was right too. There were good times.

"Poor Dad. He puts up with so much. Sometimes I think she will kill him with her tantrums and scenes."

"Oh, June he'd have left long ago if it had been that bad. I know this, we wouldn't be where we are if it had been up to him however much I love him."

"Life would have been a lot calmer. She shoves and pushes us, encouraging us to join this and that and she doesn't do it. It's family and nothing else. The Mother's Union is just a gossip shop, we couldn't go to the Brownies or Guides as they were just junior paramilitary organisations, preparing us like the Hitler Youth."

Mary stifled her laughter,

"And her teeth would have dropped out to join the W.I. and sing, "Jerusalem."

"She's there pushing us to meet men and then she sounds as if she hates them."

June mimicked.

"Men. They never grow up they only grow older. They have to have something to play like bowls, football, or golf. And have you ever heard of women keeping on dressing up. Men. They just have to keep on dressing up. Football kit, judges' wigs; swirling about as Bishops or Vicars and if they can have a job with a uniform, they are in seventh heaven. She baffles me. Look what happened when I wanted to join the Communist Party? You would think she would have been proud of that but no, she went mad saying I'd never get a job if I did that and if you can't beat them you have to join them."

"And she's right. You know she's right. Oh, come on June, snap out of it, she's really OK."

Mam ruined Mary's defence by shouting upstairs,

"When you two have finished doing your logs impressions get down here; there's work to be done"

Before Mary had time to broach the subject of living in Manchester, Mam decided that we should have a day out.

"Now that Mary is home we are going to Buttermere as a whole family."

Mary and June murmured that they weren't too bothered about a day out. Mary wanted to see some of her old friends and June simply did not want a full day in Mam's company.

Dad said that he didn't feel fit enough.

I went out to play, as I knew what was coming. I sat on the front step miserable and knowing what was going on inside the house. Mam raged that she never got anywhere, we didn't have days out as a family. With the Lake District on our doorstep we shouldn't just hang around Maryport. I'd heard it all before and it didn't matter what objections were offered; we were going. I wondered wearily why they bothered.

The day came and we all walked round to get the bus to Cockermouth.

Dad had coughed and coughed for most of the night and he coughed and coughed his way to the bus station. He coughed and coughed on the bus. He wheezed and hung on to the seat in front of him. Mary said nothing, but when we alighted in Cockermouth and moved to wait for the next bus, she simply took his arm and steered him across the road. As the bus turned to make the return journey to Maryport, she helped him on to it and came back over the road to us.

"There. He's got a key and he can get his asthma powder and lie down. The day was tainted and coloured every memory. Mary and June were quietly worrying, and Mam was high and excitable. We were exhorted to look at the lake, the fells, the colours and weren't we lucky to live near such a jewel? We sat by the beck and spread out our blanket and picnic. It was a glorious day. The sun glinted on the lake and clouds drifted shadows across the fells. We paddled in the beck and were amused by a donkey that insisted on investigating our picnic bags. It was clear that Mam was uncomfortable. She was not a picnicking sort of person. She simply tolerated sitting on a blanket and worried about her dress creasing.

"I don't know what people will think when I get back on that bus. There will come a day when we don't have to do this, and we will have a proper tea in a farmhouse. All right for those that can afford it after poncing about on the fells. We had to worry more about just getting food on the table never mind coming out here."

"All right Mam, it's not like that now."

"No, but if you've lived through the Depression, you don't forget it,"

"And you won't let us," said Mary.

"That's enough. I know what you did for me in Cockermouth but that doesn't give you licence to say what you like."

Mary and June decided to go for a walk up the fellside and Mam tried to get comfortable to read her book. I wandered along the beck. It was a long day and it seemed a long time before we were packing up to get the bus back to Cockermouth. While we waited Mam said that she thought that the Coop had a holiday place near and when it was time for the next Divvy she could get them proper boots and they could have a walking holiday. June shuddered and said that she had too many memories of school Geology trips where she was embarrassed to always be the one trailing at the back. June was always embarrassed about something. There was a long wait in Cockermouth for the bus to Maryport and we lugged our bags with us while we looked in the shop windows on Main Street.

"I'd like to live here someday," Mary commented. Mam looked at her sharply.

"What on earth for? It's nothing but a little market town that's far too above itself. "Looks down its nose at Maryport but they never suffered like us and they were happy to take our money when we came shopping."

"I still think it's a nice little town."

"What do you know?"

"Mam, June and I came to school here and we know some Cockermouth people, it's a nice place."

"That doesn't mean you have to live here. Maryport is good enough."

I ventured that it didn't have a Woolworths, but it didn't seem to help.

When we walked in the house Dad was sitting reading the paper and looked fine to me. June extravagantly showered him with kisses and Mary's eyes narrowed.

"Better then?"

"Aye, not so bad. Did you have a nice day?"

He needn't have bothered asking, as he was getting the "Silent Treatment," from Mam.

But sometimes this was preferable.

I sat at the table and picked at my meal. Mary had gone back to College. Dad was at work and I was powerless to protect.

"You're going my lady."

"No, I'm not".

"Oh, but you are. No-one is finished until they have been to College and that job at the Library is going nowhere."

"That's rubbish."

"Rubbish? For somebody with brains you are a non-thinking person. It isn't just the education you get at College. You learn to live independently, work out your own finances; experience another way of life. You are going."

"I'm not. All you want to do is split up John and I."

"Don't talk tripe. You and John. I'm sick of hearing about him. My cleverest daughter and all you can think of is a man."

"He going to get a job at the new Calder Hall and that has a works house with it."

"What? Not owning your own house? You must be daft."

"I love him."

"Love? Love? Don't talk to me about love. It's made more slaves of women than enough and when the bills come in, love flies out of the window. Men, they're neither use nor ornament. Oh, he'll smarm around you now but wait until that wedding ring is on your finger, it won't be boxes of chocolates then. Remember, 'maids are May when they are maids but the sky changes when they are wives'. And you will be wasting all that cleverness. Do you want to end up like me? Do you? I wasn't behind the door when brains were given out. I could have stayed on at school after I was fourteen. The Headmaster even came to our house to ask Mother and Father if I could stay on and train to become a teacher.

"When was that? When was it? 1926. That's when it was. Dad was on strike and it cost money to train. Everyone was on strike so we couldn't even borrow the money. "But now, now they are crying out for more teachers and giving grants for you to train. Without grants the likes of us couldn't do it but now we can at least try. Thank God, times have changed and not just the rich can go as far as possible. How many lads have gone down the mines and lasses into the factories just because they couldn't afford to go to College? June you'll never know the frustration and the bitterness. And I'll make sure you don't. Look what happened to me, married when I was barely eighteen and then the baby died, and I was stuck. Its' not going to happen to my girls."

"But maybe that's what we want."

"Maybe it is, after you have a qualification. Can't you see it's not just for a job or money? The more education you can get the better and if you choose to stay at home with your children then you can pass it on to them. And now it's free to go.

"Anyway, there's nothing more to be said. I've written away, filled in this application form and all you have to do is put your signature on it."

"I won't."

I held my breath.

Mam stood for a few seconds then lifted the cold teapot and poured it over June's head.

"Sign it."

Oh, June. Oh, June don't be diminished. Oh, my beloved June. I went away in my head as the black tea leaves slithered down and she cried.

Mary's musings about living away from home did not come to fruition. Mam decided that Mother Tuke was much too old to live alone and as Mary announced that she had somehow scraped through her exams, she was summoned home to live at Grasslot. It seemed that just as Mary returned to the fold, June left, red eyed, for College in Sunderland.

The words were scrawled in pink chalk on the gable end of Collins terrace and I stood deciphering them. Curly cuh, uh, nuh, tuh...... Cunt. And underneath this, fuh, uh, curly cuh, kicking cuh... Fuck. I'd never heard them. Across from Fuck was, buh, a, suh, tuh, a, ruh, duh... Bastard. What a funny word and I murmured it to myself. Bastard.

"Go on. You want nothing looking at that. Your Mam will skelp you if she sees."

I nearly jumped out of my skin as Mrs. Denwood came with a bucket of water and whooshed it at the wall. I left her vigorously scrubbing it with a yard brush and strolled up Collins Terrace thinking of the bad words.

"Dyu wanna photo lass?"

I had been too absorbed to notice one of the Lights, lounging by her front door.

She straightened and stood four-square in front of me.

"Who yuh staring at, Maryport snob."

"I wasn't."

Fear rose and began to colour my face.

"Stare at me again and I'll smack yer gob."

"Yeah? You and who's army,"

and I smartly nipped around her and walked on thinking,

"Don't run. Don't let her see you're frightened. Don't run."

Then she nearly stopped me dead in my tracks,

"Don't talk to me like that. I can shite bigger than you."

What an amazing thought. I screwed up my courage threw back to her one of the new words.

"Bastard."

And then I ran like the wind to Mothers'. Mary was sweeping the step.

"I hope I didn't see you talking to that Light girl. Mam would have a fit if she saw you playing with one of them."

327

No fear. There was no temptation to play with someone with the dubious talent of defecating about four foot of shit.

"Anyway, Betty McCracken is here to see if you want to go to the shore." This was a good offer and as Betty and I carried our bags with old towels, costumes, sandwiches and a bottle of Underwoods' pop, Mary called,

"Remember what Mam says, 'Take care and if you come back drowned, I'll kill you." Betty laughed and laughed. I smiled a watery smile. I'd heard it every time there was an expedition to the shore.

Maryport may be by the sea but it was an expedition getting to it. This was no pretty little seaside town and pictures of it would never have graced any 1950s calendar. The only people that lived near the sea were the ones in the small mean dock houses of Downstreet. Anyone else had to circumnavigate the slag banks, the derelict iron ore works, the two docks and the sea wall before being able to paddle in it. But it was worth it.

It was certainly worth it.

I cannot say that I found that I liked the sea. I cannot say that I fell in love with the sea.

I was the sea.

We all were the sea.

The sea was always there. It had been there before me and would always be there. It was a fact of life like breathing. It pulsed and permeated everything. It insinuated every sense. The saline air that we breathed was always moist and damp and steeped our senses in brine. It stirred the wind circulating around us. It was a stream in our blood and coursed through our genes. Its' surging, soughing sound was always there. It was no surprise to me. But any approaches to physically feel it were beset by many obstacles. From the end of Senhouse Street the road took a very steep dip down Shipping Brow. This had paving stones which were flecked with rubber and delayed anyone on a frosty winter day suddenly whizzing down into the freezing harbour. It was a very narrow harbour and the ships built there, had to be launched broadside on. Mam was very proud that Thomas Henry Ismay had been born in Maryport and begun the White Star Line which eventually became Cunard, that built the, "Titanic." I thought this a rather questionable claim to fame considering that all I knew of that ship was that it had sunk on its maiden voyage. Across the harbour was a narrow wooden bridge and I was able to peep through each slat to see the water far below me. Following the harbour wall led to the docks and what a sinking feeling if the dock gates were open as this meant that we had to walk all the way around both docks. These were working docks and were rather dark and forbidding. Small engines chug-chugged in with their wagons of coal. These were positioned to tip their load down a towering, black chute. It was deafening as the coal rattled and clattered into the blackened bowels of the Irish coal boats. There were ships' chandlers and lying around the docks, large chains, anchors and fishing nets strewn or heaped with orange floats peeping through them. Railway lines wriggled everywhere. All around the edge of the docks were large black, solid iron bollards and thick and thin sturdy ropes and chains coiled and snaked from them. When I was smaller and Mary and June walked me to the shore, Mary enjoyed leap frogging over the bollards. It was a risky exercise holding the threat of plunging into the murky oily dock waters. Sometimes they took an arm each and swung me over them calling.

"Whoops nearly in that time."

Oh, very funny.

They urged me to be Geronimo and clap my ear to the railway lines to check if a coal train was approaching, which was all very well for a brave Indian, but I didn't fancy paddling while decapitated. Leaving the docks, we scrambled up the grassy bank to climb over the sea wall and skitter down its' sloped side to find a place in the sea grass to spread our blankets and picnic. We usually wore our swimming costumes under our clothes and when we had undressed there was much flapping the blanket and arranging our clothes into pillows so that Mary and June could lounge decorously, pretending to be Marilyn Monroe and Jayne Mansfield. Of course, going to the shore had to be timed just right. If the tide was out, then there was another long walk to get to the water. If it had turned to go out, then there was the danger of it taking you with it. If the tide was full in, then there was no sand to play on. The best time was when it had just turned to come back to the shoreline. Then it was considered safe and could only bring you back with it, getting deliciously deeper with each minute. As sandshoes were only mentioned in Enid Blyton books, I grew adept at skipping in bare feet, from stone to stone to reach the sand. Either that or Mary or June carried me or hauled me with a swinging motion across them. The sand was dark brown, coloured by the coal dust and was the right consistency for making sand pies and castles or scraping words with my big toe. Dotted in the sand were little whorls left by lugworms. The larger rocks had mussels hanging from them and pyramid limpets that clung firmly, however much I chipped and smashed at them with my spade. And when I eventually read "Coral Island", I could understand the torture of keel hauling across flesh-scraping barnacles and truly sympathise. When we finally reached the sea my bucket and spade had to be left on a high rock. We were not troubled that they would be stolen but positioned them where we could quickly identify them. The sea never brought you back where you first entered it.

The first shallow rippling water was warm and on soft breeze days it plashed and sucked the sand around my feet. Further in, the weight of the water dragged against my legs and the temperature cooled. Mary usually just dived into the deeper, vital, undulating water and laughed at my feebleness as I hugged my arms around me and delayed submerging my whole body. We were not alone in all this expanse of sea. Many others were going through exactly the same motions, trying to accustom their body and the sudden surprise of someone splashing the freezing water caused much squealing. There were always lads who ran whooping into the sea and swimming effortlessly far from the shore. Dainty girls played with buoyant beach balls, squealing coyly and looking appealingly for the lads to retrieve them from the deeper water. It was so clear that I could look down at my feet and the dark sand. June taught me how to swim. Standing behind me,

"Arms out. No, straight out. Now make your hands into paddles. Shut your fingers you fool, or the water will come through. Imagine you are a duck; they don't have holes in their feet. Now, shut your fingers and don't let any water come through. Great. Now put your hands together like praying. O.K. Pull the water away and behind you and thrash your legs like a frog. Remember always away from you."

I practised and practised until I became quite slick.

"Not bad. Now try with your feet off the bottom."

Shucks.

The longer we were in, the warmer it became and only hunger drove us from the water. It was a wrench to wade back to the rippling early waves and then stand looking and looking for the bucket and spade. They were always miles to the left or the right from where we emerged from the sea. The trail home was a drag. We were always tired, the wet swimming costumes and towels weighed heavy and sand scraped my sandals.

"Where's our Edna's sock?"

Blank looks from Mary and June.

"Don't tell me you didn't notice that the little lass only had one sock on?"

"Mam, she's old enough to dress herself now."

"I send her with you, and you are supposed to look after her and you bring her home with only one sock."

"She likely didn't notice."

"Mam, my foots' sore."

"Aw Petal. You hear that you two? Now she has a sore foot."

We never came back with everything; well, just a lot of sand.

June always preferred Maryport shore and we definitely brought more than we wanted from there as there was a tar works near it. Mam was forever rubbing butter on the towels to remove the black claggy tar. This was nearly as far to walk as Grasslot Shore, but we turned right at Shipping brow and wandered through the Downstreet area like interlopers. This brought us to the Prom. A one and a half-mile strip of grey concrete, leading to the golf course. Every now and then there were intersections with sloping walks down to the beach. Here the sea had formed large slabs of sandstone that were ideal to rest on and held intriguing rock pools. Always we looked straight across to Scotland, which was just another fact of life. Some days it looked closer than others and little white houses could be seen dotting the coast and the sides of Criffel. I once asked Dad where the tide went to when it was out and after a few moments he said,

"I guess those greedy Scots have supped it all."

Sounded a reasonable answer to me.

I can remember Mary whispering,

"Shh, listen. That bird is singing, 'a little bit of bread and no cheese."

And it did seem to be repeating this. I learned which birds were terns and which were gulls, red wings, curlews and lapwings. I knew thrift, purple and white clover and certainly felt the sharp sea holly. I knew that, "White horses," were just the foam on the turning waves and none of it was taught in school.

To come home we had the choice of trailing back up Shipping Brow or hauling up the Hundred Steps. These were large sandstone steps carved into the brows that brought us out at Brow Street Church and then downhill all the way home.

"All right which one of you has our Edna's knickers?"

Blank looks from Mary and June.

"I don't believe it, now you've left her knickers on the shore."

We didn't just visit the shore when the weather was hot. On wild, wild days it was exhilarating to be blown along the Prom and dodge the waves crashing over it. Or watch them travelling fluently and swiftly along the piers and bashing against dock walls. It was impressive to watch the sea in dark humour, heaving and heavy and rolling menacingly towards the land. It was thrilling to totter in the wind nearer and nearer to the waters' edge and risk the angry surging spume turning. Then shouting, "Run away, run away," and skittering backwards when it crashed and rushed, leaving us puffing while it slithered back to begin the next attack. The large slabs of sandstone were pummelled and as the waves withdrew, they left fermenting foam, fizzing in the hollows. There was risk in picking across the slippery seaweed and a visceral thrill in being so close to such awesome power. And when we grew tired of baiting the waves and moved to safer ground, it was satisfying simply stand under the louring dull, pewter sky and watch the magnificent force. Simply running along the Prom and being buffeted by the wind was a cathartic release.

We went on frosty days and marched purposefully along the Prom, "to blow off the cobwebs." And when a bad cold had reached the stage of us being completely bunged up, Mam ordered us to walk by the sea, as the ozone would cure catarrh. We trailed in the keen, biting wind muffled in clothes with teeth chattering, alongside the rhythmic moan of the water until our eyes streamed as well as our noses. I loved it in all its humours however tortuous the walk to reach it.

Betty and I chose the safer route to the shore, down the back lane and avoiding a repeat skirmish with big lasses who had dubious talents. I told Betty about the queer words on the wall.

"Is that all you know? What a twit."

"Well, what does it mean?"

"It's, well, it's when men and women do it."

"Do what?"

"You know. "It.""

I was baffled.

"You know. What they do to get a baby."

"What? Sit on a step?"

She stopped and looked at me,

"What are you talking about?"

"I asked Auntie Lizzie once how to get a baby and she said I'd to sit on a step until the sun shone on me."

"And you didn't think that if that was right there would be millions of babies?"

I shrugged. It was nothing to do with me.

When we were in the sea we shouted and threw the dirty words to the seagulls lazily circling the blue summer sky and when we sat down to eat our picnic Betty said,

"Best not say them at home."

"I'm not that daft."

"Good job. My grandma says that your Mam is a lady."

It was gratifying to know that Mam had reached lady status. I guessed she must be very clean and anyway she knew all the things that apparently made you a lady. Mam said that only common people had curtains that only reached the windowsill. Ladies had their curtains six inches on the floor. Ladies painted their front doors black or navy or racing green. Ladies never used carrier bags; in fact, the best ones only carried a dainty basket. This showed that they had their shopping delivered leaving them with only frivolous shopping. A lady was never but never seen wearing rollers or a headscarf and only common people wore jewellery that moved. Mam knew what was "U" and "Non U," so maybe putting it all together worked.

"Our June says she's a tartar."

"A what?"

"See, you don't know everything. I think it means somebody scary."

"Ere. Did she ever find out, you know, when you tore that dress?"

"If she did, she didn't say. Come on lets' pack up and walk home now, it's starting spitting."

We did a lot of walking. Everybody did. Not particularly for economy, you just walked. Public transport was precisely that, it was very public. The timetables tied visits; and time was wasted in draughty bus stations or shelters that did very little sheltering. It was a great relief to see the bus drawing near and even more relief when there was room to get on them. They were often packed, and children had to stand for older women and pregnant women which meant that I spent most journeys standing in the aisles, swaying and hanging on the long chrome poles. The buses to Workington invariably picked up flat capped men going to the dog track with their grey hounds. The poor animals stood in the aisles flicking fearful wild eyes and enveloping the bus when fear made them give off strong pungent odours. If it was an evening bus or even worse the last bus it was an accepted fact that some of the passengers were drunk. Tottering on they weaved down the bus and slumped into a seat, giving off stomach churning fumes.

"Yawright Dahlin"

If you looked stonily out of the window with embarrassment,

"You bloody deaf or somethin? I ast you if you wuz awright?"

You were lucky if they resorted to,

"Stuck up bitch," and sank into a drunken torpor for the rest of their journey. Equally troubling was a bevy of rowdy lads and invariably one of them hurtled to the bus platform to vomit in the rushing wind, while his mates shouted,

"Nut as good coming up as it was going down eh?"

I bet he thought that was rib tickling funny.

Fortunately, Mam was not averse to venting her wrath and disgust on them and fortunate for her that they were easily quelled or maybe her imperious demeanour was enough.

"Excuse me. Are you aware that there is a young child here? Just curb your foul language."

"Sorry Missus."

Wednesday was half closing day in Maryport when the whole town quietly died. While it was looking more like the ghost towns in the Westerns and tumbling tumbleweed bowling down Senhouse Street would have been no surprise, many people defected to Workington to spend their money. Mam only visited Workington market occasionally but when we did, I thoroughly enjoyed the free street theatre and listening to the stallholders exhorting us to buy.

"Ho, no Missus. I'm not going to just put in one set of towels but here's the matching flannel and a pair of flannelette sheets. Go on now, can't say fairer than that can I?"

I agreed.

The market had succumbed to the enthusiasm for gadgets and it was fascinating to watch a man with a piece of lino that was clean on one half and disgustingly dirty on the other. One swipe of his miraculous squeegee mop and the dirt disappeared. On the next stall a man was extolling the virtues of an onion chopper which guaranteed no more tears. I watched with baited-breath, while the man at the pot stall talked up a storm while balancing more and more, "priceless," china along his arm.

"And for the lady that makes the lucky decision to own this I will throw in a vase. Not just any vase but a big one. And I know some of you ladies like a big one." Wink, wink.
Mam hurried me on but couldn't resist a sly smile and nudging Auntie Lizzie.

The day usually ended with a live variety show at the Opera House. We saw a young Betty Driver and an even younger Frankie Vaughan and Mam declared that they would, "go far." A favourite was Bobby Thompson, a comedian from the North East and we merely suffered the conjuror and troupe of dancers until he came on. His raw working-class humour and amusing descriptions of a life we recognised was always popular.

Then the bus home.

With the bus aisle already full of swaying men and children Mam lifted me onto her knee while old Mrs. Porter gratefully squeezed her bulk beside us. Mam murmured in my ear,

"Some are born great, some achieve greatness and some have greatness thrust upon them."

I turned my head and saw my stifled smiles reflected in the dark of the bus window.

"Ow's yer fettle, Mrs. Croft?"

"Oh, fair to middling."

"I see you've got another of your lasses off to College. Makin sure they good jobs eh?"

"Not at all. I want them to be better educated, a job at the end of it will be a bonus."

"Educated? Bit of a waste. Now if it had been lads that would have been different."

Even I knew that this was dangerous ground and I airily fingered the drops of condensation jerking down the window.

"Mrs. Porter, my daughters are being educated to enrich their lives. Plus, when they have children, they will be the ones who will be with them the most and can pass it on to them."

I had heard it numerous times.

"Aye, I suppose that's a thought. But they could have been making you some money at the Jam Factory all this time and then they could marry an old man with a bad cough."

Thankfully Mam laughed with her, but the mention of the factory was risky, as this was the main threat that Mam used.

"If you don't stick in, you'll end up at the factories," and another fate worse than death appeared to be Woolworth's.

"Get your head down to some swotting or you'll be spending all your life serving in Woollies."

This last one seemed a shame as I thought Woolworth's a most interesting store.

"Have you been to the market Mrs. Porter?"

"Aye. I've got some grand bargains. I got our Henry three new vests, you know one for in the wash, one in the drawer and one on. At least he can have a clean one on if he has an accident."

Mam nodded in agreement. It was good to know that Henry would be clean if he was killed. With each stop the bus emptied a little and it was relief when Mrs. Porter heaved her way off and we could spread out a little, even though I found it more than comfortable and warm on

Mam's chubby knees. It was also a relief to get off the bus and wander home.

Having a journey on a train was only marginally better, though steam trains held a certain excitement. The railway station at Maryport was a beautiful building and had the distinction of having only one platform. This was usually crowded not just with people but baskets of racing pigeons cuttery cooing anticipating their next race. It was a fine thrill to hear the train chuff, chuffing towards the station but as it drew closer the noise became deafening. I had no problem obeying Mam when I was told not to stand at the edge of the platform as the engines worried me. They seemed huge and unpredictable, as if there was a life lurking somewhere that could not be trusted to be friendly. They wheezed to a halt and just as I began to overcome my distrust, they belched smoke or loudly hissed steam from their sides. They also had a distinctive steam train smell which was not unpleasant, but it was there. Coal dust had settled in every crevice and the upholstered seats sent up a fine dust as people sank into them. And though they were slower than the buses I thoroughly enjoyed a ride on a train. Occasionally we had a day visiting Carlisle, and if I thought that Maryport station was busy, it was bleak in comparison to Carlisle. Trains were constantly coming and going. Enormous express trains from London to Glasgow steamed in. Trains waited while large canvas bags of post were slung into them and men could be spied inside, expertly, flicking letters into pigeonholes. Though the war had ended. National Service meant that troop trains still pulled in and lads in khaki tumbled off, nonchalantly carrying bags on their shoulders. People wandered the platforms fingering their Platform tickets and anxiously scanning the incoming trains to claim some disgorging passengers. We skittered aside while couples rushed together in long embraces, and we skirted the long queues at the newspaper stalls and snaking out from the tearooms. Halfway along one platform was a high balcony and occasionally the Station Master was seen in his black top hat pompously watching the heaving scene. It was exciting and exhilarating and added to the pleasure of visiting our city. And we did think of it as, "our city," almost as if it was only taking care of the castle and museums for all of Cumberland. From the station we always turned left and spent the day looking around the big shops, Binns, Marks and Spencer's, Jespers, and a giant Woolworth's. It was a great treat to ride in a lift or ride an escalator and then have a meal in a restaurant that was underneath a cinema. The day ended by going upstairs to the pictures and trailing tired along the still busy platforms for the slow wheezing train home.

Public transport stifled impulsiveness. Visits had to be planned around the bus and train timetables and for longer journeys, time had to be considered for standing waiting for connecting transport. Time was lost by having numerous stops to drop or collect other passengers. Time was important and there was a sinking feeling running to see the bus drawing away and knowing that there wouldn't be another one for another hour. June had little sense of punctuality and it appeared that John was little better. They kissed and cuddled just inside the front door while Mam wrung her hands in the living room.

"That lads' going to miss the last bus. He'll be walking back to Workington. Is that clock, right? Should I tell them the time Alf?"

"Leave them be. If he has to walk it might teach him a lesson," but it didn't teach him or June anything.

June gave a time to be home and then hurtled round the door an hour later.

"Sorry, the bus had gone so I had to wait for the next one."

"I'm telling you my lass, if there was a bus after the last one had gone, you'd be on it."

John had finally proposed and while they were on the miners' summer day trip to the Isle of Man had slipped an engagement ring onto Junes' eager finger. The buses and trains continued to run to their own timetables and gave no thought to two star crossed lovers. I wasn't very sure how June managed when she was away in Sunderland and no Mam to scold her, towards even a little punctuality. She always managed to be on time at the railway station to return to College with all her bags and baggage.

We didn't appear to know anyone who lived right beside a railway station or a bus stop and so there was always a long walk after the ride. If the ride was for longer visits, then the walk included carrying everything. People were often walking leaning to one side with the weight of their luggage or standing drawing breath and summoning the energy to pick up their suitcases to stagger a little further. Once, Uncle Stanley came from Manchester in his new Hillman and drove June, Mam and I to Carlisle for her to catch the train to Newcastle. I luxuriated in the privacy and I was so comfortable as the car became warmer. I was fascinated by a little orange lever that shot out from the side of the car whenever it was turning a comer and thrilled by the speed. I appreciated the convenience when we placed June's luggage into the boot of the car right at our own front door and didn't see it again until we were outside the railway station in Carlisle. Mam beckoned a porter and grandly slid a penny into his hand. There was a lot of flamboyant kissing beside the car and June was exhorted to "stick in and not so much going to see Al Martino at the Sunderland Empire and a bit more writing to us instead of that John." June graciously agreed to everything and hurried to catch the porter with her luggage.

On the return journey I had the back of the car all to myself and thought this form of travelling a wondrous thing. We hadn't got wet, our hair had not been blown hither and thither by the wind, our shoes were not muddied by the puddles and our chat remained our own. It was a splendid journey with the Lakeland fells to the left, the Scottish hills to the right and as we neared Maryport the Solway could be spied, glinting and dancing. As Uncle Stanley drove down the dim tunnel of trees that was Netherhall Road and turned into Lawson Street, I was reluctant to leave this comfortable cocoon. Mam quite reasonably pointed out that if we didn't, the neighbours would not see us alighting from a private car.

But in our daily lives, walking was the most usual manner of getting from one point to another. Walking with Mam always had a purpose and was often a route march without deviations. The longest walk was to visit her aunt who lived on the far side of the pit village, Flimby. The three-mile walk was complicated for me, as I had to wear Mam's latest creation and best shoes. I was either too cold or too hot and gradually the shoes pinched, and I felt the sting of skin rubbing off my heels. Occasionally my growing discomfort was diverted by Mam's chat.

"That's Battys' farm. Nice folk but farmers knew nothing of what we were suffering in the Depression, always something to eat on a farm, no wonder all farmers are Tories."

And in her sweeping generalisations she betrayed the uneasy relationship with the farming community that encircled the town. It was fully accepted that they worked hard, and we needed their produce but there was little affinity. There was agriculture and there was industry and we simply rubbed alongside each other from necessity. Nudging the farm fields was the towering Risehow pit bank. Thin clumps of grass were struggling on its' lower reaches and the odd coal grimed hawthorn bush growing at odd angles clung grimly. We crossed the level crossing where the small coal trains carried the coal from the pit to the docks.

"We had one of the first railways you know; it was called the Maryport and Carlisle Railway and the little train that picked up the miners was called the "Settaway." When it pulled into Aspatria the guard shouted:

"Speeyatree lowp out. That means "Aspatria jump out."

I knew, I had heard it over and over. I even knew that when we passed the tunnel running under the railway to the shore that I would be listening to the searingly sad tale of her brother Sydney.

"See that tunnel? That's the one Mother ran down to get away from Sydney. It was a time when there was hardly any money coming into the house and her sister Lizzie, kept begging and pleading for Sydney, as Lizzie had no children. Mother knew that they could give the little lad a much better life and so when he was three, she took him and left him there. But Sydney had spied her sneaking away and ran after her calling, "Dust a minute Mamma. Wait for little Sydney Mamma." Mother had put her hands over her ears and run down the tunnel to go home by the shore. She said that she would hear him sobbing and calling until the day she died."

349

And as Mother had repeatedly told me the same tale, she obviously had not forgiven herself for her defection.

"What happened after that?"

"Oh, Sydney had the best of everything there, but when he was ten, he got himself a part time job at the pit and came home."

I hurt for little Sydney suddenly left at another house and not allowed to return home. Mother had not visited him fearing a repeat performance of his pitiful cries. I wondered what he had thought when day followed day with no more contact with his large family. He must have deduced that the only way back was to be employed and money allowed him home. And yet he had grown into a fine man. Well, except for abandoning his Appleby family and bringing shame by living with the handsome Marie. It was relief in more ways than one when we reached Firth House. Old Aunt Lizzie did not live alone, her bird like brother Dick and her elephantine husband Joe also lived there. He lumbered around the house while she clucked around him as if his size offended her. He usually walked me over to help him milk the goats that he kept by the railway line across the main road. He majestically presented me with a tin cup of the warm goats' milk, and I struggled down the rich liquid knowing that I had been much favoured. Back in the house I confided in him that my tooth was aching, and he took me between his gargantuan knees.

"No problem. I have a good cure for that very thing. Now listen very carefully. When you go home tonight get your Mam to put on a pan of water and when it comes to the boil, she has to skim the fat off the top. Right, when that has cooled you roll it into little pills. Then you take one just after you've gone to sleep and one just before you wake up. You'll never have toothache again. Have you got all of that?"

I assured him that I had, and Aunt Lizzie chided him for stuffing a little girls' head with nonsense. Which I didn't think was very kind of her, as I was willing to try anything rather than go back to Danny Watsons. Mam said,

"I heard you've been banned from the "Biggest Liar Competition," Uncle Joe. What was that for?" He pulled on his pipe and looked over his glasses at Mam.

"Because I win it too many times Lass."

"You should be ashamed of yourself. Here's me upholding Flimby chapel and you sitting in the Sun Inn telling lies for free beer. Sometimes Edna, I am mortified by him."

Mam smiled at Uncle Joe.

"What was your last win then?"

He looked at her with innocent eyes.

"I only said that I had caught a fish."

"That's not a lie, you do go fishing."

"Aye but I suppose it was when I said that the Carlisle train had cut off its' tail as I was pulling the head into our house," and he slapped his large thighs and laughed. "Mind there wasn't many entries the other year and they begged me to have another go but I refused. The young lads in the pub kept on pestering me and blow me I won it again."

"Get away, what tale did you tell that time."

"I didn't. Honestly, I didn't. I just said that I couldn't enter the competition, as I didn't tell lies and blow me, they gave me the cup. Said that that was the biggest lie they had ever heard."

"Did you tell them about winning the races?"

Aunt Lizzie bristled.

"Excuse me Edna, that wouldn't be a lie and your family was always there as witness. They couldn't beat you lad at Maryport Regatta, could they?"

"You're right Aunt Lizzie, in fact I was there the year he sat in the pub drinking until the gun went off and then he ran along the pier ripping off his clothes, shouting, 'Wait on. Wait on.' He jumped off the end in just his underpants and won the race. Likely all your bulk doesn't slow you down in the water. I don't know how you put up with him Aunt Lizzie."

"Well, she does and has done for a long time now haven't you lass? And she can give back as much as she takes. Can you mind when we hadn't been married that long and we went to that wedding at Broughton? After the "do," Lizzie went home with the other women and all us young lads drank in the pub till we noticed it was a full moon that night. So, we decided to take off our clothes and have a swim in the Derwent. When I came out, some wag had gone off with all my clothes. There was nothing for it but to walk home stark naked. When Lizzie opened the door she just stood and said, 'Eeh, lad that's nut, the suit you went out in.' I tell you, many a wife would have gone mad."

"Oh, stop your blethering, here take this bowl and you and little Edna go and get some strawberries for them to take home after they've eaten this tea, and mind her fancy dress."

He lifted me from his corduroyed knees, and we wandered to the back garden for him to fill the bowl and my mouth with the sweet, sour strawberries.

"Go for the little ones Lass, they are often sweeter, and when you get home put a little pepper on to bring out the flavour. When you've swallowed that one say after me, 'Ifacka, lacka, hadacka gunacka, laeka woudacka shootacka yonacka birdacka onacka yonacka treeacka."

I squelched the delicious strawberries in my mouth while I practised it over and over and thought Uncle Joe Bishop great fun. I wondered why Sydney had not wanted to remain living with them; maybe it just wasn't home to him.

Limping the miles back to Maryport and clutching my bowl of strawberries in a brown paper bag, I recited my new poem to Mam.

"Oh, the man is daft, but he's certainly a character."

It seemed that we had a lot of those in the family.

The only other walking that I remember going with Mam was shopping and though it did not involve skinned heels it was fraught with its' own peculiar dangers. There was almost as much grooming before setting out as when we visited relatives for tea. Even shopping could be a minefield of how one should be seen and behave in public. Mam scorned the women that did a big shop for the weekend,

"Look at them. Nothing but beasts of burden. And men call themselves the stronger sex. Let them try carrying weeks' groceries. They don't know what it feels like."

I don't know how she knew either, as she only ever went out of absolute necessity for one or two items. Otherwise we staggered like beasts of burden for her. I spent a lot of time studying dead eyed fish in Palmers wet fish shop or counting the pyramids of tins in Liptons while she chatted to friends and relations.

"Hello Billy and John Musgrave and how are you two? Alf said that you were at the doctors the other night, is it that leg?"

"No, I've a funny lump on my neck". John nudged Mam,

"I could have saved him the trouble of a visit, that lumps' called his head."

"Oh, get away with you, you daft beggars. But you could both do with a bit more weight on."

"Greyhound breed that's us Aunt Edna. We may not be fat but we're very virile. In fact, Billy offered to show Alice his virility last night and she hit him. Some women just have dirty minds."

"Aye and I'm not as green as I'm cabbage looking. Our Lizzie would be mad if she heard you talking like that. It's time you were a bit more mature."

"Listen Edna, the only mature thing about our Billy is his socks."

And the two brothers wandered off up the street laughing. Mam was obviously very fond of them but not so her in laws. If she saw them approaching, she tried to make detours but as it was such a small town that she was often thwarted.

"Cooee. Aunt Edna. How are you my dear?"

"Fine thank you and yourself?"

"Wonderful. Never down. It doesn't do does it? Have you heard, I'm joining my husband on his ship and we will be crossing the equator."

"Very nice Gwen, and who will be caring for your children while you are away?"

The possible direct hit was wasted.

"Mummy and Daddy of course. Must fly. Take care."

I don't know why Mam bothered and she walked on muttering,

"I tell you, you couldn't dint that one with a pick. Not backward in coming forward."

It was very perplexing. I liked Gwen and her cheery outlook on life and, like Mam, was only trying to improve herself and her status in life.

"Get in this shop, here comes Mother Croft."

Too late, we were accosted by my grandmother carrying her large basket on one arm and a roll of carpet under the other.

"Hang on Edna, I'm glad I've caught you. I'm just on my way down to Lawson Street with this bit of carpet for you."

Mam stiffened,

"Thank you but I have sufficient carpets."

"In that case I'll just put in round your back door and if you don't want it, I'll have it back some time. I've just been cleaning the Baptist church for a wedding. Glamour for a day, that's what I call it. Glamour for a day. What are you doing you dirty little girl?"

I had grown so bored that I had decided to enliven just standing while they talked, by picking my nose. She thrust her gaunt face into mine,

"Don't you know that when that stuff gets down to your stomach it turns into worms."

Worms! Whaah. I couldn't actually feel them but now my innards sounded like Fathers' compost heap with all the worms wriggling together for warmth. Trust a grown up to spoil a simple pastime."

357

She straightened,

"As I said I'll chuck this in the yard. Look after that lad of mine."

She strode off with her basket full of detritus and a white loaf balanced on top.

"God knows where that carpet has come from. What do I want with other peoples' left-tovers. The woman has such a cheek. And as for you, letting the side down. I know people have skeletons in their cupboards but mine will come out and jangle. Just keep your fingers out of there in future."

No fear. Mother Crofts' methods were simple and effective, I certainly didn't want any bogey transformations in my stomach, however boring the shopping. I did a lot of just standing while others talked and it was rare if they spoke to me and if they did, it was the usual litany.

"And what do you want to be when you are grown up?"

How lovely it would have been to have answered,

"How do I frigging know, I'm a little girl?" But I didn't need to say anything, as Mam always answered for me,

"She would like to be a teacher wouldn't you Pet?"

Would I? I hadn't even thought about it, but I nodded agreement. The future was far away, and the choices were simple anyway. If you didn't pass the eleven plus you went to the factories or Woolworth's. If you did pass the eleven plus and proved to be average at the Grammar School, you became a secretary or a nurse. If you did quite well at the Grammar School, then you went to College and came back a teacher or a doctor. Somewhere in among all of this you got married and had some children. Simple. The latter seemed very important as an invisible certificate of success in society. The women who didn't marry were considered to have failed somehow and various reasons had to be found for their single state. Often parents took the blame for being too interfering, too particular, or needing their daughters' money or care, or both. Some were pitied as their intended husbands had been killed in one of the wars, or they had been jilted at the altar. Whatever the reason, they had failed to join the club and were different. It was not even considered that they may have chosen to remain unmarried, no one in their right minds would choose such a lonely state. It was assumed that they must be lonely as many areas were closed for them, even areas of conversation. As few ran their own houses and continued to live with ageing parents, then there was little point in chatting about household matters. There was little point in talking about children as they could not possibly understand, or it may be cruel to remind them that they had not fulfilled their biological purpose. And of course, intimate matters could not be alluded to in front of them because it was assumed, they could not know of such things. They were big children who had never flown the nest. I knew that I must not disappoint. Somehow, I had to get married even if I did not attain the dizzying heights of being a teacher. I could not be excluded, and I certainly did not want to be pitied. I wasn't very sure how I would join the majority and for now I was more worried about the regular Friday school tests.

CHAPTER 13
"BALM OF HURT MINDS"

I knew now that as I entered the classroom, I was not a person, particularly a person with emotions. I was not required to have opinions or display originality. As I sat down, this invisible funnel appeared on the top of my red head. It was the teachers' job to pour facts down the funnel and it was my job to regurgitate them. I had worked it out. If you just sat there and didn't make any waves, then you were a good girl. If you just sat there and didn't make any waves and occasionally churned back the facts, then you were a good and clever girl. If you just sat there and didn't make any waves, churned back the facts and added clairvoyance then you were a good and brilliant girl. If you could read the teachers' mind and churn back the very answer that they wanted, that really specific and precise answer then you were practically top of the class. Of course, not the absolute top of the class, that was always the preserve of a boy. We were told that boys were good at Maths and Science and girls were good at the Arts. The tests administered each Friday were dependent on logic, one-word answers and a plethora of Maths. Each Monday some shuffled round according to the results. Pam and I didn't do much shuffling; we stayed on the table next to the top table. Once I was surprised to hear my name called to move up and sit at the top table, but the previous Friday a spelling test had been added and a section called, "Composition." Likely my composed piece had deposed one of the

Franks and for a whole week I sat uncomfortably among the boys. Normality was resumed when the next Monday came and I had proved wanting when working out how long it took ten men carry a bucket of water, ten miles to fill a bath. I was told that I had fallen at the first fence by forgetting that the bath needed a plug. I was exhorted to learn to read questions with more care but instead felt that the adults had in some way tricked me with their daft questions.

I had moved into the calmer waters of male teachers who did not seem to have to assert their authority with aggression. Either that or Annie had softened us up for them. She could lose her temper magnificently and suddenly erupted. She pushed her way through the desks with her fists prepared. To add to the pain, she pushed the knuckle of her longest finger forward and hammered it into the back of whoever had enraged her. Usually I sat staring ahead wincing and listening to the thuds and cries or I sneaked a look and watched with horrified fascination and silent sympathy. Then the small criminal that had been singled out for the knuckled fist had to stand at the front with his back to the class. There he stood snivelling and wiping his tears and snot on his sleeve. It was always boys that received this special enlightenment but the fear that she may spread her favours was a wonderful spur to be obedient. Her method of destroying the few, ensured the subservience of the many. It was difficult to gauge what disturbed her but talking in class; not understanding or being generally thick were the main sins. Only once did I feel her wrath.

Annie had a wonderful machine clamped to her desk that sharpened pencils and she whirred the handle until it had a point that would spear the toughest steak. She and she alone was in charge of it and one day I asked if she would sharpen my blunt pencil. She returned it with a flourish and as I pressed it on my exercise book the point flew across the room. Before I could say, "Annie Robinson," she brought a ruler down on my hand. Whap! I was given a lecture on wastefulness and economy as my fingers burned and my face reddened. But by now I had learned. Unlike my first day at school, I now knew that they had some strange right to physically abuse the children in their care. In fact, education had elevated it by giving it a name. Some pupils took a peculiar pride in "Corporal Punishment," and slid past the desks slyly showing the weals on their hands and refusing to cry. It became a measure of how much they could stoically endure. This time I didn't hurry home to report the incident even though I was confident that Mam could verbally lambast a dozen Annie Robinsons. It simply wasn't worth the long-term taunting and mocking from the adults in school that resulted from any defence from home. There was no defence or protection just the hope that the next teacher used gentler methods of ensuring discipline.

"Mam my new teacher, Mr. Penn isn't half good..."

"Oh, so he is half bad?"

"Err. No. I meant he's good."

363

"In that case you must say so and not that you only half like something or someone."

She frequently interrupted with corrections making a tale disjointed and eventually hardly worth the effort.

"Then he took us into the Hall to sing, "Hearts of Oak" and "Barbara Allen," it was dead good you know......"

"No, I don't know."

"Pardon?"

"You said, 'you know', was that necessary?"

"Err no. Anyway, he said we had to lift our heads up."

"Please don't put a preposition at the end."

Grrr.

It was very disconcerting.

Well, Mr. Penn wasn't half good, you know. Not only did he introduce us to rousing folk songs but took us out of school for, "Nature walks." This was so unusual and enjoyable that I promptly remembered all the facts that he gave when he gathered us around him. Otherwise lessons continued as before but without the heart stopping fear.

I didn't understand why the school year began in September and the real year began in January. Mine was not to reason why, mine was but to attend and comply. Much was made of attending school and absences were queried and noted with pointed comments. Some received certificates in Assembly for not missing a day. I was never awarded one. Mam bustled me out to school in all weathers and in all states. I got up and vomited in the toilet and she washed my face and shoved me out of the door. I coughed and coughed all night and my eyes and nose streamed. She gave me a large handkerchief and some Victory V, tablets to suck and I sniffled my way up the hill. Attendance at school was very important. It was very important until she decided that I was needed to accompany her somewhere. If I squeaked that the teachers would be cross, she bristled.

"Excuse me, you are my daughter and I will decide what you do with your day. "We've been invited to Auntie Bessie's' at Fletchertown for tea and I can't go at the weekend.' If anything is said to you just you tell them that."

Oh.

I would not have dared, instead I stood and listened to lectures on the benefits of education and that even one day off meant that I must have missed, "something." I didn't feel that I had missed anything, having had a wonderful day with my gentle and jolly Auntie Bessie. I had enormous fun with her two children Margaret and Jim, roaming the country lanes and we returned for tinned salmon sandwiches and homemade cakes. It was always the same tea and as she set us to the bus in the evening, she always wailed that she had forgotten the jelly setting in the washhouse. When the teacher admonished me the next day, I was not in the least remorseful but assumed a humble pose. Mam stuck to her resolve not to take me to the dentist ever again but as I grew, I had the distinction of having another set of teeth growing behind my front top teeth. Danny Watson decided that the front ones had to be removed so that the others would move forwards. Mary told me that I hadn't to think about it. I had to live in the, "now." Now I was simply sitting in the waiting room. It hadn't happened just yet. But now I knew what was happening behind that door and that soon I would be sitting vulnerable and being gassed. I was terrified. This time Mary carried me home and tucked me up on the couch. Mam was nowhere to be seen but had left a note telling us that it would be too upsetting to see me in post dentist state and so she had gone over to her mothers. Mary cast her eyes to the heavens and Mrs. Routledge sympathised saying that her Albert had just had all his teeth distracted. Having so many teeth out merited two days off school and blew my chances of a certificate for that term. On the second day Dad walked me to Annovazzis' for an ice cream to freeze my mouth which I thought a much better remedy than Mary's' boiled water and salt swished around it. Returning to school I was accosted by Annie. "I believe you were seen wandering around the town eating ice cream when you should have been in school. Have you any explanation girl?"

I lowered the volumous scarf that Mary had wrapped around my face and flashed my toothless state.

"I've had thicks teeth out Mith."

She told me not to be such a dirty girl and hurried away. There was just no hiding place in that little town.

Teeth enlivened many a boring lesson. When they were only slightly loose, that became the preoccupation of the day. Back, forward, back forward and then a little tearing sound. Not ready yet, but there was the added promise of the Tooth Fairy when it did eventually give up its' moorings. Scabs were much the same and sitting cross-legged in Assembly brought a scabby knee into focus. The time could go quite quickly pick, pick, picking though sadly there wasn't a Scab Fairy. We were told that a scab was God's sticking plaster and if we picked it off all manner of disease would sneak into the open wound. They just didn't understand or remember how tempting the activity was when bored. The big scarf around my mouth was a trial. Mary said that I had to wear it when I was outside, or I would get neuralgia. At breaktime Tanis tried to tie it in a lumpen knot and by lunchtime I gave it up and chanced catching even oldralgia. Teachers didn't do clothes or anything else that brought them into physical contact with pupils. Many children ran about with buttons or ribbons flying in the wind and boys were castigated for not having their shoelaces tied. They did not seem to be a dextrous as girls and took much longer to fathom the mysteries of fastenings. If they were clever boys then it was assumed that they were too otherworldly and if they were not very bright then they were told that they were lazy. They may also have been exhorted to learn to do it themselves, as it was very possible that their shoelaces had spent time soaking in the bottom of the latrines. The fashion for windcheaters meant that the bottom of the long zip was dangerously near an unmentionable part of their anatomy and a teacher may not want to be fumbling about in that area to help him fasten it. Whatever the reasons there was no help offered which meant touching. I hated it when the Nit nurse came, which she did with regularity. We were summoned to sit on a chair while she searched our hair. To do this, one of my long plaits was loosened and after she had scrabbled about, I was told to return to the classroom. I never did master plaiting my own hair and unless a friend tried, I had to go through the day with one neat plait and the other like a shawl on one shoulder. Even though I didn't get a letter to go to the Clinic for free nit shampoo I dreaded her visits and feeling silly for the rest of the day.

Mam continued to refuse to allow me to be vaccinated, so when the other children were dismally trooping off to be stabbed in the shoulder, I sat alone in the classroom smugly reading. Though I did rather regret not being able to whinge about the pain or having the beautiful scab that erupted after a few days. The only advantage to these visits was that they made a change to the normal routine. The school day was predictable with numeracy and literacy all morning and what were considered more frivolous subjects, such as Art and Music relegated to the afternoons. In among this the bell rang and we were told to go out to play and the miracle was that we did. The adults had magnanimously provided a large rectangle of tarmac for this very purpose. We trooped out in all weathers and for fifteen whole minutes we whirled about like headless chickens amusing ourselves on the hard, black, unyielding surface. The teachers "on duty," invariably stood sheltering by the doorways to the school, looking hunched and pinched and clasping their cups of tea. We had to cease whatever we were doing just as suddenly when the bell rang again.

"Get in line. Now!"

"Miss, Miss he's pushed in."

"I was there Miss and now he's in front of me. Miss."

"That's it. To the back."

I never knew why that was delivered as a threat. This was no Butlins that we were about to enter. Even more shocking were the children who found difficulty switching off the play mode. Oh, the sin of being "over there," after the bell had gone.

"You there, go and tell those boys to come now and I mean now."

We all stood freezing while the line sinners were herded into submission. There was an unspoken desire to make us all suffer for the transgressions of the few.

It was a relief when there was the longer break for lunchtime. It was probably an even bigger break for the children who sat at the back, as few of them seemed to have breakfast. Their blood sugar level must have been so low by late morning that they couldn't assimilate knowledge even if they'd been a budding Einstein. No one ever asked when or what we had eaten or appeared to connect this with poor concentration. There was more concern given to telling us to use the toilet and wash our hands before queuing for the dinner hall. Once inside there had to be silence and then,

"Hands together eyes closed."

All together we recited,

"For what we are about to receive may the Lord make us truly thankful. Amen."

Much relieved scraping of chairs to sit and wait to be called to the hatch. These were no snack meals. It was said that there was a dietician in Adelaide Street in Carlisle who worked out the nutrition needs of children for a week. The meals were planned around this and sent to the school canteen cooks. Two solid courses. Whallop! I didn't have any problem with school dinners, I quite liked them. As Alice Musgrave was a dinner lady, she often let the ladle slip and my Chocolate Crispy was swimming in custard. I didn't complain and staggered out to the rectangle of tarmac weighed down with food. Gradually we drew away from playing with boys. I was becoming bored with being allowed to be a Desert Rat while the boys had to be Rommel or Monty. The lads still played at giving, "Jerry," another thumping and wheeled about in their mock leather flying hats like some demented Biggies. Anyway, war women were usually drippy and just stayed at home watching the skies for Quentin to come home from his mission. I still liked George and felt like a defector when I hurried away to join the girls but now you had to be careful. More and more some were saying,

"You go with him."

"I don't. I just like him."

"Same thing."

"Tis not."

"And anyway, you do go with him cos we saw you get behind him in the line the other day."

Proof if proof were needed of undying love.

371

We were moving away from having boys as friends and developing an embryonic interest in them as boyfriends. Their interests were less interesting and yet we courted their attention. While hotly denying any relationship, however naive, I knew who were the handsome lads and wanted to be popular. There was an instinctive knowledge that this was not quite the time, but we were moving towards it and testing. We were practising approaching the opposite sex with crude little notes slithered across the desks and persuading friends into asking,

"Jimmy wants to know if you go with him" and then the simpering,

"Maybe."

Nothing much at all happened for a few days after that until the devastating message.

"Jimmy says to tell you he's chucked you."

How mortifying. I was so mortified, and heart-broken, that I shrugged my shoulders and rushed out to play "Tiggy," with the girls. Life was too full, and I could not think of these sallies towards and away from the boys with any seriousness. It just added a certain frisson to the school day. And if the school day was reasonably predictable this only added to the feeling of stability in our young lives. In the Primary school we were not given a timetable but like blotting paper somehow absorbed what each day would bring. One period that always gave me pleasure was when the teacher told us to get out a book and read quietly while he marked our work or wrote the end of term reports. I didn't mind if it was some instructive non-fiction book, I just loved books. Not just reading them but the feel and the smell, especially the smell of leather books. I even enjoyed the act of reading, working out the larger words and the pronunciation of others. I was amused when I realised my mistakes and for some time read "misled," as "mizzled" and one day it dawned on me that he had pursed his lips and had not pursued them. Some fragments of sentences confused me. How on earth "all the ladies hung on his lips," I wasn't very sure and felt it must have been quite painful. But all the time I was refining my ability to decipher and decode the words and their meaning. It was small wonder that reading was a favourite pastime. Books were all around me and always had been. Probably the pram that Mary struggled from Grasslot to Curzon Street had books wedged between the pots and pans. The whole family read and not just as a private activity they talked and discussed them. They recounted various passages and recommended them to each other. They passed them around, bought books as presents and everyone belonged to the Library. Uncle George was forever telling everyone to read, "And Quiet Flows the Don," and, "The Ragged Trousered Philanthropist." Romance books were scorned and only used as a last resort by everyone and the Classics were much revered. Letters were the main line of communication and newspapers were read from front to back and then articles of interest read aloud. Our newspaper was the "News Chronicle," but Mam said that if Mary and June were asked in an interview, they had to say that we "took the Manchester Guardian and The Observer." She did buy these occasionally, but she also occasionally bought "The Morning Star." Some newspapers were not allowed in the house and I remember sneaking a look at "The News of the World," when I was at Auntie Lizzies.' There were lurid pictures of girls in bikinis and horrid pictures of rabbits dying from myxamatosis. I wasn't tempted to look again. Comics were banned. Mam said that the pictures would stunt my imagination and so I became a comic junky. At every opportunity I voraciously read the antics of Lord Snooty, Desperate Dan and Beryl the Peril at friends' houses. I read Donald Almonds' weekly, "Eagle," and thrilled to the exploits of Dan Dare and the Mekon. I knew the exact day that Topper and Beezer were delivered to Pam's' house and often ran around with her at lunchtime to take turns to read them before the bell rang to return to school. Occasionally Mary or June bought me "Radio Fun," and we all laughed at the cartoons of June Whitfield, Tommy Cooper and Jimmy Edwards. Then, in a commendable show of defiance, June marched to the Newsagents and ordered the comic "Mickey Mouse" to be delivered for me. Mam conceded defeat, as she did not have to pay for it. I eagerly awaited its' arrival each week and felt a sense of disappointment when I had devoured all the pictures and pages. In my bedroom I had a shelf for my own books that I had received as prizes or gifts and I was fond of them. "Stripy the Zebra," Randolph the Bear Who Said 'No," "Little

Black Sambo," and Epaminondas." I laughed and laughed at his scrapes and the way that he interpreted instructions literally. I had no sense of that this was connected to his colour, I would have laughed had he been a white boy. Sometimes the women around me, read me stories. When I was ill enough to merit staying in bed with the little bedroom fire glowing Mam read to me.

Hmm.

Her choices were the books that she had known as a child and more often than not, left me with night terrors or a candidate for a lifetime of depression. She solemnly read aloud, "The Little Match Girl," who turned out to be dead. This was followed by, "The Water Babies," another one who turned out to be dead. Then, "Grimm's Fairy Tales."

Grim?

I was terrified!

Mam read the story, then closed the book and wished me, "Good night and God Bless" and left me twitching about someone wearing a cloak of nettles and witches who ate motherless children. Just as I was returning to reality she produced, "Alice in Wonderland" and read this as a serial. I hated it and wished that Dodgson had stuck with his Maths instead. It was too silly, too fanciful and too potty. Someone going down a rabbit hole and meeting a dreadful Queen among other weird characters. And the cringe worthy Tweedledum and Tweedledee. I listened to, "Twas brillig in the slimey toves," and thought it was rubbish. Of course, I couldn't say so as Mam had already played the guilt card. She had given up cleaning and cooking just to read to me and so I sat and suffered.

One evening she came around my bedroom door with a very old book and sat on the edge of the bed.

"This is the first full book that I ever read. I found it on Mothers' attic. I thought it was wonderful then and I think I always will. I'll enjoy reading this to you."

She pronounced it, "Don Kwix Oat," and I listened baffled by the old man tilting at imaginary windmills and cared for by Sancho Panza. I thought it was very sad and could not understand what she found so amusing. But I knew that this was something special for her and enjoyed the intimacy of the activity.

June rescued me when she worked at the Library and brought me books by Beatrix Potter and Alison Uttley. I loved, "The Little Grey Rabbit," stories and lay in bed turning the pictures to the light to peruse the detail. I was so impressed that they had imagined a flower as an animal's hat or umbrella, and it encouraged me to view the natural world with more imagination.

As I grew a little older my tastes changed and I devoured, "The Famous Five" stories. I thought that George was the best and Ann very drippy and wet. These were adventures with more depth and the baddies were very bad and the goodies were terribly middle class. When June brought me, "Five Go Off in a Caravan," Dad looked at it and said,

"Why? How long had they been there?"

Very funny Dad.

Woolworth's had begun selling the Classics for half a crown each and Auntie May sent me them with regularity. Now a whole new world opened up with "Treasure Island," "Kidnapped," Coral Island," and "King Solomon's' Mines." With each book, I delayed beginning reading for a little while, savouring what was to come; I looked at the picture on the dust cover and opened it to smell its newness. Once I had begun reading it was a trial to put it down to go to school or go to sleep. If I read while the adults talked, Mams' passion for reading worked in my favour. Aunt Evelyn made pointed comments about how very rude I was, but Mam defended me,

"Dear God, the little lass has to do something and better that than trailing the streets."

Then sometimes, when she was annoyed about this or that, she shoved me out saying,

"You've always got your nose stuck in a book, away out for some fresh air."

"It's raining."

"Well, you're not made of sugar, you won't melt."

Which was true.

I dutifully played out for a little while, but part of my mind was wondering what was happening to 'Heidi' or, 'Heidi's' Children.'

"Mam, can I come back in? It's that sort of rain that soaks in." And soon I was back in Switzerland helping Peter and Heidi take the goats up to their summer pastures. I read whenever and wherever I could, and the adults provided a regular supply. Mary had begun a little tradition of bringing me a new book every time she came home from College and thankfully did not collide with Auntie Mays' contributions. Mam did not encourage American stories and I ploughed my way through "Little Women," "Jo's Boys" and "What Katy Did," to the accompaniment of scornful sniffs and pointed comments which often included words such as "brainwashing," and "piffle," Now, when we went to the Chapel jumble sales I squandered my pocket money on more books and read about "Dimsy of the Third" then "Dimsy of the Fourth". These made boarding schools sound terribly exciting with jolly japes and midnight feasts in the dorm. She played a lot of lacrosse and I assumed this was a posh form of hockey as I had never heard of it and neither had anyone else when I asked them. Occasionally I wished that I could somehow be packed off on the train to a school far away, tearfully waving my little white handkerchief to my family sobbing on the one platform at Maryport station. Of course, they would miss me dreadfully and send me wonderful parcels of, "tuck" that I could share with all the other girls. There wasn't any actual evidence that this last one would happen as Mam didn't send Mary or June parcels while they were at College just reams of letters bemoaning her lot and the loss of their earnings. Anyway, I already knew that I would have missed them all too much and a parcel of home-made fruitcake and sticky buns would not have compensated. Instead I curled up on the couch and read about another way of life while Dad rolled the romantic chords of Rachmaninov and the others talked around me.

Now Mary was working at Flimby school and did not live with Mother Tuke totally. She had to come home frequently not just to have a proper bath but to answer Mams' summons to help with housework or collecting rents. Mothers' large family still came to stay with her and then Mary was released to sleep at home in her own bed. Many of these collided with June's long holidays and we were all together again making it difficult to become completely absorbed in any book.

"Mam, will this do?"

Mam looked Mary up and down.

"I suppose it's clean."

379

"No, seriously. Does it look right on me?"

"Aye well, a blind man on a galloping horse won't notice."

"What's wrong with it?"

"Maybe a scarf would help."

"What round my neck, waist, head, what?"

"Try your face."

"Cheek. Pass me that perfume."

"Oh, and who was your last servant."

"You and I paid you well."

Psst. Psst.

"Phew. Something is rotten in the state of Denmark."

"Mam that's the new, "Californian Poppy." It's a lovely smell. I got some of that new Max Factor Pan Stick when I was in Briggs chemist the other day; do you want to try it? Oh, and no more boot polish for mascara, just look at this dinky little box."

Mary produced a small turquoise rectangle and when she flipped it open there was a tiny brush that she expertly scrubbed across a strip of black and applied to her lashes. "Honestly you've more money than sense. Soap and water was all we had and your Dad still courted me, didn't you lad?"

"I did that. Just a minute, I hope you're not putting that cascara on you."

Mary assured him that she was not.

"Are you three going to the pictures tonight?"

"When your Dad's had his supper."

"You'll like it. Richard Burton. Jean Simmons and Victor Mature in, "The Robe." I won't tell you how it ends."

"Will you two stop blethering, I'm hungry. Woman put the smell on the table."

Mam scurried off to the kitchen. Mary waved and her taffeta dance dress rustled off down the hall. I suffered Caligula being everything evil and marvelled at the power of Jesus' robe and on the way home listened to Mam and Dad having a very interesting discussion. We were going to have a, "function." In fact, so much so that Mam was going to hire the Coop Function room.

"When she's gone out tomorrow, I'll away round to the Coop and book it and then I'll go to Studholmes and order a cake. What do you think?"

"Sounds grand to me. See if you have time to go to Williamsons' and get some proper invitation cards and one of them big silver keys for everyone to sign on the night. When we get home, we'll make a list and then we'll know how many cards to buy."

"That's a bit much. I could just send letters."

"No expense spared Edna, she's our eldest. Have you thought of a present?"

"I thought of twenty-one pounds. You know, one to mark every year."

"If you can get that much gathered together by then, that would be a nice idea. You know that chap I have to ring each week to check on accidents a Naval Armaments Depot for the doctors? He's an "Entertainer," so I might ask him if he'd oblige. I mean I don't want to be playing at my own girls party."

"That's true, you should just be enjoying it. And you keep your mouth shut until we tell her Edna."

I wondered how I was going to eat but Mam told me to stop trying to be funny.

The invitations were sent out to all the family and friends that Mam chose to be invited. Presents began to arrive and seemed to be mainly household items like fancy jam dishes and packs of towels. I thought they were pretty uninteresting, but Mary was highly delighted and stated that they were for her bottom drawer. As she did not have a steady boyfriend Mam said that it was more like a hope chest. The twenty-one pounds still had not accumulated as the birthday drew near so Mary played safe and chose herself a red suit on Mam's Coop book. Mam didn't mind as going out and choosing gifts was not one of her attributes. On the actual day, telegrams and bouquets of flowers arrived and were displayed in the sitting room. Mam and Mrs Routledge had worked until the whole house was unusually tidy and all the gifts that had so far been opened were carefully placed on Mam's perfectly made bed, envelope corners of course. People came and went, drinking tea and trooping upstairs to view the gifts and Mam murmured to Dad,

"If that beggar's late for this special occasion, I'll flatten her."

June retained her shapely figure. She quietly opened the door just as we were trying to get some lunch. Her pretty little face was beaming. Mary squealed with delight and they hugged and hugged each other.

"Oh, what a surprise. Mam never said. Nobody said. This is brilliant. How did you manage it? It just wouldn't have been right without you. I was wishing and wishing you could be here. This is just perfect."

Mam nudged Dad and he smiled and shook his head.

Although we all seemed to be getting ready at the same time, Mam said that Mary had to come later to make a grand entrance like they did in the films. So, Mary and I walked round to the Coop in the dark November evening after the others had gone. Oh, but it was magical. The room was full of people, there were balloons floating and coloured crepe paper around the lights. As Mary entered everyone threw streamers and sang "Twenty-One Today." It seemed that all the family had come, even cousins John and Kenneth had zoomed up from Appleby on John's motorbike with their mother rammed into the sidecar. Mam had magnanimously invited a few of her in laws and it was good to see them all mingling. Uncle Stanley had spent quite a lot of time being a taxi ferrying family to the Coop and was still missing when Mary and I arrived. Though Mary was definitely the star of the evening there was another surprise to come. Auntie May came puffing up the stairs carefully guiding Mother Tuke. This really set the seal on the function as a very important birthday. When the old lady came around the door the surprise and pleasure was tangible.

"Right Alf. Now that Mother is here, I think you should announce the buffet open."

Dad rattled on the table with a spoon.

"Let's have a bit of hush please."

To everyone's surprise, especially Mam, Dad stood up and made a speech. He praised Mary as I had never heard, he spoke of his love for her without embarrassment; he stated that she had been a fine daughter and that he was so proud of her achievements.

"And I wish you all health and happiness for the future, my eldest. Everyone charge your glasses and be upstanding for Mary."

We all stood with our glasses of sherry while gentle tears slid down Mary's face and then there was a calm lull while we all did justice to the buffet. Cold collation of course.

Aunt Evelyn leaned close to Auntie Lizzie,

"Fine speech but a shame she's not spoken for. I nearly bought her a cat and a canary instead of those nice sheets off Barnsley market. Fancy, twenty-one and still nowhere near married. Leaving it a bit late if you ask me."

"Nobody's asking you. Maybe she's better off as she is."

"Get away, who's going to keep her company in her old age and if she doesn't have children who's going to look after her? "

385

"I can't say our Bill's much company and both him and your Jack are just waiting till they can leave here to go for a proper drink. The lass has plenty time and she wasn't behind the door when looks were given out. They say there's a Jack for every Jill and maybe hers' is just around the comer."

"Oh, she's a looker all right but our Edna stuffing them with all this knowledge and qualifications can't be helping, A man won't want a wife better than him so it narrows the field a bit and that must worry her."

Mary didn't look at all worried by her single state. She was too busy dancing with Malcolm, who had arrived looking very dashing in his air force uniform. He had cast a few wistful glances at June, but she was too busy clinging onto John's arm and showing everyone her ring. Soon the company gravitated into men over there and women drinking tea together while I ran around batting balloons and playing with my cousins' children.

Uncle Sydney stood with the men,

"It's grand to see Mother out and enjoying the company. She's been sad enough about Father and Uncle Joe Stalin dying. I'm glad Father didn't live to see that day. I hope they can keep as tight a rein on the country. I mean it was an achievement to feed them all in Russia, no matter how he did it."

"That's true. Same with China. Look what they've achieved by all pulling together. America must be really sweating, in fact that's all this war in Korea is for. Capitalism versus Communism. Just a shame our lads are involved. By the way, where's Marie?"

"Sh. I've left her over at Mothers'. At least John and Kenneth have passed the time of day with me, but it was a relief that they didn't ask where she was. I can't wait to get out of the same room as May. She probably came just to make me feel uncomfortable, which is a bit of a cheek as I've paid enough over the years. That's right Edna fill up my glass."

Mam poured the sherry and looked hard at him.

"What do you mean you've paid enough? Anybody can send money but who was there if they coughed in the night? Was there anybody there to give May a break now and then. A lad needs a father around for all sorts of things."

"Oh, give over on a nice night like this. They got grown up, didn't they? It's a man's job to put food on the table and I've done that. You didn't have to live with her. I can tell you now, what they are going to have on the table tomorrow. If it was Tatie Pot on Monday it was Tatie Pot next Monday and so on. I once made the mistake of saying I quite liked tomatoes and that's what I got, every blooming day. By Friday I couldn't face them anymore and she just kept shouting that I'd said I liked them. No

387

wonder I moved down South, and I could hardly take the lads with me, could I?"

Mam conceded this point but was not to be completely outdone.

"I don't know why you had to go so far. You didn't have to move to that part of the country. What with all that smog killing people and those terrible floods on the East coast. I saw it on the News at the pictures. Poor folk rowing around the streets in boats. At least we have nothing like that and plenty good clean air."

To move completely out of Cumberland was always incomprehensible and to want to do so was unforgivable.

Gradually, and some a little sheepishly, most of the men drifted away to try to catch the Labour Club before closing time. The Entertainer wished everyone well and astounded Mam and Dad by refusing any pay for his services. It had been a magical evening for me, full of gaiety. I had sipped sherry from numerous glasses and John and Malcolm had whirled me round in their arms on the dance floor. I was comfortable with all who were there and enjoyed playing with so many other children. I knew that Mam was very pleased with Dad and we would hear of his speech repeatedly. I also knew that it was a feather in Mary's' cap that Mother had left her house to be there. Mary had been a star for a night even without a man to keep her company in her old age. It had been a proper function, and everyone was agreed that Mam had "done her proud."

On the Sunday after the function Auntie May came over to Lawson Street and brought me a new volume of "Swallows and Amazons."

"I had it with me in the Coop, but I couldn't give you it as all the others were there and I hadn't anything for them. Anyway, they wouldn't have appreciated it like you Petal."

"Well, Edna, a good do eh?"

Mam banged the teapot down and returned to the kitchen.

"Still miffed because I beat her to buying that blue dress for your party I think."

Mary smiled.

"You'll just have to put up with the Wagnerian dramatics like we do for a while."

Auntie May called,

"I was wondering if anyone wanted a walk round the shops. Do a bit of window shopping and pretend we have money eh?"

This was too tempting for Mam.

"I'll come but I'll be careful what I admire, or I'll find it on your back instead of mine come Monday."

"How was I to know you wanted the same dress for Mary's' party? I'm not clairvoyant like our Evelyn and anyway if we don't hurry, she'll be coming over here and we'll have to take her with us. Anybody else coming?"

Dad declined saying that he was too full of Sunday lunch and was going to lie down for the afternoon. Mary and June reached for their coats and Mam bustled me into mine while I protested that I wanted to read my new book.

If it wasn't pouring down, window-shopping was a pastime that whiled away a few hours. As a small town the shops used their windows to woo and inform. The displays were changed frequently and some used imagination and flair making it worth the wander. There were three "walk around" stores, Woolworth, the Coop and Graves but the other shops had their own separate identity and in consequence had to compete with each other for customers. It was thought very poor spirited for the same display to be there longer than two weeks. Rather like Mam insisting on, "Tide," some people gave their loyalties to one particular Butcher or Grocer and so they often closed their windows with a sun blind or simply placed a coy model lamb in the window and that was that. The dress shops were more competitive and there were long pauses while there was much studying and commenting. There was only one Milliner, but Miss Nixon's' window always merited a long stand to study the gorgeous creations towering above the tea cosy and pork pie hats. This was no ordinary hat shop and I thought Miss Nixon a true lady. She was tall and slender with whisping grey hair and a gentle voice. Though she also made hats, "to order," I was not aware that she eventually went mad.

Auntie May peered into the large window.

"I don't know how she carries stock like that in such a small place,"

"I do, she has an arrangement with another Milliners in Carlisle and each month they swap their displays. You know, the one by the Cumberland Bus Station."

"Is that a fact? Would you look at that? Just a few long feathers draped like an Alice band. Hardly seems worth it."

"I like it. It's a Norman Hartnell style. I think he designs for the Queen Mother."

"They reckon all the top designers were keeping their heads down in case she picked them. They do say that she never pays a bill."

"Go on, and them with all that money. I'd like to see us get away with it. Our names would be in the shop window after a couple of weeks and the public shame would be awful. I tell you, there's two ends dragging at this country. There's them on the Dole, out for everything they can get without doing a day's work and them lot in Buck Palace living it up off our taxes. It's the same difference. Both ends are living off somebody else's money, but they get away with it every time. It's us lot in the middle that have to pay for both of them and even then, they can't pay their bills like we do".

I had an idea

"Couldn't they sell the Crown Jewels and pay their debts?"

"Course they can't, the Crown Jewels belong to us."

Oh …

I wandered on up the street to look in Dixon's' window. If we owned the Crown Jewels, then why couldn't my Dad have his little caravan at Silloth instead? It was all very puzzling.

Dixons was the town jeweller and more often than not his window was much the same. His display always included a large glass lamp with droplets of glass hanging from the shade. The light caught each droplet and glinted and shone on the costume jewellery considered cheap enough to be left in the window over the weekend.

"That's a funny looking clock."

"It's a travel clock. See, it folds up in its' own little case to keep it safe on a long journey."

I wondered how long the journey would have to be to merit buying a small clock or even how much use would be made of it as there were clocks all over the place. Town Halls had clocks, stations had clocks and many jewellers had clocks hanging outside. Maybe the people who needed these ingenious little clocks were travelling to uncivilised places to find King Solomon's Mines or searching for Lapis Lazuli in the exotic Far East.

"Give over day-dreaming our Edna, we're going to cross over the road to see what's on the pictures next week."

We crossed and stood reading the cinema posters.

"Not much choice there. "They Were Expendable," another blooming war film and in the middle of the week, "The Outriders."

"Dad'll want to see that as it's a Western."

"Aye well, he can take Edna, I don't like them."

By now I was tiring of these films and I didn't like to tell Dad that I was nearing an age when I hung up my holster and unpinned my sheriffs' star. Now I tried to leave the house without the cowboy costume and half-way up the street airily said that I had forgotten it. Sometimes he was very obliging and remembered it for me, proudly producing the silver six shooters from his pocket.

"There you are my lass. I knew you'd want them."

I stuffed them as far as possible into my gabardine coat pocket and smiled thinly if any of my friends came out of the first house and stared at the carved white plastic handles protruding traitorously.

"I seen you last night going in the pictures with guns."

"You never."

"I did, they were sticking out of your pocket."

"I was carrying them for somebody."

"Yeah, like who?"

"Urrm. Somebody my Dad knows."

It sounded feeble even to me. The time for dressing up and whooping unselfconsciously down the main street was coming to a close. I just wished that the grown-ups knew it too.

"Let's' walk as far as the Carlton and see what's on there and if Ognis' is open we'll have a cup of tea."

It was always a mystery to me why all these Italians had left their own warm countries to come to a little wind-blown town in the far north of England. I knew little of the poverty and persecution in Europe and it seemed a very strange choice but here they were with their Ice cream parlours and little three-wheeled ice cream cars. Ognis was shut and so we looked at the posters outside the Carlton. "Walk Softly Stranger" with Joseph Cotton and Alida Valli.

"I wouldn't mind seeing that."

"The papers said it was tripe, not half as good as "The Third Man.""

"That was creepy."

"Afternoon, Mrs. Croft."

Across the road Johnny Rafferty was leaning in the doorway of his cafe and Mam nodded over to him. Auntie May lowered her voice,

"We're not going in there however much I could take a cup of tea. They say that he takes bets on the side."

"They say a lot of things about Johnny."

"What makes me mad is that he gets the credit for fighting to bring the Labour Party. I don't know where he came from, but he just turned up one day in Maryport. I'm surprised at you acknowledging him our Edna."

"Oh, I wouldn't patronise his cafe and I'd hit the roof if any of my girls were seen in there, but his wife seems nice wherever she comes from and I won't forget Johnny. Remember when we lived in Carlisle, May? Mother sent me a letter telling me that the Hunger Marchers would be arriving there the next day and would I go out and cheer them on? I mean, I know they are called the Jarrow Marches but that was only the place where they all met up from all over the North and then marched together to London."

"I know that, get on with the story."

"Well, I got up the next morning and got Mary and June ready. June was just a baby in a pram and Mary sat on the end of it. I walked to Scotch Street and stood there. The main towns like Workington and Maryport had had collections and bought all the men new great coats and knapsacks but not boots. I mean new boots would have been too painful so instead they brought Johnny Rafferty. At that time, he was a master cobbler and his job was to repair the boots on the long march. I know you were in Manchester even then, but you know that the Depression was truly terrible up here. And if you think about it, how desperate were they to agree to walk hundreds of miles to let London know? It was said that there was plenty good coal in the mines, but the money wasn't being invested to bring it up in a more profitable manner. Instead the wages were being reduced and reduced to compensate. It got so that even with nearly all the men in a family working there wasn't enough to feed them and of course they were paying people off. There wasn't any Dole then, just the shameful Parish Relief. All that they wanted was work with a living wage. They were so sure that if London knew of the privations being suffered that some change would be made. They were terrible times and often there was nowhere to turn. I know you were sending a bit to Mother, but you couldn't send to all of us and we were all in the same boat. We couldn't help each other; in fact, we didn't even offer cups of tea. Nobody took offence; it was understood that there was none to spare.

"It was while we were in Carlisle that Alf fell sick with his asthma and they promptly gave his job to someone else. There was so many unemployed that they didn't need to wait for him getting better. And there was I with a sick man and two little girls and no money at all. One morning I left him in bed and walked the pram down to Rydal Street to beg for Parish Relief. I hadn't dared tell Alf or he would have been worse from the shame of it but I had to find food for us. Dear God May, they made me feel terrible. I had to stand there in front of a panel of people and explain our circumstances while they whispered to each other. Then they told me that they would send the Means Test man round to assess my house. Daft me hurried home and cleaned and tidied and tried to make sure Alf didn't know. I left the door open so

397

that he wouldn't hear anybody knocking and this great big man just walked in. Not a by your leave or anything.

"Arrogant pig. He just marched in, in his fine boots and walked all around the living room and the kitchen. When he made to go upstairs, I stood in his way and said that my husband was too ill to be disturbed. Then he said.

"That seems a fine three-piece suite, couldn't you sell it?"

"I just stared at him wondering if he was all there. I mean who the hangment had the money to buy it and how long would that last? May, I was really starting to worry; I'd made the house look as nice as possible and now it looked as if we weren't so badly off. Anyway, he rocked on his heels and after a silence he said very patronisingly that he would report back to the Board that I kept a clean house and I would get the money and a voucher for groceries. Just as I was going to thank him and get rid of him, he, leered into my face and said,

"You say you've a sick man upstairs? "

"I nodded and he stroked the couch and said,

"For a certain consideration I could add a voucher for a bag of coal."

"At first I didn't comprehend what he was meaning. When it dawned on me, I just opened the front door and said, "Any more of that filth and I shall report you to the

Board and if I go back this afternoon and find I have not been awarded any money then I will report you anyway. Out!"

"He looked me up and down as if he had just stood in something, but he could see that I meant every word and he left without speaking. In the afternoon I trailed all the way back and found that I was going to get vouchers for groceries and coal."

"Did you get any money?"

"Money! I got ten shillings and sixpence to keep the three of us and the rent was three shillings. There were times May, I was wrong of my head not knowing what to put on the table. Now, I look back with some embarrassment. There was a little comer shop on the end of the street where we lived and the day before the Parish relief was paid, I used to go there with a penny in my pocket. I waited until the shop was empty and then I chose a tin of meat, some potatoes and an Oxo. When I got them in my bag, I made a great play of looking for my purse, knowing full well that it was at home. Then I offered the penny for the Oxo and said that I would come back with the money for the rest. And every week that kind man said that I needn't come back until the next day if I wished. The relief was wonderful. I'm sure he knew but he didn't say anything and every week I meticulously took the money in the next day. At the time I thought I'd pulled a fine one but now I think he must have known."

"You weren't doing anything dishonest. I was reading in Liz's, "News of the World," this morning of a "Lady of the Night" saying that she was driven to it through lack of money. They know nothing."

Mam snorted,

"They can't get away with that excuse. There were people up here starving but we wouldn't have stooped to those depths. You just had to manage somehow and look what our George did."

Mary looked despairingly at June.

"We'll walk on a bit, Mam. I want another look at that Hebe Sports suit in Ewarts window."

Auntie May clucked them on and carried on reminiscing …

"Nobody knows what desperation is until they do something like George did. I couldn't believe it when Mother wrote and told me. It's no wonder she has a soft spot for him. Do you remember it?"

"Course I do. Meg took their Peggy to the doctors and he sent her out saying that there was nothing wrong with the child except malnutrition. He told her to take her home and give her good fruit and meat. Fruit and meat. I ask you, we could hardly afford bread. When George came home from the pit, Meg told him, and he told her not to

worry. The next day he went back on his shift and put his finger in the cutting machine. The bosses were so terrified they not only paid the medicals, but he got compensation. Peggy got her meals but that's his finger missing. He might be an atheist but he's a good man and there's no way he'd have stolen to feed his children."
"There wasn't anybody with anything to steal."

"That's true, but that must have taken some doing"

"Anyway, you still haven't finished your tale about Johnny Rafferty."

"Oh, that. As I said, I walked into Carlisle to watch the marchers come in. Even then Father was considered an old man, but he had marched with them as far as Aspatria. And as you know, Carlisle didn't ever suffer a Depression and they hadn't much empathy with West Cumberland, but their contribution was to offer them the Market Hall for the night and hot soup and bread for their supper. I nearly wept as they came around the comer; they looked so smart in their new coats but before I had time to cry, I was laughing. There, right at the front of them was Johnny Rafferty. His coat was about six sizes too big and he was ringing a big hand bell and shouting, "Help the hungry marchers." He didn't seem to have any idea that he should have been shouting, "Help the Hunger Marchers" and he looked so comical. It was the best laugh I'd had in some time. I saw them into the Market Hall and had a word with one or two that I knew. They were so pleased to see a Maryport person that I was glad that I'd made the effort to go and I managed a copper or two for their funds.

"By then the time was getting on and I knew I would have to go home to feed the girls. I mean I could have sweetened Mary with a biscuit, but I was still feeding June myself and I could hardly do that outside my own house, could I?"

Auntie May agreed.

"Just as I turned the pram to walk home, I heard this funny noise. Like a low hum. The crowds had begun to disperse, and the marchers were all in the market Hall so I couldn't think what it was, but I knew it was getting louder. I wandered a bit further down the street and I couldn't believe what I was seeing. May, it is a scene that will stay with me all my life. It was the marchers from the south of Scotland coming to join up with the Cumbrians and then all march together across the country the next day to Jarrow. If we thought we had it bad, it was nothing compared to them. They were shuffling down Stanwix bank with their feet wrapped in rags and bleeding. They were all mumbling as if they could not cease,

"Are we red? Yes, we're Red. Are we red? Yes, we're Red.

"Over and over and over. It was as if they had begun and could not stop. The tears ran down my face, you've never seen anything so awful and pathetic. Somehow, they wearily reached the Market Hall and Johnny Rafferty stayed up all night mending their boots. All night. He had no sleep but the next morning he was there at the head of them with his huge coat and his bell. I won't forget him and there's many on that march wont either. His cafe might be a bit seedy, but he's got a past."

"I never knew that story but a fat lot of good it did them marching all that way."

"They weren't to know that. They trusted the powers that be, to listen. The only thing that made a change to men idling on street comers and women trailing old prams to the shore to pick coal, was the war. It's no wonder we thought Russia was getting it right when we were so hungry. Mary and June don't like to hear me tell these tales, but I don't think we should ever forget. The Upper Classes would have us back there again if they could while they have their Coming Out Balls and gallop about hunting shooting and fishing. Blooming Noel Coward and the Mitford Girls carrying on as if none of it was happening."

"It wasn't happening for them."

We caught up with Mary and June.

"I think it's time we got home. Dad will be wanting his tea and it's growing dark. Come on Edna."

403

I was uncomfortable seeing Mam and Auntie May crying as they walked and talked and so I had abandoned them to look at the toys in Graves' shop window. Though I was not greatly enamoured of dolls there was a beautiful doll standing in its blue and pink box and beside it the dinkiest little pushchair. I hauled Mary and June back to see it and they agreed that it was just what a girl would want and walked down the street carrying on their conversation.

"I just thought that if I added my Birthday money to my next months' wage then maybe I could get that suit, or do you think the yellow coat would be a better buy?"

June grinned,

"Please yourself. I think the suits' too heavy looking. I'd rather borrow the coat."

And that was a Sunday afternoon in.

I went to bed that night and added the poor marchers in my prayers, then I lay in bed and lusted for the little pushchair. I don't know why I wanted it as I often found that playing with dolls short lived and boring. Sometimes I sorted my dolly pram and arranged them in it. I flapped the covers and a tucked them in, then I walked up and down the street and that was all. Occasionally I scolded them for upsetting my carefully arranged pram and the flapping and folding began again. The cold inanimate mini people didn't do anything interesting I just knew that I was a girl and I was supposed to like them. Now and then I sat them all on the fender stool and gave them a drink of cold water from my little tea set; they never even offered to try it. Boring. I still liked Sam and Alma but even they had been relegated to sitting on each end my dressing table like ornaments. But I wanted that pushchair. I wandered home from school through the town and stood staring in the shop window. I became worried that one day I would look, and it would have gone. I lobbied Mam but she said that I had to wait until Christmas. Christmas! I could be dead by then. I tried Dad but he just flapped his newspaper and suggested that I ask Mam. This was obviously going to require a full onslaught of charm mixed with shades of the pathetic and neglected child.

"What are you doing?"

"I'm writing to our June."

"Not on lined paper you're not. Only the most common people write letters on lined paper. And don't let your writing slant backwards. That's a sign of a selfish person and you don't want people to think that do you?"

Me? Selfish? I reached for some unlined paper and thought that I'd better start by asking June if she was well before launching forward with my own selfish pleas. Mary posted the letter and then it occurred to me that the pushchair could be gone before June had time to reply. This was getting serious. Mary got the full treatment and succumbed immediately. I should have tried her first. She took me by the hand, and we returned with me proudly pushing the pushchair.

What a row.

I was dismal. I knew that it was my fault that Mary was in trouble. I was not taken aside and spoken to. It was Mary that took the full blast.

"You stupid girl. There you are saving for a coat and you go and spend your hard-earned money on her."

"But Mam she wanted it."

"She can't have everything that she wants."

I sat on the fender stool with my chin in my hands and wondered why not. What would it do to me?

"She has to learn the value of money. What lessons are you teaching her? She has to learn to wait."

Why? Did waiting make you a nice person?

"It wasn't all that expensive."

"That's not the point. She was told she had to wait for Christmas."

"I didn't know that."

"The little beggars' already tried me and Dad."

"I didn't know that either."

"In future you'll have to ask. God, you haven't the brains of a hen. Christmas is only a month away and she should learn to do without."

Mary shrugged,

"She's got it now."

"I've a good mind to take it back."

Fear smote my heart. Not my new possession. Not the much-coveted pushchair. Mary looked miserable and Mam washed the dishes with gusto. When Dad came in from work he was regaled with Mary's crime.

"And you have to speak to her Alf. Our Mary has to learn not to squander her money. It's hard enough to come by without wasting it on Edna."

Wasting it? What a cheek. I manfully pushed the chair up and down the yard so that the wheels would be too dirty to return it to the shop.

Dad stroked his red hair and went to the bottom of the stairs.

"Mary. Get yourself down here."

Now I was really worried. This was serious if Dad was taking a hand in it.
"What's all this about?" Mary looked at him wearily, "It's my money and I'll spend it how I like."

"Well, it seems to me that there's a bit too much of doing what you like lately."

Mam pulled me into the kitchen, and we stood together listening.

"What's that supposed to mean?"

"It means just what I say. You are wasting our Edna to madness and some of it has to stop and this is a good opportunity to get said some other things."

Mam looked down at me puzzled and I shrugged my own ignorance.

"I've had about enough of you flying in and out of here like lodging house. You're there with the fine clothes and all that make up. It's off to this dance and that dance. And it's going to stop. I'm not having you getting a name for yourself. Your there in a respectable job and people talk."

"Nobody can talk about me. I haven't done anything wrong. I don't know how you can even think it of me."

"I don't think it of you, but a lie is round the world before the truth gets it's boots on and Maryport loves to talk. Now I've said my say. You get yourself in at a decent time in future."

"Excuse me, I'm twenty-one now and I'll come in when I like."

"I don't care if your fifty-one, this is my house and you'll come in when I say. And the next lad that you bring in here is the one you marry. Right?"

Mam and I looked at each other. Wow.

The door nearly came off its hinges as Mary slammed it and ran upstairs crying.
Mam whispered,

"She'll think I put him up to that, but I didn't know he was going to say all that lot."

"I wonder which lad she'll bring in to marry."

"Well, her Dad's spoken and for all her temper she'll not cross him. Let's see what she brings home next."

We smiled at each other and ventured into the living room.

Dad got an extra helping of supper that night and I played up and down the hall with my new toy. It didn't seem so good anymore. It was tainted and after a little while I abandoned it and went upstairs. Mary was wiping her eyes and writing to tell June.

"Sorry Mary."

"It's not your fault Pet."

I climbed onto the bed beside her.

"It is, I know it is. I'm really sorry I got you into trouble."

"It's my own fault and stop wobbling the bed, Mam says my handwriting is bad enough."

"What are you going to do? I mean about finding a husband."

Then she laughed.

"Why does everybody think I want one just yet? I'll meet Mr Right someday and if I don't, I don't. When Aunty May goes home I'm away over to stay with Mother. She doesn't know what time I come in. I know who's to blame for all that Dad said and I'm telling June."

"It wasn't Mam, honestly."

"Don't you believe it. Dad wouldn't tell me off."

"Honestly it wasn't Mam, I know it wasn't."

"Yeah sure. He's a wonderful man but he does whatever she tells him."

"Not this time."

Mary looked down at me.

"Seriously?"

"Hmm", I took the doll from under my arm and slid it under the covers. I stoked the yellow nylon hair and closed the one plastic eyelid that was a bit stiff.

"There sleeps Titania, sometime of the night."

"Oh, don't you start. Mams' bad enough. Here, does your teacher know that you know things like that?"

I was mystified. Why would my teacher know? They had never mentioned Shakespeare.

Mary shifted towards me,

"Listen. What's this?" and she hummed,

"It's that thing from "Madame Butterfly."

"Who composed it?"

411

"Puccini."

She looked at me with some surprise.

"How do you know that?"

"Dunno. Oh, yes, I do. Mam shouted of me and made me sit and listen to it on the wireless."

"She used to do that with me and June too."

"And Dad plays bits from it. I've seen the sheet music and it says, "Puccini." He told me how to say it right."

"Well fancy that. The stuff that must be in your head and the school doesn't know about it."

"Why would they? They never ask me. Anyway, that sort of thing has nothing to do with school has it?"

Mary looked down at her unlined writing paper.

"It's a sort of knowledge and maybe there isn't time for everything in a school day."

"Tomorrow I think I'll make time and go around, and ask my class some things like that, just to see what we are missing. I'll write and tell June to try it as well. Shove off now while I get this letter finished."

I stood by the door.

"I am sorry Mary. I wouldn't deliberately get you into trouble."

She smiled across at me.

"I know."

"You can take the push chair back tomorrow and get your money back if you want. I don't like it now."

"Oh, you are the sweetest thing. I'll tell June what you've just said. Of course, I won't take it back, you just enjoy it."

She didn't seem to understand that I meant it.

"Err, while you're writing the letter could you tell her she needn't send me a Postal Order?"

"Was she going to?"

"Well, I asked her to, to buy the push chair."

"You little madam. Get away downstairs before I plonk you one."

Still I dithered in the doorway.

"I wish you wouldn't go over to Mothers' to sleep. I like you here."

"I know that too but soon June will be home for Christmas and we'll all be together again."

That was a good feeling and I slid down the banister leaving Mary humming, "Mr Sandman send me a dream."

When I got downstairs Mam beckoned me into the kitchen and whispered in my ear,

"Is she all right?"

"I think so. She's writing to our June. I told her she could take it back to the shop, but she wouldn't."

"Of course, she wouldn't, bless her. She'll just have to wait to see if her coat is in the January sales."

"Mam, I don't want her to go and stop at Mothers."

"Neither do I at the moment. I'm about to start cleaning for Christmas."

June replied and as usual Mam read the letter aloud to us,

"Dear All,

"Honestly the expense being here. I've had to buy red biros for marking and I managed to get ten second handbooks for my course for one pound seventeen shillings. Then there was three pounds, fifteen shillings for College shorts and I simply couldn't find the right grey P.T. knickers under fifteen and eight pence. I need a clock, but I'd rather have a College scarf. Even though all the rooms have this central heating it is very cold here in Sunderland. Tell Dad, thanks for the blotters from the doctors and I'd be glad if you could send an extra fifteen shillings for my fare home.

"John came to stay at the weekend and we went to the pictures and on Sunday did some window gazing, but we were frozen wandering about. It was wonderful to see him, but he is so serious and intense about everything. My teaching Practice has finished in Chester Road Junior School. I had forty-two ten-year olds. I was told that two boys had just had nervous breakdowns and they did nothing but cry, so I had to ignore them. I was in charge of Reading, Scripture, Knitting and P.T. Mary's letter telling me to ask them if they had learned anything from home came too late but maybe on my next T.P. I'll try it.

"Good job I needn't send Edna money as I haven't any. It's Rag Week soon and I'm really looking forward to that. If Mary goes to the Library for you, tell her to get, "Mine Own Executioner," by Nigel Balchin as it's very well written. I've been reading Arthur Koestler's "Thieves in the Night, about Jews and their complexes.

"Malcolm is the only cousin I write to now as Robin doesn't answer. Centre stage Mr. Crellin please. Oh, hope you got the geyser fixed and it is working again, both the one in the kitchen and Dad. Ha, ha.

Thanks for Edna's report. Not bad being fifth in such a big class. Tell her to sort out her cardboard money, as there is something I want to try on her when I get home. I can't wait to be strapping up my trunk and I can't wait to see Mary again. Not long now. I'd better close as I have an essay to do critically examining the constitution of either Sparta or Athens. I chose Sparta and I hope it enjoys being critically examined. By the way, Laurel and Hardy are supposed to be coming here, fancy that, and the full London production of, "Oklahoma." I thought I'd try to get tickets for it even if the seats are in the Gods. Give everyone my love, especially Mother and I'll write to Mary soon. I get so easily depressed here but the Dexedrine helps. I might write to Dr. Robert for some more. I keep getting headaches a lot and at the moment I have a really sore throat. Still, it will be so nice to be home for Christmas."

Main folded the letter and slid it into her apron pocket.

"I'll take it over and read it to Mother and Mary. What a minx she is, one minute she hasn't any money and the next she's going to see "Oklahoma." I don't know what to think of that young man she's going to marry. He seems like an old young man to me. It would be nice for her to get someone who is a bit of fun. I might get her a clock

416

for Christmas on the Coop book but that's not very exciting. I could maybe give her the money for the College scarf instead. If she was wearing that then everyone would know that she was at College. I'll see. I don't know what she means about sending our Edna money, I never asked her to do that."

I slid off my chair and said that I was going to look for my play money before I got the third degree. I can't say that I was enamoured of June saying that she wanted to "try something out," on me. I was rapidly becoming a guinea pig for both my sisters. When June had been home for Mary's birthday, she had sat in the bath with me one night and explained why worms were necessary to oxygenate the ground. I understood but found it all quite disgusting and not a fit subject to accompany our ablutions.

When she came home for the Christmas holidays, she brought with her the display that she had made on Teaching Practice and pinned it on my bedroom wall. I lay in bed reading about different types of paper and looking at pictures, "courtesy of Wiggin Teape," showing the stages of manufacturing paper. I could not understand why I couldn't eat sugar paper, but I could eat rice paper. June took me to Annovazzi's and bought some Callard and Bowser's nougat to show me the fragile rice paper around each piece.

" Mam says that I haven't to call it, "nugget" as it's a French word. I have to say "noogarr."

June cast her eyes to the heavens.

"I bet you'll be the only person in Maryport saying it like that. And I suppose you have to say, "onvelope," instead of envelope as that's a French word too."

I nodded, as my mouth was full of the large chunk of noogarr.

"Honestly, sometimes I despise her with all this what's right and what isn't. I've been to some of my new College friends' houses and their mothers' just rush around making them good meals and telling them that they've missed them. Then they send them back with huge parcels of goodies. What do I get? Just letters telling me how hard her life is, and I'll have to come home to make some money and help with the cleaning. When she met me off the train, I asked her if she'd missed me and do you know what she said?"

I shook my head, savouring the delicious sweet taste.

"Oh, I'd miss a kettle if it had been around long enough. Would it have choked her to have said something nice?"

"We all mish you". I managed round the nuts and goo.

June got her hanky, licked it and wiped my mouth. Thanks June, I just wanted second-hand spit on me. Which still didn't explain why I couldn't eat sugar paper.

June just became exasperated and said, "Because you can't" and got ready to start her Christmas job delivering the post.

Mam had decided to go over to Mothers' to borrow one of her Benzedrine tablets.

"Eeh, one of those little tablets and I can get a room cleaned in no time. I know Mrs. Routledge is coming but I can't trust her to bottom a room properly. I thought our June would have been more help, but she's gone and got that holiday job. Good grief, here she is, back already."

It transpired that June's sore throat was Tonsillitis. She had to go to bed and Mam had to use the white telephone to ring for the doctor.

The only cereal that we ever had was Cornflakes. In the summer I enjoyed it with the thick cream from the top of the bottle of milk but in winter Mam insisted we ate it with hot milk. She reasoned that a hot meal was like central heating for, "your insides." I got quite used the soggy steaming cereal, but the best thing was the mask on the back of the packet. I couldn't wait for it to empty so that I could awkwardly cut it out and pester for some string to poke through the holes at the side. That night I made the gruesome mask and had a brilliant idea. I put on Dad's white cotton surgery coat, which came down to my ankles, then the mask and then rammed his bowler hat on my head. I crept upstairs and slowly round the bedroom door with my arms outstretched just like the zombies.

"Whooo. Whooo."

June let out one, long; piercing scream and Mam rushed upstairs and bundled me out.

"You naughty girl. Can you imagine anything more frightening than a little ghost?"

I can't say that I had ever thought of it.

"You know how sensitive she is. You've probably set her back a day or two from getting better with your antics. Get up those stairs and say you are sorry."

I took off my brilliant costume and stomped back up the stairs. I didn't feel very sorry. You make an effort to give someone a laugh and they respond with histrionics. I sidled round the door and said mechanically,

"Sorry and I hope you're not going to be ill longer."

June accepted my apology but wiped a hand across her brow.

Mam was not pleased.

"The last thing that I need right on Christmas is you lying in bed. Blooming Lady of Shallot. Either that or you

420

think you're Ophelia drifting away. And you'll not have any pocket money for all the dances. I can't be expected to provide that as well. I'm not sending your Dad out in all weathers to collect the rents. He's just had his spell in the hospital and if he loses any more work, they might dock his wages. Fine Christmas we'll have. Come here Edna, get your coat on and go over to Mothers' and tell our Mary to come home when she comes in from Flimby. Lizzie will have to pull her weight and see to Mother. I need Mary to do a bit more here."

She loudly flapped the bedside mats and dusted around June who was looking very pale and troubled.

"I've only been ill two days."

"Aye, it's a queer thing that those new antibiotics work on other people, but you just lie there watching everyone run around you. What did your last servant die of?"

"Oh, give up, I'm not well. I don't need this."

Mam stiffened,

"I would never have spoken to my mother like that. After all I've done for you. 'How sharper than a servant's tooth it is to have a thankless child.' And you, what are you doing standing there as if dead lice was dropping off you? I thought I told you to go to Grasslot."

I skidaddled.

421

Oh, great; now Mary was mad. She dragged me after her back to Lawson Street.

"I come in from work, get Mother some tea and then you come with that message."

"What a life. I wish I'd stuck to my guns and stayed in Manchester after College."
"It's not my fault."

"Don't worry I know whose fault it is and it's not our June neither. I've a good mind to tell her."

"Oh, don't. Please don't. You'll only make it worse and it's nearly Christmas. Maybe she'll be ill too. Maybe she'll get a headache."

Mary stopped and looked down at me,

"What rubbish. Mam doesn't get headaches, she gives them."

Her eyes twinkled and then we both laughed.

"Aw come on. Don't worry. I'll smooth things a bit and she's right. Dad isn't fit to go for the rents."

Thank goodness Mary's temper plummeted as fast as it rose.

"Can we walk a bit slower and I wish you'd stop strangling my wrist."

When we got home, June was up and dressed but looking decidedly green around the gills.

What are you doing up? The doctor said you'd to stay in bed till those pills got a hold.

"Did Mam make you get up?"

June looked a little sheepish,

"Err, no. John rang to say that he was coming through. Lend me some of that rouge you bought, he can't see me like this."

Mary and I cast our eyes to the heavens.

It was that Christmas that I lost Father Christmas. He chucked me, never to return. I had never been very sure of him anyway. I scrawled my little lists and watched them burn. If they didn't oblige and float up the chimney. Dad gave them a helping hand with the poker. I stood and solemnly called my wishes up the chimney. I loved the pictures of this kindly old man and each year I was taken to Browns' Department store in Workington to actually see him. I never quite got right up to him. I was terrified. Once I got as far as the queue and braced myself. This year I would do it. I wanted to be there whispering in his ear. I so envied the other children, sitting on his knee but my courage always failed me, and I simply could not speak to him. My stomach fluttered, my knees were weak and the excitement so unbearable that I thought that I was going to be sick. Every year I just hoped that my little notes in the fire would do. The burning lists were my only way of communicating with him and giving any indication of my desires. And so far, it seemed as if he had got the message. I was a very lucky little girl. For some reason Mam had kept all of Mary and Junes' toys and produced some of them each year as well as new ones from my lists. The hand me down toys were actually better and sturdier than the new ones. Toys just after the War were very poor and, in many cases, downright dangerous. I was completely unaware that Mary and June had loved Sam and Alma too, I just thought that Santa left these extras for me. For some time before the great day I listened to the half-hearted threats that if I wasn't a good girl, I would only receive a turnip. As December was a good month for me, it wasn't difficult to be all sweetness and light for a while. The month began with my Birthday and Mam always made these very special days. She said quite reasonably that it was the only day of the year that we could call our own and so it should be remembered. It also made my Christmas list easy as I simply flowed on with all that I hadn't received then. I loved December and not just because it was my month. Now it was growing dark as I walked down the hill from school, and I did not mind if I walked into the inevitable note.

424

"Dear Edna, Gone over to Mothers'. Go to the Coop and get some bread and half a pound of lard. Mam." I defected and went to buy the items at "Liptons' or "Home and Colonial" just so that I could wander around the town with the shop windows lit and all the goods shining. I idled in the warmth of Woolworth's and stared at the dolls positioned high above the counter. Their exquisitely pretty faces framed by golden hair with an artificial shine and their arms stretched beseechingly, stared into the middle distance. The shop assistants seemed to have perfected this art too. It was their silent statement that they had done the job for so long or could do it so well that they needn't concentrate. They laconically handed over the goods, rattled the money in the till and slammed it shut and all the time looking across to somewhere or something else. I decided that if I totally failed in life and didn't pass the Eleven Plus that I would serve children first. Trying to make a transaction as a child was a long drawn out affair while the adults took precedence. I was never very sure why I was not found clutching my pennies, ossified by the counter. But at Christmas I didn't mind the waiting as it gave me more time to look around for likely candidates for my list. Every shop was decorated in some way and the effect of the colours and fairy lights was heightened by the glooming darkness. The lights spilled onto the streets and painted a sheen on the rain-wet pavements. Oil filmed puddles rippled into rainbows and the neon Bata sign shone claret red. I was fascinated by Chemist shops and slowly searched their windows. Now there were large gift boxes of toiletries on display, the lid opened obligingly to show talcum powder, soap and creams, nestled in their own satin cushioned hollow. Luxurious boxes of Max Factor and Yardley tantalised, and I gawped at the prices and wished and wished that I could afford them. How I would have loved to have seen their faces when they opened them on Christmas morning. I stood by the Electricity shop window and fantasised. Mam said that a Hoover would help Dad's chest so if I had the money for one of those it would help both of them. On one of the films at the Empire a family had clubbed together and bought their mother a television and on another film the teenager had opened an envelope only to find a key. He had rushed to the front door to find a Cadillac parked, complete with a massive red bow. I wanted to be generous; I wanted to astound with flamboyance, and I didn't want to be the one always taking. I wanted my gifts to shout just how much I loved them all. But lack of money made for lack of choice. My Christmas shopping was simple and unsatisfying. Boxes of bath cubes for the women and a packet "7 o'clock razor blades, with triple ground edges for a closer shave," for Dad. I trailed home with them and awkwardly wrapped them in red crepe paper. Even that was dispiriting. My finished gifts looked nothing like the ones in the shop windows and bits of crepe paper stuck out in all the wrong places. They always opened them and gasped their surprise and gratitude and I always knew that they were being kind.

People scurried and bustled and carried home luxury items. It was a period of anticipation. It was also a period of doubting my own sanity. Parcels arrived and completely disappeared. I wandered in to murmured conversations that stopped with, "Shh, she's here." Now the solitary little nutmeg rolling around the pantry shelf was joined by bags of nuts, tins filled with fruit loaves, boxes of sugared almonds and boxes of dates. None of them could be opened until Christmas. Mary and June teetered on ladders fixing the dripping paper decorations from the comers of the room to the big light in the middle and Mam searched the house for the nutcrackers. She took down the mirror from above the fireplace and carefully scrolled the words, "Merry Christmas" in soggy glue and then sprinkled artificial frost over it. The wine decanters came out for their annual use. They were lovingly washed and upended to dry. One was filled with Port and the other with sherry then they stood on a tray by the telephone with the matching glasses arranged around them. Underwood's pop man delivered full crates of lemonade to stand on the cellar lid and the coal man rattled extra bags into the coalhouse. We were exhorted to get everything in the wash that we might need as there was to be no more washing until after Boxing Day and Mary and Mam began to bake. Just before Christmas Eve Uncle George landed down with a big cock chicken and it lay in the washhouse, its mahogany feathers gleaming and its beady eyes staring at nothing. One night, as I went up to bed, I spied a box on the top of Mams' wardrobe. It was pink and blue, and the cursive writing said, "Pedigree." How curious. It was very similar to the one that I had seen the doll standing in Graves shop window. When I heard Dad coming up to bed, I naively asked him to hand me the box on the wardrobe. After a few minutes he came back and said, "What box?"

I scrambled out of bed to find that it had gone. Life could be very strange. Maybe wishing so hard had made me imagine it there.

Every Christmas I hung my stocking by the fire anchored with one of the brass candlesticks and Mam placed a mince pie and a glass of sherry on the table for Santa. By now the excitement was intense. I could not get to sleep. I listened to Mary and June coming in from the dance at the Freemasons' Hall and willed the night to be over. I hoped that this would be a straight Christmas with no messing about from my two sisters. One year they had found it very amusing to leave an empty stocking and a turnip on my chair. I was amazed. What Santa edict had I contravened? Shivering and clutching her dressing gown around her, Mam suggested that maybe the old man had got muddled and maybe I should try the sitting room. Very funny my charming sisters. Another year Mary had thought it a great wheeze to place a pound of sausage meat in the top of my stocking. I plunged my hand into the gooey mess while they all fell about laughing. I snuggled up with my hot water bottle and wished that the butterflies in my stomach would go to sleep too. Now, much recovered from her Tonsillitis, June had begun telling Mam that it was posher to hang the stocking on the end of the bed and posh people had their toys left in a pillowcase. I didn't care for the change in our traditions but placed a pillowcase at the end of my bed as she instructed. Just as I was drifting into a fitful sleep, I heard June and Mam whispering on the landing.

"I'm not sure about this."

"No, this is the way to do it. I saw it in a film."

"Have you remembered that doll out of the wardrobe?"

"Sshh,"

And they crept round my door and swapped my empty pillowcase for a full one. I watched them and sadly closed my eyes. Father Christmas had gone. One of my illusions gently, kindly and quietly shattered. It was never the same without him. I don't know why but it wasn't. I grew up a little that night and wished that I hadn't. Oh, I continued to play the game, I was good at that. I pretended for their sake, but I knew. I pretended with my relations and friends and occasionally wondered if they too knew and thought that I was as daft as I thought that they were. I didn't feel that I had been deceived, it was as if I had suspected all along and now it had been confirmed. I didn't resent Junes' innocent revelation, as I knew that she would not have knowingly taken anything away from me. It was almost as if I instinctively understood that it was something you learned eventually like how to get babies. Christmas was still exciting, but it had lost that extra intensity forever.

The next morning, I made my own little stand and carried the pillowcase downstairs unopened. I silently stated that presents were meant to be down there by the fire and not opened alone in my bedroom and it never happened again. Whatever Mams' faults she always got up early that morning and had the fire blazing for us to sit and open our gifts together.

"Well, which one of you knew that I was running out of razor blades? That's just grand."

I smiled gratefully at him.

"Would you just look June, bath cubes. Just what I needed. I hope that you have some too because I'm not letting you have some of these very special ones."

Gosh, maybe they meant it.

June scrabbled among her parcels and lifted the badly wrapped present.

"We've both struck lucky and just when I needed some smellies for the bath. I think I'll keep a couple to show off at College."

I began to go pink with pleasure.

Aunty May had added a large compendium of games to "Jane Eyre." I enjoyed looking at each game in their own compartment but doubted whether anyone would play

Chinese Checkers or Tiddly Winks with me for long. Auntie Lizzie had bought me a toy Post Office and for a few days I stamped everything in sight until I stamped Junes' sleeping forehead and she confiscated it. Killjoy. I always looked forward to the presents from Auntie Bessie as they were usually quite fabulous. One year it was a large box of magic tricks. I astounded them all by losing a plastic egg in a black bag and then making it reappear. They gasped when I tapped a fancy box with the small magic wand and their watches appeared in the other side of it. I "Abracadabrad," their earrings away and amazed them with a variety of card tricks. Then they told me to get lost. There weren't any presents from Auntie Evelyn as she was too poor. With the exception of the year of the squidgy sausage meat, I loved delving into the lumpy stocking and there was always a sense of disappointment when I reached the tangerine and nuts filling the toe. The morning always paused to stand on the front step to listen to the Salvation Army band playing Carols in the street. One year, Mary and June slipped silently back into the house and closed the door. I was left shivering in my skimpy nightie for the entire world to see. Ho, ho, ho. Then began a ruse that they all found very funny.

I knocked on the door and June opened it but just stood there,

"Yes?"

"I want in."

"What for?"

"Because I live here."

"MAM."

Mam joined her and looked at me curiously,

"What?"

"There's a little girl here saying that she wants in."

"Why?"

"She says she lives here."

"Oh, what a shame, poor little thing. Now go on home to your Mammy pet."

Once or twice it had worked, and I had been rather puzzled; now I just played it out with them while my bare feet froze and almost stuck to the reddened step.

Although the Christmas dinner was special, we seemed to eat all day. There were no restrictions and I munched walnuts with Dainty Dinah toffees. The radio blared alongside Mary and Junes' new records until Mam switched it off saying,

"I wish you lot had a knob somewhere to get a bit of peace."

Sometime in the day, Mam and Dad wandered over to see Mother but usually we all stayed in our own houses. There was no public transport, no newspapers and certainly no shops, public houses or cinemas open. Everything closed down and stopped. I liked it. I enjoyed the temporary stillness of the streets and the warmth in the house. I loved it being so full of food whether I wanted it or not. There was hardly a ledge that wasn't laden with plate cakes or the remnants of the big chicken dinner. The lid had been put on the set pot in the washhouse and jellies, trifles and extra pints of milk stood on it. It was a wonderful blow out that punctuated the long winter months and made them all the more bearable. I couldn't understand when some said that they wished it was over or that they could do without it. I wondered how it would have been if we had simply gone through from October to April without anything to lift the dismal months.

Gradually people began to emerge from their houses. Children clunked their new prams across the pavements; some wobbled their new bikes around the streets or crashed into walls on their shining roller skates. This was the time to don new Christmas clothes and visit relatives and friends and eat their trifles for a change.

I'm not sure how Mam managed to suddenly gauge and buy enough shopping to fill the house for a few days but for that once each year she did. Mary had been delighted to open her Christmas parcel and find the yellow coat and June found the little travel clock and the money in an envelope for a College scarf. My special gift was an artificial Christmas tree and a model Nativity. Not bad, but I preferred Mary's doll and Junes' wind up motorboat for the bath. We had struck lucky that year, as Mam was not good on present buying. She impressed on me that I had come along when she was too old. She was tired of filling stockings now. How could she be expected to prepare for Christmas and go out buying gifts as well? She recited her youth and how you were lucky to get a sugar mouse in those days. Each year Mary and June rescued me and my stocking was filled and presents wrapped and piled on the couch. We were all together enjoying our family togetherness.

CHAPTER 14
"WHEN ICICLES HANG BY THE WALL"

The week between Christmas day and New Year's was not restful. It seemed to me, illogical and unnecessary to visit family that had only just visited us the day before. But much was made of these return visits supposedly to view *their* decorations or Christmas gifts. I was perpetually getting washed and changed and traipsing off to another house to eat chicken sandwiches followed by trifle and of course mince pies. I didn't mind the latter as the tradition was that twelve mince pies had to be eaten between Christmas day and New Years' day to ensure twelve happy months ahead but the cold trifle with the ghastly cold custard was always a trial. I began to imagine that the whole world was on the move from one house to another. And of course, all this visiting the family interfered with meeting my own friends and enjoying my Christmas gifts. Now that they were older, Mary and June were able to make their own arrangements until Mam decided that they should be accompanying us. They came up with various imaginative alternative arrangements to avoid these expeditions and Mam summoned a few mild miffs and mutterings about her family not being good enough now that they had their own fine friends. But it was an easy time to woo her with promises that the housework would be done while she was out, because of course the house had to be cleaned all over again to greet the New Year.

Throughout the year Mam and Dad did not drink alcohol. Mam had lived with and witnessed the darker side of its effects and though Dad had not, he stayed true to his religion. He also maintained that he did not need artificial help to have a good time. They both relaxed their views at this time of year and accepted the glasses of sherry or homemade wines offered when visiting. The decanters in our own sitting room had to be refilled once or twice after being depleted from offering Christmas drinks and always had to be full ready for New Year's Eve.

It was important to stay up at least until midnight to see out the old year and welcome the new. It was a gesture of hope and there was an intensity about those first handshakes and kisses as Big Ben tolled out the midnight hour. There was something rather solemn when Mam and Dad raised their glasses to each other with the silent hope that surely this one would be better than the last.

"I wish you good health Lad."

"Aye, that would be a grand thing if nothing else."

As I raised my glass of ginger wine to join their toast to the coming year, I wished that the eleven plus would disappear into infinity and my class could stay together. Good health was all very well in its place but a little spell of bad health around the time of the impending exam could have been a bonus. Nothing too life threatening of course just a little something where I could pick at the bed covers and evoke sympathy and a few sweets. Why even my teachers would clasp their hands to their bosoms and say,

"Oh no, not Edna Croft. The Eleven Plus cannot possibly trouble her when she has been struck down so dreadfully. We will simply give her a Pass and that may assist her recovery."

A broken left wrist would be good. I wasn't sure how to achieve this but now was not the time and I shelved the idea as the front doorbell rang.

"Alf, if that's our George don't let him in yet and don't you go out on that step either." "I know, I know."

It was very important that the First Foot didn't have red hair and it certainly hadn't to be a woman with any colour of hair. Both were death to any good luck coming into the house.

"It's all right it's our Rodney first."

As Rodney had very black hair slicked to a greasy sheen with Brilcream this was a very good omen and he was ushered into the sitting room and made very welcome.

"Ay Lad you get more like Richard Todd with each passing day. Now come and sit down here and have a nice glass of Port. Oh, thank you."

Mam took a bag from Rodney as he mumbled,

"Happy New Year Aunt Edna."

I knew what was in the paper bag. It was always the same. A bit of coal to wish us warmth and a little salt in a screw of paper to wish us wealth.

"I can hear you've got your Dad with you, is he a bit worse the wear for the drink?"

"Oh, you know me Dad he doesn't know when to stop. Our William and Ian are with him."

And Dad brought them into the sitting room as the bell rang again and he turned around to go and answer it.

"You can let anybody you like in now Alf seeing as how Rodney had done the honours with his black hair. Now who's for a glass of Port?"

Mam was always more generous with the Port than the sherry as she didn't mind the sherry being left over to be used for trifles throughout the year.

"Dear God, Edna is that the best you can do? It's the same every year. Blooming Port, that's a woman's drink.

438

You'll have folk thinking I'm a right Sarah. Now here's a real drink, a proper man's drink."

And Uncle George slid a bottle of whisky from his coat pocket.

"Here, get some of that down you. Forget the coal this'll warm your insides better."

"Well it looks as if it's warmed yours already. Just find a seat lad before you fall down. Oh, hello Amy and you've Alice, Billy and John with you, that's grand."

William pulled me on his knee,

"You alright Blood nut?"

I nodded, almost overcome by the whisky fumes from his breath. It didn't matter I was enjoying the sitting room filling with family while Mam whirled giving dainty glasses of Port and accepting awkward kisses. As we lived in the town centre and as many came there for the celebrations it was obviously thought to be a great idea to end the evening at Edna and Alf's for another drink and use the toilet. Mary and June eventually appeared saying that they were flushed from all the dancing while Mary furiously sucked strong mints before giving Mam a New Year kiss. They draped around me balloons and streamers that had been released at midnight from a great net high on the Palace ballroom ceiling.

"Give over our Mary, you are as daft as a brush."

"God, William, if I can't be daft on a night like this it's a pity."

"Talking of brushes did you hear what Mrs. Routledge said the other day?"

Mam had centre stage.

"She said that she had a really good brush that had been her mothers' and her grandmothers. Fancy it lasting so long and it had only had four new heads and three new shanks."

As they all laughed young Ian looked puzzled,

"But that means it wasn't the same brush at all."

"Ian, that's what's funny, how much have you had to drink?" "Not enough by the sounds of it."

"Here Mary, make yourself useful and give Amy another Port."

Mary topped up Amy's glass.

"Yawright Amy?"

"Aye, nothing stronger?"

440

"You know Mam, she won't have it in the house. Away and see if Uncle George will add to your glass or has John brought some?"

"You're joking. Nothing but a blooming wuzzganner that one. You know, he wuzz gamier do this and he wuzz ganner do that. Well, he wuzz gamier bring a bottle but forgot."

Sitting on Williams' knee I watched them. Uncle George was leaning against the wall sipping from his whisky bottle and saying to no one in particular,

"Come fill me with the old familiar juice, methinks I will recover by and by."

June was sitting on the arm of a chair talking to Alice but her fluttering hands betrayed her discomfort with the amount of people and the flowing drink.

Poor June always worrying ahead. Always conjuring some hypothetical disaster. To me the room was full of well-wishers who were chatting and enjoying a New Year drink with each other. I had no doubt that June was already visualising one of them spewing all over and another falling and crashing the glasses and of course there might be some grossly embarrassing confrontation. Occasionally her eyes flicked to Mary and I guessed that she was worrying that Mam would smell the drink on Mary's breath. As Mary was now downing her allotted Port, I couldn't see what there was to worry about. June

441

had the "I'm a good girl, I am" look as she refused another offer of a swig from Uncle Georges' bottle.

"No thank you it gives me a migraine."

"Aye but at least you'll know why you've got one. Did you hear that Billy? I said, you'll know why you've got one, did you hear?"

"With a voice that loud I couldn't fail."

"Now I know you all think I'm drunk but you know it's called the water of life and it is and that Omar Khayam was nothing but a drunken old reprobate and when I leave here you'll all be saying that George is nothing but a drunken old reprobate. I know what you'll all be saying. Just you try a drink of this amber liquid and you'll see the world take on a rosier glow. I know you don't like to see me like this our Edna but if you knew the privations, I've had in life you'd excuse me. Mother always does. See that finger. See that finger. Now that's hunger for you. The things I've done. It's a bad job if a man can't have a drop now and then."

We'd heard it all before. Always looking for confirmation of disgust and if he didn't get it he talked until he was disgusted with himself.

"Shut up George we've all suffered in one way and another but tonight isn't the night to talk about it. In fact, come and sit down before you fall down. The bell rang again, and Uncle George's daughter Peggy and her husband Clifford squeezed in wishing everyone a good New Year.

"We thought we'd find you all here. Put my glass on the piano Alf. I'll have to go a place, I'm desperate. Either that or I'll wet myself."

June winced

Billy Musgrave started laughing,

"Talking of toilets, tell them what happened to you the other night Uncle George."

All eyes turned to him perched non-too steadily on the arm of a chair.

"Oh, I was coming down Ewanrigg the other night when this voice called out. "Evening, Mr. Tuke." Well I stopped and looked round. Couldn't see anybody. Then it came again. "Nice night Mr. Tuke." I nearly jumped out of my skin. Well, it was actually a beautiful moonlit frosty night and I was just about to move on when I realised it was Mary Southwoll. Would you believe she was sitting on the outside lavvy. No door on it and there she was in the moonlight sitting."

He shook his head laughing.

As they all laughed Mam said,

443

"Probably used the door for firewood. I hope you just walked on."

"Oh, I waved and wished her good night. They're harmless."

"Harmless! They're a bloody scream."

"Enough of the language Billy. But you're right, what a blooming family."

I lapped it up.

Maryport didn't just have characters they had full families of them. They roamed in packs and there always seemed to be an Auntie Violet somewhere among them. They lived in council houses or rickety old pit houses and their gardens had the odd old push chair leaning on its side and a bicycle wheel sunk among the knee-high weeds. Sometimes at night they could be seen streaming over the New Road, heads down scurrying somewhere. Mam and Dad leading the fray, the others hurrying to keep up and always a little one at the back wailing for them to wait for him; his cheap jacket and snot flying behind him. They were not villains or fearsome they were just there providing much fodder for amusement. For some reason they had all acquired their various nicknames and Bogey was the tall, lean patriarch of the Blaylocks

"Hey, I was stood at the bar in the Bounty the other day when Bogey came in and stood beside me. Jokingly I asked him if he was working and he slowly turned and looked at me incredulously and said.

"Listen Billy, if I thought there was a bone in this body that would work, I'd break it now"

When there was gap in the laughter John Musgrave said,

"Not strictly true. He does go around doing this tarmac stuff now and then. In fact he was working at Distington High Duty Alloys doing the new entrance when the foreman said,' Bogey, couldn't you get some false teeth in', and Bogey looked at him for a minute and then said, ' You're joking I tried the wife's' once and they were bloody uncomfortable".

Everyone had a tale to tell and I was just enjoying listening, but I could have added my own. In the summer Betty and I had meandered up Ewanrigg and I was much struck by watching Bogey clumsily hammering a sign into the front of his garden. The sign bore the immortal words

"Whitewashin dun in all colours"

"Talk about 'neither work nor want' I tell you ...."

"Oh, not now George. Alf get on that piano before he starts with the politics. And make it cheerful like "When Irish Eyes are Smiling" or something."

"Irish. I'd give them Irish. Blooming Celts, always whining. They come over here and then whine about home. I'd pack them all off home in a wire netting boat. Scots are the same. Happy to take our National Health Service and any other good ideas and then singing "Will ye no come back again.""

"That's enough George and I think you've had enough. Go on Alf play something if only to stop his tripe."

Dad nestled on the piano stool and began to play "The Laughing Policeman." We gathered round and joined him in a medley of silly songs as the fire drooped lower and the Port decanter emptied. Gradually they began to drift away and Mam commandeered Mary and June to collect and wash glasses. Uncle George was always the last to leave with his sons helping him down the front steps.

"I know, I know. You good folks are wanting to get to your beds. No doubt you'll be up and about Alf for church in the morning. Well you'll not see me there. You'll not get me in no church."

And just as we thought he was finally going, he always tottered back.

"Here I'll just tell you one last tale. I was walking to my allotment last spring when I saw the Vicar leaning on the fence and as I got up to him, he said, 'My goodness you have a fine plot there. You must constantly thank the Lord for it.' Well, after a minute looking at the neat rows and thinking of all the back breaking work that had gone into getting it like that I said, " All I can say is the Lord wasn't doing too well before I came along." No, you won't get me in church, however much you ask."

Dad smiled,

"You go your way and I'll go mine George. Good night Lad."

And as he closed the door Uncle Georges' voice could be heard calling to the clear night sky,

"Tis all a chequer board of nights and days"

The old year had gone and the new one was in and now we entered a period of nothingness. People returned to work and June to college. Mam grumbled her to the railway station.

"And don't you go wandering around that place in bare feet. People will think you never knew what slippers were. Don't tell me it's healthier, how can it be healthy when your feet are perpetually landing on a new cold place? And get wrapped up when you go out, nobody looks smart if they are cold and we all know it's a coat colder over there. And not so much mooching about that John, I haven't sent you to college to waste time writing to him or trailing around in the cold with him at weekends. This is the final bit so don't you go making a hash of it. You're nothing without those bits of paper to prove you did it so make sure you get them".

At least when she streamed on like this, she didn't require an answer. June just set her little face and hitched her heavy suitcase a little higher. There was always ill feeling when Mam set them to the station. It was as if she resented them going and had to make it as much of a trial as possible. I hugged the station buildings as the train hissed to a halt but moved forward to reach up and kiss June. Once the door had slammed Mam and I stood stamping our feet and I wished that the train would move out without this pregnant pause.

"I don't know why you're just standing there. You could go and find yourself a seat."

"I'm standing here to say: "Goodbye to you both."

June's face looked pinched and troubled.

"Aye well, the whistle hasn't even blown yet. All the seats will be gone, and you'll be the one standing all the way to Carlisle."

"Couldn't you just say a nice goodbye?"

"Pardon? What do you mean? I've given up going over to Mothers' to see you off on the train. All right for some. I'm just telling you to keep warm and stick in."

"Hmm and getting a dig at John while you're at it. Honestly you say such things and in all my life I've never heard you apologise."

"I'll apologise when I've something to apologise for. It'll be a sad day when nobody cares for you and that's all I'm doing telling you to wrap up."

I spied the guard waving his green flag and I hurriedly moved away from the train before it belched steam around my legs. It jerked and pulled towards the bridge ahead and June waved and then disappeared inside to gather what could be salvaged of herself. Mam clasped my gloved hand.

"Right that's her off. Little ingrate. Now we'll go over and see if Mother is all right," and I was yanked along beside her; she in a happy state of indignation and my feet nearly numb from standing.

Oh, but January was a cold month and there was nothing to enliven it. No, birthdays or anniversaries in the family. No traditions to observe. It was just the start of the long haul up to summer and a dismal, spluttering start at that. The sun crawled low in the sky and smoke rose straight in the still, bone chilling air. Frost lay in pockets by the roadside and puddles shone with cracked ice. I looked down my nose at my steaming breath escaping from my mouth like my own personal exhaust and wondered if this was death by freezing. Mam walked with her head down to shun the cold and to make sure she did not have to acknowledge anyone and then stand in the keen piercing air. And I knew that she hadn't wanted June to go. Why couldn't she tell her that? It was as if she thought that she had to be overly critical. If she stopped pushing and chivvying, we would stop trying to achieve. Without her repeatedly pointing the way ahead then we would splutter to a halt and be doomed to a life of being common or ordinary. She had made them go to College and then betrayed a lingering resentment when they went. She had known to let them go but the constant reminders of her subsequent sacrifice was debilitating. With each exhortation to go further she was silently claiming their success as her reward for her martyrdom. Or maybe it had become a habit and she assumed that we did not occasionally need to be told of her love. I had so far escaped some of the motivating barbs. I was Little Edna and as such my role was simply to be dressed and paraded occasionally. I had not been required to give evidence of academic ability and as Mam usually stated that I was just a plodder I had assumed that I could just plod on. All Mam's energies had been poured into Mary and June to achieve more than simply looking good. But my time was coming. Now, while brushing my hair she made the odd musing comment as to what I would do in the future. She betrayed a worry that people were no longer allowed to pay for their children to attend Cockermouth Grammar so what would happen if I did not pass the Eleven Plus? I did not tell her that I was planning a diplomatic illness even though this may have eased her concern.

It was a relief to lift the latch on Mothers' door and be enveloped by the warmth.

"Has she got away then?"

"Hmm. Last lap for her so I've been telling her to get her head down and do some serious studying. By but it's perishing out there today. Pour me a cup of tea if there is one."

Which was a daft thing to say as there was always hot tea at Mothers.

"I'm telling you Mother it's cold enough for snow."

Mother pulled her cheap Bri Nylon cardigan closer.

"Oh, I hope not. They've got snow in Yorkshire. I've just had a letter from Evelyn. You can read it if you want. Apparently, Malcolm will be home soon. It must have been a real sickener when they added six months to the National Service because of that war in Korea."

"I'll give him Malcolm. Do you know what the beggar has been doing? Ringing and reversing charges. I nearly had a fit when the phone bill came in and here's me so delighted when he rang to wish us Happy New Year."

"Didn't it say he was reversing charges?"

"Of course the operator tells you but if Alf picks it up first he just accepts the call as if we are made of money and when he shouts of me I don't know by then and just go on talking to the lad. I wonder what he's going to do when he gets back to Yorkshire." "There's one thing for sure, our Evelyn won't let him go down the pit. Not only is Malcolm her baby but he had that Rheumatic Fever when he was little if you remember. No, it'll be a nice office job if she has her way."

"If he was mine, I'd try and get him to College. He's a bright lad is our Malcolm."

"Oh, you and your College Edna. Not everybody can do it you know."

I don't think that really occurred to Mam. The major hurdle was simply getting in and being accepted. The Government paid for almost everything after that and when Mam talked of sacrifices, she was meaning that they could have been earning good wages at the factories to add to the household coffers and helping her at home. In fact, wages had jumped and risen as never before, and manufacturers were not slow to respond to the spending power of the workers. It was no longer accepted that a couple got married and lived with their parents and whole new towns were being built around the country. "Make do and mend," had gone out of the window and even

June was talking of having a refrigerator when she got married. Mam's generation were uncomfortable with this new prosperity. They ricochet from being pleased and boastful to muttering that the growing generation knew nothing. It was as if material possessions shouldn't be acquired too easily. They couldn't be worth much if they hadn't been saved for first and they definitely weren't worth much if they had to be bought on the "Never, Never." There was a general fear that without pain and suffering, items were without an intrinsic value. Another favourite was waiting and delay to add to the appreciation. The longer you had saved and waited then it was assumed that the coveted possession would be all the more valued. Even small children were not exempt; something had to be paid before the getting and usually good behaviour was the price demanded. Now, some workers were opening pay packets that were allowing a better standard of living than simply putting basic food on the table. Mam and Mothers' generation were too afraid that this would not last and some dire event would occur for them to be returned to the clutches of the Means Tests man or rationing. They were too frightened to throw their caps in the air and embrace their new spending power and were shocked by the recklessness of those who could. It was all very nice but there was no guarantee that it would last. But others were watching the films, reading newspapers and magazines and not only did they want more than simply getting by, but they had the money to buy more. I watched the Movietone News and saw houses that were being built with heaters in every room. Of course, we had radiators in school and other large buildings, but I had never imagined them being installed in a private house. In January this seemed a far more sensible thing to aim for than a little car for Dad to drive to Silloth. Mam didn't appear to have the same desires and I continued to dreamily marvel at the Jack Frost patterns inside the windows at Lawson Street.

Somewhere in January and February it snowed all over Maryport. The distinctive shape of Skiddaw had been covered with snow since about November and gradually Criffel across the water had a blanket of white. Mam said that it would never be warm as long as the wind was coming off them.

Mam said that snow wouldn't lay in Maryport because the salt from the sea would melt it. But it always snowed heavily enough to beat the salty air and I loved it. I especially loved it when it came stealthily in the night. I knew as soon as I awoke that it was there. There was a solemn stillness and all noise had been dampened and muffled. I scrambled out of bed and hoppity skipped across the icy lino to open the curtains. Then I just stood with my elbows on the windowsill and gazed at the wondrous view. The sky was grey and heavy and the backs of the large houses of Curzon Street were like Robins' photograph negatives. Snow had gathered on the ledges of the rough-hewn sandstone and etched every detail. Below I could see where Mams' little boots had crunched down the yard to the coal house and the smell of Cumberland dry cured bacon was rising and tantalising my senses. Above me I could hear Dad coughing and hawking and spitting in the bathroom. I wrenched on my clothes and tumbled downstairs.

"If you think you are going out in that without a wash or some breakfast you've another think coming. Get back up those stairs."

"Dad's in there."

"Not for much longer. What will people think of us if you go out bleary eyed?"

Shucks. What did it matter when there was virgin snow waiting? I trudged back up all those flights of stairs.

"Dad. It's snowed, can I come in for a wash?"

"Frizzling Hexam. You'll be wet enough out there before long. Come on I'm nearly finished."

At least Dad had some understanding.

As I washed. I peered again out of the bathroom window. Beautiful, just beautiful. It was falling thick and fast and the heavy flakes whirled and danced with no specific pattern or route. It had a hypnotic effect and I lingered just watching.

Later, filled with bacon I still couldn't get out into it. The answer to any form of cold was more clothes and Mam

455

conducted an inspection. Yes, I'd remembered my Liberty Bodice and she added a scarf wrapped around my chest and pinned at the back while Doris Day sang of her Secret Love on the radio.

"Now to do your hair even though 'I see you stand like greyhounds in the slips, straining upon the start."

Getting out of that house could be a trial in itself.

So, there I was with more skins than an onion and this expanse of snow in the long backyard. It was not long before gloves were sodden and my hands were stinging with the sharp, wet cold. It didn't matter as I had a creditable snowman and not far to look for coal for his eyes and a rotten carrot for his nose. I had no sooner ventured out to inspect the snow in the back lane when wallop! Snow landed and crashed around the back of my neck. I didn't need to even turn, as I knew it would be Faffy Gill.

Though there were few children living on the street, Faffy lived next door but one to me and her family was a similar set up to my own. Her brother Billy was training to be a doctor at St. Andrews University, her sister Maureen was at College training to be a teacher and Faffy was the same age as myself. She was in the same year at Camp Road School but not in the same class. All the ingredients were there for us to be good companions. The ingredients only came together now and then; otherwise we waged our own war of attrition. Faffy had even devised her own version of Pooh sticks that had its own sequence. First run after Edna Croft always remaining behind her ready to wrench the ribbons from her hair. Swiftly turn around with Edna Croft now running at the back and move with all speed to the bridge over the river Ellen. Fall about laughing while waiting for the ribbons to appear floating under the other side of the bridge and Edna Croft watching them dismally.

I never caught her as she was slender and lithe and seemed to be able to accomplish the most amazing physical feats. She could climb the highest walls, ride her bike waving her arms in the air and she was willing to take risks to add extra excitement to any activity. Somewhere deep inside I rather envied and admired her. She was neat and elfin pretty and though I wasn't fat, I felt lumpen and stodgy beside her. Her boldness and daring made me feel serious and feeble but it was when I joined forces with Faffy that I had my greatest small-town adventures. Otherwise we were a challenge to each other, and we taunted and tantalised more than we played together. Often, we met with children from further up the street and from Selby Terrace and Curzon Street that ran parallel to ours. There were few arranged meetings but like flotsam and jetsam we came up against each other to play or to walk to school. We drifted together and apart. If we did decide on a game and were dividing into teams Faffy lead one team and I the other and our rivalry added urgency to the need to win. Either that or we desperately tried to sabotage the game to bend it in our own favour. If we were playing, "You can't cross the golden river," and

Faffy was the caller on the other side of the road I could guarantee that she would shout, "You can't cross the golden river unless you are wearing red," and those wearing red edged forwards across the road. On and on it went with every colour under the sun except the one that I was wearing. "Ha, ha. Edna Croft you're the loser, you're the loser. Na, na, nana, na." But there were times when we called a truce and found that we had much in common. We should have been friends then; and on some occasions we were but Mam didn't help either. There were never any friends good enough, smart enough, behaved well enough or came from just the right class and as Mam kept herself aloof from all but her close family I only remember her speaking to Mrs. Gill if they happened to collide when cleaning the fronts. Mam had decided that Faffy was not a very good girl and her constant remarks were like water dripping on stone. And of course, Faffy didn't help herself.

She was doomed as soon as Mam had solved the mystery of the frequently missing ribbons. We struggled with a fitful friendship. Mam often complained that she didn't want her gentle baby infected by that girl and her hoydenish ways.

Dusting the snow from my coat and shoulders I marched towards Faffy and stamped on the rather sweet little snowman that she had made just outside her own backdoor. Hostilities were declared once again, but this was an ideal time. There was little point in forming a pile of snowballs and then no enemy in sight. It was brilliant.

No holds barred and the snowballs whirled and flew until Mrs. Gill appeared and yanked her inside their backdoor.

In the early months of the year the walk up the long hill to school could be particularly hazardous and many times I've unintentionally slid halfway home. Lads seemed to have a particular talent for creating slides and Church Street was an ideal candidate for their version of the Cresta Run. As the school playground was also on a slight slope it was quickly striped with glacial rows. Queues formed to slide down them and the waiting was a good time to crunch the snow into snowballs. The slope was perfect for rolling the snow until the ball got bigger and bigger and we slithered about warmed by all the activity. It wasn't long before it dawned on the teachers that something enjoyable was going on out there. We were lectured on the dangers of the long slides, they cited broken limbs, fractured skulls, something called concussion and described the dreaded sneaky snowballs that had stones hidden in them. The slides were banned, snowballs were banned, and we huddled in miserable groups looking at them until the thaw set in. I wondered if June was at that very moment having a lecture on how to crush exuberance and stop all signs of happiness. Instead we stood around while the cold seeped into our bones and the wind from the sea slashed our cheeks raw. This was the only time in my life that I experienced chapped legs. Mam had decided that when it was so cold, I should have long lisle stockings. She carefully sewed suspenders to the edge of my Liberty Bodice, and this squelched the flesh of my upper thighs together. Not only was this the most ignominious thing that I had ever worn but created such pain as my thighs rubbed and chaffed against each other when I walked to and from school. The stinging agony was only marginally better than when I slid into the bath in the evening and the warm water touched the raw flesh. Hitler could have used this as a means of torture instead of feather quills down the fingernails. And when Mam saw the reddened area, she was very pleased that she had thought of long stockings to keep me warm. It was a paradox and a circle of agony. It didn't matter how much I wailed,

"Mam, nobody wears these. Everybody has white ankle socks."

"Well, I'd like to meet this family with the surname, "Everybody.""

Very funny.

It was much preferable to be nondescript and to go unnoticed and by the end of the day the stockings had begun to dangle round my ankles like concertinas. Faffy derived much amusement, pointing and leaning against the back wall with laughter until I grabbed the lapels of her gabardine and leered in her face. We never actually came to blows but the threat was always there that we would provoke each other until there was some physical explosion. In winter the snow provided useful ammunition instead. There were many advantages to snow not least being giving Faffy a good pelting.

CHAPTER 15

"A LITTLE WATER CLEARS US OF THIS DEED"

Valentine's Day was very important to Mary and June. It was a badge of honour to receive more than one or two cards and there was always the hope of telegrams or flowers being delivered. Of course, the most important man in their life had to come up with the very large padded cards delivered in their own slim white boxes. I shared their curiosity and anticipation but had no expectation of a card for myself. One year I was startled to received one and Mam, Mary and June teased me about it. I airily showed it at school, eyeing the boys in my class for blushes. I was deeply disappointed to later find that Auntie Lizzie had sent it. The week before Valentine's Day Mary opened an invitation card and turned it, perplexed.

"What's that?"

"I'm not sure Mam. It's an invitation for supper on Valentine's night."

"Very nice."

"Hmm. I don't actually know this couple very well."

"Who is it?"

"Oh, a couple that were at the Grammar school. Now they are married and live at Cockermouth, but I didn't really know them."

"Likely they know you well enough to invite you. Cockermouth eh? Didn't I say you'd get to know the right people from the Grammar School?"

"Give over. I said I only know them vaguely and what would I talk about? Hardly "old times" considering my time at the school."

"Oh, that. People have short memories and anyway you've done all right since. You haven't anything else lined up for that night, so you make yourself look a right bobby dazzler and just go and show them. Sounds very nice to me. Supper at Cockermouth. Funny night to choose though."

Mary returned. Mam looked up from her book.

"Was it a nice supper?"

Mary flung herself on to the sofa.

"Supper? Oh, it was so lovely, I couldn't be ladylike and dainty and just nibble a little."

"Poor conversation eh?"

"Gosh, no. We never stopped. They were very interesting, and it was good to laugh about the old teachers and reminisce a bit. This Bill that was there had been at the Grammar too. Would you believe he'd been a prefect when I was in the third form and had to tell me off for something. I would have been really embarrassed but he made it sound so amusing."

"Ugly chap this Bill then?"

"Phew no, far from it, in fact he has the loveliest blue eyes I've ever seen outside Hollywood, Course he was one of these really clever ones and got Scholarships for this and that."

"What made them ask you?"

"Apparently he has done his National Service first and now he is at University. He worked his Christmas holidays at Workington and saw me going on the bus to Flimby. So, his friends at Cockermouth had done a bit of sleuthing and come up with the idea of getting us together."

"Lives at Cockermouth, does he?"

"No, he lives at the Moor, so he got the bus so far back with me."

The telephone began to ring, and Mary jumped up to go into the sitting room to answer it.

Dad looked over his glasses at Mam.

"Sounds like a nice night eh?"

"University eh, that's more like and she seems rather taken with him".

It was a long time before Mary came back into the living room and though she was rubbing her hands together from the cold, her cheeks were flushed.

"Was that our June at this time of night?"

"Err, no it was that Bill wanting to know if I'd got home safely."

"What a gentleman. But that took some time to ask didn't it?"

"Oh, we were just talking and arranging to meet again. I think I'll just go up to bed now. Goodnight."

Mam smirked at Dad as he said.

"Now you let her be. Don't go making too much of it, you know how contrary she is."

"Me? But you've got to admit he sounds very nice in fact she may just have met her fat as they say."

Mr. Sandman had obliged and sent Mary a dream. If they weren't meeting as much as possible while he was home from University there were long, long telephone calls and letters dropping in the vestibule. The sun was shining in Mam's heaven and she frequently commented that he'd been a good Saint Valentine that year.

We didn't celebrate Saints days but certainly embraced Pancake Day. Mam whirled in and out of the kitchen sliding the golden, brown treasure out of the frying pan onto our plates and I was always sorry when I had to concede defeat and leave the table bloated. On the next day the Roman Catholic children wandered around the town with a smudge of ash on their foreheads, which seemed very strange. But we agreed that throughout Lent something had to go and in consequence this was always a period of slimming. Now this had absolutely nothing to do with a healthy diet, this was slimming with a capitol S. and as such had to be a painful as possible. It had to be endured and if you didn't suffer then it couldn't possibly work. If you weren't grindingly hungry or eating foods that were bordering on unpleasant, then it wasn't true slimming. On Ash Wednesday Mary, June and Mam went up to Briggs chemist shop to weigh themselves on the large scales and the plan was to return each week at the same time until Easter, keeping a chart of how they were doing. They always began with optimism and good intent. There was to be no bread, no potatoes, no biscuits or cakes and definitely no chocolate or sweets. In fact, nothing could be eaten that brushed up against being remotely enjoyable. They winced and shivered though grapefruit for breakfast and I was sent into the yard to fling lettuce round and round in a clean tea towel. They ate plates of cold meats or fish accompanied by Energen rolls that looked like grey sponge. They looked longingly at Dad and I with our bacon and eggs and Dad muttered that he didn't know why they bothered, as they were all bum heavy. Mam huffily said that we were pear shaped. Mary invariably insisted that physical exercise was added to make the agony end a little sooner. Each evening the dining room table was pushed back against the wall and they jumped up and down, flinging their arms to the sides. They touched their toes and bent from side to side and agreed that they were looking hollow eyed in fact their clothes were nearly dropping off them and Mam began quoting,

"Let me have men around me that are fat. Yon Cassius has a lean and hungry look."

It didn't last. Long before Easter Sunday the frying pan resumed its rightful place and the Energen Rolls were flung out in disgust. Even the birds avoided them. Mam returned to saying that it was impossible for a woman to lose weight after a certain age and her girls needn't look as if they'd just come out of Belsen.

467

Soon after the slimming was abandoned came Carlin, Palm and Pasche Egg Day. Mam didn't keep Carlin Sunday but at school the lads sniggered and recited,

"Carlin Sunday, farting Monday."

By now the Coop was doing a roaring trade. All children had to have new clothes for Easter Sunday, in fact it seemed to be new everything to celebrate the new life on that day. At Sunday school I liked the story of Palm Sunday and sang "Hosanna," with gusto and was given a palm cross to bring home. I still preferred the sweets from Bob Harris. For quite some time Mam had been saving onionskins and in the week before Easter they were tippled out onto the kitchen table. Then they were gently folded around eggs, which were wrapped in a small piece of cloth to hold the onionskins in place, and gingerly tied with another strip of cloth. The egg parcel was slowly and carefully slipped into a pan of water and boiled. I watched with anticipation as they were equally gently lifted from the pan and the cloth and onionskins removed. They were a miracle of patterns, brown, gold and fawn mingling and striping the shells. Mam rubbed them with butter while they were still warm to make them shine and then carefully lifted them onto the ledge half-way up the window. Sometimes we braved the weather and wandered along the Sea Brows savaging our hands picking gorse to put in the pan to make yellow eggs and sometimes Mam tipped in a bottle of cochineal to make red eggs. I was more fascinated by the genuine onion eggs and the wonderful striations left by the onionskins. As my Easter eggs came, they joined the Pasche eggs on the window ledge or along the windowsill. It was quite a scoop to receive an egg that when opened revealed a tiny layer of chocolates. With television becoming more popular the thing to have was a "Television Egg." These were made of sugar and had a piece of cellophane across one end. Held up to the light you could peep into the egg and inside was a scene of sugar flowers.

Mother Tuke was always rather solemn about Easter as she felt it keenly that Jesus had been crucified. She truly believed that the weather would be rain on Good Friday to show that the world was weeping for Him and then about three in the afternoon of Easter Sunday the sun would shine forth to celebrate that He had been born again. She believed without question, a simple belief that was endearing. On Easter Sunday the new clothes were laid out and breakfast was always a Hot Cross Bun and a Pasche egg. Then the visiting began, to show off the new clothes and to collect more Easter eggs. Well, that was the reason given and I usually did return with a brown paper carrier bag of more eggs and having been twirled this way and that by Mam. Auntie Meg and Peggy stuck to the tradition of giving one of their own Pasche eggs and an orange. These went together as it was a known fact that the eggs made you egg-bound and the orange sent you to the toilet. A reasonable combination. There was an improvement at Auntie Emily's' and Aunty Lizzies'. Not only was there a proper chocolate egg waiting but they slid money to me for my "Fairing" and

469

this was the real reason for visiting. I was trained to shyly refuse the money and proffer it back and all the while, praying that they wouldn't take it. At teatime all the Pasche eggs were put into a large bowl on the centre of the table. Everyone chose one of them and the egg dumping began. Choosing a near neighbour at the table, the dumb end of the eggs were tapped together first and then the sharp ends. The egg that survived unbroken was declared, "One a Cockatee" and if the same egg lasted more tapping without the shell breaking then it was, "Two a Cockatee," and so on. The champion egg was returned to the window ledge while the shell shocked, dumping failures were peeled and eaten. It was an Easter pastime that could take on darker shades with heavy betting in the pubs. One Easter Monday Auntie Lizzie came hurrying up the yard.

"Our Edna, have you heard about George?"

"George? What's wrong now?"

"He's in Workington Infirmary with a broken nose."

"Get away. Oh God he hasn't been singing, "Land of Dope and Tory," outside the Free Masons' again has he?"

"No, no, nothing like that. He went to the Bounty for a little relaxing libation and whap! This chap smacked him in the face."

"What just like that?"

"Well, not quite."

Mam rolled her eyes.

"Now come on Lizzie, you know he spouts his views all over the place. You and Mother think he can't do any wrong, but he must aggravate some, I can't believe he was just sitting there sipping a drink when someone set on him."

Aunty Lizzie shifted uncomfortably.

"They said it was the eggs."

Mam looked at Dad bewildered.

"Eggs? What eggs?"

"Well, the Bounty had ordered their eggs from him for the egg dumping competitions. When the Bounty won and the other pub teams lost, they blamed poor George even though he wasn't playing and just enjoying a pint."

"That's crackers. Or was it? Lizzie there's more to this isn't there?"

Auntie Lizzie stirred her tea slowly,

"Now don't tell Mother but Big Billy says there was a lot of money changing hands and those eggs were rock hard.

Then somebody accused him of feeding the hens salt and chalk to add to the calcium and harden the shells."

"He denied it of course?"

"I don't think he had a chance before they burst his nose and gave him a right pasting and then they had to send for the ambulance. Poor little fellow is a mess, so we'd better think of something to tell Mother before he comes home."

"Just tell her the truth."

"That might be a bit difficult."

Dad smiled as he shrugged on his jacket to go for a walk

"Edna waken up. You'll just have to bend the truth for Mother."

Egg dumping could be a very serious business, and in Uncle Georges' case, downright dangerous.

And of course, in among all this passing time Mam declared open season on dirt again and we were all back in action, tearing the house apart and putting it back together. Mrs. Routledge was summoned more often although she did cry off one day for her sisters' funeral and returned to tell us that there had been a lovely corsage. I tried as much as possible to escape. Not only was I not enamoured of housework, but the upheaval disturbed me. I hated the upturned furniture and constant washing draped all over; I simply wanted things back in their place and calmness restored.

I wandered outside and found Faffy sitting on the low wall outside her house. I joined her and we pondered going for Donald Almond to play. As we mooched around wondering what to do, a herd of beasts were being hurried along Station Street, which crossed the end of Lawson Street. Faffy suggested that as there wasn't much else doing, we could wander up and follow them. We trotted up and moved behind the cows and the men whistling, shouting and prodding them. The cows ran awkwardly, their teats swaying and lumps of manure dropping from their hindquarters. Their large brown eyes were flicking fearfully here and there and reminding me of the greyhounds on the Workington bus. Crossing the road, we ran after them down Mill Street, copying the men calling "Cush, Cush." We slowed while the cows were ushered through a gap that opened to a large yard behind the bus station. We sidled round the comer as the cows were being coerced into a cavernous looking building. Now they were exuding fear. I could feel it coming off them. They balked at the entrance and some tried to back away, merely to collide with all the cows behind them. They gushed urine and manure and then slipped and slithered against the rest of the herd.

"Did you see that Faffy? That man slapped its rump with his stick."

"Probably hardly felt it. Remember their skin is leather so maybe it just felt like a tickle or a tap would to us."

"All the same, they don't seem too keen."

"True. Maybe they don't understand about being sold to other farmers eh?"

The cows were taken to the very end of the building and penned in as we crept towards the opening. No one queried our presence, so we simply leaned by the doorway. As our eyes became accustomed to the gloom, I could see that they were looping a rope around the cow that was nearest to hand. Two men yanked and pulled it forward towards the daylight as it repeatedly raised and dropped its head and bellowed. They were really close to us, but I was rooted to the spot by the spectacle. Two more men joined the others and they all held the thick ropes to steady the beast as one man strode forwards and placed himself smack, bang in front of the cow. Very interesting; this was becoming an adventure.

"Steady lads, come on hold it, hold it. Are you right?"

"Aye, get on with it".

And from behind him he drew a large gun and shot the cow square between the eyes. I froze.

What had they done?

I couldn't even look to see what Faffy was doing. I just stared and stared at the blood exuding from the small black dot as the beast's head slowly drooped down.

"That's it, Lads, hold it, keep it up."

And another man rushed forwards with a huge enamel bowl in one hand and a massive knife in the other. With the knife he sliced the cow's neck open and at the same time expertly slid the bowl under to catch the gushing blood. He looked up at me and smiling said,

"That's for black puddings."

I stared until my eyes ached. I could not move. I knew that Faffy was still there beside me, but I could not turn. I just stood in that doorway and watched the bowl filling with the thick, dark red liquid. Slowly they lowered the cow and dragged it unceremoniously across the floor as two more men led another roped and bellowing cow to the same place and the man was reloading his gun. I felt Faffy pulling at my coat.

"Let's go."

We trudged back to Lawson Street in silence and then sat on our wall.

"That must be the Slaughterhouse."

"I didn't know that's why they ran along Station Street."

"I thought they were going to be auctioned."

"They knew Faffy. Those cows knew."

"Don't be daft, how could they know?"

But we were uncomfortable.

"I'm telling you they knew. I think if you don't mind, I'll go in now. Best not tell our Mams eh?"

"See you later then."

I went into the sitting room and pretended that I was reading but the book could have been upside down for all I looked at it. I kept telling myself that it was just a cow. Crikey we had to eat. A meal wasn't considered a meal without meat. Blood, all that blood. How could its body have held so much? And it had been so frightened. It had somehow known what was to come. This wasn't like the cinema; there had been no rescue, no reprieve at the last minute, no happy ending. Hollywood had taught me that somehow the cavalry rode in, the escaping prisoner reached Switzerland, and the hero saved the heroine at the last minute. Something happened. Something always happened. But in that place, it hadn't, and I had just stood and watched. I felt as if I had somehow colluded and ignored those big, brown beseeching eyes and I thought of Mam saying, "All the perfumes in Arabia would not sweeten this little hand."

The next day I caught up with Faffy on the way to school. We were awkward with each other.

"Did you tell your Mam?"

"No,"

"Me neither. It was horrible. I won't forget that in a hurry. I felt as if we should have done something."

"Don't be daft. What could we do and any way it was only a cow."

"I know I just felt like that."

"Oh, give over. It's nearly Fair Time so stop being so..."

She searched for a word,

"Maudlin."

Phew, it was a good word and I didn't even know what it meant.

Whitehaven and then Friday it came to Maryport and stayed all weekend. It was exciting to see their lorries, trucks and caravans lumbering over the New Road and up through the town to set up around the old butter market in Fleming Square. Dad and I wandered up to watch the garishly painted rides being lifted and secured and stare at the huge caravans with their ornate lace

477

curtains and occasional views of crystal and Crown Derby inside them. But the fair was better in the dark that hid the chipped paint and coarseness. Mam, Dad and I scurried up the street with the blaring music getting nearer and louder and the fair lights winking and flashing in and out of view. I had saved and saved my money since Easter and now there was to be an orgy of spending my "fairing." It was never enough, and the choices were numerous and difficult. I had graduated from simply wanting to ride on a fire engine or a train, to daring the larger rides. It was a two-edged sword as I knew that I was too old for the roundabouts where I eagerly clanged a big bell and waved at Mam each time she came into view and yet I was afraid of the bigger rides.

With many of my friends also roaming around enjoying the sights and sounds, I could not be seen squashed into a model double decker bus, never mind naively waving. It had to be the Jungle Ride or the Waltzer and this had to be taken with nonchalance and not a glance towards Mam standing on the cobbled square waiting to flap her hand to me. Sitting on the long sofa like seats of the Jungle Ride with my friends I felt distinctly unsafe, but I laughed gaily and hurriedly clutched the large chrome bar as it began to move. Oh, how I admired the young lads who waited until the ride was moving, to collect the money. They balanced with their feet, planted on the painted slats going up and down and around and held out a calloused hand to drop our money into a leather shoulder bag. Which was all very admirable, but it meant that I had to let go of my only means of survival to hand over the money. Of course, Faffy didn't hold on to anything and occasionally stood up to see if she recognised anyone in the crowd as we whirled past. My giggles became more high-pitched and my knuckles whiter as the ride gathered speed and the desire to feign indifference only returned as it began to slow. The Waltzer was even worse but I galloped on as if I had been waiting six months for death by whizzing round. I tottered off it with all of Fleming Square still moving and the ground seeming to lurch under my feet. I shrugged my shoulders and said that it was all right, but the Rib Tickler was better and went to join Mam who was wondering if we should have a toffee apple or candyfloss. My stomach heaved and churned but I stoically accepted the pink fluff on a long stick, tasting the sweetness as it melted into nothingness in my mouth. Dad took me on the Dodgems and the best part was when we didn't dodge anything at all but careered around being thumped and bumped and the Candy Floss made admirable efforts for a return journey up my gullet. Naturally Mam couldn't ride on anything. Not only was she a mother and her role was to stand and wave but it was not ladylike to be seen cavorting on the rides while the music blared, "I'm a knock kneed chicken." She did agree to come and see the, "Wall of Death" but rather spoiled it by declaring that the fearless motorbike riders whizzing up the sides made her feel faint. At least wandering around the stalls gave me a chance to regain some of my air of apathy and my stomach to settle enough to accept a toffee apple. I waited with anticipation as Dad tried the shooting galleries or the

479

darts and usually wandered home with a pathetic goldfish in a bag. Mary and June went on Saturday night and as Mary proved to be a whiz with the rifles Mam was becoming the dubious owner of a collection of cheap chalk ornaments. I often found a cocoanut on the table on Sunday morning; I also often found the poor goldfish dead and floating belly up. It was a fair swap. We knew the score. The fair was rather like the tart with a heart of gold. You knew that you were being ripped off somewhere. You knew that it was all a facade, which was one reason not to go in the daylight. It didn't matter. It was lights and colour and noise and a flurry of excitement, twice a year.

The months of May and June were kind to Cumberland and Mam said that the "powers that be," who plotted school holidays must have had the south of England in mind. We trailed to school overheated in the fresh sun and waited impatiently, to be released, into the lengthening days. Though Pam and Miriam's Mothers' always made me welcome in their houses, now we preferred to trail around the Sea Brows or sit languidly on the wall around the long buried, Roman camp. At Grasslot I sat on front steps with Betty; too hot to climb the pit bank. Instead we sat and chatted and seriously and laboriously made long tubes of wool. We achieved this by having a cotton bobbin with four nails hammered in the top and the wool wound around them, and then we used a pin to pick the wool over the nails in sequence. The various coloured wool snaked out of the hole in the bottom of the bobbin getting longer and longer and that's all; but we were very busy doing it. Others joined us and we squashed together on the step picking at the wool while the lads watched.

"Whoops there goes a slipper."

As everyone laughed, I was puzzled.

"What's a slipper?"

"Are you thick or what? One that just slips out is a slipper but a noisy one is a fart, like this."

And the lad edged up his bum and let rip.

I thought it was the funniest thing that I had ever heard and could hardly breathe from laughing. Then they decided to go over the factory wall to the field high with corn to play "You show me yours and I'll show you mine." Mam shouting to me that it was time to go home as Uncle Bill Musgrave had come home from his shift at the Chemical works, spared me this delectation.

"It's nice to see you playing a nice game with that lot for once, but we had better go and get your Dad's supper."

I just agreed as there were some things it was better for Mam not to know. On the walk home we met Aunty Lizzie going in the opposite direction.

"Have you left Mother in by herself?" she asked sharply,

"No of course not, your Bill is there and don't you get at me. I do enough and so do my girls. I don't see your Kath moving in to live with Mother like our Mary does sometimes."

"All right, keep your hair on. And anyway, our Kath is a married woman she couldn't just up and live with her. It's just since Mother had that heart attack, I don't like to think of her on her own and it's getting difficult to make sure she's O.K."

"Well, you know I tried to have her in with us and she wouldn't stay. I did everything to make her comfortable but no, all she would have was back in that old house. I'll not make the same hard work for my girls when I get old Lizzie. I hope we can learn a lesson from this and somehow make life easier for them. She thinks she's living independently but it's taking all of us to let her think that and I don't know how long we can keep it up. Mary seems to be courting strong and you know June's getting married so we can't expect them to help for much longer. I don't know what's going to happen."

Auntie Lizzie brightened up,

"Here, are we having a "do" for June being twenty-one like you had for Mary. That was marvellous and I could just do with something to look forward to."

Mam shuffled about,

"Err, no. I did suggest it, but June says she doesn't want a fuss made. And her Birthday is just as she sits her Finals so she couldn't come home anyway. And of course, there's her Wedding next Easter to plan and pay for so we can't do so much."

"Now that's a shame. I could have just done with a family "do." Still, she's a different calibre to Mary and you're right, there's no point in going to a College and flunking it right at the end. Not that our June will do that, you've always said she was the brightest. She'll go far that lass. What about this one? What are you going to do with her?"

They looked down at me as if I were a lump of lard stood there.

"I just don't know. She seems to get by all right but nothing like June was at the same age. Eh, Lizzie I can remember getting the train to Manchester and of course our June was so petit I didn't buy her a ticket for years. Then just as the ticket Inspector came along and was studying our tickets June read the Headline from a newspaper a man was reading opposite us. "Hitler invades Czechoslovakia". I nearly blocked her." "Did he charge you?"

"No, I think he was too busy laughing or maybe he thought she was a child genius. Anyway, where have you been?"

"Oh, I went to see if old Mrs. Ismay was all right. Those sharp summer showers have made it flood Downstreet again. I tell you the Council should get something done about it, but they don't."

"If I'd got onto the Council, I'd have made something happen. But I didn't, I got that instead,"

And again, they looked down at me.

"Maybe it was meant to be."

"You mean Alf meant it to be. He was frightened to death that I was going to have a life of my own. I knew Lizzie. I knew the morning after that he'd done it and that was my political career finished."

"Aye so you keep telling us. Oh, you never know she might be a comfort to you in your old age."

"You might be right but at present she hasn't a care in the world."

Fat lot she knew!

Not only was even longer division mightily puzzling me but also a lad at school had decided that I was an ideal candidate to bully.

I had not even been aware of his existence until one day he leapt from behind a wall.

"Yarrrgh. Ginger."

I shot to one side and walked on shaken.

"Ginger nut. When I get you, I'm going to tear that ginger right off your head."

I walked faster. However much I hurried, he kept walking just behind me, his calm voice insidiously threatening.

"One of these days I'm really going to get you Ginger. I'm going to batter you and sit on you and shave that hair till you are bald."

I slithered into Mrs. Williamsons' paper shop and idled around until I could not see him lounging outside and then set off along Curzon Street.

"Wharrrh. Ginger!"

He jumped from the corner of John Street and blocked my way.

"So, what you gonna do now eh?"

I turned and ran across the wide road and down Lawson Street. That was all. That's all he ever did. And I was terrified of him. It was all the more disconcerting as it only happened now and then. I never knew when he was going to appear to taunt me. He was much bigger than me and obviously could "batter," me had he wanted to. I didn't know how long it would be before his fists and a pair of scissors or a razor blade to the scalp would replace the words. It was also demeaning and somewhat ignominious to wander along with someone behind you muttering threats and insults. He instinctively knew what to say to trouble me and tapped into my mortification with seamless ease.

"Saw you on Annie's concert, you great fat slug. Saw you prancing in that frilly dress. "Think you're it, don't you, swanking around with your stupid bloody ginger hair? How you gonna look without it? Eh? Think cos you live on Lawson Street you're better than anybody with your posh school blazers. I'm going to get my gang and tear it off you."

On and on he leered and sniggered, and I hurried on feeling silly and humiliated.

Occasionally I saw him at a distance, and I was filled with fear. The only thing that I could think to do was to always arm myself with a companion but one morning I set off for school earlier than usual. As I began my way up Church Street alone, I heard him close behind me.

"Now I've got you, you carrot topped..."

With a rush of relief, I saw Annie Robinson marching up the other side of the road and I nipped smartly over to her.

"Miss, can I carry your basket?"

"No."

What? Here was me grovelling enough to make myself sick and she wasn't falling for it.

"Well, can I walk to school with you Miss."

"Get away with you, Edna Croft. I'll have enough of other people's children once I get into school."

Finally, I blurted out,

"But Miss, that boy over there is calling me names."

She looked down at me as if I had taken leave of my senses.

"Calling you names? What's wrong with that? How very poor spirited of you. Just remember, 'Sticks and stones may break my bones but calling names won't harm me'. Go on, you silly girl, you are big enough to know better."

And she marched ahead of me. I hurried to walk behind her, as near as I could without offending her again but enough to ward off my tormenter.

She was wrong; it was harming and intimidating me. I was very worried and frightened. I was having nightmares that I appeared bald and bruised. I hugged my own area to play and even then, I could not trust the street corners. There was nothing that I could do to stop it; I knew that I could not tell anyone. No one would understand the heart stopping fear he generated. If I had walked into the house with a black eye, all Hell would have broken loose. The school would have been informed and a thorough search made to find his identity and some punishment given, but as there was no obvious physical harm then it would be assumed that I was simply being a bit dramatic and silly. What a fuss over a few words. I didn't tell anyone, not even my friends. It didn't seem enough to merit the pounding fear that engulfed me when I heard his voice viciously murmuring, close to me. There was also something about it that made me feel that it was my own fault or that I should have dealt with it without another's intervention. I felt diminished and his snide slithering manner was making my life a misery. It didn't occur to me that he could hardly have sat on a girl in the middle of a small town and calmly shaved her head. There was so much fear engendered by the threats that there was no room left for logical thinking.

One Sunday afternoon I was wandering home from practicing my piece for the impending Anniversary when he shot out from a shop doorway.

"Got you now, you little shit. Nobody about eh? But my mates are waiting down the street and the lot of us are going to smash your shitty little face in."

I was startled, and none too happy with God. I mean you give up your Sunday afternoon to painfully recite a trite little poem and what do you get? Nothing but a walk home in severe dread. I did what I always did and just picked up my heels and ran and ran. I never answered him, just ran away with my heart pounding and not knowing if I was actually running toward his gang or to safety. I ran until I hurt for breath and my brown eyes were flicking with the same overwhelming fear as the cows at the Slaughterhouse. He did not follow me. There were no other boys and as I turned at the bottom of the street to look back, I could see him leaning in the same doorway laughing. I didn't hate him. I was too miserable for that and when it happened, I was frightened and bewildered. I thought you had to do something to merit enmity, but I didn't even know him. It puzzled me and I wanted it to stop. And it did.

As he was in the top class his taunting ceased when he moved to Netherhall Boys School. It was as if he had suddenly lost interest. I had been a pastime and now he was too lofty for such things. I occasionally spied him around the town, and I looked away and hurried on, even though I knew that it had stopped without anything being said. After a while I knew that I could walk to school without looking over my shoulder, but his few moments of sadistic pleasure left a lasting impression of hopelessness and mistrust and recurring nightmares of somehow being out of control and vulnerable.

So, completely unaware that I had some cares in my own little world, Mam said her goodbyes to Auntie Lizzie and marched home with me.

It wasn't often that I was wandering around alone so the startling shock and worry that suddenly entered my life only happened now and then. Neither did it happen on my own territory and I was relatively carefree when I was playing around Lawson Street. It seemed as if we had an invisible area that was all ours and we felt uncomfortable when we strayed further. This was also a place where parts of it were banned but like the factories that only added to their attractiveness. I had not, never, never, ever to go near the River Ellen. In fact, none of the children that I played with were allowed to go near the river. It was a river so old that it had developed many meanders on its' journey to Maryport. And once there it gushed and gurgled its way right around the town and hurried to the sea, forming a narrow, natural harbour. It was never lazy and even on the hottest days moved with some speed, as if it knew that it was reaching its destination and could not wait any longer. But it was a pretty river, with sloping banks and trees dipping towards and in the moving water. Sudden circular ripples came, as fish snatched at flies and the water was so clear that the fish could be seen weaving and darting beneath the surface. Standing looking down at it from the solid sandstone bridges was simply not enough.

The trick was to get out of the house wearing wellies before anyone noticed and asked why wellies were needed when the sun was splitting the trees. This footwear alone usually signalled an expedition to the river and we gathered troops along the way waiting while they too hurried home for suitable footwear and then out again. The main garage in the area was on the town side of the river but on the other side was their work yard. This was called the "Brickyard" and was a very large rough space filled with piles of building sand, railway sleepers, old cars and lorries, piles of rubble and of course, bricks. This too was banned but was a must as a means of reaching the river. When we got there, we divided into teams and used whatever we could find to build rafts. We staggered about hauling wood and old tin drums, spying on the other teams' efforts, encouraging the more gullible to run home for some rope or string, and hiding when any adult appeared. This activity could take days before something resembling a raft took shape. We seemed to agree to wait for the other team to have theirs ready and then Faffy and I stood on our rafts and ceremoniously imitated the clipped tones of the Queen. "I name this ship..."

Heaving and pushing we got the strange contraptions down the bank into the river and called, "All aboard", and "God for Harry and St George" and all piled on. They always sank.

And I usually squelched home with my wellies full of river water. We were never daunted and the next day saw us furtively leaving home in damp wellies determined that this time we would make modifications and sail away.

When raft building went out of fashion for a while, there was so much in the brickyard to play with that it still drew us there. We went on safari up the piles of sand and climbed Everest on the mountains of bricks and rubble. Again, we had to split into teams as Faffy adamantly refused to be my Sherpa Tensing and I certainly wasn't going to be any other than Edmund Hillary. There just had to be two conquests and two Edmunds. When this palled, we clambered into the old lorries or the rusting cars slumped morosely around the yard. We drove to Monte Carlo or raced around Silverstone peering intently through the missing windscreens. Or we divided into Cowboys and Indians and hid behind the sleepers ready to make it a town "fitten fer wimmin and children to live in", calling,

"Hey! The Cisco Kid's back in town."

"Not the Cisco Kid"

"Yup."

"Yeehah."

We galloped around the heaped sand, slapping our thighs and twirling our six-shooters. Pching! Pching! We were very good at noises and the drawling voices. "O.K. I'm going to mosey along down to the old corral."

"Gimme a shot of red eye,"

and an invisible glass whizzed along a railway sleeper and we rode off into the sunset. We divided into teams and raced, and of course hadn't Faffy perfected the Bannister Burst so I just had to be Chris Chattaway. Then we wandered home. "You've been out a long time."

"Hmm."

"Where have you been?"

"Out."

"I'm fully aware that you've been out. Out where?"

Mam really should have been around to be employed by the Spanish Inquisition. It usually ended with,

 "You've been told and better told."

I suffered nobly and lay in bed preparing for tomorrows assault on the river.

I was at a distinct advantage in that Mother Croft lived in the little toll bar cottage beside Crow Park. This was an area of woodland divided by the river from the Netherhall Estate and just around the corner from our house. If Mother Croft was not out scavenging for coal and orange peel or stoking church boilers, she would produce a very large key and open the gates for me. It was dim and green with the smell of the onion flowers growing by the river. I often went there alone and enjoyed walking the narrow path that fishermen had made alongside the river and wallowed in its' calmness and serenity. I saw the leaning trees make spider webs of shadows on the water and dust motes danced and drifted in the shafts on sunlight. There was stillness there, except for the river slapping and sloshing and moving with a sinuous motion. I could try climbing trees without anyone to witness my failures and explore the far reaches before anyone suggested a game. Now that a tormentor had entered my life, I made sure that I was not alone on these expeditions and having Faffy with me meant that we explored further into the woods. Wandering along the hard-trodden path we found that the river took a large bend leaving a levee of stones and there ahead of us was a small manmade waterfall. Naturally Faffy thought it very wet to just stand and admire it and we slipped and slithered across the top ledge of weed flowing stones. This brought us onto the Netherhall Estate, and we pushed through long grass and weeds until we came to the manor house and peered through the murky windows. We already knew that the Senhouses had long removed themselves to live in London and simply left the grand house to weather and crumble but we were surprised to see a large kitchen and there on the table a knife stuck in a green, mouldy loaf of bread. We climbed on the steps by the stable walls and pretended that we were ladies mounting our steeds and then found large stones slumped here and there with peculiar carvings. Some had been stood upright by the mansion walls, but others were falling to the side and some had completely fallen over and lay with weeds growing around and over them. We felt the inscriptions reverently but could not make out the language and then sensing that we had been there quite a long time, we decided to go home but promised that we would come again the next day to investigate some more.

That evening I puzzled how to ask anyone about the stones without betraying that I had been there.

"Urm. You know in the Netherhall Estate there are supposed to be some stones Mam."

"Stones?"

"Yeah, like big stones with writing on them."

"Don't say, "Yeah", that's American slang."

"All right but what about the big stones."

"What about them?"

"What are they?"

Mary looked up.

What stones? Where are they at?"

"Mary, how many times have I told you, there is absolutely no need to put, "at," on the end of a sentence. Where are they would have done, at is completely unnecessary. You'll never get anywhere if you don't speak properly."

"O.K. where are they?"

"That's better."

I was beginning to wish I hadn't asked but I manfully began again.

"They say that there are stones in the Netherhall Estate with writing and pictures on them."

"Who says?"

Quick thinking was required.

"Annie Robinson."

"Oh, her. I think you must mean the Roman stones, do you?"

I was losing the will to live.

"I don't know, that's what I'm asking."

"Not so much lip young lady. There are supposed to be some Roman artefacts that were taken from that field where there was a Roman Camp, but I haven't ever seen them. I mean what would we be doing on the big Estate. Our role in life was simply to work and pay for them to have a grand lifestyle and then go off to London and spend it. They finally went and didn't come back. That's' how much they thought of the little town that gave them a good living. I do remember seeing the Lord of the Manor rounding Netherhall corner in a coach and horses when I was a little girl and some people curtsying as he went past. Our Evelyn said that she would give me a good hiding if I so much as dropped my eyes, so I stood straight and stared and stared. I think they called him Hugh Pocklinton Senhouse but none of us was "in service," there."

"But what about the stones?"

"I think they are like altar stones or something. They must just be lying around there."

"They are."

"How do you know?"

"Err, Annie Robinson said."

"Actually, it's a crying shame. Any Council with any sense would see that we have treasures in the town and do something about it instead of leaving them to rot away. I mean look at York, they must make a mint from people just going to see the very same things that we have but they had the sense to put them on display. Somebody could get in touch with any Senhouse that is left and suggest that we do the same. If I'd got on the Council that's the sort of thing that I would have done."

Mary and I cast our eyes to the heavens.

"So, what's the writing on the stones?"

" Lord, I don't know, as I said I've never seen them and if I had I don't know Latin. But I would really like to see them; I mean think of the age of them. Once long ago some poor Italian was sent over here in the Roman Army and had to put up with this cold climate. That must have been a shock to his system."

"Like Annovazzis and Cuetos?"

"Well, I never really thought of that." Mary said,

"Cuetos are Spanish not Italian."

"I know but it's very hot over there as well."

I gave up.

The next day dawned hot and still so Faffy and I persuaded Mother Croft to open the gate of Crow Park and let us in again.

"Mind you two be careful in there and don't go far."

As if we would.

This time we hurried straight to the little waterfall and dithered and slithered across. Just as we were about to fight through the long grass to make our way back to study the Roman stones and old lady suddenly rose up in front of us and screamed,

"I thought I saw you two here yesterday. You're trespassing. Did you know that? And I'll get the police. Something told me you'd be back, you little beggars. Right tell me your names."

We had been rooted to the spot with shock but at this request, Faffy grabbed my top and yanked me with her. We battered our way back to the river and slid down the small bank. Faffy sped over the submerged stones like a gazelle while I gave up the "not over the top of the wellies," rule and jumped right in. It was deeper than I had thought but not deep enough to swim. I lunged and gasped in the cold running water while Faffy stood on the other side urging me on. I floundered and pushed with my feet slipping on the river bed and the old lady jumped up and down shaking her fist and still shouting that we had been trespassing and we were, "for it" when she found out who we were.

As I scrambled up the other side Faffy pulled my arm, helping me up the riverbank and we ran and hid behind a tree.

"What the heck was that?"

"I don't know but she looked like Old Mother Riley."

"Do you think she has legs?"

"You daft lump, course she has legs it's just the grass is so long all we could see was her top half. You're soaking. God, your Mam'll go mad if she sees you, what are you going to do?"

I hadn't a clue but slopped my way back to Mother Crofts' more worried about the strange old lady taking us to court than being wet. When we knocked on her door to ask her to relock the gate, Faffy decided that she would just go home herself and we promised not to say anything even if the police came to throw us in a dungeon.

Mother Croft stood in her doorway and looked me up and down.

"So, what happened to you then? Fall in the river, did you?"

Now that was a solution to one of my problems and I resolved to tell Mam the same story simply missing out which side of the river I'd fallen in from.

"I just slipped down the bank Mother."

"Aye well it's easy enough done."

Was it? I wondered how she knew and if she had ever done it. I dripped behind her into her living room.

"Right me lass, get them wet clothes off and I'll hang them on the clotheshorse in front of the fire." I peeled of the sodden clothes and stood in my vest and knickers. "Go on, they're wet too."

I squirmed at the thought of standing naked until she laughed and said,

"Hang on I'll get you a pair of my L.T.Bs to put on."

She came from the bedroom with a large pair of salmon pink, silky knickers that smelled strongly of mothballs.

"Here, these are big enough to pull under your oxters."

I dried on her rough towel and stepped into the slithery knickers and pulled them up under my arms while the legs came down to my ankles.

"Sit on that copy and I'll get you some bread and jam while they dry enough for you to walk home".

"Mother, what's 'L.T.B?"

"It stands for, "lastic, top and bottom". I suppose your Mam's too fine for them, but they fair keep you warm. Nothing much blows up there I can tell you."

And she flung a few more coals onto the fire.

"There you go lass. 'Every little helps,' as the old woman said when she peed in the sea."

I choked on my jam sandwich, laughing and thinking of Mam saying that her mother in law was, "simply too crude for words." My clothes began to steam dry and I was uncomfortably hot and steaming too. It didn't matter that the day was hot and sultry. Mother Croft had a fire going whatever the weather. Her little house was amazingly untidy, unwashed dishes were piled in the sink and overflowed onto the tables. Ashes had tumbled out of the grate and threatened to spill across the carpet and newspapers lay on the floor where she had left them. There was a green speck of mould on the crust of my piece of bread and I picked it off and flicked it onto the fire.

I was very comfortable. I didn't feel that I had to sit up straight, not touch this or that, mind my manners or speak correctly. She busied about at the table cutting vouchers from washing powder packets and placing them in an envelope to send away for another voucher to get a free packet. Then she amazed me by swiping some of the detritus aside on the sideboard and lifting a stamp. I felt that it was truly clever to find something so small among the vases, papers, candle sticks, reading glasses, broken clocks, saucers, a gravy boat lying on its side and a dying geranium. I watched as she spit on the stamp and thumped it on the envelope.

"Right, get your clothes on and you can post this for me on your way home."

My clothes weren't quite dry, but I pulled them on, trying not to mind my fingers sticky from the jam. Mother Croft's kitchen was not the most savoury of places and I may have come out stickier than when I went in.

"Mother. Who's the old lady that lives over the river?"

"Old lady? Oh, you mean Mrs Graham. She's not old. Her and her husband are supposed to look after the place. Why?"

"Just wondered. Mother would you walk me so far home?"

"Now what's the point in me asking you to post a letter and save my old legs if I'm going to walk you home, you daft lass? If you're that frightened of your Mam, I'll tell her you just fell in the river and kept an old body company while your clothes dried, next time I see her. I'll remind her that it's lucky you didn't drown. Don't you be scared of her, she means well, even if she goes about it the wrong way."

I couldn't tell her that I had my own devious means of placating Mam and I was actually afraid of a boy jumping out at me. It sounded pathetic. Neither could I tell her that I may be accosted by Sergeant Harrison, clapped in handcuffs and then chained in a dark cell, for trespassing on private property. As I ran home, I thought of when Mam had taken me to Carlisle Castle and shown me the Licking Stone, licked smooth by thirsty prisoners. Maybe that would be my only source of water in jail, as I waited until the River Eden rose and fill my mouth and nostrils. I shook my head. Surely, they wouldn't. Surely, they wouldn't put me in Carlisle Castle wearing a suit with arrows and sewing mailbags. I would die of heartache from missing Mary and June and they would sigh and shake their heads in sorrow and miss me too. But even worse than that, my name might go in the local paper and the whole family would be damned forever. Mary and June would never be able to get married and all of them would have to move far, far away and never tell that there had been another girl that had brought shame on the family. I hurried home, peeled off the damp clothes and chose some completely different as a disguise.

I had reached home without being accosted and insulted and day followed day without Sergeant Harrison banging on the door and demanding a criminal be delivered into his hands. Faffy and I eventually agreed that it had been quite an adventure but not one that we wanted to repeat, and Mam vaguely wondered why there were damp clothes in the washing basket.

CHAPTER 16
"SUMMERS' LEASE HATH ALL TOO SHORT A DATE"

"Mam, Where's my shorts?"

"Burble, burble, blah, blah, mairy, cupboard."

"What?"

Mam came to the bottom of the stairs and said,

"If you want to speak to me, come down the stairs, a lady does not shout."

"Aw, Mam, I'm way up on the top floor."

"What?"

I ventured one flight down and leaned over the banister saying more clearly.

"Where - are - my - shorts?"

"There's no need to enunciate to me young lady. And never mind your shorts, where's the magic word?"

"Perleese."

"That's better. But remember, "sarcasm is the lowest form of wit". The shorts are in the airing cupboard."

"No, they're not."

"Yes, they are."

"No, they are not, I've just looked."

"Did you look under anything? If I come up those stairs and find them, I'll block you with them."

Wharrgh.

I stomped back up-stairs and rummaged around finding them under Mary's neatly folded blouses. I pondered telling Mam that the shorts had been somewhere else just to be right but as I was almost convinced that she had an all-seeing eye I pulled them on and ran downstairs.

"What did I tell you? You don't look properly. Men are just the same. If a thing isn't under their nose, they can't see it. Now they look nice and show off your fine fat legs."

Thanks Mam, I just needed that.

"Is our June still doing her Lazarus impression?"

"Dunno."

Forgetting that ladies didn't shout Mam stood at the bottom of the stairs,

"JUNE. Are you up?"

"Mumble, mumble," drifted down.

"This is the third time I've called you and when I ask you if you are up, I don't mean are you upstairs. Come on or we'll miss the bus."

"It's nowhere near time for the bus."

"Mary, I know that, and *you* know that, but she doesn't, and I always shout of her a bit earlier. How she manages at College I don't know."

"Likely she does and it's nice to have her home before her exams so don't get at her."

"Me? Me? I only say what has to be said. Mind sometimes I don't know where we got her from. She was saying last night that she has come home to swot, not to have days out and she finds the Carnivals embarrassing. I can't understand that. People do their best to put on a good show each summer and they are definitely worth seeing. The work that goes into some of those floats; real artistry and I don't know how they afford all the crepe paper. Remember the Ivy Queen at Broughton Moor Carnival last year? Now that was a sight to see. Nothing embarrassing about that, and if she can't have a day out as a family it's a bad job. 'All work and no play makes Jack a dull boy' as they say."

She pointed to the stool and stopped her mouth with hairgrips and ribbons.

I climbed on and sat waiting while she brushed my hair and parted it.

"Dear God. Come and look at this."

Mary and Dad crowded behind me and stared in silence. I looked ahead down the long yard and wondered if I had finally got the nits.

"That's it. That's it! Get her up to Jeans' hairdressers and get it all cut off."

My eyes grew larger and still stared down the yard. What had they found in there? A mouse?

"Dad, we can't do that. She's almost sitting on it."

"If you won't take the lass, then I will, even though I've never been in a Ladies Hairdressers. I'm telling you it's coming off. You can't leave the little lass in that state, just because you like it."

"Alf, it's her crowning glory."

"Tripe. The beads of sweat are standing on the back of her neck and you are bothered about the length of her hair. It's like a great shawl lying on her shoulders, and too hot for her, you can see that. She'll be ill from overheating of the brain. I don't know why the long faces, it'll grow again, sure as eggs are eggs. Mary stop primping in front of that mirror, go and get dressed and make an appointment for it all cut off."

"We're going to Cockermouth Carnival today and hairdressers are always shut on a Monday, you know that."

"And you know what I mean; if they are shut Monday then take her Tuesday and she can miss school. Now I've spoken and it's coming off.

Gosh, I couldn't imagine myself with short hair and found the thought rather exciting. Mam slowly plaited my hair and the air was as sombre as if a telegram had arrived with bad news. Mary's voice came down the stairs,

"Mam. Our Edna's messed up all my good blouses."

"Aye well, if you'd put them away, she couldn't have done it."

But her voice was dulled as if the heart had gone out of her.

June wandered around the door frowning.

"Honestly there's no peace in this house. First chance I have for a long lie in and there's our Edna shouting about shorts and then Mary and what's all this about our Edna's hair?"

"Oh, stop your grumbling, you had to be up anyway to catch the bus for Cockermouth. I know they put extra buses on for Carnival day, but it's still hit and miss whether we can squash on one. Go and get some toast while I finish this hair. I may not be doing this much longer."

"What's been going on, has she got head lice?"

"June! None of mine have ever had head lice or fleas for that matter. No, I just parted her hair and the sweat was standing on her neck. Then your Dad said she has to have it cut off or her brain will overheat. But June it's so beautiful."

She let one plait fall and lifted the hem of her apron to wipe her eyes and June moved over and put her arms around her.

"Oh, don't Mam. Don't cry. You know Dad's right. You can get brain damage from a high temperature and it will grow by the winter comes. Don't cry."

"Aye well, I suppose she has quite a nice face. And look at her, sitting like patience on a monument smiling at grief."

"Aw, listen Mam there's bigger losses at sea. Come on cheer up we'll have a really nice day today and don't think about it as it hasn't happened yet."

At least the drama caused by my overheating brain had made June more amiable about having a day off with Mam.

The Carnivals were a great tradition in the area and brought a day of colour and fun. Again, there was a sequence and order and they usually began at the village of Seaton and ended with Maryport Carnival. Many were disappointed when some villages simply had to have them on the same Saturday. Then there was deep discussion as to whether to go to Flimby Carnival this year or to Dearham. It was a day to visit relatives who lived there, to wander around different shops before the Grand Parade or meet friends and family in the streets. Even the Grand Parade had an order and sequence and began with a young girl riding bareback and dressed as Britannia. Following behind were the dignitaries of the area, the town Councillors and Fred Peart the local M.P. looking distinctly uncomfortable and out of place but nobly waving to the crowds as if that's all he ever wanted to do each Saturday in the summer. After this came the Queens. The Carnival Queen, the Snow Queen, Gipsy Queen, Ivy Queen, Rose Queen and floats depicting the four seasons. The lorry, tractor or wagon that had been commandeered to carry the displays was completely disguised with decoration and the driver struggled to peer through a small rectangle left clear in the windscreen. It was thought very poor to leave the cab or the wheels undecorated. The local brass and silver bands played, and the dance troupes marched and occasionally stopped the whole parade by giving a short display in the middle of the street. Punctuating the larger floats were the smaller entries of bicycles, scooters and decorated prams. And no Carnival was complete without fun characters, invariably men dressed as women with impossibly large bosoms, violent red rouge and lipstick smeared awkwardly across their faces. Particular public houses made their own entries that were often tribes of Zulus stained with coffee and shoe polish. Gorilla costumes were popular and gave an added thrill when they rushed towards the waving crowds. The Police were very tolerant and were often running through the Parade looking for their missing helmets. The weather was very important for the success of the Parade. Too hot and some were fainting and needing copious quantities of liquid. Rain gave great concerns, but some bravely went ahead while the dye from the crepe paper ran down the floats and the Zulus became pale-faced warriors. Strong wind was almost as bad and could ruin the delicate frames entwined with leaves and paper while little children shivered in their thin, frilled clothes.

Though the Carnivals had their origins in the pit villages, Cockermouth had condescended to be infected and though not the first or the last in the Carnival timetable, it was always the prettiest and the most sophisticated. It was important to be there with enough time to find, "a good stand," on Main Street and then clap in appreciation as the floats glided past. There was a certain disappointment to see the ambulance trundle along, as that signalled the end of the Parade and then we walked to the field near Millers Shoe Factory to sit by the banks of the River Derwent. All in agreement that Rio could not do any better. Mam sat awkwardly on the grass and drew the picnic from her bag while little children ran races for lollypops. A large stage was always erected, and the dance troops vied with each other for cups and trophies and gorillas wandered languidly, loathe to lose their costumes. All those that had been in the Parade were given a picnic in a brown paper bag which always looked infinitely more interesting and appetising than Mam's attempts to use up whatever she had come across in the cupboard.

On the following Tuesday Mam took me to Jean's to have my head lightened. It was a doom-laden walk, and, in the shop, Mam was given a cup of tea to fortify her. She cried on the way home; carefully dabbing her eyes with a lace handkerchief that was usually threaded through her watchstrap. At home I kept looking and looking at myself in the mirror, feeling very odd and being reminded by Mam, that I must tell them at school that I had not had nits but perspiration.

When the time came for Maryport Carnival, the shops usually entered into the spirit by decorating their windows for a window dressing competition. We were surprised to find that my hair was in Jeans' window. It was attached to a very large doll and tumbling into a bowl of cotton wool soapsuds. Around it, in coloured letters were the words, "Friday Night is Arnami Night." Mam was much gratified to see that it had won Third Prize and was sure that it was the luxurious red, hair that had won and not the actual display.

The Carnival at Maryport was known to be the biggest, probably because it was the last one of the Season. Invitations were extended to all the other villages and towns to enter the Parade once again and where possible they did. The visiting Carnivals Queens donned their robes and this time rode in limousines instead of on their floats, waving majestically to the crowd from the back of their car. As many bands as possible took the chance of one last march and the dancing troops swelled until their dancing displays split the Parade and made it seem even longer. Many of the vehicles used were working vehicles so it was not always possible to keep them decorated and in a convenient barn to wait for the last Parade but those who could trundled them out once more. Oh, but I enjoyed Maryport Carnival the most of all. Not just because it was longer but there was an added raw humour that was missing from Cockermouth. There were more fun displays and groups to delight and amuse and often shock with their crudity or daring topical comment. It was almost obligatory for a man dressed like a pantomime dame and looking very pregnant; to be hurried along squashed in a pram. At certain points they all stopped and after much shouting, water throwing and flapping sheets the "husband" triumphantly held aloft a doll; then they cheered and hurried on their way. While some clapped, June looked away and Mam announced that there was simply no need for such things, but she couldn't resist a smile at their antics. Maryport also seemed to have cornered the market for homemade bands, and groups marched along playing pans, kazoos, paper and combs, anything that made some semblance of noise. One year, Cockermouth had re-entered their float of a towering golden pyramid. At each corner an Egyptian guard stood solemnly and from an impressive opening in the centre of the pyramid, a boy sat immobile as Tutenkamun. Everyone gasped and clapped and cheered and just as they were nodding and agreeing with each other that nothing could cap that; a little chap came running behind, dragging a battered, handcart. He was blacked up and wearing nothing, but a chamois leather sewn into a loin cloth. The hand-made cardboard sign, flapping on his bareback stated, "Maryport King Footenmouth."

This was Maryports' answer to Cockermouths' serious and very beautiful effort. It promptly destroyed any pretensions of grandeur and prestige and it mocked the hauteur and arrogance of one town to another. In its' small way it acknowledged and accepted that Cockermouth had an elevated opinion of itself and saw the port with all it's dirty industries as white trash neighbours. And unabashed we did not care.

The annual Carnivals were a sudden burst of outlandishness and bravado and someone's chance for their few minutes of fame. There was a freedom about them; a colourful expression of release for many who had worked deep underground with the weight of the Solway not far above them. It was one more outward sign of the industry affecting the social make-up of the area.

The day ended with the grand Carnival dance at the Palace Ballroom and now Mary and June were making foursomes with John and Bill. As they jostled over the mirror in the hallway, Mam, Dad and I got ready to go to the pictures to see the new film, "Genevieve."

"Move over June and pass me that powder; looking wonderful isn't easy you know,"

"Go and use the mirror over the fire and give me a bit of room. Do you think Bill will wear his smart dinner jacket and bow tie?"

Dad paused in the doorway,

"Isn't about time you brought this young man with the fine clothes home to meet us?"

Mary looked round startled,

"You said I hadn't to bring another home until I was definitely going to marry him."

"And I think it's about time you made your mind up. There's more talking on the phone and flying off to see him, he must be something special and I think we need to vet him, so you and your Mam plan a nice Sunday tea and get him down here for our verdict."

Mary flushed.

"He hasn't proposed yet and even if he does, I might not be ready to settle down to marriage."

"Listen you can't go through life just enjoying yourself.

"Alf!"

"You know what I mean. Any man who gets our Mary is getting a good catch, so I don't know what he's waiting for. She might not be ready to settle down but I'm ready to have a bit of peace in this house. By, I'm already looking forward to the day when I'll look down that yard and say, 'Here comes our June with those five bairns of hers again.' She'll tumble in with them and I'll have them all over me until I take them off to the Sea Brows."

June's face was puce, but it was obvious that she was enjoying the imagined future':

"Give over Dad and get yourself off to the pictures."

The three of us walked up Senhouse Street to the Empire. Mam nudged him,

"You fair embarrassed June there."

"Aw, come on you know yourself it would be nice to have a few little ones around. In fact, if we got that caravan, we could take them on there and give them a break and then hand them back when we got fed up."

"True. Oh, I don't know, I had such hopes for June. I thought she'd have a proper career and go far. I didn't want nothing but housework and churning out children for some man."

Dad ignored her tactlessness.

"She has got a career and one she can always pick up if she needs it and if she wants a house and children instead then that's good enough for me. As long as she's happy."

Mam stood stock-still.

"It might be good enough for you but not for me. You'd just let them hang as they grow. If we all did that we'd still be in caves and running about painted with woad. We have to move forwards and keep on moving forwards or else we'd stagnate. She thinks leaving College is an end but it's only just a beginning."

519

"And so is marriage. As I said she'll have her job to come back to when her children are older."

"You know Alf, I sometimes think all that the Suffragettes got for us was the right to do two jobs instead of one. And if they were getting married, I had hoped that it would be to someone with enough so that they didn't have to do anything."

I pondered the logic of this beside her desire for us to have career.

"Come on Mam, I want the toilet."

"You were told to go before we left the house. And stop hopping about. Decorum Edna decorum."

I thought that it was a brilliant film, but it had simply left Mam grinding her teeth.

"I agree it was good acting and a catchy theme tune and I didn't know that Kaye Kendal could play the trumpet but wasn't it just typical. Two men following their hobby and dragging the women with them. I mean would you ever see women tinkering with vintage cars and making others suffer so that they could race them. Not likely. Playing, that's all those men were doing, and we are supposed to admire and sympathise with them. If women weren't keeping the serious things in life tacking over, I don't know where the world would be. Who do you think did all the work to get the Carnival up and running? The women. I tell you, there wouldn't be Father Christmas if there wasn't Mother Christmas."

Dad wandered on with my hand in his, ignoring her. He nodded to some people over the road.

"Isn't that Mrs. Graham?"

"Mmm. They do say that her daughter has T.B."

Mam looked shocked,

"I thought we'd nearly got rid of that. How do you know, did one of the doctors say?"

"No, Big Billy Musgrave said that she had Two Beauties."

On the Sunday after that particular Carnival we were all seated in our allotted places at the table eating the Sunday lunch.

"Does this meat seem tender enough?"

"It's very nice Mam."

"It's a job to get a bit of decent meat nowadays."

"I thought things were better since Rationing stopped."

Mam shrugged grudgingly, unwilling to admit that everything at the table was just fine.

"The vegetables could be a bit sharper."

"Mine are O.K."

Mary wiped her brow,

"I think they call that, "al dente," or something."

"What?"

"When vegetables are only half cooked."

"Are you saying that my vegetables are only half cooked?"

"No, no of course not. I was just looking at a French cookery book the other day and it said that we cook them too far."

"Oh, so mine are cooked too far. There's nothing wrong with a good British meal, in fact there's an art to cooking this food properly. We do ourselves down thinking foreign food is better. I remember our May at Appleby making mince without an onion or gravy browning, it was just like a grey mess and I thought then that even mince had to have some care taken to cook it. I didn't think it possible to get that wrong. Anyway, men are such

children that they prefer a good plain meal, so you are as well just learning that."
June said,

"There's a girl at College who's a vegetarian."

There was a scandalised silence.

"What no meat?"

"No, she doesn't eat meat at all."

"That's crackers. You can't have a meal without a bit of meat. Well, it wouldn't be a meal would it?"

"Is she a funny religion?"

"No. She doesn't like the texture and she likes animals."

"What's that got to do with it? By Jove, we should have tried that when the Depression was on and you had that allotment Alf. There was one night, all that I had in the house for you two little lasses for your supper was a cauliflower from the garden, so I grated some cheese on it and gave you it on toast. I felt terrible and I cried when I went to bed. I cried and cried. Those are days you never forget."

To try to stem the sinking tone of the conversation I said brightly,

"Did Bill propose at the dance?"

All of them turned and frowned at me.

"You don't ask questions like that and anyway Mary would have told us, wouldn't you?"

"Too true. But I'll tell you what he did ask me. He asked me if I'd go with him to the Graduation Ball."

Mam put her knife and fork down.

"Oh, my goodness. The Graduation Ball. Now, that's serious."

I could see that already she was mentally picturing flowing gowns and long lace gloves.
"Well, if he didn't propose, did he wear his posh dinner jacket?"

Mary smiled at me,

"Yes, he did."

"What just the jacket and no trousers?"

Even June laughed but when the laughter was subsiding Mam looked at me reprovingly,

"I don't know what's going to become of you. They say that there's a Charley in every gang and it seems to me that it's always going to be you. It's no compliment to be the clown in the group and maybe people are laughing *at* you and not *with* you."

I felt squashed and then dismal. I thought it was good to make people laugh and I liked the feeling when it was me that had achieved this. I fell silent and when they were clearing the table, June put her arm round me,

"Don't take any notice of her. Pet. You are sweet and funny and just go on being you."

Which was very nice other, but I hadn't realised that possibly some were mocking me when they laughed. Maybe being me was a silly person and not a witty and amusing person. I had never considered it and Mams' statement made me thoughtful. I liked Bob Hope and Tommy Cooper and it seemed such a great gift to make people happy and smiling. Her thrown away comment had only taken her a few seconds to voice, but it stayed inside me and stained like indelible ink. It made me self-conscious and aware that I may just be a figure of fun, but it did not stop me. It was as if visualising the ridiculous or pricking pomposity, bubbled up inside me and could not stop tumbling from my mouth. I found that humour also made a good camouflage for sensitivity or deflecting delicate situations and using it became a compulsion that I found hard to resist. Her words haunted me on and on and sometimes I tried, I really tried to be serious, sagacious and wise. It didn't last. Even hearing me speaking profoundly, palled after a few moments and

I was overtaken by the absurdity and could not check the urge to throw in the facetious and fatuous. Now I was sad that, possibly I was just a someone to snigger about and resolved that I would try to become a grey person that no one noticed at all. I would grow up and wear my hair in a bun, and dull coloured clothes that hid any semblance of the female figure. I would have heavy glasses and quietly scurry from some sensible office each night with my head down. And even as that thought was rippling through my mind I wondered if Rock Hudson or James Mason would bump into me and knock off the glasses. As they apologised and hurriedly collected my bag from the pavement they would look up and have the temerity to gently remove the hairgrips. My hair would come tumbling down turning me into the town beauty and they would be compelled to whisk me away to wondrous foreign parts.

Dad leaned down behind me and whispered in my ear,

"When my dinner's settled, we'll go off to Saltpans."

It was as good an offer as I was going to get so I smiled at him gratefully and wandered in the kitchen to help dry the dishes. Mam and Mary were busy in there, clearing up and wondering whether mauve satin or ivory taffeta would be sophisticated enough for a grand ball. This had to be something super special for, as Mam said,

"The apparel oft proclaim the man."

Dad and I walked everywhere and anywhere but he preferred walking towards the sea, which wasn't difficult at Maryport. The walking was always amiable. He strolled, slapping his walking stick gently against his leg, humming to himself and sometimes holding my hand in his hard, warm grip. Often, we stood still while he gathered the remnants of his breath and coughed into a handkerchief. His heart weakened with toll and toil, he was giving me what he could, his time and his love. On these simple walks he was the heartbeat of my life, just Dad and I. They were tranquil with no particular time limit. We just walked. We walked through the dim tunnel of trees along Netherhall Road. Tall and lush, they were on both sides of the road and bent and met to form a green passageway along and past the gates of the Netherhall Estate. These were rusting and leaning inwards and the carved popinjays on the gate columns were greening and spattered with bird dirt.

The road made a sweeping bend and to the right was the new Netherhall Boys School. It had been designed and built with no consideration to the local architecture and materials, so it stood glaringly in violent pink new brick. Its' only claim to originality was a tall, "Pepper Pot" chimney, otherwise it was an unimaginative design planted in large, wind-blown, playing fields. Again, it perpetuated the passion to place children away from civilisation but this time the planners had gone one better by placing it on the main trunk road to Carlisle. Mam said that it was a recipe for hordes of young lads to try to prove their manhood by playing, '"chicken" along the busy road. Soon after the school, the road divided; the larger one turning to the right towards Carlisle and the smaller one sliding to the left and along the Solway coast. Dad and I always meandered away from the main road and to the sea. We walked past the cemetery and the golf course; we walked until the pavement petered out and then onto the soft springing sea turf. We turned and jumped down to the lapsing, soft, top sand and followed the tide line. It was so interesting, with bird bones bleaching or whole birds sightless and twisted in the drying seaweed, their circled flights ended. Dad filled some empty spaces in my mind naming shells and stones. He lifted seaweed with his stick and showed me the best type to squeeze until it made a satisfying popping sound. He told me to hunt for a lucky stone that was usually the most beautiful tiny stone lurking among the common ones. Then we rubbed it, shut our eyes tight and made a wish. If it was white with coloured striations, he declared it truly lucky and slid it into his pocket for it to join all the others in a pot in the back yard. When we reached larger flat stones he sat down, with his hands hanging carelessly between his knees and simply watched me meandering, studying this or that. There were no unreasonable demands, he just sat enjoying the sea air, seeming assured and composed and I was his future. Dad was love and tolerance and dignity. Mam was just Mam. Not a relaxed person, always leaving the impression that it was a precarious relationship and sometimes I loved her through fear. Fear of the dramatic scenes, fear that I would be the cause of her being found floating in the dock, fear of losing her approbation and fear of just losing her. For I knew that she loved us, but it was a fierce, passionate and sometimes suffocating love that was hard to gratify. Dad was warm and easy going and as he sat smoking a Woodbine and gazing around the long bay, I knew that he did not need any more than this. I also knew that it would not last, I had Mary and June going ahead of me, silently showing me that I would stop walking with him and walk in other directions. I would go to the Palace ballroom and find another man to walk with, while Dad took Mary and June's children to Saltpans. And that would be right but for now we were here and comfortable. Dad would be a good grandfather.

We walked to where there was a hollow of land and he told me that the Romans had made it to catch the sea and then when it had evaporated, they used the salt left there, to pay their soldiers. Across the road the land rose steeply, pitted with badger sets and in the late spring it was so covered in bluebells that from a distance it looked totally blue. This was our turning point to go back home. We took this particular walk in all seasons and in all weathers. We walked even when the waves were shattering and smoothing the stones. The spume and spray reaching out to us while we pushed on together with our heads bent downwards against the buffeting winds. Dad's rheumy eyes picked our way home in winter glooming as well as summer haze. Only once were we caught out by a truly heavy storm and he hurried us to the shelter of a straggling hawthorn bush that had bravely grown by the shore. It cowered against the salt-sprayed winds and had grown bending landwards. We crouched in its' sharp thorny shelter, conspiring against the cold and the lashing rain. Through the thin branches I could see the clouds looming with menace and the sea birds arced and halted and stumbled in the fitful air. The cold seeped miserably in while I huddled further into his rough tweed jacket and his rasping chest. Just as I was wondering if we were so wet that we may as well be walking home Dad jumped up and ran towards the road. He waved his stick and shouted at the little bus that had trundled around the corner. I watched him, knowing that we were very far away from a bus stop and his gyrations would have little effect on officious drivers. To my surprise and relief, the bus slowed and stopped. I disentangled myself from the thorns of our small sad shelter and ran across the turf. As the warmth of the bus enveloped me, I felt that I really should have known better. Dad knew the bus driver and the conductor well and he swayed on the platform laughing and chatting to them while the rain slipped down his ruddy hair. Occasionally our walking included a something of significance to remember like the day Dad gently pulled me down and crouching together he put his fingers to his lips and pointed. Behind the large house where the road divided, a fox was picking its' way across the field. It was rusty red, its' brush held straight out behind it and was oblivious that anyone was there. We hovered together and watched the privileged view until it disappeared into the trees. Then it was home, plodding through the long tunnel of trees with a pleasant tiredness and knowing that I was too big now for a piggyback.

As the summer blazed the family began to gather to celebrate Mother Tukes' birthday. Her mild heart attack had troubled them, and they came towards Maryport to be with the old lady. Mam and Auntie Lizzie baked and carried their offerings into Collins Terrace, and we had a party tea with everyone squashed into the living room. Those that had travelled far decided to make a holiday of it and stayed on for a while and Aunt Evelyn had made an appointment to have her wig redesigned.

I was lying across Mothers' couch with my head resting on Mary's' lap while she flipped through a magazine above me. I squinted up and read,

"Why not knit this jaunty jacket for your man"

And I knew that Mam would probably have wondered why a man didn't knit a jaunty jacket for his woman. But they didn't, it wasn't like that and Mam saying it, didn't make it so. The fire was laid but not lit yet and it had been covered by a nice clean piece of newspaper. In the summer evening, I was warm and drowsy and happy to just lie there and listen.

Uncle George was puffing on his pipe and sitting comfortably in Fathers' old chair and the others were sitting round the table. The dominoes clattered and clinked as they swirled them around and then selected them to manoeuvre across the palms of their hands.

531

"All I'm saying is that when the war ended, we had two challenges. We had to repair the damage of the ravages of war and at the same time make sure Germany could not rise up again. Churchill might have called it our finest hour, but we ended up bankrupt and exhausted. And the laugh of it was that we ended up feeding the blooming Germans. I mean Monty sent tons of wheat over there, while we were on Rationing. The Marshall plan must have been one of the biggest free gifts in History." "Aye and did we see any of it? No. We were too busy thinking we were still a great power and that Lord Keynes went over to America thinking they'd just give us money and found that things had changed a bit. I don't know who he thought he was, but America wasn't falling for his arrogant manner and we ended up with a loan with interest we couldn't afford."

"Mind you could hardly blame Churchill for the austerity. Clement Attlee was in then and that Stafford Cripps thought we should all have cold baths and live on whale meat."

"Say what you like, I'll vote nothing but Labour. You've got short memories if you can't remember what it was like before National Assistance or the National Health. At least now we have a safety net if you fall sick or out of work."

"But even with that, the rot has started to set in with charges for glasses and false teeth. It's no wonder Nye Bevan resigned."

Mary smiled down at me and pointed to an advert that asked,

"Are you weary and out of sorts, then take Bile Beans."

I smirked back to her as others came up the lobby laughing.

"Hello Sydney. What's tickling you?"

"We've just come from the Bounty and I was leaning on the bar enjoying a pint when in comes Bogey. He stood and looked at me long enough and then said, "Was it you or your brother that was killed in the First World War"?

 "Oh, get away with you."

"No, straight up. I nearly choked on my pint and even funnier he couldn't see why I was laughing. Any tea going?"

"Try the pot we're in the middle of this game. Oh, Mother sit down, surely he can pour himself a cup of tea?"

But Mother rose to get it for her son.

"God, Mother this tea's so weak it's a fortnight. Make some fresh eh? What's the crack then?"

"We were just saying how well Germany has done since the war."

"Aye well, with wily old Adenauer at the helm and siding with the West they were bound to go forwards. It was sad to see Russia move back into itself but I suppose they've never had a history of having friendly neighbours so it would be hard for them to suddenly start trusting. It's a queer old world at the moment. I mean we're sending folk over to Australia like mad and then bringing black people from Jamaica because we haven't enough cheap labour."

Uncle Stanley chipped in,

"Phew, you want to see Manchester now, there's loads of black faces around. May and I were thinking of buying a couple of houses and renting them out to them."

"Nice if you can afford it, mind our May isn't looking too well. Is she all right?"

"Far as I know, she doesn't say much."

Mother sat down at the table and said sharply,

"Aye and no doubt you and Robin don't ask either."

Uncle Stanley shrugged.

"I've told her if she carries much more weight, she'll be like Queen Salote of Tonga."

"'Well, I bet you were popular saying that".

"Mary, that's enough to your Uncle. Anyway, we can't all have wasp waists and hour-glass figures."

"Oh, May has, it's just, the sand's all sunk to the bottom."

"Stanley! That's terrible."

But they were all laughing.

"Is it back to Silloth again this year Edna."

"Too true, but this time we've got a big caravan at Skinburness. Going up market a bit."

"Nice for those who can afford it, to you too. If you tell our Evelyn, she'll think you're rich as Creosus."

"She can think what she likes as long as she doesn't stay long enough to try to join us. And I've done a lot of hard saving for our holiday; the money didn't just magic itself there. At least Alf doesn't go to a pub and pour it down his throat to pee up a wall later."

Uncle George shifted uncomfortably in his chair,

"That's enough now. There's no need to be vulgar. We all have our little weaknesses and maybe yours' is holidays. I laughed at Big Billy Musgrave. He was telling me that

Little Billy had been asking for a holiday, so he tipped a quart of sand and a bag of salt in the bath for him and told him it was the seaside."

"Oh, give over, he never did. Honestly those two lads of yours Lizzie are as daft as brushes."

Auntie Lizzie smiled and began carefully placing the dominoes back into their box.

"You all right Mother?"

"Hmm, I was just wishing Ben had lived to be here."

"Never mind, he died peacefully or so his wife said, and we're all here."

"Aye it takes a lot to make up for one missing."

"Our Evelyn said that she knew he was dead before the telegram arrived."

"She blooming would, how did she make that out?"

"She said she dreamt he climbed over her bedroom windowsill and stood at the end of her bed saying his goodbyes to her."

"Now what the hangment would a fellow be doing climbing walls when he was busy dying?"

"I don't know, ask her."

Mam was pulling her coat on.

"Come on Edna, it's time you were home and in bed."

I didn't want to sleep at Mothers but the thought of the long walk over the New Road was not very inviting.

"Aw, Mam, can't we get the bus?"

"Are you joking? Get the bus for a couple of stops, I've never heard of such a thing."

"You'll be home, and in your bed before you know it. 'For our little life is rounded with a sleep."

"Oh, for God's sake who gave our Edna that book of Shakespeare"

Mam smiled,

"You can blame May. She bought me it when I was in my teens and I thought I had never seen words so wondrous. I read it and read it until it fell apart and then June bought me another to replace it. I can remember seeing Lawrence Olivier doing at the Lonsdale in Carlisle and it was amazing after reading it for so long to see it properly acted. Sometimes I wonder if things are going to get so good that I may be able to go to Stratford on Avon and really see it. I know that's a bit silly, but you never know."

She was embarrassed and fastened my coat roughly and I went to kiss Mother.

We walked down the long street and turned for Maryport. I had never thought of Mam having hopes and aspirations for herself and that night it just seemed an impossible dream for her to travel so far and then be able to afford to go to a real theatre. Mary said,

"Isn't it just typical of Uncle Stanley to not see that there's something wrong with Auntie May."

Mam shrugged,

"I don't think they ever really loved each other. He was turning into nothing but an old bachelor and May wanted his name, so it suited them, I suppose."

"What a way to get married."

"Oh, times change Lass. Then, it was almost a disgrace if you didn't get married and it was certainly a disgrace to be born out of wedlock. May felt it keenly all her life. There wasn't money for romance, and it was always, 'two can live as cheaply as one,' thrown at you. I remember walking out with Nicky Winter and thinking that nothing could be finer. That was after I knew that I would never make anything of myself with the cost of education, so I started looking at lads and he was so handsome. He brought me some flowers one day. I think of that now and then"

"What happened to him?"

"Nothing. I thought it was the "done thing" to play the field and your Dad wanted to walk me home from a dance. I thought it would make Nicky jealous and then he would declare himself."

"And he didn't?"

"I suppose he didn't get much of a chance. I fell wrong with that first baby and that was me off to Cockermouth Registry Office. I still think of him though. Oh, don't get me wrong, your Dad was handsome and tall, and he came to meet me once wearing a purple suit. Oh my, that was smart and went with his red hair wonderfully."

It sounded terrible to me. A purple suit. How ghastly.

Mary must have been feeling particularly charitable that night, or particularly stupid when she said,

"I can't think of having an older brother. I wonder what was wrong with him?"

My heart sank, as I knew the tale was coming again.

"I don't know that there was anything wrong with him other than being more than two months too soon and there wasn't any incubators or even any thought of going into a hospital. He'd have probably lived now. Alf and I had gone over to Mothers' and all afternoon I couldn't get easy. I moved from one chair to another until I started to have these terrible pains. Mother kept telling Alf to go for a midwife, but he just sat there saying it was only November and it wasn't to be born until the end of January and I was just making a fuss. Finally, Father said he would go. What a night I put in and when it was born it just kept making this funny repetitive little noise. I was trying to get some sleep and I said to the midwife, 'When is it going to stop doing that?' and she just said quietly. 'Oh, not long now Lass'. I was drifting off when it dawned on me what she meant. I sat bolt upright and gathered the little thing to me saying, 'Well, do something about it'. She was a nice woman and she rubbed it with olive oil and wrapped it in cotton wool. It didn't seem to know how to suck so we just fed it with a dropper. That woman did everything she could think of and it lasted ten days then it died. Your Dad had been to tell the Vicar, but he didn't come so the doctor christened it. I asked for it to be called Bernard and you know Mary, I never knew whether it was properly registered or not. I never asked Alf, as I wasn't exactly speaking to him at the time. Poor little thing had red hair just like him. People might wonder why I dislike Mother Croft so much but the things I've taken from her and that time was one of them. When I felt a bit better, I went back to that first little house your Dad and I had up Kirby Street and she walked in one day when I was crying. She put her hands on her skinny hips and asked what was wrong with me. The daft woman. There was I, barely eighteen, just lost a baby and now tied to a man for life and she asks what's wrong. When I said I was sad about the baby she just sniffed and said, "So what, you can make more." Old bitch. But she was right because before long I had you and June. Three babies in three and a half years. One day when I went to the doctors, he weighed me, and I was six stone. He just quietly said that I had to send my husband in to see him. Well, I don't know what was said but I know he told Alf to lay off me for a bit. It was a blessed relief I can tell you because there was nothing in it for me. How could you enjoy something when you are too worried that you may be making another mouth to feed and us in the Depression? But your Dad was good about it. I'll give him that much and I was so upset myself at the time I didn't think that he might have been sad about losing a son. We weren't much help to each other. No, I don't think there was anything really wrong with that baby. It just came too early but sometimes I console myself thinking it might have grown up having asthma as bad as Alf so maybe it wasn't meant to be. We never mention it."

My lost brother was a bit like Bunty; something that hadn't to be mentioned but was mentioned every now and then.

"Cheer up Mam, maybe it *was* meant to be. Just think if you hadn't had to marry Dad then there wouldn't have been any June, Edna and me. We three are here like we are, because of that little baby and having me is so wonderful how could you be sad." "Give over, you daft lass. Mind I'd never thought of it like that. Funny how one thing leads to another. And if you think you were a bonus you've another think coming." They laughed their way past the bus station with its' new roof and under the new electric streetlights glowing orange. Mam said that at least the Queen coming up here to open Windscale had brought one or two modern benefits, but she didn't think that Lizzie and Phil would notice. I trotted beside them and felt a sadness for the little baby with the red hair being exhorted to live on when he could not do so. I wished Mam would not tell the tale. It was as if Dad was to blame for everything and not a nice person, but he was, I knew that he was and everyone else seemed to think so. Mam was always saying if only this person had let her do this or not stopped her doing that and the major villain was always Dad. As all had happened long before I was born, I could not offer a credible defence for him, but it was uncomfortable to listen when I loved him so much. Still, it was funny to think that without that little baby I would not have been born and then my children and their children. Who knows, out of all of them may come a one wonderful person to change the world? It was all too deep for me and I gave up thinking.

When we got into the house Dad didn't look like the villain from, "Maria Martin and the Red Barn." He didn't even have a twirling moustache. In fact, he was just sat there looking at his paper and listening to the radio. Mam tutted as she moved his used crockery from the table to the kitchen and called back.

"Got your supper then?"

"Aye it was a nice bit of tongue you left."

"Couldn't clear away eh?"

He just looked over his glasses to Mary and shrugged and smiled.

"I did, I cleared the tongue off it."

"Oh, very clever. I'm working over at Mothers and I come home to more work."

I smiled at him and mimed the playing cards and the dominoes, and he smiled back.

"Was there only you over there?"

"No there was ... oh, blast, here comes our Evelyn."

Aunt Evelyn and Auntie May came up the yard and bustled in.

"We've just been to the pictures and thought we'd have a cup of tea before going over to Grasslot."

"And you couldn't ask me to go with you. Nice one. I'm good enough to make the tea but not to take to the pictures. Some sisters I've got."

"Stop twining, you weren't there to ask when we decided, and May's been sick twice. Nearly spoiled the film for me."

"Who's bothered about you? It can't have been very nice for May. I hope she reached the toilet in time."

"Thankfully, yes. I would have been mortified if she'd done it in the actual cinema. There's something wrong with her stomach and she hasn't been to see a doctor yet. All that Stanley and Robin keep going on about is buying more houses in Moss Side and she doesn't look fit enough to be doing it. Her stomach is out here, and it doesn't even look right."

"Don't say that to her. You don't think she's got that..."

And Mam whispered in Aunt Evelyn's ear.

"Our Edna, trust you to turn a bit of sickness into that. All she wants is to lay off the frying pan for a while and lose a bit of weight. No will power that's what's wrong with her and always has been."

It's all right for you to talk with your slim figure. I can't seem to shift it. 'Oh, that this too too solid flesh would melt'.

They came from the kitchen carrying the freshly brewed tea. Auntie May was sat with Mary looking at photographs of the grand Graduation Ball and they turned them to show Aunt Evelyn. Aunty May sipped the tea.

"I don't know what's wrong with me, nothing tastes the same, as they said in the war, this tea tastes like coffee so it must be cocoa. I like your pelmets Edna. They are becoming all the rage. Have you got them all through the house?"

Mam preened,

"Of course. Now, what do you think of that Evelyn? A Graduation Ball eh?"

If Aunt Evelyn could have spit feathers she would have done.

"Well, I don't know where I've gone wrong. You, squandering money on new things for the house and our May queening it in Manchester. And I'll have you know my children have done all right even if they haven't been to fancy Balls. Cyril can turn out smart as paint when he comes to see me. And my daughter wouldn't be seen in such a low-cut dress. I'm surprised you encouraged her Edna to flaunt herself in public like that. Her face is painted up to the nines, I can see eye stuff and what's on your face?"

Mary looked taken aback and said, "I've got a tan,"

"Tan? You look more like a smoked kipper to me."

Auntie May fluttered her hands and said feebly,

"I think she looks wonderful. If I'd had a daughter, I'd have wanted her to look just as Mary does on that photograph and standing there with a nice young man in a proper dinner suit. You look a smasher Pet."

"A smasher? She won't when her face dries to parchment and she looks like a walnut. That's what happens with too much sun. All that money gone on fancy clothes and weekends away. I'd say you're going to have to be careful with your bosoms hanging out on a photo."

Dad got up and took my hand.

"I think it's time Edna was in bed."

I heartily agreed as Mam stood up, ominously placing her hands on her hips. Dad and I pulled faces of alarm to each other as we climbed the stairs and heard,

"That's enough out of you, you sharp tongued beggar. Coming in here, demanding tea and then insinuating my eldest is a trollop. How dare you speak of my girl like that? It's a very smart evening dress, bought in Binns in Carlisle. Now, that's enough. Finish your tea and away you go. I'm sorry May but I don't have to listen to my lass insulted in my own home by her."

Aunt Evelyn had already jumped up and snatched her coat from the back of the couch.

"Come on May, it'll be a long day and a short one before I drink tea in this house, and you'll be eating your words our Edna when Mary walks in six months gone."

Bang! Mary's' fist hit the table,

"Out! Away over and see if your husband is out of the Station Inn yet before you throw bricks at any of us. I earned good money for that dress and Mam saved hard for those pelmets and there'll be no six months gone in this house. You've a nasty mind, that's what."

The front door nearly came off its hinges as Aunt Evelyn slammed it. Dad and I hovered on the landing.

"Just you calm down Mary. You shouldn't really have spoken to her like that. You should have left it to me."

"Are you joking? It was me taking all the insults. Kipper indeed. Making out I'm a harlot."

"That's enough of rude words like that. You know fine you didn't look like a kipper and she's just riddled with jealousy. Go and wash your face with cold water and calm down. Take no notice, they'll be back."

"Who wants them? Well, I love Auntie May, she spoils me rotten and doesn't come out with such rubbish."

"I want them, Mary. They are family even with all their faults."

I undressed and climbed into bed. When I reached the God Blesses, I left Auntie Evelyn out.

CHAPTER 17
"A MINISTERING ANGEL SHALL MY SISTER BE"

June had not had a "function" for her twenty first birthday, and so Mam and I had risen very early and got the milk train to Carlisle and then caught the connecting train to Newcastle. I had been surprised to find Carlisle Station just as busy early in the morning as at other times of the day and held close to Mams' hand as we walked over the bridge to the next platform. The noise was deafening with shunting, steaming trains and we watched the impressive Glasgow to London express snaking in and sliding to a stop before boarding our own smaller train to travel to the North East. I thoroughly enjoyed the longer journey and was so pleased to see June waiting to meet us. We wandered up towards the city centre and on the way, June chose a table lamp as her birthday gift, which I thought extremely boring when there were giant chemistry sets and fabulous Silver Cross doll prams for sale. Then we looked around Fenwick's and C&A stores and had our tea in Carricks restaurant, which was very sedate and posh. They were both on their best behaviour, though Mam managed a few quotes from King Lear about serpents' teeth and ungrateful daughters but not enough to spoil the day. June had suggested that a telephone call would have been enough if Mam was so busy, but Mam always felt it important that she actually saw us on our birthdays. I had to be dressed in new clothes and a ghastly matching soup bowl hat as Mam said that she wasn't having me showing them up if we met any of June's lecturers. We didn't and I bore the hat stoically to preserve the pleasant atmosphere. It didn't seem much of a very special birthday, but June now knew that she could have the key of the door and go to vote. She walked with us to the station and hurried away before the train pulled out. I had the feeling that she was relieved to see us go.

Though Mam felt that all her exhortations to, "stick in," had made some impression, Junes' natural ability did not fail her, and she left College as a qualified teacher. She had particular success in Music which was a relief as we were mightily sick of her practicing Manuel De Fallas,' "Ritual Fire Dance," throughout her visits home. She must have been bored with it too as she flung it in the piano stool. I pulled it out one day and placed it on the piano. It looked extremely difficult and I picked out one or two notes and chords and then decided that the effort was too great. I had found learning the piano almost too easy, the worst part being the long walk to the top of Crosby Street, clutching my half crown and my music case. Miss Graham had a unique approach to teaching the piano. I had to play the piece that I had been given the week previously while she sat and smoked and gossiped with a friend and then she selected a new piece for me and told me to go away and practice it. Occasionally I asked Mary, June or Mam to decipher notes for me and I played the piece over and over until I had memorised it. Dad took no part whatsoever. It was almost as if he found it such a natural skill that he simply could not understand anyone having difficulties or the need to be taught. My own method was now proving redundant as the pieces became longer and more complicated. When I reached, "Jesus Joy of Mans' Desiring," I became decidedly disillusioned with the whole business. I whined when I had to trudge out in all weathers, and I manufactured reasons not to sit in the cold sitting room practicing for an hour. Mam was not to be budged or fooled.

"Listen, there might not be much else to you lass but this you can do. And do it you will."

Oh.

I had pranced home with my school report and waited nervously and curiously while she opened it. Then she handed it to me. There were a few "Tries hard" and the end comment left me with a sinking feeling, "Edna has a lot of common sense but can be a little silly." I was not complimented in the slightest, what was the good of common sense? Why everyone knew that the cleverest people hadn't any; and "Tries hard?" Tried hard doing what? It implied that if I hadn't tried hard then I couldn't do anything. And "silly," well, that was just fuel for Mams' fire. I made myself scarce for the rest of the day. In the evening Dad came in and read it while I pushed a bit of liver around my plate.

"Well now, if that isn't the grandest report. Just look at that will you?" I looked up to see if he had his glasses on. He was turning it to Mam with his thumb on the top lines.

"Would you look at that number in Class = 46. Position in Class = 5". By Jove; fifth out of that lot is going some. Did you see that?"

Mam sniffed,

"Of course I saw it. It isn't first is it?"

"Aw get away with you woman, she can't hope to beat them the lads and there will always be lads in her class."

"That's true. No, she hasn't done so bad. You could have a word with her about acting daft in school and maybe I should go and ask if she can sit with somebody more serious than Pam."

Fear smote my heart and I earnestly stated that I would be a model pupil in future. Being separated from Pam was as unthinkable as was being serious so I was careful not to use the word, "promise". June bought me the latest in water pistols as a prize and Mary gave me some smacking kisses and a Mars bar. Mam watched and then announced that if I failed the eleven plus, she would buy me a new bike. She reasoned that if I failed then I would need a cheer up and if I passed then that was enough to please anybody. At this time the Raleigh bicycle company must have been doing a roaring trade with this one exam and must have been delighted with its' inception. Now I wandered home and paused to stare at a new bike called a "Pink Witch" that was shocking pink with the new butterfly handlebars and pondering that it may be worth throwing away a life of honour at the Grammar School.

As usual, our annual holiday in Silloth was a great success. The caravan was on a large field and I quickly found others to play with and made a particular friend from Carlisle called Pat. At the end of the holiday we vowed to be friends forever, we would be pen pals and never, but never lose touch with each other, as if Carlisle was the ends of the earth. And as usual, Dad returned from the holiday much improved, in fact we all were. Whatever was in the air at Silloth it certainly seemed to make everyone sleep better and longer. All of us were revived to move towards winter.

Mary continued to spend ages on the telephone and writing numerous letters to Bill until one evening Dad said,

"Right, that's it. I want to meet this man that takes up so much of your time."

Mary flounced about but agreed to invite him to tea with Dad sincerely hoping that this would be, "the last." The china was lifted down and washed, the silver cutlery polished and the Irish linen washed and pressed. Plate cakes and sponge cakes were baked, and trifles and jellies placed out to set in the washhouse. Best ham and tongue was set out on plates and red cheese was cut into chunks and put into the dish. Oh, but the struggle Mam must have had after Bill left that day to find something derogatory to say. She was ready to call the banns there and then. I couldn't blame her; I fell for him right away. He was so easy and such fun. And when he left telling Mam that her hair shone like a lavatory door on a frosty might she blushed coquettishly and simpered back into the living room. When Mary came back in that evening Mam was waiting for her,

"Well, I've heard of 'Mary, Mary, quite contrary but you beat the band. It's high time you settled down and if you are waiting for better than that, well, you are just crackers. If you don't want him, I don't know what you want. You think you've got the life of Riley picking up you're wage and prancing about on the Operatics with our Gwen. Mollycoddled that's what you've been. A man won't wait forever and who do you think you are? You'll end up and old maid, dry as a biscuit. I don't know what you are dithering about for. And if he hasn't asked then I don't know why. I mean you're a good-looking lass, and a man doesn't always want a woman with brains."

That's it, Mam, you go for the jugular.

Mary almost gave back as good as she was taking, doors and drawers were slammed, and I sloped off to practice the piano. It was ironic that my piece that week was, "A Maiden's Prayer." It was all very confusing. Mam was shouting at Mary to do the very thing she was telling June not to do, and I wondered which one was being contrary. I couldn't see anything wrong with John. He was quiet and gentle and certainly handsome. Now he was working

554

at the new Windscale, so it wasn't as if June was engaged to one of the feckless. June simply wanted all that Mam was pushing at Mary, but she saw marriage as a new beginning and freedom from all the atmospheres at home. She thought that she would have the ability to make her own decisions and regular sex without all the scuffling and guilt. She had been sold the image of the homemaker and playing house while at the same time men were being sold the image of the strong man making decisions for their little women. When neither could live up to this it was a collision course that many could not avoid and bred future disillusionment and dissatisfaction. For now, June dreamed her dreams and imagined her future. He would take her "away from all of this", forever. They would marry in a charming country church and move into their own little cottage. There she would cook hearty meals for her man and wear checked gingham aprons with frilled straps going over her shoulders and matching the gingham kitchen curtains. Now and then they would have an evening out together sharing their love of the cinema. Later she would prepare dainty suppers for them to eat while their many children lay in bed, pink and clean and flushed with sleep. Almost every night they would lie in the privacy of their own room, the waves would crash on the sand and trains would rush through tunnels. He would make June impregnable to the pinching shoe that was her mother. Of course, she would not abandon her father and would bring her children back to dangle on his knee. I guess she got the curtains.

Occasionally Mam sighed and said,

"Poor Edna, she must think that she has three mothers with us all correcting her manners and her behaviour."

I could not join her in her sighing sadness, as it simply was not true. I had one mother. Just the one. I knew and always knew that Mary and June were a different something. They did correct my manners and behaviour, but they were moving through a great period of their own growing and changing. They swirled around me and in and out of my life. I knew that they did not have the ultimate responsibility and I knew that they had their own identities Mam was the queen of the colony and we were the drones and workers. But the three of us were linked and intertwined. There was the knowledge that the same blood ran in our veins and we knew what shaped us. It was truly love at first sight. We did not wait to assess whether we had nice personalities or the same tastes in music, politics or religion. Love did not need to grow and ripen. I never had to seek their love, I was accepted, and I accepted them. They gathered me to their hearts with an uncritical love and held me in their shelter. There was no jealousy, envy or resentment. We were three different people pursuing our different paths through life but still threaded in each other. They did not deny me my own uniqueness but reached out and eased my crawl from my chrysalis while they were still edging out their own new wings. Neither of them were my mother. They were my sisters.

There were many times when Mam commanded that they wash, dress or feed me. There were many times when she expected and insisted that they take me with them, whether they wanted to or not. But there were other times. There were times that I would never forget. I would never forget walking with June. Oh, my most beloved sister.

Born in the month of June at the summit of the year. The beauty of that month was reflected in her name and in her personality. She was not the brash rose of June or the searing, blazing summer heat firing her veins. She was the gentle wind that stirred the long growing grass meadows. She was the small flower that peeped among the lushness. Generous and sensitive with her mouth puckered with brushing kisses. She was pretty, excruciatingly pretty, her small round face edged with dark, dark hair and grey green eyes twinkling from long lashes. She was the soft, fragrant summer evenings when twilight stayed all night and she dreamed her dreams. And sometimes in her febrile and flurried pursuit of her future without ambiguity and angst she would look down and take me with her.

June whispered in my ear,

"Tomorrow I'm going to the Coop for the stuff to make a picnic. Are you game?"

I grinned and nodded, and she didn't need to put her finger to her lips, as I knew not to say anything about it. I also knew what was coming the next day. June was taking me for a walk and one, which would last all day and had to be our small conspiracy until we were almost ready to go. It was a bonus if Mam had already gone over to Mothers' and all we had to do was leave her a note. It wasn't so bad if June could get into the kitchen and prepare the picnic while Mam was upstairs or out doing the washing and then we just announced that we were going. But if Mam knew in advance, she was torn between the advantages of being rid of us or sabotaging the whole expedition. It was touch and go sometimes whether we got away without Mam manufacturing something to delay us. It was amazing how much she, "suddenly" remembered just as we were heading for the front door.

"Oh, are you two going somewhere?"

"Err, we thought we'd have a walk up Flimby woods. It's all right I've got a picnic and we thought you might like some peace."

"Well, you could have said. I might have had some jobs that I wanted you to do."

"Oh, I'm sorry Mam, I never thought, but you just save them for tomorrow."

"I might not want then done tomorrow. Maybe they need done today. Now I'm left to have to do them. And did it not enter your head that I too might have liked a walk?"

Actually yes, it had, but Mam would have wasted time getting herself and us ready, just in case we met someone. Then the walk would be severely shortened by her bad feet, headache, funny turn, or expecting too much for someone at her time of life. "Sorry Mam, I thought you'd be too busy."

"Well, I wouldn't be if you had given me some help, now would I? Anyway, you can take a message up to your Auntie Meg for me while you are going."

"But we aren't going in that direction."

"You are now, young lady. Goodness, I ask you to do one message. Me? I was happy to do messages for my mother. You see I loved her, and I hated seeing her with too much to do."

Total resistance to that would have been a statement that we did not want to do things for our mother and even worse, we did not love her. If it wasn't to go to take a message to somewhere obscure, it was our appearance.

"June! You are not taking our Edna out in this heat without a hat? You know very well that red heads cannot take the sun, in fact it draws the sun and then she'll be ill. "She'll be coming back weakened with sunstroke and who will have to look after her? Me, that's who. Selfish or what? I'll have more work and you'll have had a nice stroll with a fancy picnic. I've never known anything like it. Get on this stool Edna while I sort your hair and June looks for you a hat."

Hats. I hated them. With a rather small head they had to be secured with something or they fell over my ears and that was a cue for Mary to clap her hands and say, "Come out, I can see your feet."

Sometimes Mam made adjustments to them with nips and tucks here and there until my head was throbbing from the tightness and a red line seeped around my neck from the shortened elastic. No, it was far better to plan our escape when Mam was occupied elsewhere and leave a dainty considerate little note on the table. It was better because June was powerless to resist Mam. She had her own theory that if only she could find a way to "manage," Mam then life would be hunky dory. The greater truth was that it was wasted thinking, as there was no way to manage Mam. If we jumped one way, then she jumped another and knew and used every ploy to achieve whatever she wanted. We were sitting ducks, even when Mam wasn't sure what she wanted but simply had to exercise some control, however small the triumph.

So, June listened carefully to Mam's plans and then made her own. June made wonderful picnics. It was always a model picnic and just as one should be. Gone were the stale, softening biscuits and the hard bread with a sliver of whatever might be left over to fling between the slices. June boiled too many eggs and then chopped them into too much melting butter until the sandwich filling overtook the bread and squelched from the sides. Fresh crisps and some fresh salad and large Kit Kats that were wrapped in copious pieces of paper to stop them melting. There was a damp flannel to wipe sticky fingers and bottles of Ginger pop and of course a quarter of boiled sweets. These were to ensure that we didn't drink too much and need the toilet too often. Then June encouraged me to wear my most comfortable clothes and shoes and somehow forget the hat.

We always walked towards Flimby, rapidly through Grasslot just in case Mam happened to be in Lairds' grocers, past Battys' farm and then a sharp turn left. We left the pavement and crunched onto a wide, hard, blackened cinder track. We walked alongside the towering sullen, pit bank and smelled the sulphurous fumes from the nearby Chemical Works. Old railway bogeys lay rusting on reddened rails with slithering bramble branches twining in and around them. High above our heads hung rusting giant buckets strung on thick, thick metal cables that had carried coal from a smaller colliery in the woods. Now they dangled useless, like some dirty mockery of a ski lift. We could see and hear the winding machines and men pitted with coal dust, their eyes gleaming from the dirt and a white stripe on their foreheads where their helmets had rested.

Climbing a farm gate, we walked around the hardened tractor tracks at the side of the field. The hedges grew tall and straggling wild and it was not unusual to hear something scurrying, disturbed by our laughter. The trees of the deep wood drew nearer, and we slipped easily from the open fields and into it's cool dappled light. Now June was calm and relaxed and seeming more assured. I trusted her. I never wondered how she knew the way or if we would reach home safely, I simply walked with her. We walked through the summer spreading trees; the path now brown and soft and the loamy scent of wood and decay seeped into our senses. Fallen logs were greening with mould and paling cream and fawn with crumbling rottenness. Shafts slanted through any openings and dust motes danced in their spangled stripe of light. We walked until we reached a part of the woods that always surprised me. The trees fell away leaving a clearing and a small lake partially surrounded by large slabs of high stone. The reeds grew tall around the edge of the water, but June led us with confidence to a flat piece of ground to share the picnic. She spread some of the paper on my knee and I sank the oozing egg sandwiches, licking my fingers and between each one as the egg slithered down. The silence was only punctuated with, "Pass the Pop" and then we lay in the grass looking up at leaves in fans of five, June's body relaxed against mine.

"See that, its' clover."

"I know."

"Clever Dick, I bet you don't."

"I do. Dad told me that on the shore."

"That's a different sort of clover."

Sometimes I wondered if my brain had room for anymore.

"Now these ones are onion flowers, smell them."

"I know that too."

"You do not."

"I do they grow in Crow Park."

"Oh. Did you know there's a new film coming to Maryport with Danny Kaye in it and its' all about Hans Christian Anderson. You know the man who wrote the fairy tales".

"Err, they don't have bits chopped off do they?" June leaned up on one elbow,

"What on earth are you talking about?"

"Well, if not bits cut off, wrapped in nettles or fattened for a witch to eat them."

"Oh, God, has she been telling you those Brothers Grimm stories? I had nightmares after she told them to me."

"Me too."

"You poor little thing. But they are what Mam thinks of as children's stories and I suppose they were in her day. Don't think about them they are not true just keep thinking that they are only stories. Anyway, this new film hasn't anything like that in it and it has good music too. On the way home I'll teach you one of the songs called, "Thumbelina," and you will know it when you go to see the film. In fact, I'll buy you the sheet music and you can have something different to play."

"Teach me it now."

"No, not now because right now we are in a special place so I'm going to do another song. Say after me 'Little Sir Echo, how do you do?"

I dutifully copied and copied and copied as she said each line. Then we added the tune and June said that I had to stand up and shout it across at the big rock. "Gerroff."

"Go on see what happens."

I shouted a bit self-consciously,

"Woohoo."

It came back to me almost before my voice had stopped. I was amazed and woohooed and Little Sir Echoed until June got sick of me. She explained that the sound was bouncing off the rock and back to us, so I decided to call it Echo Lake.

We packed the bags and wandered on; tramp, tramp in the solemn stillness. June was calm and untroubled.

"Not long now before we leave the woods and come out at Broughton Moor, so go and find somewhere to have a wee."

"I don't want one."

"It doesn't matter go and try."

"Why there isn't any in me?"

"For goodness sake go and do something. There isn't anywhere after this to hide and you can hardly do it going through the Moor or Ewanrigg."

I had to concede a point but couldn't do it gracefully,

"Well, I'll go but I don't think I've even any drips."

"Go, you cheeky minx."

I wandered behind a tree and squatted feeling the grass on my bare body.

"I told you I haven't..."

"Shut up and get on with it."

June's voice came from somewhere much further away. Not even in front of me would she have done such a thing. Hitching up my clothes I found her waiting.

"Come here, you look like the wreck of the Hesperus," and she straightened my clothes and combed my skimpy hair.

"That's better, you can't walk where there are people, looking like that."

"You're as bad as Mam."

"Don't ever say that. Don't ever, ever say that. If I thought I was going to turn into her I'd, I'd…"

"Jump in the dock?"

She laughed,

"No, I wasn't going to say just what Mam says. It's a sort of blackmail and the worst sort. She keeps saying that she is going to kill herself but if she carries on, she won't have to because one of us will do it for her."

It was funny because we both knew that that would never happen, and we laughed our way out of the woods and across the field to the stile. Now our feet beat on the hard road as we walked through the mining village and down the long hill towards Ewanrigg.

"See Ewanrigg Hall? It used to be a fine mansion named after a Northern king called Ewan. The Christian family lived there, in fact Fletcher Christian used to come and stay with them".

"He lived there as well."

"No, he didn't, he was a cousin and he lived at Cockermouth. Who told you that?"

"Annie Robinson."

"Well, she got that wrong."

Fancy that. I had never thought that a teacher could be wrong and as our June was the cleverest person in the whole world then she must be right. Life could be very confusing.

"Wilkie Collins came to stay there as well and he wrote a spooky book about the ghost in there. It's called, "The Woman in White."

"Mam said that he stayed in the Golden Lion in Maryport."

"Maybe he stayed there too. She's usually right. See that building over there? It's the old fever hospital. That's where people went if they caught something other people didn't want to catch". For a sensitive soul, our June knew some weird things. The thin road led us to Ellenborough,

567

and we tipped with it, past a terrace of houses that was always known as, "Shiny Row". The houses were built on a hill and the angle meant that their windows caught and reflected the sun setting. June and I had wandered so long and so far, that now the day was creeping into evening and the Solway Firth was beginning its' own spectacular display. The sun, sliding down the sky slowly and majestically was a regular, natural and impressive scene. The yellow deepened as it sank languidly, and peach hues rippled in the few clouds and around the Scottish hills. They gradually darkened to purple and navy as the massive claret orb began to slide behind them and the sea was blushed and spangled. As it seeped down, the huge circle became even more florid and rouge fevered, flooding the water crimson. It lowered to a semi-circle and gradually disappeared leaving a fading coral film gauzing the view. The Solway was left shimmering in the half-light and swallows screamed their way home. June and I turned into Lawson Street exhausted and hungry, but she was calm, and she had given me the gift of her time.

Walking with Mary was altogether different!

"Are you two going for a walk?"

"Yes, why?"

"You could take this message to..."

"Oh, pot with that Mam,"

and Mary winked, snatched my hand and yanked me down the hall.

"I only thought that..."

"Yeah, yeah, maybe when we get back. See you."

Oh, but Mary was such fun. Mary was all laughter and bustle. She was too busy living for too much introspection and her eyes twinkled with mischief. She had the attitude that life was too short to have a specific knickers drawer or to replace lids on her jars of make-up. There were more important things to do and cram into life. Mam was forever trying to imbue in Mary some soberness and sophistication.

"Mary a lady doesn't laugh raucously."

"I do."

"Then you are no lady."

"True."

Mam would shake her head, deflated but not defeated.

"Mary, you are the eldest and as such I expect a little more composure and decorum."

"Dee what?"

"I'm telling you, you're the one that's taken after the Crofts with your, "hail fellow well met", outlook. And that's not necessarily a compliment, you want to settle yourself a bit."

Mary was capricious and impulsive and then impulsively decided that she wanted to be a more serious person.

"Now, as I am the eldest,"

"Only by a few months."

June retorted witheringly.

"Shut up June. I am the eldest and I have decided..."

"You can decide what you like, I'll do it my own way."

"What's going on here? "

"Mam, I'm telling our June and she won't listen".

"Right I don't know who started it, but I know who's going to finish it. June get upstairs and read your book and Mary come and help in the kitchen."

It was about the closest they ever got to arguing and even that was just a pale shadow of altercation. I don't remember them ever falling out with each other. When

June wasn't there Mam would put her arm on Mary's and say,

"You can give up lass, she'll do whatever she pleases and persuade herself it's what others want. You'll never beat that one."

Mam's opinion that Mary was singularly lacking in brains had, over the years, soaked in and was accepted by her. In turns they clashed and crackled against each other, but it was a marriage made in heaven. Mam struggled with her role as dominating matriarch and knowing that Mary was a good companion. She was puzzled by the idea of a daughter as a friend; but knew that she wanted to be with her and share. Mary knew her as a mother but she herself was a carer and excelled in all practical areas and Mam wanted to be cared for and served as well as enjoy her company. Neither could relinquish the roles of mother and daughter.

"Tell you what, while you're out, go up to Huntingdon's and get one of those Maudella dress patterns and tonight we'll have a squint and see what material we need." "Mam, don't be daft, I'm taking our Edna up Cherry Wood. If I'm back before the shop shuts, I'll get one."

"You know we can do that together. Our June hasn't a clue about dressmaking she's always got her nose stuck in a book, which is as it should be and our Edna's left-handed and all fingers and thumbs. Did you see that pincushion she made at school? What a ham-fisted attempt. I don't know why they get them to do that I mean who uses a pin cushion anyway"

But we were out on the street and away.

"Honestly I don't know how she always manages to think of a conversation as we are halfway down the hall."

"She might be mad when we get home."

"If she is then she is but for now we are going around by Craig's to get a fishing net and then we are off. Do you want to call on a friend to bring them?"

"Bit late now."

"O.K. We'll see if my friends are coming."

Mary had lots of friends. We seemed to collect people along the way, and I trotted beside them with my new fishing net, listening.

"Here what do you think about Princess Margaret. Seems a crying shame to me. Did you read it in the papers?"

"Hmm, but if she really wants him, she should have him no matter what. That's what her Uncle did."

"I don't know about that. Fancy even at twenty-five she has to ask the Queen's permission to get married."

"Well she should have given it."

"They're saying she was bullied by the Archbishop of Canterbury. The old goat should have kept out of it. I mean Townsend is so handsome."

"Handsome is as handsome does. He's married."

Mary mimicked,

"I am mindful of the churches, teaching that marriage is indissoluble. The decision is my own. I realise I owe it to the Commonwealth." What bilge. We never asked her to do that. I bet she doesn't want to give up the fancy Royal life. Anyway, what does indissoluble mean?"

"I think it means you can't get a divorce and Townsend would have to so that they could get married. Like saying you can't dissolve a marriage."

"Well, why didn't she say that, honestly the way they talk isn't natural"?

"I can't see that her Uncle has given up any of that."

"Any of what?"

"Partying and playing and having a rich life without doing anything for it."

"Shh."

"Why?"

"You can't talk about the Royal family like that."

"Why not? My Mam does it all the time. Do you think somebody like J. Edgar Hoover is listening and will clap me in the Tower?"

"No, but I just don't think we should criticise them. I mean they are Royal after all."

"Phoo, they go to the toilet like anybody else."

"Mary! That's terrible."

"It isn't, we live in a country where we can say what we like."

I pondered that one and felt that it didn't apply at school or home at times.

We climbed the stile and followed the railway line and the river until we came to a flat area where we sat with Mary's version of a picnic. As she handed me my swimming costume, she also produced a clean empty jam jar with string wound around the lip and fashioned into a handle.

"Away you go and catch something for our tea. I'll shout of you when Ramadan has ended, and you can have something to eat."

I wandered into the river while they settled to sunbathe. Minnows darted and flashed in the green fronds and I scooped and paddled after them. It seemed that I was almost as good at fishing as I was at making pincushions, but I enjoyed the cool of the water while they lounged and chatted.

"I like that song, "Lay down your arms and surrender to mine," oh, and the 'Warsaw Concerto.' Did you see the film?"

"Did I see the film, it was dreamy. You know I think I might try my hair in a chignon like in the film."

"I'm trying to grow mine so that I can have a pony-tail."

"What like the Bobbysoxers?"

"Well hardly like the Beatniks. You know, I don't think you get a tan unless you lie very still."

"Right I'll try that. I'll have to do something I look like Biddalls' Ghost at the moment"

I shouted,

"Who's Biddalls' Ghost? Was he in Ewanrigg Hall?"

"You what? No, it was some sort of show before there was the pictures and what has Ewanrigg Hall got to do with it?"

"Our June said there was a ghost there."

"That's a woman ghost. Come and let's see what you've caught."

I proudly showed them two dead minnows floating in the jar and they kindly sniggered, dived on me and reorganised my vital organs. It was noisy and fun and by the time Mary turfed out whatever she had put together for a picnic I was ready to eat it.

I knew however hot the day or dream drowsy we were after the food Mary would be home before the shops closed or to do whatever Mam had requested. She would only go so far in her bid for assertiveness and Mam knew it.

As we walked home, we gradually shed her friends and she delivered me home.

"Right what was it you wanted?"

Mam forgot to be peevish,

"Dear God, look at her she's in a worse state that Russia. Did you come down Lawson Street with her like that?

And what's this in this jar. Yuck, tip it down the outside toilet as you go past. Here's the money and I want the change. But if there's enough, get one of those Toni home perms, and we'll have a go tonight."

My heart sank. Whenever they decided to stay in and play hairdressers, it was my job to stand and pass the tiny tissue papers while they daubed the pungent smelling liquid on each roller.

CHAPTER 18
"THE MORN IN RUSSET MANTLE CLAD"

Lady Macbeth had sharpened her dagger once again. Quotes about serpent's teeth rang around the house. The air was charged and poisonous and it was mainly directed at June. She had begun working at a school at the nearby town of Workington which Mam said was not a job but a, "position." June repeatedly told Mam that teachers were paid backwards and so she would not receive any wage until the end of the month. Mam corrected her and said that it was not a wage but a salary. Whatever it was called didn't seem to make it come any faster. Dad had long ago capitulated and his little brown wage packet was meticulously placed on the table for Mam to open. She pocketed the majority and magnanimously gave him his pocket money. This was not without voicing that she could not see why he needed any, as she provided everything. Then she complained if he did not pay for gifts, flowers, cinema or any other expression of devotion that all other men in the world appeared to do for their wives. Now June was living off the fat of the land for free. The end of month could not come soon enough.

The end of the month came, and Mam waited for her to walk in from school and pour money all over the table. June wandered up the hall and dropped her bulging bag of marking.

"Any tea Mam? Honestly that class today, it's been so windy, and they are noisier for some reason. What's wrong?"

Mam placed her hands on her hips,

"Money?"

"What money?"

"Where's your pay?"

June looked for a few moments as if she did not understand and then it slowly dawned on her.

"Oh, Mam our wages are paid straight into the bank. We don't get a wage packet or anything like that. I don't actually see any hard cash."

"And you can't get it out?"

"Well, I suppose tomorrow I can withdraw some, but John and I have put aside some G Plan furniture in Listers shop, so I'll have to go down and pay for that. Gosh there's so much that we need, it's frightening. I'll see what's left over"

I felt a certain weakness.

Mam was incredulous.

"You have lived here since College ended and been kept like a lady and you have the temerity to walk in talking about furniture. And as for, "what's left over" what do you mean, "What's left over"? I'm afraid I resent being nothing but an afterthought. Particularly coming after an inanimate object such as furniture. Was I consulted? Was I asked to go with you to choose this furniture? It seems as if everything is going on around me and I am the last to know. If you think that you can go on like that then you have another think coming. I haven't put you through College for me to be treat like a skivvy, putting food on the table, cleaning and washing. Do you know how much electricity costs? Things don't just magic themselves into a house, you know. Don't imagine you can have free board and lodging to pay for fancy furniture You can get yourself right up to that bank when it opens, draw the lot out and we'll see what you can have out of it and I'll decide what that will be Madam."

It wouldn't have been so bad if Mam stuck to the daughter that she was lambasting but as her ranting became more hysterical, we were all drawn in somehow.

"And you sitting there,"

Me?

The unkindest cut of all.

"You're another one that does nothing but take. Sitting on your backside, waiting for meals to appear and clothes to be clean."

Emboldened by her new status June roundly told her that she would decide how much she would pay for her keep and there was no need to take it out on little Edna.

I could see that this was not going to calm Mam in the slightest and decided that a wander over to Mothers' was called for. I folded my book and as I pulled my coat on in the doorway, I felt I should do something for June, but I left them. June merely aggravating the situation by trying to be assertive and Mam mistaking this for outright revolution. Her anger was raw against the daughter that she had invested so much hope in and June was like a moth batting against glass. I knew that I could not help her and wondered at her being so naïve as to choose finance as the area to make her stand.

"If you had any love in you for me, you would want to give me your wage. I'm nothing in this house and your actions today just prove that I come last in everything. All that I've done for you and this is the thanks I get."

This was only a beginning and so I shrugged my shoulders to June and sloped out of the room.

At Mothers' I slumped onto the couch and dragged Darkie nearer to me. The butt of his old head was comforting.

"What's wrong with you then?"

"Mam and June are falling out, so I've come over here."

Auntie Lizzie paused slicing the loaf.

"Aye well you do right lass. They'll work out their own salvation. Poor June, she's a sensitive soul. Here, I'll make you a bit of bread and condensed milk and that'll sweeten your humour."

She handed me a plate and I bit into the bread and felt the thick milk slither between my fingers.

"Mother, have you got a flannel?"

"What a lass you are for clean hands. There you are, and don't get any on the cat or the sofa. Lizzie seeing as our little Edna's in, you go down and get me ten Capstan. "Now then, what's going on?"

I wiped around my lips and hands and thought it a shame that something so delicious could be such hard work to eat.

"Our June hasn't paid any keep or something and she got paid today."

"She will pay, she will. She's a good lass, there's no way she'll not give your Mam something."

"I think Mam wanted it all and then give June some back first."

"Dear God, the girl is getting married. I don't know, your Mam was spoilt rotten growing up with brothers and sisters all around her paying for her dancing lessons and clothes. We thought at least one of us could have it all. We even let her stay at school until she was fifteen, but we couldn't stretch to her staying on any longer with the General Strike going on. I think we were making a rod for our backs, or rather, your backs. I don't know what to do with her. I know I should, but she is my youngest and I'm too old now to start."

She plumped on the couch beside me and cuddled me close.

"She doesn't get it from me, I know that. She gets it from her Dad. Ever the firebrand both of them and sometimes that's a good thing."

"Get away."

"No, it won't seem like it when it's you that's in the firing line but when your Mam turns it on something worthwhile some good gets done."

I was puzzled,

"Like what?"

"You won't remember because you weren't even a twinkle in your Dad's eye, but it was your Mam that was instrumental in getting school medicals brought to Cumberland."

So, my mother was the cause of the nit nurse coming to school. I was not impressed.

"She'd heard of them in other parts of the country and poor old Cumberland is always last to get anything, so she started a committee. She organised meetings and wrote letter after letter. She never took any credit for it and I suspect her name won't be down anywhere, but it was her that drew attention and finally got it. Then she turned her mind to getting school meals here and did the same thing. Of course she had to move to Carlisle when your Dad got a job there and she had Mary and June babies so she couldn't do much but one night she got your Dad to baby sit and went to a meeting about the Spanish Civil War. Well, that was it. She made great friends with somebody called Margaret Cohen and her brother Nat. They had jumble sales to raise money to get a child or a woman out of Spain and there was little enough money around then, but your Mam managed. God love her, she had next to nothing in her own cupboards but that was a terrible war. It was brother against brother and such atrocities were committed. Just a rehearsal for the Germans really but we weren't to know that. Of course, your Dad didn't like all this going off to meetings and writing letters, well no man would. Still she did more than her bit for those poor unfortunate people and it will never be known. She didn't take any credit for that either, bless her. I bet if you look in your piano stool you'll still find, "Songs of the Revolution" and "La Passionata" or something. So, you see, sometimes being brave and fiery is no bad thing."

Hmm. I wasn't very sure what Mother was talking about. I'd heard of Agincourt and I'd heard of the Battle of Hastings, I knew that one of our Queens died with the word "Calais," stamped on her heart but nothing called the Spanish Civil War. At that time, I was thoroughly enjoying History at school. We were learning about the Tudors and I thrilled to hear of the exploits of Drake, pinching gold from Spanish ships and bringing it home. And as for Good Queen Bess standing there saying that she had the body of a weak and feeble woman was to my mind a masterstroke of oratory. But we were not told anything about a recent war in Spain. Just as I was about to ask Mother what it was, we heard someone coming up the lobby. June came around the deep red chenille curtain that served as a door.

"Where's our Mary?"

"She came in from work, had a bit of tea and then went over to one of her friends. Oh, and I think she was going to the Library to change your Mam's books."

June slowly sat down at the table, put her head in her hands and began to cry.

"She can't even do that for herself, however much she likes to read can she? Oh, Mother it's terrible. I'm so sick of it. Its' money, money, money as if that's all that matters,"

and she cried and cried. Auntie Lizzie came in and looked at the scene. She fired the small packet of cigarettes over to Mother and bent to put her arm around June.

"Never mind lass, never mind."

"But I do mind, I do. I've been so busy starting this new job and looking at the house and furniture and stuff. I just didn't think. Of course, I'll pay for my keep, I just didn't keep track of the dates and time flew past and now this. She has no idea how hard it is getting to grips in a new school, trying to get to know your pupils and please the Head. We aren't fully qualified until we do this first year in a school and I'm mindful of that so I'm trying to impress from the word go. On top of that there's the wedding to think of. Well, I'd like to think of it but she's organised this and she's organised that and we have to go here for the Reception and I needn't think I'm inviting this person or that person. I'm beginning to wonder if it's my wedding or not. If I hear one more time, "he who pays the piper, calls the tune," I'll tear my hair out".

Mother struggled up from the couch and thrust a handkerchief into her hands. June gulped and dabbed her eyes and Auntie Lizzie kept on stroking her and murmuring,

"Never mind."

"She's shouted and shouted and then she flung herself out, so I came over here. I just never thought. I'd have got around to it. I never thought."

"Edna go and put the kettle on and make a cup of tea. Lizzie you go out and bring those blankets in that are airing on the line and June go and wash your face, you can't walk through Grasslot looking like that. After we've had a good strong cup you can walk Edna home."

June looked horrified.

"She walked herself here, she can walk herself back."

"No, she can't; the nights are drawing in a bit and there's more cars around and hiding here isn't going to sort out things is it?"

June wasn't too sure about that. All she wanted to do was avoid confrontation as simply as possible. She didn't actually want to resolve anything with any effort. I struggled the old kettle under the tap, and then scooped the musty, aromatic tiny black leaves into the teapot. Auntie Lizzie came around the back door with the heavy blankets and made a face to me.

587

"What a carry on eh? I'm sorry for her but she should have thought. God, she knows what her Mam is like, the dizzy lass."

After the strong tea June and I walked slowly home. Dad was eating his supper; Mary was taking books out of a bag. Mam looked up and walked into the kitchen. The air was electric and crackled.

Mary said,

"Come on upstairs June I've got a Marshall Ward catalogue, we could have a flip through it", and off they went. I sidled into the kitchen.

"Mam. What's the Spanish Civil War?"

She looked up sharply from washing dishes,

"What?"

"I said,"

"I know what you said, what made you ask that?"

"Mother was telling me about it."

"Well, if she was telling you, why ask me?"

Diverting Mam was not going to be easy.

"She just mentioned it."

"I don't know why she would do that, out of the blue. Filling a little girl's head with that. It was a terrible war where horrible things happened, I don't know what she was thinking of."

"She was saying you'd helped. I didn't know you'd been to war."

"Oh, get away with you, I've never been to a war. I just raised some money and sent it there."

"And what happened?"

"It helped to pay for them to get out of the carnage."

"Like Cuetos?"

"No, of course not Cuetos. I don't know who it helped, and they don't know me; the money just went over there."

"Why did you stop?"

She hung the tea towel on a peg and looked out of the window,

"Oh, Franco and the Fascists won, helped by Germany. Then our own war started."

"We had enough to do trying to save our own skins and of course you came along and that put paid to anything like that."

"Mother said you are a good woman."

She flushed as she folded her apron.

"She never."

"She did, that's why she was talking about the war."

"Well, I don't know what brought that on,"

And I couldn't tell her.

"Still it's nice to hear."

She stroked my hair and I never quite knew whether it was the hair that she was admiring or a gesture of love for me. She had calmed considerably.

"Our June will pay something, Mam, you know she will."

"Hmm, I know. It just hurts that I come last every time. It'll come right."

And it did. A few more days of an icy, uncomfortable atmosphere was the price, though June did bring in flowers, which were flung contemptuously into a vase. June left a cheque on the table as she went out and it was ignored for some time. Then it disappeared. Mam was proud that she had a bank account at the Midland bank and could teach us how to write cheques, so I guessed that it had gone there. I don't think either of them apologised or even mentioned it again; day just followed day while June fluttered around and desperately tried to chat brightly about curtains and bridesmaids' dresses.

I didn't understand the rush, as the wedding was not going to be until the next Easter. Now when we went walking June talked of radiograms, and kitchens with Formica tops. I crunched through the leaves and thought that it looked as if God had shaken a giant box of cornflakes down to earth. She said that she wasn't going to wash dishes with washing powder, but she would have the new Squeezy washing up liquid and I reached the arching tangled bramble branches and tasted the sweet-sour succulent berries. She taught me the words to the song "In Gilly, Gilly, Osenpeffer Bogen by the Sea", between musing whether to have peep toe or court shoes to wear on the day. Arrangements forged ahead and I was horrified to find that it had been decided that I was to wear a long creation in white net with pink rosebuds. As American denim jeans and chunky jumpers were all the rage, I was miffed that I had to parade in all that froth. Dad said that it was a grand dress for a little bridesmaid to wear. Which was all very well but he wasn't going to be the little bridesmaid wearing it. It was reverently folded in black tissue paper to await the event. Mam struck fear into my heart by saying that when the wedding was over, she would shorten it and I could wear it to parties. As if I could ever appear in front of my friends so ignominiously. It was very important not to look different and I wanted to be liked. Popular would be good but just being liked would do. Parties were rather like the concerts. I wanted to be invited but I really didn't care for them when I got there. Boys were always rowdy and noisy. They descended into rough and tumble games and thought making a mess of the jelly excruciatingly funny. The girls simpered through Postman's Knock and I sat passing the parcel never winning a bean. But I would have been deeply wounded to be left out. I laughed gaily and left clutching my bag of goodies agreeing that it had been a smashing party and went home with relief.

Mary and June organised wonderful parties for me. I enjoyed handing out the invitations and welcoming my friends. The furniture was pushed back, and Mary thumped the piano while June directed the games. They arranged a Halloween party with apples strung across the living room and the large jam pan full of lemonade with apples bobbing in it. As we knelt and dipped towards it, Mary gave us an extra push into the sweet liquid. The centrepiece on the table was a large black witches' hat and at the end of the party they opened it to reveal a present for each child. They decided that ten was going into double figures and so was a very special birthday. I was to have my own function. They booked tea at the Waverley Temperance Hotel and I stood at the door greeting my friends and feeling pleased that it was me that was offering a good time. It was a small price to have to wear the frothy bridesmaids dress for June.

They continued their own lives of working and playing. They were still very enamoured of dancing and took every opportunity that they could to, jive around any dance floor available. Bill was now working at the big Iron and Steel works at Workington and so the foursomes were a regular event.

"Are you and Bill coming to the dance at the Freemasons' Hall next Saturday?"

"Dunno, I'll ask him. You know he's setting off for the steel works in Dusseldorf on the Sunday so he may want a soon night."

Mam had enjoyed telling others that Mary's boyfriend was going abroad, though she said that it was a pity that it had to be that particular country.

On the Saturday evening, Mary and June were upstairs getting ready for the dance when the front doorbell rang. Dad answered the door and I heard Bill murmur,

"May I have a quiet word with you Mr. Croft?"

and they went into the sitting room. After a few moments they came out and came into the living room as Mam came from the kitchen,

"I didn't know you were here Bill. The girls aren't ready yet, would you like a glass of sherry while you are waiting?"

He did and was still sipping it when Mary came down.

"You're here early?"

"Shall I go out and come back in then?"

"Don't be daft. I'll just finish my make-up and we can all walk up together."

Dad shrugged at Bill.

"Embalming early, I think."

As they left the house, June put a ten-shilling note on the table and said,

"It's Saturday night so you three have some fish and chips for your suppers."

And Mam smiled and murmured,

"Gentle, generous June. I think we'll just do that Alf. Edna, get your coat on and away up to Cuetos'. Mind you ask for fish and chips three times, not three fish and chips or else we'll only get one bag of chips. Oh, and ask for your Dad a fish with the bone in. Nearer the bone, the sweeter the meat. I'll be setting the table while you're out."

I hurried up to the chip shop and saw the long queue for the Empire. We three had been the night before, and thoroughly enjoyed watching Fred Astaire and Cyd Charisse hoofing their way through, "The Band Wagon." In the middle of the film, Mam had appalled me by whispering that if I had been born a day earlier, she would have called me, "Sydney" after her brother, as that was his birthday. Thank goodness I had hung around for one more day.

My heart sank as I rounded the corner and saw another queue for chips. There was nothing for it but to stand and stand as it wound round and along the wooden counter with the succulent smell tantalising. It was as if the whole Cueto family whirled and cooked and served, even old mother Cueto seemed to have permanent residence in a corner, gutting fish. When my turn came, I dutifully repeated Mam's instructions and added a request for some, "scrapings" as I loved the little bits of golden batter that they sprinkled over the package. Philip Cueto called,

"Is that for Mr. Croft?"

Clem answered that it was, and more chips were scooped onto the pile. It made me feel good inside.

I ran back down the street clutching the hot parcel to me, up the long yard and into the house where we three sat down to the tasty take away.

Mam and Dad talked. No matter how unromantic their marriage had begun, it was as though time had created a companionship and warmth for each other.

"Mind, our Lizzie said that I hadn't to tell anyone this and I haven't but..."

And she told Dad. It was obvious that the trust that they had in each other meant that they could tell anything and that didn't count as revealing a secret.

"Well, I'm telling you Edna, Dr. Rattrie asked me to go in his surgery the other day while he examined this chap. Stinking, he was. Not Dr. Rattrie, I mean the old fella. When he asked him to bare his chest, he was wearing five shirts. Honestly, five shirts. Said it was warmer and he'd sort of forgotten to change."

"Scandalous. I'm telling you there's no need for it. Nobody knows what those doctors have to put up with at times."

They didn't even bother to say, "don't say anything" or "this is in confidence," they just knew when it was and when it wasn't. They were comfortable with each other.

"I'll get these dishes washed up and then we'll have a listen to the radio. I think Frank Chaksfield is on. And we could have a game of cards. I hope they are all having a good time. By you've played in that hall a few times lad, haven't you? Still, they won't be late in tonight with it being a Saturday dance. Good job there's special bus on to Workington and John needn't walk home."

Though some dances were until two and three in the morning, the ones held on Saturday had to stop at midnight, as there could not be any dancing on a Sunday. We played Rummy on and on and as I didn't have a specific bedtime on a Friday and Saturday, I cuddled up on the couch with Mam while she read her book. It didn't seem long until June wandered in and looked around with surprise.

"Where's Mary?"

"I don't know, why?"

"Well, her and Bill left the dance early so I thought they were here."

Mam looked troubled but Dad just smiled,

"Leave them be, she'll be home soon enough."

"I don't know, do you think we should go and see if everything is all right?"

"Don't be daft woman, we wouldn't know where to start looking. I'm telling you they'll be in soon."

"Just a minute, do you know something that I don't?"

Mary coming up the hall spared Dad the third degree. She came into the living room and held out her left hand, revealing an engagement ring. I disentangled myself from Mam's arms and Bill stood in the doorway looking sheepish and pleased.

"What do you think then?

"Oh, Mary it's beautiful. It's just beautiful. Would you look at that Alf? Now what do you think? Hang on, you beggar, did you know?"

Dad smirked,

"That's why the lad came early. Came to ask me first. Of course, I said it was fine."

"You mean we've sat here eating fish and chips and playing cards and all the time you knew, and you never said."

"He asked me not to, in case she wouldn't have the ring. And this time I didn't want to steal Mary's thunder."

Mam smiled back at him indulgently.

"What a man you are."

The sherry reappeared and finally Bill left to walk all the way home. Not only was Mary 'spoken for,' but Mam had the added bonus of being able to say that Mary's "fiancée," was going to Germany.

Autumn was well in and the trees along Netherhall road bent and tangled with each other and shed crinkled leaves. Mam said that with my colouring I would be lost among them. The weather dipped with the occasional warm day as if God had found one left over from the summer and flung it in. Seasonal games came and went with no particular beginning or end. Someone just began playing marbles and then the whole world was very seriously flicking glabbies and claiming their winnings. Someone began skipping and then everyone was flinging ropes over themselves and I was slapping myself smartly and painfully around the back of the head.

Someone could be seen playing with two balls up against a flat door and soon the ropes disappeared, and everyone was reciting,

"Mickey Mouse, built a house," while they flung balls and scurried after them. This was one pastime that I thoroughly enjoyed and proved quite dexterous, often adding a third ball to add to the challenge. Mother Tuke's back door made from wide planks was excellent to practice and hone my skills.

599

"Little Edna, get yourself in here and do something useful."

They just didn't appreciate that I already *was*.

After helping to lift the hearthrugs back into the house from the washing line, I set the table while Mam peeled potatoes then I sat down beside Mother.

"Did you play two balls when you were little?"

"I don't think I did lass, but I had a top and a whip and I was very good with a Diablo. I once got a beautiful coloured ball from my Grandparents when they came up from Cornwall. My they were smart. My grandfather wore a stovepipe hat and we thought they were very rich. But I can't remember playing like you are doing."

"Do you miss Cornwall?"

"Heavens no, I was just a very little girl when we came here. I don't remember it."

It was no trouble getting Mother to reminisce and I enjoyed listening. As Mam came in and out of the room, she smiled at me and cast her eyes to the ceiling. We'd heard it many times before, but Mother was a good raconteur and weaved her life into an interesting story, so we enjoyed hearing it again and again. Unlike Mam she did not dwell on the darker side or descend into tears. I led her on.

"Where was it in Cornwall?"

"Oh, it was a little hamlet called, "Little Sins," just north of Redruth and not far from, "Great Sins," so I don't know what they got up to there! My father was a mine sinker, which was a very superior job to just being a miner. Well, when the tin mines began to fail, he came up here to sink coalmines. I was only about three and my name was Minnie. As we were Quakers, I was allowed to choose my own name later and so I chose Mary. "I was Mary Wills. Here, see that cigarette packet. If you turn it over and look at the small print it says, 'W.D.& H.O. Wills. "Now that stands for William David and Henry Oliver and they are part of my family that moved to Bristol."

We'd heard that one a few times too. Somehow the family must have declined in Cumberland as the story made a jump to living in a pit house near Flimby when she was thirteen and went to work as a maid servant for a family called Tuke. She fell head over heels in love with the son, John who was a "callow youth" but very handsome of course.

"Give over now Mother, I think the tale has gone far enough; come up to the table for your tea."

Mother stuck her tongue out at Mam's receding back.

"They were very grand people and when I was having your Aunty May they wouldn't let him have anything to do with me. They sent him off to join the Army, but he wrote to me and I wrote back telling him that we had a little girl. He said she had to be called Mary, but his handwriting was so bad that I mistook it for May. Talk about hard times I had to go picking coal for a bit of money and oh, I used to get desperate to feed May, so I had to run home. When he came on leave, he got a message to me to bring the baby and meet him at Maryport station. You see the railway didn't go as far as Flimby then. Well, I carried May all the way and there he was so tall and handsome and that was it. We got the train to Carlisle and then another to Scotland and we got married. I tell you, you couldn't make it up."

"No, and this tea is going cold and you stop encouraging her."

After tea Mam and I walked home. As we turned into the street Faffy was sitting on her wall. She wandered up as Mam let herself into the house. She held out her flat palm with her other fist balled onto it.

"Smell cheese."

I'd fallen for that painful one before, so I scrabbled in my pocket and conked her with my conker.

In the October half term Mary went to Manchester to stay with Auntie May, as she still wasn't very well. June and

Mam were drooling over the new ballerina length wedding dress that she had bought and Faffy and I had called a truce to collect for the bonfire. I really did seem quite popular at this time of year with having access to Crow Park. This meant that we could gather good material to drag around the street and pile into a heap. Neighbours saved anything that would burn, and we begged cardboard boxes from shops. We also made the occasional raid to other bonfires. The few weeks and days before the actual night were almost as good as the night itself. I repeatedly opened my box of fireworks and counted them and studied the patterns on the wrappings. My favourite was a Jumping Jack that caused havoc in a crowd. We worried about the weather and couldn't wait for it to get dark. Mam said that everyone had fireworks to show that they were happy that it was Mary's birthday and for some years I believed her. She usually took a flask of homemade soup and potatoes were flung into the reddened embers to bake. The next morning, we always ran around to see if it was still smouldering and Mam grumbled that the Catherine wheels had burned the trelliswork.

Then came the telephone call to say that Auntie May had died. I felt bad inside. I could not grasp that I would not see her bustling up the long yard anymore. For some reason Dad had always given her the nickname, Mrs. Maybrick, we were all very fond of her and she had been kind to me. It was decided that June would stay at home to look after Dad and I, leaving Mary and Mam to go the funeral. Mary had loved her dearly and in turn Auntie

603

May had pampered and fussed over her; her eyes were red from crying. Auntie Lizzie didn't know what to do.

"I think if you two go then that will be like representatives from Cumberland. What do you think? I mean somebody has to stay here and look after Mother and June can't do it all. Evelyn will go from Barnsley. Talking of Evelyn, she says that things go in threes and old Mrs. Wordsworth has just died so I wonder who will be the third."

"Give over Lizzie. Blooming old-wives-tales. We don't need anymore. I just hope there's no falling out at the funeral."

"Hmm, you can't guarantee that where Evelyn is. I don't know, I shouldn't really be leaving Bill. It's very expensive on the train but she was my sister and I still don't think we should have told Mother."

"Get away with you Lizzie. She had to know. It was her first born and she'd think it funny if May suddenly stopped writing and coming. She might be very old but she's not daft."

"I know, I know; but it was awful telling her. You shouldn't outlive your own children. "She just keeps saying that she should have gone first. It's awful seeing her big brown eyes so full of tears and remembering. One of us will have to stay with her. I don't know what to do."

Mam finally obliged and assured her that she should stay at home. While they were away, I slept with June and heard her weep her own tears for a much-loved Auntie.

With the funeral over they returned saying that an argument with Aunt Evelyn had been touch and go when she had realised that Auntie May's clothes wouldn't fit her slender figure, but they would do very nicely for Mam. We moved on with our small lives in the long dark days before another Christmas.

CHAPTER 19
"NOR ALL THY TEARS WASH OUT A WORD OF IT"

"Has anyone seen my Acme Thunderer? I've P.E. today so I can't do without it,"

"It's on the hall table where you left it. Honestly, what you are going to do when you are married and have to look after your own stuff? And get a move on or you'll miss that bus. Come here Edna and I'll sort your hair. Your parting is like a dog piddling through snow. Mary tell your Dad he can come down if he wants, I've got the fire going. June put a muffler or something on, it's cold as charity out there."

I hated the dark mornings and it was cold and damp. Though I was too big for the fender stool I sat scrunched up on it and feeling the licking warmth from the fire.

"Edna, get a move on, here's Valerie for you."

I had made a new friend. She had come with her family to live in the Waverley Hotel until their house was built in the nearby village of Crosby. While she lived there, we walked to and from school together. I was unwilling to go out into murky air but was pleased to have some company. As she walked with me, she said that they were moving the next day and when they were settled in, I could go to stay with them, her Mum had said so. Since the holiday at Skinburness, Pat and I had kept a correspondence and they had invited me to stay with them in Carlisle. Mam had put me on the train with strict, imperious, instructions to the guard to, 'keep an eye on her'. Pat and her mother had met me off the train and then we had boarded a bus to their home. I thought that Carlisle was vast, and their home was full and cosy. I enjoyed their kindness and the adventure of one night away from my family. It was a small practice at being independent, but I airily told Valerie that it was used to staying away from home.

When I got home Mrs. Routledge was sitting at the end of the table carefully drinking from and china cup with her little finger jutting out. She slowly dipped her ginger biscuit in the tea while Mam winced.

"Hyah lass."

I opened my mouth but before a sound came out,

"I sincerely hope that you were not going to reply, "Hyah," we'll have no American talk out of you."

I closed my mouth and Mrs. Routledge apologised for her commonness.

"Right, your money is there and there's some of Edna's clothes in the carrier bag that she has grown out of and I can't thank you enough, you're a good worker. By the way how is your husband, we've been so busy I've forgotten to ask."

Mrs. Routledge gratefully pocketed the envelope of money and pulled her coat on,

"He's fed up of the bandages, but they are coming off before Christmas thank goodness. I told him, I said he looked like one of them mummies raped in bandages and he did have a good laugh. Oh, is this for me?"

She blushed as she picked up the prettily wrapped Christmas gift and pushed it into the carrier bag. Mam often gave her things, usually gifts that she had received and didn't want; but Mrs. Routledge didn't know that.

Mam saw her out of the door; the back door of course and then came to turn the Roly Poly pudding, steaming in the large pan.

"Not long now."

"Aw Mam, I'm famished."

"You're always famished. You'll have to wait until the girls come in and your Dad gets up from his afternoon nap. Here, go and get another pint of milk from the Coop for more custard and if there is threepence left over you can buy a Wagon Wheel, to put you on."

I didn't want to go out again, but I loved the large biscuits, and this was an offer not to be missed. I also treated myself to another slow look in the brightly lit shop windows wishing that I could have a bite out of the Wagon Wheel. I didn't dare as Mam said that we had not to eat outside in public with the exception of holidays. I began to peel the wrapper as I wandered up the yard. Mam was busy manhandling the pudding out onto the large oval meat plate. She gingerly peeled away the cloth revealing the steaming grey suet pastry and the jam bubbling from its sides. Dad lounging in the kitchen doorway commented that it looked like Big Bertha and half an hour later it certainly felt as if a bomb had fallen into my insides. Dad staggered out to work announcing that he didn't want another thing to eat for a month of Sundays and the rest of us tottered to the nearest seat. I loved it, the different textures, the surprise of the sweet jam and moistness of the yellow custard. Mam kept apologising that it was a very ordinary meal and not one that could be offered to visitors, but we didn't care. We were full and warm all over.

That Christmas Mary bought me a real tent. It was set up in front of the fire in the sitting room and in the afternoon, I solemnly sat in it eating my tea and dreaming of taking it to Silloth in the summer. I was planning sleeping and eating in my new abode while the others were snug in the caravan when the doorbell rang. It was the town band and they asked if Dad wanted any specific Carol played. He pondered for a few minutes and then asked for "Silent Night."

"And if you don't mind, I'll go and listen from the sitting room as it's perishing out here."

On the day after Boxing Day Valerie was as good as her word and I went with them in their car to stay at the new house. It even snowed and snow at Christmas was almost unheard-of outside Hollywood. We played in the snow making slides and snowballs. The new house had radiators and I was luxuriously warm. Behind the house Valerie's' parents had a piggery and on the day that I was supposed to go home her mother took me into the dining room and suggested that I stay a little longer so that I could see the piglets when the large sow obliged. She thought that that would be good, and I supposed that it would, but I was becoming sick to go home however kind they were. She took both my hands in hers and said that I hadn't to mind if one or two of them died, in fact sometimes people died. I was suddenly very uncomfortable and to escape this strange conversation I assured her that I already knew that as my Auntie had just died. The big sow seemed to have dozens of piglets and their wriggling curly tails and their pinkness fascinated me. I was allowed to hold one and was surprised by its' warmth and fleshy feel. Their New Year wasn't a bit like ours. No-one staggered in and quoted Omar Khayam and Valerie's' Dad didn't belt out silly songs on the piano. In fact, we even went to bed before midnight, which I thought was a very poor show. I lay in bed and pined for the blackened frying pan and the lonely little nutmeg rolling about in the pantry. It had been very nice, but it had gone on too long and I was pleased that I was going home the day after New Years' Day, to my freezing bedroom and the noisy chaos.

Valerie's Dad drove me home and rang the bell. As Mary opened the door he just shrugged and got back in the car. She thanked him and steered me towards the sitting room. I had so much to tell them about the snow and the pigs and the radiators. I was surprised to see that the decorations had gone and instead the room was full of flowers. Mam was in the chair by the fire with her head down. Oh, dear, was this one of her Wagnerians dramas just when I was bursting to relate my own adventures? She didn't look at me but said,

"I can't do this Mary."

Mary sat me down beside her on the couch.

"I can't Mary. I can't do it. You do it. You tell her"

and she drew her lace handkerchief from her watchstrap.

Tell me what?

Mary turned to me and said,

"I don't know any other way to say it Edna, but Dad died on the twenty ninth of December."

Dad?

Died?

But he couldn't, he had said that he was going to take me to the new Doris Day film of, "Calamity Jane." He wouldn't have said that if he had been going to die.

I didn't speak.

"The day you went to Crosby, he had to go into hospital, and he died the next day."

What was she talking about?

Dad? He always went into hospital, but he always came back out. He was always ill.

I didn't say anything.

Mary was cold. Her hand on mine felt cold.

Mam looked across at me.

"We thought it best that you stayed where you were. We had the funeral yesterday on New Year's Day; he'd have liked that. It was one of the biggest funerals that Maryport has ever seen. The chapel was packed in fact there was standing room only and there were people stood outside. Maryport band followed the coffin all the way to the cemetery. There's going to be a memorial service in Grasslot chapel and Brow Street Methodists and what do you think even Dr. Rattrie is having Requiem Mass for him in the Catholic Church? Do you see all these flowers? There was so many for the grave that we had to bring these home."

She looked helplessly at Mary,

"I don't know what to say to her Mary. I don't know what to say. Oh, God this is terrible."

Mary slowly got up and put her arm around Mam. I just sat on the edge of the couch.

The fire was blazing but I was cold.

"Here lass, read this, it was in the paper."

I dumbly took the cutting from her and read.

"PIANIST, MEDICAL CLERK AND FIREMAN

Maryport Death.

Last Saturday the funeral followed a service in the Brow Street Methodist Church, taken by the Rev. B.P. Marks, of Mr. Alfred C. Croft of Lawson Street, Maryport.

Mr. Croft, a native of Broughton had lived in Maryport for many years and few people were better known or liked. He was the medical and filing clerk for four Maryport doctors, the three Dr. Rattries and Dr. Bird. Thus, Mr. Croft came into contact with thousands of local patients. Despite his own poor health, he gave cheerful and obliging attention to people attending the surgery.

In pre-war days he was engaged in haulage contracting and was called up to the fire service. He had his worst experience during the blitz in Barrow. He was blown from a fire float into the water and suffered injury and illness. He was a trustee of the Grasslot and Brow Street Methodist Chapels. A singer and very fine classical pianist, he was also leader of a Maryport dance band and was associated for a number of years with the late Mr. Stephen Mossop (violin) and Mr. Fletcher Graham (trumpet) in playing for concerts and dances. A vice president of Maryport Albion Band he was keenly interested in its progress. Members of the band acted as bearers at the funeral. They had played outside his home for him at Christmas. Two days later he was taken to hospital where he died."

I stopped reading. I already knew whom he was survived by; I didn't need to read that.

It must be fact. It was there in the papers. If it was in the papers it must be true.

Mary rose,

"I'll go and make a cup of tea."

"I'm awash with tea but it's something to do, go on."

After a little while I wandered through to the kitchen leaving Mams' peevish voice saying,

"Don't leave me, don't any of you leave me alone."

Mary was standing in the kitchen leaning her closed hands on the table and her head bowed.

"I don't know what to say to you either pet. But I know this; you'll be all right. You will. You have us."

The kettle boiled insistently.

I didn't know what to do. I was overcome with a great tiredness. I made my way back to the sitting room as if I was walking through treacle and slumped on the couch. Mary came back carrying a tray and looking grim.

"Here, get that down you, you'll feel better."

What was she talking about? Tea to make it better. It was all crazy. There wasn't any making it better. She groped the cup to me, and I wrapped both my hands around it to warm them. It didn't matter how much they stoked the fire. I was cold. I had wanted to come home so much and tell them of my holiday. I wanted Mam to know how kind they had been to me and I realised that while they were being kind they must have known. They must have known the terrible thing that had happened in Maryport. Now it didn't matter. It was stupid to even think of talking about snow and piglets. None of it mattered. It was so trivial against this enormous event. After a few sips of the tea, I wandered out of the room and up the stairs. I went into Mam and Dad's bedroom. No, there was no Oxygen cylinder. It was too correct and tidy. He was gone and I didn't know what to do. With Mary's words in the sitting room my world had savagely stalled. My whole known world stopped and shuddered on its axis. I slid back out of the room and as I reached the bottom of the stairs June came rushing into the house.

"Oh, God are you back? Oh, my poor lamb, I meant to be back in time. I wanted to be here for you getting home but I've been at Johns'. Come here."

She crushed me to her, and I stood and let her. She pulled me back into the sitting room and sat me down beside her, holding me close. I wanted to push them all away, but I could see in their eyes that they were hurting. I wanted to be with them, and I wanted to go away, I didn't know what I wanted.

"Do you want to know what happened pet? Should I tell her Mam?"

"If you want lass, maybe she should know. I don't know whether I've done right or wrong leaving her at Crosby".

"Dad went into hospital, as usual, you know how he did? We didn't think much of it. "Mam asked me to go and do the visiting as she'd been in the afternoon. When I walked round the ward door, he had just died there and then. His heart had given out with the asthma dragging at it. I ran over and gathered him into my arms and the nurses didn't stop me. He was still warm, and I held his cheek against mine. I rocked him and rocked him until the nurses had to pull me off. Then I suddenly realised that I was the only one with this terrible news. I worried and fumed all the way home and had to break it to everyone. Terrible, it was terrible."

Poor June, poor gentle June, to be the one to have to do that.

I was cold. My certain and stable world had been violated and they kept patting me and telling me that I would be all right. It would never be all right. I didn't know why they kept saying it. Now and then they looked helplessly at each other. Mary suggested that we had something to eat and we four sat at the table going through the motions and it was like sawdust in my mouth.

That night as I lay in bed, I had a pain. I didn't know that grief could be a real pain, a real physical pain. It was somewhere just below my throat and down my chest. Dull, unmoving and leaden. I knew then that Auntie May and all the other deaths had not been a rehearsal. Nothing had prepared me for this. I knew then that death was not something that you could practice. I just lay there with no other feeling but the pain.

Mam insisted that she could not sleep alone and as they passed my door, I heard Mary say,

"Do you think I should look in on her?"

"No let her sleep. "Sleep that knits the ravelled sleeve of care."

"She hasn't shed a tear."

"She will, she will, leave her."

I turned over. I had been so wrong. He had not been nothing in the house. He had been love and laughter. He had kept Mam even. He had been her stability. Together they had been the positive and negative. How could I have been so wrong? How could I have thought that he had just been there, without influence or strength? He had been the artery; the backbone and he had held us all. If Mam was the steering oar, he had been the balance. I was so cold. I stared into the darkness. A simple man. He had been content with so little. He had never had a meal in an hotel or a flight in an aeroplane. He had never felt a foreign sun on his back or craved expensive clothes and entertainment, but he had played his part. He had always solemnly donned his best suit to go to vote. He had followed his religion in a gentle and devoted manner. He had supported and raised money for local charities and gave of his talent and his time. He had never promoted himself or been boastful of his wonderful ability to make music. He had never been insulting or nasty to others; he just meandered through life with a sharp sense of humour and a ready smile. He had been a good and faithful son to a difficult and irascible mother. He loved Mother Tuke and was pleasant and welcoming to his fractious in laws.

And to us?

He was there. He was always there. There was never any suggestion that he would leave us, that he preferred another woman, that he had another interest that took his mind away from us. Apart from his music he did not have any particular hobbies that drained the money and his attention. He was always there. If he disagreed with the way that Mam approached us, he never said so. From the moment that they were married, he was married, and he remained loyal. There was never any suggestion that he would have discussed Mam in a negative manner or that he would not have supported her if we had appealed to him. That was where his loyalties lay. He exuded a pride in us simply because we were his. He asked nothing that we could not give. Just by being there he gave a certainty. His gentleness tempered Mams' volatility and held her in check. She knew that he was always there to provide and bear the ultimate responsibility. Now he was gone.

The days dripped past with inertia. Many people came and went with their condolences. Some seemed to feel the need to tell me that he was all right now, that he was in Heaven, that he was still watching over me. I knew that I had to help them to feel comfortable and I nodded and agreed with them. It sounded hollow and stupid. When one of them said that my Daddy was now with the angels, I could have been sick. What was he doing there when we needed him here? And we did. Oh, how we needed that man. Another assured me that he would never leave me, and I felt a surge of anger. Of course, he had left me. He had let me go to Crosby and he had left me. He had gone. But I smiled and nodded and went through the motions of politeness. A neighbour of Mothers' brought me a kitten saying that it would take my mind off things. A kitten. As if anything could make up. It disappeared of its own accord and I made a desultory stab at looking for it, but it had gone too. Maybe it sensed the depressed atmosphere under the artificial smiles. My world had suddenly gone mad, but I knew that people were trying to be kind. Mary, June and Mam seemed to have a compulsion to go over and over the death to anyone who would listen and even just to each other. As if going over events would change them.

No one seemed to know what to do. We drifted through the days making tea and seeing visitors in and out. Mam sent me for some shopping, and I hurried to the Coop fearful of meeting someone, anyone, who may mention it. I was aware of the people serving me nudging each other and giving me pitying glances. Part of me wished that he had not been so well known and liked. I seemed to do a lot of going for bits of shopping and I gradually I could see that there were some who avoided me. They put their heads down and crossed the road. They were embarrassed and we were tainted. School had begun again but Mam would not let me go, she said that I had to build a little wall around myself before facing everyone and anyway she needed all of us around her. But this meant that now nothing was normal. I did not realise that Dad had taken normal with him. We had to be careful that whatever we did, did not upset Mam as she saw so many things as insulting to his memory. She cancelled the papers and said that the radio had not to be turned on. She was appalled when Mary and June suggested that they go out with Bill and John and so instead they came to the house and stood about awkwardly in the face of such grief. Mam noticed those who did not come with their sympathy and made a mental inventory of all that he had done that should be recognised and appreciated. She fretted about what she should wear for the memorial services and spent most of the time just sitting by the fire. She said that grief was a form of laziness and I could not argue. We all seemed to have slowed in our movements and thinking. After so long measuring the day according to Dads' pattern at the surgery we had lost the focus of time and could not adjust. The regular jaunt to the cinema stopped making another evening of just sitting in the house. The piano lid was closed. I went into the sitting room and opened it; I stroked the keys gently, not allowing them to sound.

I don't remember what we did, we four women in that cold house. I don't know what we ate. There was an oppressive torpor. Mams' grief was terrible to see and all the more bitter for her that they had reached some understanding of each other and love. We knew nothing of nervous breakdowns and could not see that she was unravelling before us. How could we know, when all had our lives were filled with her exaggerating situations and demanding attention? Now it was hard to decipher whether this was a glorious opportunity for her to be the grieving widow in her widows' weeds or genuinely shocked and afraid. Official people came and talked to Mam in the sitting room about pensions and she obliged for a while and then wailed that she could not be expected to make any decisions so soon. She could not remember where important papers were kept and then she was galvanized into action and produced whatever was needed. After a few days she took his jacket from the peg and began to go through the pockets.

"Mary, in all my married life I have never done this. I feel awful doing it. Here put these hankies in the wash and I'll give these few cigarettes to Mother. Oh, God some of his Long Lasters. Throw them out. Trust his blooming wallet to be on the inside pocket next to his heart."

We gave a watery smile as she slid it out and began to remove the few pounds notes and his wartime identity card. Mary said,

"What's that slit in the lining?"

Mam carefully slipped her hands into it and drew out an old, small, piece of cloth. She looked at it for a long time and then sat down as if a great weakness had come over her. Her large brown eyes filled as she looked up at Mary. Mary took it from her and straightened it out. It was a baby's tiny bib.

"I never knew. I never knew that he had kept that. The midwife sat and made it for our first baby. I never knew he'd kept it. He must have had it with him all these years. Oh, Mary we should have talked. I thought the grief of losing it was all mine."

I watched them with the little revelation of a man's memory of his only son. But here we were again not talking, just talking on the surface, talking in platitudes and clichés and simply hoping that time would move. June assumed that this overwhelming need for us would go on and on and fretted that she may have to cancel her wedding. Mam just quietly said that it would go ahead but smaller than intended. She did not say that she could have done with the company or the extra income for a little longer. Both of them had to go back to work and Mam was very gratified to receive a hand-written letter of condolence from Gordon Bessey, the Director of Education.

I desperately wanted things to be as they were. The house tumbling with all of us. The noise of the radio and the gramophone. Dad belting six bells out of the piano and the telephone ringing. Mary and June rushing here and there, putting on their make-up and leaving bags to fall over. Mam grumbling at all of us, and lying in bed reading Shakespeare, before jumping up to go over to her Mothers. In my innocence I thought that it would happen. People said things like, "Times' a great healer" and I assumed that they were right. I subconsciously thought that if we could only get this close time over with, then we would be the same but without him. No one really talked to me, it was assumed that I was too young to understand, and few talked of death anyway. Those close to me were ravaged themselves by this cataclysmic event and we could not help each other. I returned to school and it was not mentioned at all. It was as if I had simply had a longer holiday and had to catch up. No one took me aside or offered anodyne words. I didn't know then that there was no healing; that I would have to wrap layer upon layer over it and then take care that none were ripped away to reveal the rawness still there for that man.

And at night when I listened to Mam crying and Mary storming up the next flight of stairs saying,

"I can't sleep with you, you know I can't stand the light on all night. You'll have to pull yourself together and get used to it."

I wasn't angry with them. I was angry with him. I felt like shouting,

"Look at the mess you have left. Look at us. Look at us now without you"

I wasn't angry with Mary; I thought that she was right. It was as if Mam said the words that she was sorry for us, but her actions were shouting that she was not seeing anyone's need but her own.

My days staggered forwards, convulsed and bruised. The sands of my time were swirling and settling and his new non-living sponged into the sediment. I felt like a kaleidoscope that was being shaken and when I settled the slivers would always be dyed with him. But he was not there. We were smarting so much that still we could not truly help each other. His steadying presence had gone. His leaving left us stepping into an abyss with darkness for the future. How could such an unassuming, gentle, sick man leave such a devastating effect? What was to become of us? What would happen to the four women that he had left so suddenly?

Tired of the oppressive grief in the house I wandered over to Grasslot. Mother looked up and then pulled me onto the couch and held me close and all she said was,

"He's left his kiss upon your hair lass."

I wept. At last I wept.

Daddy.

Oh, my Daddy.

Oh, my most beloved Daddy.

Time was without him.

Printed in Great Britain
by Amazon

58908394R00357